ISBN 978-0-428-17792-8
PIBN 11307546

1 MONTH OF
FREE
READING

at

www.ForgottenBooks.com

By purchasing this book you are eligible for one month membership to ForgottenBooks.com, giving you unlimited access to our entire collection of over 1,000,000 titles via our web site and mobile apps.

To claim your free month visit:

www.forgottenbooks.com/free1307546

English
Français
Deutsche
Italiano
Español
Português

www.forgottenbooks.com

Mythology Photography **Fiction**
Fishing Christianity **Art** Cooking
Essays Buddhism Freemasonry
Medicine **Biology** Music **Ancient
Egypt** Evolution Carpentry Physics
Dance Geology **Mathematics** Fitness
Shakespeare **Folklore** Yoga Marketing
Confidence Immortality Biographies
Poetry **Psychology** Witchcraft
Electronics Chemistry History **Law**
Accounting **Philosophy** Anthropology
Alchemy Drama Quantum Mechanics
Atheism Sexual Health **Ancient History**
Entrepreneurship Languages Sport
Paleontology Needlework Islam
Metaphysics Investment Archaeology
Parenting Statistics Criminology
Motivational

THE EARLY HISTORY OF BANKING IN ENGLAND

BY

R. D. RICHARDS

Ph.D., B.Sc.(Econ.) Lond.

LONDON

P. S. KING & SON, LTD.

ORCHARD HOUSE, WESTMINSTER

1929

PRINTED IN GREAT BRITAIN BY
RICHARD CLAY & SONS, LIMITED,
BUNGAY, SUFFOLK.

TO
M. C. M. R.
AND
H. B. R.

276405

"We must erect a Bank, which well computed doth almost double the Effect of our coined Money; and we have in England Materials for a Bank which shall furnish Stock enough to drive the Trade of the whole Commercial World." — SIR WILLIAM PETTY, *Quantulumcumque concerning Money* (1682).

PREFACE

THIS book is an attempt to bridge certain gaps in the early history of English banking. It deals primarily with the operations of the pre-Bank of England bankers, the evolution of English paper money, and the remarkable transactions of the early directors of the Bank of England during the first six years of its eventful history.

The main inquiry is, therefore, confined to the sixteenth and seventeenth centuries, with particular reference to the second half of the latter century. A brief survey, however, is given of English banking in the eighteenth and early nineteenth centuries.

The first chapter describes the activities of the pioneers of English banking. The second and third chapters give a detailed account of the part played by the goldsmith bankers in the development of banking technique, in the trade expansion of Stuart England, and in financing the Government of the day. The fourth chapter examines the earliest English banking schemes, including the ill-fated experiments of the City of London, the short-lived Million Bank, and the extraordinary land bank projects of the closing years of the seventeenth century. The fifth, sixth and seventh chapters deal with the foundation and early history of the Bank of England. The eighth chapter describes the salient features of English banking between 1700 and the Bank Act of 1833. The ninth and concluding chapter examines the economic, political and religious conditions under which banking emerged in England, and traces the evolution of English banking theory and practice.

Though use has been made of the contemporary printed books and pamphlets, and of the newspapers of the day,

ix

the inquiry is based to a great extent upon the study of a large number of contemporary manuscripts which have not hitherto been examined by historians. Full details of the manuscripts and of the printed material used are given in the bibliography section.

I am particularly grateful to the Governor and Company of the Bank of England for granting me the unique privilege of examining in detail the Bank's earliest Court Minute Books, and for allowing me to make use of a great deal of valuable and hitherto unpublished material relating to the Bank's early history, its methods of business, its internal organisation, its issuing experiments, its connections with the goldsmith bankers, its " accommodation " of traders, its transactions with the Lords of the Treasury and with the Exchequer, its continental agencies, and its financing of William III's campaigns in the Low Countries.

This valuable new information with reference to the Bank's early activities has been supplemented from two other important sources : the contemporary Minute Books of the Treasury, preserved in the Public Record Office, and the Ranelagh Report preserved among the Harleian Manuscripts in the British Museum, which throw further light on the Bank's methods of financing the campaigns of William III.

Use has also been made of the Early Records of Chancery Proceedings, the Exchequer Bills and Answers, and the Records of the Exchequer of Receipt, all of which are preserved in the Public Record Office. These documents have yielded much new and interesting information relating to the transactions of the goldsmith bankers, and to the early forms of English paper money.

New and interesting information with reference to the technique of goldsmith banking has also been obtained from the earliest ledgers and other documents of the historic banking houses of Hoare and Child. Messrs. Hoare and Messrs. Glyn, Mills and Co. (in which firm Child's Bank is now incorporated) have given me every facility and assistance during the course of my investigation, and I have to acknowledge their kindness in allowing me to publish many curious excerpts from the ledger accounts of their early customers.

I desire to thank the Clerk of Parliaments, Sir Arthur Theodore Thring, K.C.B.; the Chamberlain of the City of London, Sir Adrian Pollock; the Rector of St. Mary Woolnoth, Lombard Street, the Rev. H. A, Raynes, M.A.; and the Master and Wardens of the Goldsmiths' Company of London for granting me permission to examine some of the valuable documents in their custody. I wish, also, to express my thanks to the editors of the *Quarterly Journal of Economics*; the *Journal of Economic and Business History*; *Economic History* (the annual Supplement to the *Economic Journal*), and the *Banker* for allowing me to include certain sections which have appeared in these periodicals.

The assistance on special matters which I have so freely received from various experts is acknowledged in the context.

R. D. R.

Cambridge,
   August 1929.

CONTENTS

CHAPTER I

THE PIONEERS

CHAPTER II

THE GOLDSMITH BANKERS AND THE EVOLUTION OF ENGLISH PAPER MONEY

CHAPTER III

THE GOLDSMITH BANKERS AND THEIR TRANSACTIONS WITH THE EXCHEQUER

CONTENTS·

CHAPTER IV
TUDOR AND STUART BANKING SCHEMES

CHAPTER VII

THE EARLY TRANSACTIONS OF THE BANK OF ENGLAND (continued)

CHAPTER VIII

THE SALIENT FEATURES OF ENGLISH BANKING HISTORY IN THE EIGHTEENTH AND EARLY NINETEENTH CENTURIES

CHAPTER IX

CONCLUSION

APPENDICES

CONTENTS

LIST OF ABBREVIATIONS

Addit.	Additional MSS.
B.M.	British Museum.
Burr.	Burrow, *Reports.*
Cal. S.P. Dom.	*Calendar State Papers, Domestic.*
Cal. S.P. For.	*Calendar State Papers, Foreign.*
Cal. T. B.	*Calendar Treasury Books.*
Cal. T. P.	*Calendar Treasury Papers.*
Carth.	Carthew, *Reports.*
Ch. P.	Chancery Proceedings.
C. J.	*Journals of the House of Commons.*
C. M. B.	Court Minute Books of the Bank of England.
Cott.	Cottonian MSS.
Croke.	Croke, *Reports.*
D. N. B.	*Dictionary of National Biography.*
D. P. E.	*Dictionary of Political Economy* (Palgrave).
Enc. Brit.	*Encyclopædia Britannica.*
Eng. Reps. Ch.	*English Reports, Chancery.*
Ex. Accs. V.	Exchequer Accounts, Various.
Harl.	Harleian MSS.
H.M.C.R.	Historical Manuscripts Commission, *Reports.*
Holt	Holt, *Reports.*
Keble	Keble, *Reports.*
Lansd.	Lansdowne MSS.
Ld. Raym.	Lord Raymond, *Reports.*
Lev.	Levinz, *Reports.*
L. J.	*Journals of the House of Lords.*
Lutw.	Lutwyche, *Reports.*
Mod.	*Modern Reports.*
N. E. D.	*The Oxford New English Dictionary.*
Parl. P.	*Parliamentary Papers.*
P.R.O.	Public Record Office.
Recs. Ex. R.	Records of the Exchequer of Receipt.
Recs. T.	Records of the Treasury.

Reps. D.K.P.R.	*Reports of the Deputy Keeper of Public Records.*
Salk.	Salkeld, *Reports.*
Show.	Shower, *Reports.*
S.P. Dom.	State Papers, Domestic.
S.P. For.	State Papers, Foreign.
Trans.R.Hist.S.	*Transactions of the Royal Historical Society.*
Ves. sen.	Vesey, senior, *Cases.*

THE EARLY HISTORY OF BANKING IN ENGLAND

CHAPTER I

THE PIONEERS

"In his [Henry VII's] tyme the bankers had their begininge who did invente the merchandisynge exchange, makÿngè of money a merchandise."
—G. MALYNES, A Treatise of Tripartite Exchange (1610), B.M., Cott. MS., Otho, E.X., fol. 94.
' The 'Gentlemen of England . . . have too often their houses filled with Scriveners and Sollicitors, who entertain them with the croaking Musick of Procuration and Continuation till they have devoured their Estates."—J. CARY, Essay on the Coyn and Credit of England (1696), pp. 25–6.

OUT of the business of dealing in foreign moneys, a business indispensable to the traders who frequented the great mediæval continental fairs, there had emerged before the thirteenth century not only a system of offsetting mercantile debts, but also the method of assigning these debts by means of the bill of exchange. Before the third decade of the fourteenth century the Venetian money-changers had developed into recognised keepers of deposits, while a little later they were settling the debts of their customers by book transfers of credit.[1] " It is tolerably clear," writes a well-known authority,[2] " that private banking began in Venice as an adjunct of the business of the *campsores*, or dealers in foreign moneys." The money-changers, *changeurs*, or *campsores*, were the exchange specialists and financial intermediaries of mediæval Europe; the fairs were their clearing houses.

[1] See E. Lattes, *La Liberta delle banche a Venezia dal secolo XIII al XVII secondo i documenti inediti del R. Archivo dei Frari* (1869), pp. 26–29; F. Ferrara, " Gli antichi banchi di Venezia," in *Nuova Antologia*, XVI (1871), pp. 435–66; and P. Huvelin, *Le Droit des Marchés et des Foires* (1897), pp. 534–37.
[2] C. F. Dunbar, " The Bank of Venice," *Quarterly Journal of Economics*, VI (1892), p. 310; and *Economic Essays* (1904), p. 145.

B

The assigning of mercantile debts by means of the bill of exchange [1] was practised in England in the fourteenth century by merchants of continental extraction,[2] the wealthiest of whom were important Royal money-lenders.[3]   But though the Englishman was using this instrument with increasing frequency before the end of the following century,[4] he does not appear to have carried out any major operations in the " business of exchange " prior to the age of the Tudors. With, however, the expansion of England's trade during the latter part of the Tudor period the transactions of Englishmen in this particular sphere increased so rapidly that by the end of the Tudor régime they were of an outstanding nature.   It is, therefore, not surprising to find during the reigns of Elizabeth and James I certain English business men gradually developing into recognised money-lenders, money-changers, bullion merchants, exchange specialists, and financial middlemen.

Of these business men four types—the merchant, the broker, the scrivener, and the goldsmith—became prominent as financial intermediaries.   They are the pioneers of the banker's trade in England; the origins of English banking must be sought for in their transactions.

Even in the early years of Elizabeth's reign the term banker, connoting an exchange specialist, was in use in England, and the Elizabethan traders and writers were well acquainted with the operations of these specialists.   In 1572

[1] The early history of the English bill of exchange is discussed in Chap. II, pp. 43-47 *infra*.

[2] See A. H. Thomas, *Calendar of Early Mayor's Court Rolls preserved among the Archives of the Corporation of the City of London* (1924), pp. 94, 200-1.

[3] For the operations of Italian financiers in pre-Tudor days see Sir Edward A. Bond, " Extracts from the Liberate Roll relative to loans supplied by Italian merchants to the Kings of England in the Thirteenth and Fourteenth Centuries," *Archæologia*, XXVIII (1839), pp. 207-326; R. J. Whitwell, " Italian Bankers and the English Crown," *Trans. R. Hist. S.*, New Series, XVII (1903); W. E. Rhodes, " The Italian Bankers in England and their Loans to Edward I and Edward II," in T. F. Tout and J. Tait, *Historical Essays* (1907).

[4] In the reign of Edward IV, for instance, by the merchants of the Staple.   See *The Cely Papers, 1475-1488* (1900, ed. by H. E. Malden for R. Hist. S.), No. 128; *The Stonor Letters and Papers, 1290-1483* (1919, ed. by C. L. Kingsford for R. Hist. S.), Nos. 150 and 223, and E. Power, " The English Wool Trade in the Reign of Edward IV," *Cambridge Historical Journal*, II, No. 1 (1926).

that remarkable critic of the financiers of the day, Dr. Thomas Wilson, carefully examined, in his earnest and thorough *Discourse uppon Usurye*,[1] the methods of " bankers and exchangers," [2] while eight years before the publication of this learned treatise, an observant English economic writer described in detail how " the bankers do cunningly fall the exchange at Antwerp." [3]

But the transactions of the Antwerpian bankers were of an extensive nature much earlier in the sixteenth century than the reign of Elizabeth. The Flemish loan negotiations of Sir Stephen Vaughan during his tenure of the office of Royal Agent are striking evidence of the extent of these transactions in the first half of the sixteenth century.[4] " Two days ago," wrote the Queen of Hungary on 25th May 1544 to the Imperial Ambassador in London with reference to Vaughan's arrival in the Low Countries, " came one who calls himself the King's Commissioner and seeks in Antwerp to raise for the King [Henry VIII] 100,000 ducats monthly." [5] An interesting letter written by Vaughan, which describes how this loan was obtained,[6] is a typical illustration of the dealings of the Tudor royal agents with the continental bankers.[7]

In Vaughan's time the securities usually accepted by the bankers of Antwerp for English loans were those of Italian mercantile firms established in London, such as the houses of Vivalde and Bonvyce.[8] This is evidence of an exotic predominance in the embryonic London money market of

---

[1] Published in 1572. [2] P. 114 *b*.

[3] B.M., Harl. MS., 660, fol. 107.

[4] That the overseas financial operations of the Tudor royal agents were extensive in the first half of the sixteenth century is proved by the fact that at one time the annual interest on Henry VIII's Flemish loans amounted to £40,000. See J. W. Burgon, *The Life and Times of Sir Thomas Gresham* (1839), I, p. 68.

[5] *Letters and Papers, Foreign and Domestic, of the Reign of Henry VIII*, arranged and catalogued by J. Gairdner and R. H. Brodie, XIX (1903), Pt. I, 578.

[6] *Ibid.*, XIX, Pt. I, 630.

[7] For a detailed examination of the activities of Vaughan see F. C. Dietz, *English Government Finance, 1485–1558* (1920), pp. 167–74. See also R. H. Tawney and E. Power, *Tudor Economic Documents* (1924), II, pp. 138–42.

[8] *L. and P., op. cit.*, XIX, Pt. I, 630. For other Italian mercantile houses in London " known and abled upon " the Antwerp Bourse see *ibid.*, XIX, Pt. I, 725.

the first half of the sixteenth century, a predominance which declined in the second half of the same century when Englishmen began to play an important part in international finance. Sometimes, however, even in the first half of this century, English merchants and members of the Privy Council guaranteed the integrity of the Italian house in London whose securities for loans were accepted in Antwerp.[1]

Antwerp reached the height of its prosperity between 1500 and 1560,[2] and during this important period of European commercial expansion its great financial magnates, the Fuggers, Hochstetters, Welsers, Tuchers, Van Dalls, Prowens, Hoffemans, Lyndenas and Rantzaviuses appear to have been always ready to negotiate with the English royal agent.

The wealthiest of these continental financiers were the Fuggers of Augsburg.[3] "The Fugger is never from me," wrote Vaughan to the English Privy Council in September 1546, " the house of Bonvyce . . . pulls me hourly by the sleeve ";[4] and it was with the firm of Fugger, which by 1508 had established an agency in Antwerp, that more than one of the English royal agents, particularly Sir

---

[1] *L. and P.*, *op. cit.*, XIX, Pt. I, 759.

[2] For a description by modern writers of Antwerp at the height of its prosperity see Burgon, *op. cit.*, I, pp. 75–77; J. L. Motley, *The Rise of the Dutch Republic* (1885), II, pp. 95–98; H. Pirenne, *Histoire de Belgique* (1900–1920), II, pp. 399–403, and III, pp. 259–72; J. A. Goris, *Étude sur les Colonies Marchandes Méridionales à Anvers de 1488 à 1567* (1925), particularly pp. 338–409; R. H. Tawney, *Religion and the Rise of Capitalism* (1926), pp. 73–76; and R. Ehrenburg, *Capital and Finance in the Age of the Renaissance* (English trans. by H. M. Lucas of *Das Zeitalter der Fugger*, 1928), pp. 233–80.

A contemporary writer, L. Guicciardini, *Descrittione di tutti Paesi Bassi, altrimente detti Germania inferiore* (1567), pp. 82–115, gives a detailed description of Antwerp and its merchant houses. For a lengthy excerpt relating to the trade of Antwerp from the French translation of this work see Tawney and Power, *op. cit.*, III, pp. 149–73.

[3] For the House of Fugger see W. Jacob, *An Historical Inquiry into the Production and Consumption of the Precious Metals* (1831), II, p. 26 *et seq.*; Ehrenburg, *op. cit.*, I, pp. 64–132; Burgon, *op. cit.*, pp. 60–63; A. Stauber, *Das Haus Fugger* (1900); P. van Dyke, " A Captain of Industry in the Sixteenth Century," *Harper's Magazine*, European ed., 59 (1909–1910), pp. 276–84; V. von Klarwill, *The Fugger Newsletters* (1924); and *ibid.*, Second Series (1926).

There are numerous references to the transactions of the Fuggers in *L. and P.*, *op. cit.*

A detailed list of recent works dealing with the history of the Fuggers is given in the *Economic History Review*, Vol. I, No. 2 (January 1928), p. 342.   [4] *L. and P.*, *op. cit.*, XXI, Pt. II (1910), 51.

Thomas Gresham, the greatest of them all, conducted large transactions.

Gresham [1] commenced his loan operations in Antwerp in 1552, operations which have been described in great detail by Burgon.[2] During the ensuing fifteen years, with the assistance of Sir Richard Clough, his able and zealous Welsh "factor," he raised in this great financial centre many large loans for the Tudors. Before 1570 this famous "Court banker of Elizabeth"[3] had also succeeded in obtaining very substantial State loans in London, loans which are of considerable importance in the genesis of the London money market,[4] and which prove that by the 'sixties of the sixteenth century Englishmen undoubtedly possessed the power to engage in high finance.

The surviving records of Gresham's financial activities in the City of London show that he obtained large sums for the use of the State from Englishmen. The following interesting item [5] illustrates his method of recording these London loans :

---

[1] For the career of Gresham see *D.N.B.* See also Burgon, *op. cit.*; H. R. Fox Bourne, *Famous London Merchants* (1890), Chap. II; and F. R. Salter, *Sir Thomas Gresham* (1925).

[2] *Life and Times, op. cit.* See also H. Buckley, "Sir Thomas Gresham and the Foreign Exchanges," *Economic Journal*, XXXIV (1924), pp. 589–601.
Among a large number of contemporary documents dealing with the overseas financial transactions of Gresham the following are interesting :— S.P. For., Eliz., 14, letter dated 12th May 1560; 15, letter dated 24th June 1560; 30, letters dated 2nd and 8th September 1561; 40, letters dated 11th and 16th August 1562.
A number of Elizabeth's letters to Gresham are contained in B.M., Addit. MS., 5755.

[3] B.M., Addit. MS., 5755.

[4] Evidence of the increasing importance of London as a monetary centre is contained in an interesting letter from Gresham to Cecil, dated Antwerp, 12th May 1560. Gresham states that he is confident that large loans for the use of the State could be raised in England at interest not exceeding 5 per cent. S.P. For., Eliz., 14.
A little later in the same year Gresham informed Cecil of the large number of bankruptcies in Antwerp, the most startling being those of Lixhall and Fleachamore (*ibid.*, 14, letter dated 30th August 1560); and in September 1561 he reported a great scarcity of money in Antwerp (*ibid.*, 30, letter dated 2nd September 1561).
See also *Cal. S.P. For., Eliz., 1569–1571*, no. 1416, p. 373, and no. 1755, p. 463.

[5] From B.M., Lansd. MS., 12, fols. 28–29. Even so early as 1561 a loan of £30,000 at 10 per cent. was raised for Elizabeth in London. This sum was obtained from twelve Englishmen. S.P. Dom., Eliz., 19, no. 2.

Item of Sr Rog^r Martenn,[1] Knyght, the xxvj daie of Novemb^r 1569 to paie the xxvj daie of Maye an^o 1570 the somme of xvc^{li} : more for the brokerage after one p cento some xv^{li}, more for thinterest after vj upon the hundrethe for vj monethes some iiij$\overset{xx}{}$ xi^{li} .... lmvjcvj^{li}.

There is a great deal of further documentary evidence relating to the flotation of State loans in the London of Elizabeth. In a list of London residents who in 1589 contributed to a Royal loan of £15,000 at 10 per cent.[2] there are over a hundred subscribers, Englishmen with hardly an exception. Still later Elizabethan loans lists, compiled by the actual Royal " collectors," show that in the last decade of the sixteenth century large sums were raised in London by means of the Privy Seal demand note, " loanes," as they were termed, " upon Privie Seales." [3] These well-preserved later lists [4] are cogent proofs of the capacity of Englishmen as contributors to State loans in Elizabethan times, and of the striking development of London as a monetary centre after the eclipse of Antwerp and its famous Bourse.

The Privy Seal demand note was usually issued in printed form to specially appointed " collectors " who entered on the note the lender's name, the amount advanced, and the receipt for the same. A Jacobean specimen,[5] dated 31st July 1604, is headed with the words " By the King "; commences with the phrase, " Trustie and well-beloved "; and demands the sum of £30 to be delivered to John Wyn, Esq., " our collector in our Countie of Carnarvon . . . the loan whereof we do desire to be untill the twenty fourth day of March 1605[6]." Moreover, the note was " an immediate warrant to our Exchequer " to pay the contents

[1] A London " mercer," i.e. general merchant, who became Lord Mayor in 1567.

[2] B.M., Lansd. MS., 60, fol. 45.

[3] Many details of Elizabethan " loanes upon Privie Seales " are contained among the State Papers, Domestic, e.g., S.P. Dom., Eliz., 71, no. 4; 71, no. 9; 71, no. 24; 71, no. 77; 73, no. 43; 73, no. 70. Also in P.R.O., Recs. Ex. R., E. 401/2583 (dated 1597); E. 401/2584 (dated 1604-5); E. 401/2585 (dated 1620); and B.M., Addit. MS., 27877 (dated 1611–12).

[4] Particularly in P.R.O., Recs. Ex. R., E. 401/2590, a parcel which contains several Elizabethan lists of receipts of " money upon Privy Seales."

[5] In P.R.O., Recs. Ex. R., E. 401/2590.

to the lender or "his assignes" upon its delivery at the Exchequer of Receipt [1] when the loan was due for repayment. It could thus be assigned, and among the extant specimens there are actual examples of assignments. An Elizabethan specimen for £50,[2] duly receipted by the "collector," is indorsed with the signature of an assignee, who received the sum specified on the note at the Exchequer of Receipt. The assignability of the Privy Seal demand note in Elizabethan times is an important monetary phenomenon, for it must be remembered that the bill of exchange payable to order was not recognised as an assignable instrument by the English Courts of Common Law until the post-Restoration era.[3]

The surviving Royal "collectors'" lists of the subscribers to the State loans [4] and the Wardens' Accounts and Court Minute Books of the Goldsmiths' Company of London [5] contain numerous illustrations of the financial activities of Elizabethan merchants and goldsmiths.[6] There are, also, a number of contemporary documents among the Records

[1] The old English Exchequer was divided into the Exchequer of Receipt, the department which was concerned with the actual receipt and payment of public revenue, and the Exchequer of Account or audit department. For contemporary accounts of the Exchequer in the seventeenth century see Sir Thomas Fanshaw, *The Practice of the Exchequer Court and its severall Offices and Officers* (1658); and P.R.O., Recs. T., T. 43/6, The Lowndes Papers. See also T. Madox, *The History and Antiquities of the Exchequer* (1769), I, Chap. VII; F. S. Thomas, *The Ancient Exchequer of England* (1848), Chap. IV; H. Hall, *Antiquities and Curiosities of the Exchequer* (1898), Chap. IV; H. Jenkinson, *A Manual of Archive Administration* (1922), pp. 206–19; M. S. Giuseppi, *A Guide to the Manuscripts preserved in the Public Record Office* (1923), I, pp. 178–81.

[2] P.R.O., Recs. Ex. R., E. 401/2590.

[3] For the emergence of assignability in the bill of exchange see Chap. II, pp. 44–45 *infra*.

[4] In addition to the receipted Privy Seal demand note a kind of verbose promissory note, termed a "bill obligatory," was sometimes given by a Royal financial intermediary as a sealed acknowledgment of a loan. Some of the Tudor sealed bills are still extant, and one of these, dated 1581, acknowledging a loan of £1,000 received by Leicester from Sir Richard Martin, a powerful Elizabethan goldsmith, contains among other words the following promise :—"I the said Erle doe by this bill confesse that by her Maties appoyntment I have receaved the said some of one m li to be repayd to the said Richard Martin or his heirs executors and assigns by the end of three monthes next ensuying the date hereof." B.M., Lansd. MS., 32, fols. 31–44.

[5] Preserved in Goldsmiths' Hall, London.

[6] See W. S. Prideaux, *Memorials of the Goldsmiths' Company* (1896–1897), *passim*.

of the Exchequer of Receipt which show that certain of the later Tudor goldsmiths were important bullion merchants.[1] It was this type of goldsmith—craftsman, bullion merchant and money-lender—who was the immediate forerunner of the goldsmith banker of Stuart London, a banker who became generally recognised in the metropolis and in the provinces as a keeper of deposits, an issuer of promissory notes, and a dealer in bills of exchange and various types of Treasury-Exchequer money orders.

But it does not appear from the available contemporary evidence that the goldsmiths were outstanding figures in the London money market of Elizabethan and Jacobean times. Though always ready to lend money for a " consideration," the Martins, Hoares, Heriots, Spilmans and Williamses of the reigns of Elizabeth and James I were primarily jewellers and lapidaries, makers and sellers of gold and silver ware, cutters and vendors of precious stones. Their financial activities were overshadowed by those of the merchants, the brokers and the scriveners. In the last decade of the Tudor period the English " exchanging " merchants carried out large operations in bills of exchange, and in the actual transference of coin and bullion from England to France and Flanders, or from these countries to England. " These Bankers, these money men, and merchants," writes Wilson, " doe set what price they list of money and make it eyther of highe value, or meane value as they please, for their owne singular commoditie and private gaine." [2]

Both in the State Papers and in the Records of the Exchequer of Receipt appertaining to the reigns of Eliza-beth and James I there are many instances of the large transactions of English merchants in the business of " de-livering money beyond the seas by bills of exchange.' Among several references to these operations in the forme documents is a special report, submitted to Burghley ir 1597, which deals with the affairs of William Beecher whose profits as an exchange specialist amounted in a com-

---

[1] *E.g.* Sir Richard Martin's transactions, P.R.O., Ex. Accs. V., E. 101 Bdles. 296/4, 304/12; and those of Sir Martin Bowes, *ibid.*, Bdles. 302/24 and 27, 303/5, 7 and 8.
[2] *Discourse uppon Usurye*, p. 114 b.

paratively short time to £40,000.[1] But the evidence among
the latter documents is overwhelming proof of the fact that
during the Elizabethan and Jacobean periods, English
merchants not only carried out extensive exchange transactions, but also advanced a great deal of money to the
State. It is only necessary to examine the first of the Pell
Office [2] Order Books, dated 1597–1599,[3] to find that large
sums were paid by Army paymasters on active service
overseas to English merchants " for so much money by them
made over by exchange " ; [4] and there are entries of many
such transactions in the remaining Elizabethan and Jacobean
books of this well-preserved series of Exchequer records.
The Order Book dated 1610–11 [5] may be taken as a typical
Jacobean specimen. It contains several entries which are

[1] S.P. Dom., Eliz., 264, no. 145. A Jacobean Chancery bill of complaint, P.R.O., Ch. P., Series II, Bdle. 337–70, *Beecher* v. *Quarles*, states
that Beecher was " employed in the years 1595 and 1596 to make over
money by exchange " for payment of the English forces in Flanders and
France. Details of the transactions of Beecher are contained in S.P.
Dom., Eliz.; 261, no. 36; 262, no. 114; 263, nos. 9 and 10; 264, no. 145;
and of other such Elizabethan merchants in *ibid.*, 244, no. 33; 251, no.
80; 262, no. 97; 262, no. 109; 262, no. 135; 263, no. 8.
[2] The Pell Office was that department of the Exchequer of Receipt
which recorded all issues, and was presided over by an official called the
Clerk of the Pells. After the restoration of this office in 1597, separate
books for this purpose known as Order Books were commenced. The
Clerk of the Pells also recorded all payments in the Issue Books. See
Reps. D.K.P.R., VI, App. II, pp. 218–25, and III, App. II, pp. 173–87;
also Giuseppi, *op. cit.*, I, p. 185.
[3] P.R.O., Recs. Ex. R., Order Books (Pells'), E. 403/2721.
[4] The method appears to have been as follows :—Under the authority
of the Privy Seal a payment order representing a certain sum, signed by
the Lord Treasurer, was issued by the Exchequer of Receipt to the Army
Paymaster, who gave it, or sent it, to the merchant who " made the money
over by exchange," and the latter presented it for payment at the Exchequer of Receipt. The payment order is described in Chap. II, pp. 57–
58 *infra*.
The following is a synopsis of an entry in the Order Book (Pells'), dated
1609–1610, P.R.O., E. 403/2729, fol. 14*b*, relating to the above method :—
Order dated 22nd March 1609[10] under Privy Seal for £5,895 6s. 10d. to
Richard Weight, H.M. Paymaster in the Low Countries, " in prest to be
by him paid to Edward and John Meredith of London, Merchants, for so
much money by them made over by exchange and paid to the hands of
his deputie for the paie and imprests."
The English merchants " made the money over " in three ways :—
(1) by the actual transfer of metallic money; (2) by selling English goods,
usually wool, in Flanders, and thus obtaining ready money locally; (3) by
means of bills of exchange drawn on Flemish merchants. See E. Power,
" The English Wool Trade in the Reign of Edward IV," *Cambridge Historical
Journal*, II, No. 1 (1926).
[5] P.R.O., Recs. Ex. R., E. 403/2730.

remarkable illustrations of the financial activities of London
merchants in the reign of James I.   One, for example, refers
to the repayment on 24th December 1610 of a State loan of
£30,000, with £3,000 interest,[1] a loan which had been
advanced by six English merchants; another relates to a
State loan of £10,000 advanced by one English merchant;[2]
and there are a number of entries relating to the big exchange
transactions of Edward and John Meredith " of London,
merchants." [3]

We know also from Wilson that exchange transactions
were of an important nature in the Elizabethan period.
He points out that in dealings of this kind the " bankers
and exchangers " made a deduction known as *collibos* in
return for their services, or as a recompense for the " damage
and losse " received " by the money which they deliver by
exchange." [4]   He divides what he terms " the bankers
art " into " exchange reall " and " exchange by bills," the
former indicating the exchange of metallic money, and the
latter including the artifice known as " dry exchange," [5]

[1] P.R.O., Recs. Ex. R., E. 403/2730, fol. 96b.   [2] *Ibid.*, fol. 66b.
[3] *Ibid.*, fols. 14b, 125b, 150b, 159b, 211b.
The Company of Merchant Adventurers were also active in the business
of exchange during Elizabethan times, *e.g.* S.P. Dom., Eliz., 262, no. 96;
249, no. 54.
It is true that in the later Elizabethan and the Jacobean periods a few
of these " exchanging " merchants were either " merchants strangers " or
merchants of foreign extraction resident in England.   Such, for example,
were Horatio Palavicino, in Elizabethan times, and Philip Burlamachi,
in the reigns of James I and Charles I.   The latter, however, always
appears to have regarded himself as an Englishman.
For examples of Palavicino's transactions see S.P. Dom., Eliz., 241,
no. 38; 265, no. 121.   See also W. H. and H. C. Overall, *Analytical Index
to the Remembrancia* (1878), I, 513; I, 615; II, 219; III, 6; VI, 67
(pp. 185–94).
For some of Burlamachi's accounts see B.M., Addit. MS., 18674, fols.
19–23.   See also H. V. Judges, " Philip Burlamachi, a Financier of the
Thirty Years' War," *Economica*, November 1926; and *H.M.C.R., MSS.
of the Marquis of Salisbury*, Pt. I (1883), p. 163, No. 10; and Pt. II (1888),
p. 153.   [4] *Discourse uppon Usurye*, fol. 110b.
[5] *Discourse uppon Usurye*, fol. 114b.   Wilson explains " dry exchange "
by stating that it was " practised when one doth borrowe money by ex-
chaunge for a strange Region, at longer or shorter distaunce of time, to serve
his turne the rather thereby, not myndynge to make anye reall payment
abroade, but compoundeth with thexchanger to have it returned backe
agayne accordyng as thexchaunge shall passe from thence to London, for
suche distaunce of time as they were agreed upon."   See R. H. Tawney,
Wilson's Discourse upon Usury, intro., pp. 73–74; M. Postlethwayt, *Universal Dictionary of Trade and Commerce* (4th ed., 1744); and W. Forbes,
A Methodical Treatise concerning Bills of Exchange (1703), p. 2, for further
details about " dry exchange."

which has been described as "nothing more mysterious than what to-day would be called a finance bill."[1]

But though in Elizabethan and Jacobean times the "business of exchange" was to a large extent in the hands of certain wealthy English merchants, the English brokers and scriveners had also developed into important financial intermediaries, and in some instances into actual money-lenders. "John Davenant, broker, of London, for certeyne money men and merchants," we are told in a Jacobean Chancery document[2] which refers to the Elizabethan period, "made divers offers in loans or otherwise by way of mart to deliver money to Robert Gyttens," one of Elizabeth's chaplains, who, "by subtile intimacions and sinister practices," was "drawn to enter into divers bonds and statutes unto the said John Davenant," "in great trade" as a broker.

Many English brokers by the end of the sixteenth century seem to have specialised in the "business of exchange." Many, on the other hand, were simply common pawnbrokers, and these, undoubtedly the most vicious of Tudor and Stuart money-lenders, are referred to by contemporary critics as the "retayling" brokers, thus distinguishing them from the "exchanging" brokers, who were termed "sworn" brokers if they traded under official authority.

Malynes, in his *Lex Mercatoria*,[3] has a high opinion of the "sworn" brokers, and regards "the testimony of a sworn broker and his booke together" as "sufficient" to end any differences with reference to mercantile contracts.[4] There were a great many complaints about the dealings of the other class, the "retaylinge broggers," "fripperers," or "thievinge brokers," particularly in the reigns of Elizabeth and James I. Huniman, writing in the latter reign,[5] refers to the large number of "pawnes" taken by such brokers upon "unlawful, intolerable and unjustifiable considera-

---

[1]. Tawney, *op. cit.*, intro., p. 73.
[2] P.R.O., Ch. P., James I, Bdle. G. 16/75, which gives a lengthy and vivid description of the methods of an Elizabethan money-lending broker.
[3] First ed., 1622.
[4] *Lex Mercatoria*, p. 201.
[5] B.M., Royal MS., 18 B. XVIII. "A Project for raysing of a Stocke out of the iniquity, the dangerous proceedings and the unlawful dealings of thievinge brokers to supply the most urgent occasion that the commons dailie have for loan of moneye upon their pawns."

tion." They were big receivers of stolen goods, and by carrying on this trade, in spite of laws and proclamations, became a great danger to the public weal. "This dunghill trade of brokerie," wrote Stubbes in Elizabethan times, "newly sprung up and coined in the devil's minting house the shoppe of all mischiefe hath made many a theefe more than ever would have bin." [1]

The "intolerable consideration" of the retailing brokers is also emphasised by Malynes, who states that these brokers were often financial middlemen borrowing from the monied men in order to lend to the needy at extortionate rates. He quotes their "most favourable extortion by Usurie upon pawnes" as "sixpence for 20 shillings for one moneth of 28 days which is about thirtie in the hundreth by the yeare." [2] He suggests certain remedies for such exactions, one of which, copied from Italy, is the erection of *Monts de Piété*, or "Banks of Charity," for receiving legacies from which advances could be made upon the security of pawns at low rates of interest.[3] He refers to the Venetian exchange office,[4] of which only brokers were members, and thinks that its adoption in England would remedy many abuses, while he strongly advocates the establishment of "Counting-Houses" with "masters" and assistants for dealing "in five severall matters, by Exchange, Banke, Mount of Charitie, *Mensa argentaria*, and Houses of Vendition." [5]

Huniman is more emphatic. He would "bridle ' the "retayling broggers" and their "devilish proceedings," by placing them under arrest until their accounts were compared with the bills of their customers. He urges a strict

---

[1] *The Anatomie of Abuses* (1583), Pt. II, no pagination.
[2] *Lex Mercatoria*, p. 337.
[3] *Ibid.*, p. 341. See Chap. IV, p. 95 *infra*, for further details about *Monts de Piété*.
[4] *Ibid.*, p. 202.
[5] *Ibid.*, p. 204. Even so early as 1601 Malynes in his *Treatise of the Canker of Englands Commonwealth*, pp. 20–26, described the banking of his time as practised on the Continent, a description which is reproduced in *Lex Mercatoria*, Pt. I, Chap. XX, and entitled "Of Banks and Bankers." He defines a "banke" in the former work, p. 20, as "a collection of all the readie monies of some Province, Citie, or commonwealth, into the handes of some persons licenced and established thereunto by publike authoritie of some Prince, erected with great solemnitie in the view of all the people and inhabitants."

search of brokers' houses throughout the whole of London and the contiguous areas, a search which he thinks would reveal the names of the " money-masters " from whom the brokers obtained the money for their money-lending transactions at rates which, he tells us, varied from 20 to 25 per cent., while they charged their customers 60, 80 and even 100 per cent.[1] For eradicating such exactions he, like Malynes, suggests the erection of *Monts de Piété*, " King James his Bancke Houses of Piete," which he regards as of more importance than the Charterhouse, founded in James I's reign, and all the other London hospitals.[2]

Gerbier, writing in 1641,[3] and Cooke, in 1648,[4] refer to the " horrible usury," and the " cruelties " of the pawntaking brokers. Both these writers follow Huniman and Malynes as advocates of *Monts de Piété*, while Gerbier draws attention to the striking increase of usurious practices among the servants of brokers, and emphasises the fact that " such as doe take pawns " were " multiplying daily."

The unofficial brokers greatly increased in number during the 'sixties and the 'seventies of the seventeenth century. A proclamation of Sir Richard Ford, Lord Mayor of London, dated 7th November 1671,[5] states that " of late years " the " franchises and liberties " of the City had been " much invaded and violated by Foreigners, Stranger Aliens, and others taking upon them the employment of brokers upon the Royal Exchange." His Lordship, therefore, forbade any but " sworn " brokers " to deal or intermeddle " between merchant and merchant. " Exchange," wrote John Scarlett, " merchant of the Eastland Company " and legal expert, eleven years later, " is concluded by Mackelers or Brogers alone betwixt themselves, or by bringing the Parties face to face." " Brogers," he adds, " are Persons Sworn and Authorized by the Magistrate, whose work and Trade it

---

[1] Huniman, *op. cit.*, fol. 11.
[2] *Ibid.*, fol. 12.
[3] S.P. Dom., Charles I, 478, no. 96.
[4] *Unum Necessarium*, p. 29.
[5] B.M., 21. h. 5 (48). For an interesting account of the activities of the brokers in the 'seventies of the seventeenth century see J. Vernon, *The Compleat Compting House* (1678), pp. 108–11.

is to enquire of Persons that have Moneys to remit or to draw, and to agree such Persons concerning the Conditions, acting impartially between them both." [1]

In the last decade of the seventeenth century some of the brokers appear to have developed into bullion dealers, [2] and some into stock-jobbers. Both Houghton and Defoe, writing in this decade, refer to the emergence of stock-jobbing. Houghton in five numbers of his curious newspaper [3] gives " an account of the main things that relate to Stocks and Stock-Jobbing." ." The forming of public Joint-Stocks," writes Defoe, [4] " which together with the East India, Africa and Hudson's Bay Companies before established begot a New Trade which we call by a new Name, Stock-Jobbing."

Evidence of the emergence of the stock-jobber, and also of a further increase in the number, and in the transactions, of the brokers before the end of the seventeenth century, will be found in a statute of 1697, entitled, " An Act to restrain the Number and ill Practice of Brokers and Stock Jobbers." [5] In the early part of the following century the nature of the broker's business is clearly defined in an Act of 1711. [6] A section of this Act forbids a broker to receive more than 2s. 9d. per cent. in any contract or bargain in connection with the selling or buying of " tallies, orders, Exchequer bills, Exchequer tickets, Bank bills, or any share or interest in any joint stock enterprise." This is striking proof not only of the nature of the brokers' activities at this time but also of the development of English credit technique.

The other outstanding figure in the London money market

[1] *The Stile of Exchanges* (1682), pp. 7–8. Chap. II, pp. 7–13, of this detailed treatise is entitled " Of the duty of Mackelers or Exchange-Brogers."

[2] See 6 & 7 Wm. III, c. 17, s. 7 (1695).

[3] *A Collection for Improvement of Husbandry and Trade*, Nos. 98 to 102, dated 15th June to 13th July 1694.

[4] *Essay on Projects* (1697), p. 29.

[5] 8 & 9 Wm. III, c. 32. Compare this with 7 Geo. II, c. 8 (1734).

[6] 10 Anne, c. 19, s. 121.

These later Acts should be compared with 1 Jas. 1, c. 21 (1604), which attempted to curb the activities of the brokers, and 21 Jas. 1, c. 17 (1623), the earliest attempt to fix the broker's fees. See also 12 Anne, Stat. 2, c. 16, s. 2 (1713); and 6 Anne, c. 16, s. 4 (1707).

of Tudor and Jacobean times was the scrivener, whose original business was the writing of bonds, bills obligatory,[1] and contracts. In this position of clerical intermediary between trader and trader, buyer and seller, and lender and borrower, the scrivener had every opportunity of acquiring an intimate knowledge of financial and mercantile transactions, and of developing into a monied man and a money-lender.[2]

Indeed, there are strong grounds for concluding that the scrivener was the earliest English pioneer of the banker's trade. He appears to have preceded the goldsmith as a keeper of money deposits for the express purpose of loaning such deposits to his customers, and he continued to act in this capacity even after the goldsmith had developed into a banker.

There does not appear to be any evidence to show that the goldsmith, the broker, or the merchant made a practice of receiving deposits in Tudor and Jacobean times. A few instances of merchants keeping deposits occur in the Elizabethan and early Stuart Chancery Proceedings, though not as a regular and specialised business, with a view to re-issuing the money deposited in the form of loans, but for the purpose

---

[1] The terms ' bond" and '" bill obligatory " were sometimes used as interchangeable terms. In Ch. P., James I, Bdle. D. 7/63, *Harman* v. *Wild*, dated 1622, it is stated that Richard Wild, a London goldsmith, accepted as security for a loan of £50 a " bond or writing obligatorie " for £100. Often termed a " bond," a money bond, however, was generally regarded as a sealed writing acknowledging a debt in which the borrower usually bound himself for twice the amount of the loan. Such bonds appear to have been frequently transferred by indorsement by merchants in Stuart times. See *Buller* v. *Crips* (1704), 1 Salk., p. 130; and Chap. II, p. 48 *infra*.

Copies of the Tudor bills obligatory are given in W. West, *Symbolæographia* (1590), sect. 38; and I. B., *The Merchants Avizo* (1607), p. 55. The latter treatise also gives a copy of a Tudor bond. For details of pre-Tudor bills obligatory see *Select Cases concerning the Law Merchant, 1270–1638* (1908, ed. for the Selden Society by C. Gross).

For a good contemporary account of bills obligatory see Malynes, *Lex Mercatoria*, Chap. XIII. Malynes states that these bills were used as transferable instruments in the Low Countries. In the 'nineties of the seventeenth century, Sir Josiah Child, *New Discourse of Trade* (2nd ed., 1694), Chap. V, advocated the passing of a law for transferring these bills. For a modern description of bills obligatory see Sir J. Comyns, *A Digest of the Laws of England* (5th ed., 1822), Vol. 5, F. 2.

[2] For the stages in the evolution of the scrivener into a financier see H. C. Gutteridge, " The Origin and Historical Development of the Profession of Notaries Public," *Cambridge Legal Essays* (1926).

of personally using such money in trading transactions.[1]
Evidence, however, of the scrivener functioning as a deposit
keeper early in the seventeenth century is revealed in an
Act of 1621,[2] which refers to this intermediary as a person
who received " other men's money or estates into his trust
or custodie." There is also in existence a well-preserved
Chancery Bill of Complaint, dated 1616,[3] which describes in
detail the " shoppe ' 'and methods of a metropolitan
scrivener. This interesting document states that one John
Hedges, of Mitcham, Surrey, had on many occasions as
" he had spare in money . . . delivered the same unto one
William Gregory citizen and scryvener of London," and
that on or about Michaelmas 1615 had " delivered unto "
Gregory £200, such " divers sums " " remaining in the
scrivener's hands " and " at his disposition." We are also
told that these deposits were made use of by the scrivener
as loans to his customers, and that he kept a " servant or
apprentize " who was his " principal dealer," and " by him
imployed for receavinge and payinge of divers somes of
money." [4]

Throughout the seventeenth century the scrivener, or
" money scrivener " as he is sometimes termed by con-

[1] E.g. P.R.O., Ch. P., Early, Bdle. 608/24, Brown v. Thomas and Agnes
Doughty.
There are, however, instances in the latter part of the seventeenth
century of merchants forming partnerships and accepting deposits as a
specialised business. The deposits were invested in various trading enterprises, and the depositors received joint bonds as securities. See The
Case of Richard Thomson and Company (1678).

[2] 21 Jas. I, c. 19, s. 2. See also Herbert v. Lowns, Eng. Reps. Ch.,
XXI, Chap. I, pp. 495–96.

[3] P.R.O., Ch. P., James I, Bdle. H. 13/4, Hedges v. Gregory and Atwood.

[4] Further details of the money-lending activities of the scrivener in
Elizabethan and Jacobean times are contained in Ch. P., Early, Bdle.
407/44, Fulwoode v. Mayor and Sheriffs of London; and ibid., James I,
Bdle. H. 2/29, Hodges v. Chubb.
Descriptions of the activities of the scrivener are also given by Wilson
and Stubbes. The former, Discourse, p. 108, refers to the scrivener's
house as a kind of money-lending agency, while Stubbes, Anatomie of
Abuses, pp. 78b–79, deals with this intermediary as a deposit keeper, a
person to whom money " is committed " upon " good securities to the
owners for the repayment thereof " and a " certaine allowance for the
loane thereof," such deposits being afterwards loaned with interest to
" poore petitioners."
B.M., Lansd. M.S., 113, fol. 9, points out that not only did the merchants
entrust the scriveners, and also the brokers, with large sums for insurance
purposes, but that they also were accustomed to receive a great deal of
credit from these intermediaries.

temporary writers, was not only a particularly active money-lender but also a recognised custodian of deposits. In the " Act for the restraining of excessive Usury " [1] of 1660 he occupies pride of place among the usurers of the day, and even so late as the reign of Anne he again appears first in a list of financial middlemen in an Act of 1713.[2] Carefully compiled treatises intended for his guidance appeared in Stuart times,[3] and his business methods and artifices are frequently discussed in the writings of contemporaries. " The Country Gentleman," states Powell in his curious little book, *The Art of Thriving*,[4] published in 1636, " he is by this time come up to London and has brought his Atturney with him, one that professes the taking up of money by right of writ. His Atturney brings him to the Ship behind the Exchange and leaves him there while hee goes to fetch the only *Noverint* in those parts, whom hee prepares at his shop with the purpose. . . . Hee then brings the Scrivener into the taverne . . . and the Scrivener according to the true practice of most of them at the first meeting, especially while they were with the borrower in the taverne, was more easie in promising than they in proposing. . . . Let me see, saies the Scrivener, there comes in this night Sir Samvan Skynkers money, five hundred, and to-morrow much more. I can supply you one hundred to a thousand out of that as your occasions require : how say you ? "

The facile pen of Dekker, one of Powell's remarkable contemporaries, gives us a similar picture. " The Gulgroper," he states, referring to the scrivener or " moneymonger " in his *English Villanies*,[5] " takes him (the young gentleman) to a side window, and tells him he is sorry for his hard lucke . . . yet for his fathers sake (whom he hath known so long) if it pleases him he shall not leave off play for a hundred pounds or two. If my young Ostrich gape to swallow downe this mettall . . . then is the gold poured

---

[1] 12 Chas. II, c. 13.
[2] 12 Anne, Stat. 2, c. 16, s. 2.
[3] *E.g.* T.B., *The Several Forms of Instruments relating to the Affairs of Merchants and Traders* (1674); G. Billinghurst, *Arcana Clericala* (1674).
[4] P. 138.
[5] Section marked C. 2. Dekker's *English Villanies* was published in 1631.

on the board, a Bond is made for a repayment at the next quarter day." [1].

And so, also, that shrewd commercial writer Sir Dudley North refers, in a description of the banking methods of his time, to the scrivener's financial activities. " The Merchants and Gentlemen," he remarks, " keep their Money for the most part with Goldsmiths and Scriveners, and they, instead of having Ten Thousand Pounds in cash by them as their Accounts shew they should have of other Mens Money, to be paid at sight, have seldom One Thousand in Specie; but depend upon a course of Trade whereby Money comes in as fast as it is taken out; Wherefore I conclude that the Specific Money of this Nation is far less than the common Opinion makes." [2]

In addition, however, to the scrivener, the " retayling " and " exchanging " brokers, and the " exchanging " merchant, two other types of middlemen became more conspicuous with the expansion of English trade in the late Tudor and early Stuart periods. These were the wool " brogger " and the corn " bodger " of provincial England. [3] The former, who was " in effect the banker of the cottage weaver," [4] may be regarded as the precursor of the old-fashioned country banker. Invaluable as an agent of the

---

[1] Vernon in his *Compleat Compting House,* which appeared in 1678, thus describes the scrivener's methods (p. 128) :—" Suppose a man want *l.*100, he goes to a Scrivener and tells him his wants; the Scrivener tells him he hath a Friend hath *l.*100 lies by him, and if he will give him anything for his pains and trouble, he will endeavour to possess his Friend . . . that he will procure the said *l.*100 to be lent him for six months, or twelve months, or as they do agree; this is called Procuration, and many times 40s. 50s. *l.*5, is given to a Procurer to obtain the lending of *l.*100 for twelve months."

[2] *Discourse upon Trade* (1691), p. 20. See also J. Cary, *An Essay on the Coyn and Credit of England* (1696), p. 25; and A. Justice, *A General Treatise of Monies and Exchanges* (1707), pp. 20–21.

[3] For details of the activities of wool " broggers " and corn " bodgers " see R. B. Westerfield, *Middlemen in English Business* (1915), pp. 265–66 and 134–36; N. S. B. Gras, *The Evolution of the English Corn Market* (1915), particularly Chap. VII; W. Cunningham, *Growth of English Industry and Commerce* (5th ed., 1921), *Modern Times,* I., pp. 85—100; and Bland, Brown and Tawney, *English Economic History, Select Documents* (1914), pp. 367–69, 373–80, 385.

The business of the wool " brogger " is dealt with in several Tudor statutes. See, for example, 4 Hy. VII, c. 11 (1487); 37 Hy. VIII, c. 15 (1545); 1 Ed. VI, c. 6 (1547).

[4] Tawney, *Wilson's Discourse, etc.,* intro. p. 49.

exporting merchant or the wool-jobbing capitalist,[1] the wool " brogger " was a particularly helpful intermediary to the wool-grower and small clothier of the countryside. To the wool-grower he advanced money on the security of future supplies of wool, and to the clothier he sold wool on credit. Loans and credit sales of this nature were quite common in Tudor times,[2] and even much earlier.[3]

But the expansion of English trade was not the only factor which gave an impetus to the activities of financial intermediaries. Another important reason why these activities increased in the late Tudor and early Stuart periods was the change of public opinion with reference to the ethics of usury.[4] In the antecedents of English banking the legalisation of usury is an event of considerable importance. The Act of 1545,[5] which allowed the taking of interest up to 10 per cent., increased the transactions of " moneymaster " and money-lender.[6] They, however, received a set-back in 1552 when the Act of 1545 was repealed,[7] but

[1] See G. Unwin, Industrial Organisation in the Sixteenth and Seventeenth Centuries (1904), App. A. II.

[2] The operations of financial middlemen in industry are also very evident during the Tudor epoch in the organisation of the tin mining of the Stannaries. See G. R. Lewis, The Stannaries (1908).

[3] There is evidence which shows that the advancing of money to English wool-growers on the security of future supplies of wool was practised in the thirteenth and fourteenth centuries particularly by Flemish and Italian merchants, and that the granting of credit in connection with the sale of wool and cloth was an ordinary feature of English trade. See M. Postan, " Credit in Mediæval Trade," Economic History Review, I, No. 2 (1928).

[4] For further details about this change see Sir William Ashley, An Introduction to English Economic History and Theory (3rd ed., 1894), Pt. II, chap. vi; Cunningham, op. cit., Modern Times, I, pp. 153–59; Tawney, " Religious Thought on Social and Economic Questions in the Sixteenth and Seventeenth Centuries," Journal of Political Economy, XXXI, Nos. 4, 5 and 6 (1923); and Tawney, Religion and the Rise of Capitalism (1926), particularly pp. 36–55.

[5] 37 Hy. VIII, c. 9.

[6] It is also possible that the activities of financial intermediaries were increased as a result of Henry VIII's dissolution of the monasteries and Edward VI's confiscation of the gild lands. Though the documentary evidence is not conclusive it is very probable that the small farmers, for example, who were accustomed to receive from the monasteries and the gilds loans of seed, cattle or sheep, and who often obtained money from the monastic authorities on the security of future supplies of wool, would, after such sources of assistance had disappeared, be compelled to make increasing use of the services of financial intermediaries. See R. H. Tawney, The Agrarian Problem in the Sixteenth Century (1912), pp. 109–10.

[7] By 5 and 6 Ed. VI, c. 20.

were again stimulated by the Elizabethan Act of 1571,[1] which revived the maximum rate of 10 per cent.[2]

With this increase in the activities of financial intermediaries the earliest English joint-stock companies made their appearance,[3] and so also did the financial terms stock, share, dividend and capital. The terms stock and share occur in connection with the Tudor mining enterprises.[4] An early instance of the term dividend appears in the documents relating to the privateering expeditions of Frobisher, documents in which the term share frequently appears.[5] The earliest English examples of the economic term capital are to be found in certain curious Tudor treatises relating to accountancy.

These early English accountancy books are also evidence of the development of credit organisation in England during the late Tudor period, and, indirectly, of the non-existence during this time of an English bank of the type then functioning in Venice. The earliest specimen that has survived is a valuable book written by James Peele, " citizen and salter " of London, and published in 1553.[6] In another book-keeping manual written by Peele, entitled *The Pathe Waye to Perfectnes in th'accomptes of Debitour and Creditour,*

---

[1] 13 Eliz. c. 8.

[2] The various laws dealing with usury in the sixteenth and seventeenth centuries are : 3 Hy. VII, c. 5 (1486); 3 Hy. VII, c. 6 (1486); 11 Hy. VII, c. 8 (1494); 37 Hy. VIII, c. 9 (1545); 5 & 6 Ed. VI, c. 20 (1552); 13 Eliz., c. 8 (1571); 21 Jas. I, c. 17 (1623); 12 Chas. II, c. 13 (1660), which was confirmed by 13 Chas. II, Stat. 1, c. 14 (1661).

In the seventeenth century the Act of 1623 limited interest to 8 per cent., and the Act of 1660 reduced the limit to 6 per cent., which was further reduced to 5 per cent. by 12 Anne, Stat. 2, c. 16 (1713). All the usury laws were repealed in 1854 by 17 & 18 Vict., c. 90.

For a list of the most important contemporary treatises relating to the subject of usury see Cunningham, *op. cit., Modern Times,* I, p. 154, footnote 3.

[3] The first two joint-stock organisations were the Russian or Muscovy Company and the Guinea Adventurers, both formed in 1553. For full details of the origin and development of such organisations up to 1720 see W. R. Scott, *The Constitution and Finance of English, Irish and Scottish Joint Stock Companies* (1910-12).

See also Cunningham, *op. cit., Modern Times,* pp. 214-84; and W. A. S. Hewins, *English Trade and Finance chiefly in the Seventeenth Century* (1890), Chap. III; H. Pirenne, " The Stages in the Social History of Capital," *American Historical Review,* Vol. 19 (1914).

[4] E.g. S.P. Dom., Eliz., 36, no. 95.   [5] Scott, *op. cit.,* II, p. 79.

[6] *The maner and fourme how to keep a perfect reconyng after the order of the most worthie and notable accompt of Debitour and Creditour.*

which was published in 1569,[1] occurs what appears to be the first instance of the term capital in a treatise written by an Englishman.[2] "Then," writes Peele in this treatise in describing what he terms "an inventorie of traffique," " substracte the some totall of the creditours from the totall some of money, debts, and goodes, and the remayne is the net substaunce, stocke, or capitall by thowner put in traffique of merchandise."

A third of the Tudor accountancy books, the *Brief Instruction and maner how to keep bookes of Accompts after the order of Debitor and Creditor*, issued by John Mellis in 1588, also uses the term "capitall" as equivalent to that which remains—the "remaine," "net rest," or "substance "— after a person has "substracted" the "totall summe" of his "creditours" from the "whole summe" of his "ready money, debtes, and goods." But this book is chiefly interesting because it is a translation of the accountancy section of a Venetian treatise, Lucas Pacioli's *Suma de Arithmetica, Geometria Proportioni et Proportionalita*, which was published in 1494.[3] Pacioli's lengthy section on accountancy[4] deals in some detail with the Venetian banking methods of the day, but in the translation issued by Mellis the chapters relating to banking have been omitted. Even so late as the reign of Charles I, Richard Dafforne stated in a voluminous accountancy treatise entitled *The Merchants Mirrour*, which appeared in 1636, that the " Banck-Account " was " needless here in England."[5]

---

[1] Both A. Anderson, *A Historical and Chronological Deduction of the Origin of Commerce* (1787–89), I., p. 130, and D. Macpherson, *Annals of Commerce* (1805), II, p. 149, state that "the new book-keeping" was introduced into England in 1569, referring to Peele's second work.

[2] See E. Cannan, "The Early History of the term Capital," *Quarterly Journal of Economics*, XXXV (1921), pp. 461–81; and R. D. Richards, "The Early History of the term Capital," *ibid.*, XL (1926), pp. 329–38.

[3] Mellis's book is also interesting because it is a revised edition of an earlier translation of Pacioli by Hugh Oldcastle, which was published in 1543, but, unfortunately, no copy of Oldcastle's book has survived.

[4] This is Section IX, Treatise XI of the *Suma de Arithmetica, Geometria Proportioni et Proportionalita*, and is entitled, " Particularis de computis et scripturis."

[5] Dafforne deals with " bancks " because, as they functioned on the Continent, he thinks that English merchants should possess some information about them. " Banck," he writes, *op. cit.*, p. 10, " is a name used at Amsterdam where all Bills of Exchange of 60l. sterl. and upwards, ought to be paid and received."

Such is a brief description, with particular reference to Tudor and early Stuart times, of the transactions of the English pioneers of credit technique. The recognition, after the eclipse of Antwerp and its famous Bourse, of the London money market as a factor in international finance, and the consolidation of this market in the Royal Exchange [1] are events of outstanding importance in a century of great economic changes.[2] The commercial expansion of the Tudor and early Stuart periods stimulated the activities of financial middlemen and increased the use of paper credit. The change of view-point with reference to the taking of interest resulted in a release of more capital seeking investment, and in the beginning of joint-stock enterprise. The passing, before the end of Elizabeth's reign, of the first English statute relating to insurance [3] lessened the risks of traders, and thus made them more ready to invest in mercantile "adventures." The genesis of modern capitalism made the monetary specialist indispensable, and there emerged as pioneers of a new financial régime the merchant, the broker, the scrivener and the goldsmith, pioneers of a credit technique which developed so rapidly under the ægis of the goldsmith in the age of the later Stuarts.

[1] Ready for occupation in 1568, opened by Elizabeth on 23rd January 1571, and followed in 1608 by the New Exchange, which James I called "Britain's Burse," and later in the same century by the Middle Exchange and Exeter Exchange. See J. Stow, *Survay of London* (1598), pp. 150–51; E. Howes, *The Annales or Chronicles of England* (1615), pp. 868–69; E. Leigh, *England Described* (1659), p. 133; T. de Laune, *Angliæ Metropolis* (1690), pp. 148–50; and C. Knight, *London* (1875–78), II, Chap. XLIII.

[2] See W. Cunningham, "Economic Change," *Cambridge Modern History* (1902–11), I, Chap. XV; J. E. Symes, "The Economic Revival," *Social England*, III (1901), ed. H. D. Traill and J. S. Mann; Tawney, *Religion and the Rise of Capitalism*, pp. 66–79.

[3] 43 Eliz., c. 12, An Act concerning matters of Assurances used among Merchants.

For the early history of insurance in England see C. Walford, *The Insurance Cyclopedia* (1871–80); and F. B. Relton, *An Account of the Fire Insurance Companies* (1893).

CHAPTER II

THE GOLDSMITH BANKERS AND THE EVOLUTION OF ENGLISH PAPER MONEY

" That the Goldsmiths, the Goldsmiths,
The Gold and Silver Goldsmiths may
With Gold and Silver Plenty,
And Treasures never empty,
Thrive on 'till the latter Day."
T. JORDAN, *The Goldsmith's Jubile* (1674).

IT has hitherto been generally assumed that the English goldsmith bankers of the first two decades of the second half of the seventeenth century were very rudimentary exponents of banking technique who came to a disastrous and untimely end in the twelfth year of the post-Restoration epoch. Historians have devoted little attention to their activities, and have usually regarded Charles II's partial suspension of cash payments at the Exchequer of Receipt—the so-called " Stop " of the Exchequer—as an artifice which immediately ruined all these bankers. Such conceptions are primarily due to the complete neglect of that vast field of documentary evidence, the Stuart Records of the Exchequer of Receipt.

In the light, then, of this new evidence, and of other important contemporary manuscript material, there are strong grounds for concluding that the private banking of the goldsmiths was a powerful factor in the economic development of the England of later Stuart times. The " shops " of the wealthiest of the London goldsmiths of the post-Restoration period were really important banking establishments, and in some of these the banker's trade was undoubtedly greater than that of the *aurifaber*. Interest was paid on deposits; loans were supplied; bills of exchange, tallies and various types of Treasury-Exchequer payment orders were discounted; promissory notes, which circulated freely, were issued; cheques were used; bullion was bought and sold; foreign coins were changed; system-

atic accounts were kept in special ledgers. " Public
Banks," wrote that observant contemporary economist
Dr. Nicholas Barbon,[1] " are of so great a Concern in Trade
that the Merchants of London for want of such a Bank have
been forced to carry their cash to Goldsmiths, and have
thereby raised such a credit upon Goldsmiths' Notes that
they pass in Payments from one to another like Notes upon
the Bank." " Some ingenious goldsmith," declares Mr.
Hartley Withers,[2] " conceived the epoch-making notion of
giving notes, not only to those who had deposited metal, but
to those who came to borrow it, and so founded modern
banking."

There is, in fact, an embarrassing wealth of contemporary
manuscript evidence which proves that the goldsmith
bankers were widely recognised keepers of deposits,
patronised by many thousands of provincial and metropolitan customers; powerful bullion merchants; big dealers
in both " inland " and " outland " bills of exchange, and
in Treasury-Exchequer payment orders; and important
" accomptants," " cashiers," " receivers "[3] and " farmers "
of the public revenue. Some even ran their businesses in
the form of partnerships; some had acquired an international reputation; while at least two anticipated one of
the modern functions of the Bank of England by acting as
bankers to the other goldsmith bankers. " The Goldsmiths
in Lumbardstreete," wrote a London " working " goldsmith
in the year of the " happy " Restoration,[4] " . . . are just in
the nature of Bankers at Amsterdam . . . keeping at this
day many great Merchants of London cashes."

Nor were the goldsmith bankers all immediately ruined
by the " Stop " of the Exchequer. There is documentary
evidence to show that some of them received not only
payments of interest on their loans to the King, but also
repayments of such loans shortly after the " Stop " was
declared.[5] Only five bankruptcies are known to have

---

[1] *A Discourse of Trade* (1690), pp. 28–29.
[2] *The Meaning of Money* (1916 ed.), p. 24.
[3] See Appendix 18, *infra.*
[4] T. Violet, *An Appeal to Cæsar* (1660), p. 22.
[5] See Appendix 13, *infra.*

occurred among those who financed the Government. Sir Robert Vyner, who suffered most, managed to carry on his business for twelve years after the " Stop," for it was not until 1684 that he became bankrupt. Lindsay collapsed in 1679, Backwell in 1682, Rowe in 1683, and the " shop " of Price in 1715. Moreover, it must not be forgotten that there were a number of goldsmith bankers like the Hoares, the Childs, the Pinckneys, the Heriots, the Williamses, and the Stokeses,[1] who were not directly affected by the " Stop," while new goldsmith bankers emerged, such as the powerful combination of Duncombe and Kent,[2] which was advancing large sums to Charles not long after the " Stop." Kent, for instance, was financing the army in 1674 and 1675,[3] and in 1676 he announced that he was prepared to advance money up to £50,000 at 6 per cent. interest plus 2 per cent. gratuity, for the service of the " land forces." [4]

Of the group of bankers which advanced large sums to the Exchequer, Sir Robert Vyner " and partners," Alderman Edward Backwell, Francis (afterwards Isaac) Meynell " and partners," [5] and Gilbert Whitehall were, in the order named, easily the most powerful. Evidence of the remarkable nature of the transactions of the members of this group is contained in five important classes of contemporary documents :

(1) Certain surviving personal ledgers and account books.
(2) The Records of the Exchequer of Receipt.
(3) The Records of the Treasury.[6]

---

[1] Details about these will be found in Sir Richard C. Hoare, *Pedigrees and Memories* (1819), pp. 19–20; A. Suter, *Worthies of St. Dunstan* (1856), pp. 30–31; T. C. Noble, *Memorials of Temple Bar* (1869), Chap. VI; 'F. G. Hilton Price, *Handbook of London Bankers* (1876), *passim*; F. G. Hilton Price, " Some Notes on the Early Goldsmiths and Bankers," *Trans. of London and Middlesex Archæological Society*, V (1881); C. M. Collins, *The History, Law and Practice of Banking* (1882), Chap. IV; W. Chaffers, *Gilda Aurifabrorum* (1885), pp. 60–84; W. Howarth, *Some Olde Curiosities* (1890), Chaps. V and VII; A. F. Baker, *Banks and Banking* (1896), pp. 4–5; B. B. Turner, *Chronicles of the Bank of England* (1897), Chap. I; W. G. Bell, *Fleet Street in Seven Centuries* (1912), Chap. XXII; Sir Charles J. Jackson, *English Goldsmiths and their Marks* (2nd ed., 1921).

[2] See Chap. III, p. 86, *infra*.
[3] B.M., Addit. MS., 28078, fol. 298.   [4] *Ibid.*, fol. 284.
[5] Francis Meynell, Alderman and Sheriff of London, died in 1666.
[6] The numerous transactions of the goldsmith bankers as recorded in these records may be traced in Dr. Shaw's monumental *Calendar of*

(4) The Early Records of Chancery Proceedings.
(5) The Exchequer Bills and Answers (London and Middlesex).

Most of the evidence is in the first three groups; the fourth and fifth groups contain a number of records of cases appertaining to some of the goldsmith bankers and their customers.

Unfortunately, however, not one of the personal ledgers of the Vyners,[1] the Meynells, or Whitehall has survived. Therefore, despite the fact that their affairs are examined in great detail in various books in the second of the preceding groups of records, anything approaching a complete survey of their financial transactions is not possible. But several of Backwell's ledgers are still extant,[2] are in excellent state of preservation, and, as will be shown a little later, are valuable not only on account of the detailed information which they give about the business of this banker, but also because they contain a great deal of material appertaining to the financial activities of most of the other important bankers of the day.

Indeed, Backwell's ledgers appear to be the only surviving original account books of a member of this powerful group of bankers which financed Charles II in the early years of the post-Restoration period, the group which was directly concerned in the " Stop," and without whose assistance the second Dutch War (1665–67) could not have been waged. In addition, the affairs of Backwell are examined with meticulous care in certain important books among the Records of the Exchequer of Receipt; the various Treasury Books contain numerous details of his transactions; and there are several references to his business among the Chancery Proceedings and the Exchequer Bills and Answers. Thus the surviving documentary evidence with reference to

---

Treasury Books. The affairs of the group that was involved in the " Stop " will be found in Vols. I, II, III, IV. For Duncombe and Kent see Vols. VI, VII, VIII.

[1] Sir Robert Vyner was preceded in the business of goldsmith banker by his uncle, Sir Thomas Vyner.

[2] In possession of Messrs. Child (Messrs. Glyn, Mills & Co.). Backwell's grandson, Tyringham, married Elizabeth, the daughter of Sir Francis Child (1642–1713), and their sons William and Barnaby became partners in the banking house of Child.

this important banker is much more complete than that relating to the other bankers.

For this reason the transactions of Alderman Edward Backwell,[1] " The Unicorn," Lombard Street, banker to the Commonwealth of England, Charles II, Prince Rupert, the Duke of York, the Earl of Clarendon and the East India Company, to name but a few of his important customers, are examined in some detail in this chapter and the next. " To Alderman Backwell's," wrote Mr. Pepys on 5th June 1662, " to see some thousands of my Lord's crusados weighed, and we find that 3,000 comes to about £530 or £540 generally." " The King and the kingdom must as good as fall with that man at this time," the famous diarist was told, " as a great secret," three years later, by Sir George Carteret, the Treasurer of the Navy, while discussing the possible effects of a " run " on the " shop " of Backwell during the banker's temporary absence " abroad upon some private score with a great sum of money." [2] " Edward Backwell, alderman of London," remarks Granger,[3] was a banker of great ability, industry and integrity; and, what was a consequence of his merit, of very extensive credit." The account of Backwell's banking business which follows is based entirely upon an examination of a number of important documents selected from the preceding groups of contemporary manuscript sources.

Backwell's surviving ledgers cover eight important years (1663–71) of the post-Restoration period, years which include such critical events as the Great Plague, the Great Fire, and the second Dutch War. These books are remarkable evidence of the commercial and financial activities of wealthy contemporary merchants, and of the rapidly expanding bill market of Carolean London. They contain countless illustrations of the business transactions of hundreds of traders, among which are interesting details of the affairs of certain Jewish merchants who were conspicuous figures in the international trade of the second half

[1] For details of his career see *D. N. B.*
[2] *Diary*, 6th July 1665.
[3] *Biographical History of England* (1824), V, p. 185.

of the seventeenth century.[1] Striking features are two series of special accounts entitled " Exch[a] Acct," [2] and " Interest alias Discount Acct," occurring at frequent intervals, and made up of items collected from the various personal accounts of customers. The large number of entries in the " Exchange Accounts " prove that dealings in bills of exchange formed an important part of Backwell's business. Many of his customers' accounts relate largely to dealings of this nature, and there are even instances of such accounts relating entirely to bills of exchange.[3]

The various types of entries in these ledgers reveal the exact nature of Backwell's transactions. On the debit side, for example, of the two earliest ledgers, the following constantly appear : " to him," " to order," " to him in part," " to interest," " paid in full for interest " ; and on the credit side : " by money," " by money at consideration," " by money at 5 per cent.," " by him," " by note," " by my note," " by your bill given me ye 15th April for Antwerp," " by money at 3d. per diem at a weekes warning," " by money at interest," " by money paya. at demand," " by bill drawn on him at 5 da. sight payable Mr. X value of Y," " by so much you remitted me on Mr. Z," " by note payable at demand," " by fine bars," " by tallies." The later ledgers also contain a very large number of entries of the following type which are evidence of big dealings in Government money orders : " by an order," " by an order on the Customs," " by an order on December 1670 £2,000 p. Squibb," " by an order on March 1670[1] £2,000 p. Gregory." [4] It is quite clear from these selected examples that notice was

[1] *E.g.* Ferdinando Mendes da Costa has four separate accounts in the ledger dated 1664, which contains details of big transactions, and numerous items relating to bills of exchange and the import of bullion.

Other important Jewish commercial accounts which occur in these ledgers are those of John da Costa, Alfonzo Mendes, Isaac Alvarez, Henricus Alvarez, and Alfonzo Rodriguez.

Such items as " By fine silver 675 lb. 5 ozs. at 65s. 6d.—£2,212 4s. 3d." frequently occur in these accounts.

[2] See Appendix 4, *infra*.

[3] There are many hundreds of entries in Blackwell's ledgers in the individual accounts of his customers of the following type : " By bill drawn at sight paya. to Mr. G. Horton value of Mr. Bulstrode—£100." See Appendix 3, *infra*.

[4] Squibb and Gregory were tellers of the Exchequer of Receipt.

sometimes required before the depositor could withdraw his money, or, in other words, that a distinction was made between what are now termed demand and time deposits.

In addition to some hundreds of the personal accounts of prominent English and foreign merchants [1] of the day, Backwell's ledgers contain a large number of other important accounts which are further evidence of the part played by this powerful banker in the development of England's home and overseas trade, and which show that he was not only constantly advancing money to,[2] and discounting the bills of, traders, but was also frequently investing in trading enterprises [3] and acting as the banker of many well-known trading companies. A few instances of these latter types are the accounts headed : " The Owners of ye Ship Eagle," " Adventures in ye Royal Company," " The Muscovia Comp^a," " The Hamborough Comp^a," " The Glassiers Comp^a and Wardens," " Sir Thomas Russell and Comp^a," "Sir William Rider and Comp^a," "The Ironmongers Comp^a," " The Goldsmiths Comp^a, Wardens and Commonalty," and, most important of all, " The East India Company."

Some of these company accounts contain numerous examples of big financial transactions. In the ledger dated 1670-71, for example, there are several accounts of the East India Company,[4] the first of which,[5] appertaining to April 1670, has a total on the debit side of £27,190 2s. 6d., and on the credit side of £43,115 0s. 6d., many of the items relating to the subscriptions of City merchants, and of prominent goldsmith bankers. This particular ledger shows that the receipts of the East India Company for the year ending 25th March 1671 amounted to £237,900.

But Londoners and London companies form only a section

---

[1] Among the well-known City merchants of the day who kept their accounts at Backwell's were Michael Godfrey (afterwards Deputy Governor of the Bank of England), Sir Richard Ford, Sir Hugh Myddleton, Thomas Papillon and Peter Vandeputt.

[2] *E.g.* in the ledger dated 1663, fol. 479, " The Owners of the Ship Marchant Delight," " To them lent—£450 "; *ibid.*, fol. 392, " Samson Allen & Comp^a," " By money at consideration 5 p.c. repay @ Feb. 1663—£250."

[3] *E.g.* ledger dated 1664, fol. 669, " By the shippe Royal Katherine for my owne 32nd part of her stock—£37 10s. 0d. See Appendix 3, *infra*.

[4] *E.g.* fols. 82-83, 260, 401, 423, 485, 568, 570.

[5] Fols. 82-83.

of Backwell's numerous customers. The ledgers show that he possessed many hundreds of provincial depositors, that he functioned as a private banker to Charles II,[1] and also as a State banker duly authorised to receive and make payments on behalf of the Exchequer, and that his transactions as a banker to the other goldsmith bankers were on a very large scale. The last feature is overwhelming evidence of the important financial position occupied by, and of the great resources of, the bank of Backwell, which was undoubtedly both the central or reserve bank and the clearing house of the post-Restoration period. It was the indispensable precursor of the Bank of England, a precursor which was of paramount importance in this outstanding era of English economic expansion.

Backwell's provincial customers came from all parts of England; he kept their deposits of money and of plate, and discounted their bills, both " inland " and " outland." Devonians and Novocastrians, Oxonians and East Anglians, men of Kent and of Somerset all patronised this famous banker. Merchants of Newcastle engaged in the coastwise coal trade drew " inland " bills on London merchants which were discounted at Backwell's; West-country clothiers and a Cambridge College [2] kept their surplus cash at " The Unicorn." There are many accounts in the ledgers which show that as the banker of the farmers of the Customs, Backwell frequently made direct payments out of the Customs revenue on behalf of the Exchequer of Receipt.[3] Some of his big advances to the Exchequer on the security of certain revenues are dealt with in special accounts under such headings as : " Exchequer Loan on ye Crown Lands," " Exchequer Loan on ye Fee Farms," " Exchequer Loan on Wines "; and in these are recorded payments of interest, or repayments of part of the principal, received from the

---

[1] E.g. in the ledger dated 1664, folio 432 is headed, " The King's Most Excellent Majesty Ac."

[2] One of the accounts of the ' Masters and Wardens " of Trinity College, Cambridge, appears in the ledger dated 1664 (fol. 662).

[3] In the ledger dated 1664, " The Farmers of the Customs " account, fol. 199, the entries on the Dr. side show that Backwell made direct payments out of the Customs receipts; e.g. 5th May 1664, " To Capt. Rainford for ye Tower Garrison—£361 4s. 0d."

Exchequer officials. Among the other bankers of the day who kept accounts with Backwell were " Alderman Francis Meynell [afterwards Isaac Meynell] and partners "; John Colville; Robert Welstead; Humphrey Stokes; " Sir Thomas Vyner [afterwards Sir Robert Vyner] and partners "; Jeremiah Snow, the first of the banking Snows; George Snell; John Lindsay; " Mr. [Benjamin] Hinton and Comp^a "; Joseph Hornby, Thomas Rowe and Thomas Kirwood. These accounts are evidence of the big banking businesses of his banker customers. They contain hundreds of such entries as : " by him," " by cash," " by money," " by note," " by several notes," " by my note," " by Sir Robert Vyner," " by Mr. Snell," " to Mr. Rowe," " to Mr. Colville," " to Mr. Snow," " to Mr. Stokes." [1]

Like the other goldsmith bankers, Backwell was, of course, a big pawnbroker, therefore it is not surprising to find in these ledgers many special pawn accounts. Another striking feature is a series of valuable farm accounts appertaining to his country estates, which contain some remarkable details relating to English agriculture in the latter half of the seventeenth century. In the ledger dated 1669 one of these, headed " Creslow Acc^t," [2] gives interesting information about the wages of farm labourers; the market price of oxen, sheep, hides and seed; ploughing and sowing expenses; the expenses of driving cattle to and from the market; household expenses, and the wages of mowers and of haymakers.

The account books just discussed are known as ledgers I, J, K, L, M, N, O, P, Q, R, S. The series is not complete, for there are in Ledger I references to a preceding Ledger known as H; and it seems very probable that there was originally a Ledger A. Therefore so far as the surviving books of this particular series are concerned there is no information about Backwell's transactions either in Crom-

---

[1] The following totals on the credit side of the accounts of some of the most prominent of the other bankers all appear in the ledger dated 1664 : Sir Thomas Vyner & Co., £50,561 9s. 11d.; John Colville, £15,835 6s.; Jeremiah Snow, £20,704 14s. 3d.; George Snell, £14,208 18s.; John Lindsay, £15,659 2s. 8d.; Benjamin Hinton & Co., £34,159 8s. 10d. A large number of these accounts appear in the various other ledgers.

[2] The Creslow estate was situated near Aylesbury, Buckinghamshire.

wellian times or during the years immediately following the " Stop." Fortunately, however, another of Backwell's books still survives, and is in an excellent state of preservation. This appears to be a rough account book, which, though commenced in 1657, apparently for the purpose of recording Backwell's big advances towards the maintenance of the English garrison at Dunkirk, was not finished until 1678.[1] It is, therefore, particularly valuable for two reasons : it proves that Backwell conducted a big banking business in Cromwellian times; and it contains new evidence with reference to his transactions after the " Stop " of the Exchequer.

On the cover of this important book is written, " Copies of Dunkirke Affair," and for this reason it is known as " The Dunkirk Ledger." But it was used for a double purpose. One section contains copies of the Privy Seals, warrants, certificates and payment orders relating chiefly to the Dunkirk transactions. The other section is devoted to what appear to be rough copies of the accounts of customers, and these usually appertain to the three years immediately preceding the Restoration.

Among the accounts of the latter section the most important is headed " The Commonwealth of England," and this shows that between 1st August 1658, and 7th March 1659, the " moneys transmitted to the Governor of Dunkirk " by Backwell amounted to £65,260. Two interesting facts emerge from the credit side of this account : (1) £54,889 11s. 3d. of this loan was quickly repaid by the Exchequer in a number of instalments; (2) the instalments were paid both in cash and in plate,[2] Backwell crediting the Government with the market price of the metallic content of the latter. This section also contains two curious accounts: a plate account entitled, " His Highness Richard, Lord Protector," an item in which refers to a " loane of plate to

[1] Backwell and Sir John Shaw functioned as Paymasters to the garrison of Dunkirk between 1661 and 1667. For details of their transactions see *Calendar of Treasury Books*, I and II, *passim.*
They were also " Treasurers and Paymasters of the forces in Flanders " in 1662–3. See *ibid.*, I, pp. 411, 432, 441, 498.
[2] *E.g.* " Rec^d of the Committee of Parliament by old Plate—*l.*1529 11s. 3d.''

entertaine the French Ambassador "; and a mercantile account headed, " The Owners of the Ship Katherine," showing both principal and interest columns.

The other section of the Dunkirk Ledger, though chiefly relating to " the Dunkirke affair," contains many valuable and interesting entries illustrative of the big dealings of Backwell. The first is a copy of " a certificate of all such sumes of money as have been paid at ye Receipt of the Publique Exchequer unto Edward Backwell Esq." These particular sums, which amounted to £43,067 5s. 4d., were paid up to 7th May 1660, " in satisfaction of moneys transmitted " by Backwell for the use of the garrison at Dunkirk. Other interesting items in this section are : (1) a copy of a Privy Seal to Backwell granted by Richard Cromwell, dated 20th September 1658, and authorising payment of £350 for a jewel supplied to Oliver Cromwell; (2) a copy of a Privy Seal authorising repayment of a loan of £3,230 which Backwell " sent to Dunkirke for ye Protector "; (3) a copy of an order of Lord Treasurer Southampton, dated 6th December 1662, for the delivery of a number of " Dunkirke chests "[1] to Backwell as security for a sum of £20,000 advanced to the Treasurer of the Navy; (4) a copy of a " Privy Seale for £8,000," dated 14th September 1667, granted to Backwell " in consideration of interest " for the sum of £286,042 advanced on various occasions for the use of the navy, the army, the Household, and " other extraordinary expenses "; (5) a copy of a Privy Seal, dated 18th April 1664, authorising payment of £13,363 12s. 11d. as interest on money advanced

---

[1] Backwell, on behalf of Charles II, had acted as receiver of the money of the sale of Dunkirk. See *Cal. Treas. Books*, I, *passim*.

A warrant issued by Lord Treasurer Southampton on 15th October 1664, for the drawing of " several orders of payment for the several sums of 8,000 li and 1,500 li " which is recorded in P.R.O., Recs. Ex. R., Warrant Books (Auditor's), E. 403/3032, fol. 12, is of peculiar interest. The orders were issued to Backwell. Those amounting to £8,000 were the " reward " on a loan of £286,042 " for several occasions of His Maties Navy and Guards for which he received the ordinary consideration of six pounds p. centum His Matie being sensible that the said Edward Backwell . . . was forced to admit larger pporcons of other mens monies in Banck (which he payes interest for) than otherwise he would doe which puts him upon greater uncertainties than others who deale in common loanes where a precise day of payment is fixed." Those amounting to £1,500 were an " allowance " to Backwell for his services in connection with the Dunkirk money. This warrant is given in full in Appendix 7, *infra*.

D

by Sir John Shaw and Backwell " joyntly and severally ";
(6) a copy of a warrant from " His Maties Comm^rs for ye
affaires of Tangier," authorising their Treasurer, Mr. Samuel
Pepys, to deliver to Backwell " in tallyes, orders or assignments the summe of ten thousand pounds sterling . . . and
also satisfieing him ye usuall interest allowed," in consideration of a loan of £10,000 to the Governor of Tangier, which
was delivered to the said Governor in " fortie foure thousand
foure hundred fortie four pieces of eight and a halfe being
computed at foure shillings six pence each "; (7) a copy of
a " Privy Seale for £6,657 16s. 4d.," dated 30th March 1668,
interest on a loan of £128,896 19s. 3d.; (8) a copy of a very
important letter of attorney, dated 6th April 1674, from
Charles II to Backwell, in which the latter is appointed the
King's special financial agent in the Low Countries.[1]

The preceding letter of attorney is striking proof of the
financial activities of Backwell after the " Stop " of the
Exchequer. " Whereas," it states, " we have found it
necessary to employ a fitt person to our good friends and
allyes the States Generall of ye United Provinces for receiving the sume of two hundred thousand pattacoones being
the first fourth part of eight hundred thousand pattacoones
covenanted and agreed to be paid unto us according to the
tenth article of the treaty concluded between us and the
said States Generall on $\frac{9}{19}$ February last past [167$\frac{3}{4}$] . . .
Edward Backwell is herewith appointed our true and lawful
attorney and procurator for us in our name to demand of the
said States Generall and for our use to receive the said sume
of 200,000 pattacoones. . . ."[2]

But this letter is not the only evidence of Backwell's
operations after the " Stop " which the second part of the
Dunkirk Ledger contains. There are, for instance, a number
of copies of Treasury payment orders belonging to this
period, and one of these, for £3,401 4s. 2d., representing
interest and gratuity (6 per cent. plus 4 per cent.) " for

---

[1] All these eight items are contained in fols. 1–65.
[2] The Dunkirk Ledger, fol. 64b. Fol. 70 contains a copy of a second
letter of attorney authorising Backwell to receive on behalf of the King the
remaining 600,000 pattacoones, " wee being well satisfied with the integrity
and great discretion of the said Edward Backwell."

moneys advanced to His Ma[ties] service " was actually issued to Backwell on 6th February 1672' five weeks after the " Stop." [1] Later copies of payment orders of this type, together with the second of two accounts headed, ".The Kings most Excellent Ma[ties] Dr.," show that Backwell made several loans to the King between the " Stop " and 1677, when Charles commenced the regular payment of interest on the total debt due to the bankers.

Such are the salient features of the surviving ledgers of Backwell. They are overwhelming proof of the large resources of a leading Cromwellian and post-Restoration goldsmith banker. In addition, some of the account books of another important post-Restoration goldsmith banker, Richard Hoare, who, however, was not concerned in the big loans to Charles II, are still extant, and are carefully preserved in the historic banking house of Hoare. They contain, as will be seen later, further valuable information appertaining to the private banking of the goldsmiths of later Stuart times.

There is also in the possession of Messrs. Hoare a curious old pre-Civil War receipt, dated 11th December 1633, which appears to indicate that deposits were kept by the Hoare of that day. This rare document, the earliest known goldsmith's receipt, was only recently discovered. It is signed by Lawrence Hoare of " The Golden Bottle," Cheapside, and acknowledges the receipt of £3 5s. 0d. from one William Hale for a " post ffyne charged upon Rowland Hale upon the accompt of Henry Coghill," High Sheriff of Hertfordshire.[2]

But though some of the London goldsmiths accepted money and plate in trust prior to the Civil War, there does not appear to be any documentary evidence to show that this was a general practice. The Mint in the Tower, however, was, during the four decades preceding the outbreak of this war, increasingly used as a repository. In 1640 Charles I requisitioned £200,000 in coin and bullion belonging to London merchants, which had been thus deposited, an

---

[1] The Dunkirk Ledger, fol. 64. For a description of the various types of Treasury orders, see pp. 57–63, *infra*.   [2] See Appendix 1, *infra*.

act which destroyed the Mint's reputation as a safe custodian of surplus cash. Strong protests by those concerned, forwarded to Strafford and the Privy Council, resulted in the King agreeing to return the amount taken, on condition that the depositors granted him a loan of £40,000 on the security of the Customs.

This incident, followed by the general insecurity accompanying the Civil War, paved the way towards a system of private banking. Merchants and others naturally began to seek places where their plate and surplus coin could be safely and regularly deposited, a search which resulted in a number of prominent goldsmiths developing into recognised deposit keepers.[1]

Even, however, prior to the Civil War important changes in the nature of the business transactions of certain goldsmiths began to appear. A State document advocating the retention of the Royal Exchanger, dated 1628,[2] states that at this time the London goldsmiths were divided into : (1) "goldsmiths about the Cittie Exchanges," and (2) "working goldsmiths," and adds that the business of exchange was " a new kind of trade sprung lately up among them."

This demarcation between the "exchanging" and the "working" goldsmiths had been emphasised in a striking way four years earlier. In 1624 the "manual working goldsmiths" of London petitioned the Wardens and Assistants of the Goldsmiths' Company for the immediate establishment of a yeomanry company of "working" goldsmiths, the said yeomanry to be established by Act of Parliament and to be allowed to "keep Courtes" in Goldsmiths' Hall for the redressing of abuses. This petition was

---

[1] The anonymous writer of a curious pamphlet entitled *The Mystery of the New Fashioned Goldsmiths or Bankers* (1676), states that goldsmith banking originated during the Civil War, which resulted in apprentices leaving their masters and becoming soldiers. The apprentices, according to this writer, previous to the war were responsible for the custody of their master's money, therefore many of the masters after hostilities commenced began "to put their cash into Goldsmiths' hands." A reprint of this pamphlet is given in J. B. Martin, " *The Grasshopper*" *in Lombard Street*, pp. 287–92, and its contents are examined in E. T. Powell, *The Evolution of the London Money Market* (1915), pp. 58–63.

[2] S.P. Dom., Charles I, 107, no. 17.

made because, in spite of the fact that the goldsmiths had been incorporated by Edward III as metal workers in a " gouldsmitherie," a " kind of trade " had recently " sprung up " among them whose members were " but changers of gold and silver, and hucksters and sellers of plate, jewells and other goldsmiths' wares." [1]

But in addition to being money-changers, some of the goldsmiths, as has already been mentioned, also functioned as custodians of money in trust,[2] which was returnable on demand to the depositors, and which could not be used by the custodian. From being a bailee of money was but a short step to the accepting of demand deposits with full authority to make use of such deposits as loans to customers, a stage which, as the Dunkirk Ledger shows, was undoubtedly reached during the Cromwellian period.[3]

That the goldsmiths occupied a powerful financial position not long after the Civil War is shown in a special report, dated 1652, from an English agent in Amsterdam to Sir Robert Stone of London.[4] This report describes the monetary importance of the English metropolis, and draws attention to the wide prevalence of counterfeiting and clipping. " I wondered at first," states the writer, " how the merchants transported all weighty and culled English money to Holland until one of the bankers told me.". He explains that this exportation was due to the activities of the goldsmiths, the " cashiers " of the merchants of London, who kept reserves, or " banks," of " all ye principall coynes in Christendom " for the needs of their customers and whose assistants were always busy melting the heaviest coins they received.

Stone's correspondent prepared his report just eight years before the Restoration. The two decades which preceded this " happy " event are of particular importance in the

---

[1] S.P. Dom., James I, 163, no. 10, a petition which is signed by sixty-nine " working " goldsmiths.

[2] This is proved by the Wardens' Accounts and Court Minute Books of the Goldsmiths' Company of London, where instances will be found of goldsmiths accepting money deposits in trust.

[3] The evolution of the goldsmith into a banker is examined in more detail in Chap. IX, Section iv, *infra*.

[4] S.P. Dom., Interregnum, 24, no. 21.

genesis of English banking. They include, in addition to the Civil War (1642–49), the administrative system of special Parliamentary Committees,[1] and the first Dutch War (1651–54), events which greatly increased the financial activities of certain outstanding members of the goldsmith's profession.

The administrative system of Parliamentary Committees was accompanied by an extraordinary delegation of the functions of the Exchequer to separate Government sub-treasuries, such as those established at Goldsmiths' Hall and at Haberdashers' Hall, into which during the Commonwealth period up to 1654, when an ordinance of the Protector in Council brought this "multiplicity of Treasuries" to an end,[2] large sums raised by these committees were paid.

Functioning as Exchequer banks, these sub-treasuries made many payments on behalf of the Government out of the revenues they received. The contemporary State Papers show that large sums were paid in this way through Goldsmiths' and Haberdashers' Halls to Government pensioners, and as ambassadorial expenses.[3] Goldsmiths' Hall thus became an important centre of financial activity which reacted on some of its members, while the Cromwellian Council of State's constant need of money, particularly during the first Dutch war and immediately afterwards, gave the wealthiest goldsmiths of the day, such as Sir Thomas Vyner and Backwell, opportunities for advancing large sums of money for the use of the State.

Proofs of the activities of the goldsmith bankers of the

[1] *E.g.* the Committee for the Advance of Money, the Committee for Compounding with Delinquents, the Committee for Indemnity. See preface by M. A. E. Green in *Cal. S.P. Dom., 1649–50*, pp. vii–xii.

[2] S.P. Dom., Interregnum, 72, no. 34.

[3] H. Scobell, *Collection of Acts and Ordinances, 1640–56*, II, p. 86, shows that Goldsmiths' Hall and Weavers' Hall "bills" were accepted by the Long Parliament in payment for the bishops' lands from 24th July 1649. See W. O. Scroggs, "English Finances under the Long Parliament," *Quarterly Journal of Economics*, XXI (1907), pp. 463–87.

These "bills" appear to have been either payment orders similar to those issued by the Exchequer, see pp. 57–58 *infra*, or what were termed "Public Faith bills," which were receipts for loans paid into the sub-treasuries. See *L.J.*; V, pp. 533–35.

A copy of "the forme which was first given of publique ffaith bills" will be found in S.P. Dom., Interregnum, A. 59, last folio.

The writer of the article entitled "Goldsmiths; Goldsmiths' Notes," in *D. P. E.*, confuses Goldsmiths' Hall "bills" with goldsmiths' promissory notes.

Cromwellian period are, as we have seen, to be found in the important Dunkirk Ledger. Further proofs of the activities of these bankers are contained in the contemporary Records of the Exchequer of Receipt, which show that both Sir Thomas Vyner and Backwell were prominent figures in English public finance as loan agents, bullion merchants, and money-changers.[1]

The Records of the Exchequer of Receipt also contain, as will be shown later, abundant details of the big financial transactions of the goldsmith bankers in the post-Restoration period. In addition, the Records of Chancery Proceedings for this period contain much valuable material with reference to the part played by the bankers in the trading enterprises of the day. The documents, for instance, relating to *Vyner* v. *Joyner*, dated 4th July 1681,[2] contain interesting information with reference to a goldsmith banker's assistance to a trader. They show that one Christopher Joyner, a London merchant, "having occasion to use considerable sums of money in the way of trading," and knowing that Sir Robert Vyner could supply him with such sums " as he should have any sudden occasion for," did " often desire " this wealthy banker " to furnish him with several sums " upon security of " bills charged upon other persons and payable to himself." It is stated that Vyner " frequently advanced moneys . . . upon receiving of such bills "; that he always entered the details of such transactions " in a certain book kept for that purpose "; and that, " on or about 4th December 1665," Joyner left at Vyner's shop " a bill of exchange for 200 French crowns, at $59\frac{1}{4}d$. per crown, drawn upon Richard Fuller, another London merchant, and payable to Joyner," a " deposit " which was entered in " the aforesaid book," and credit given to Joyner for the same " as was usual " for the banker to do in these circumstances.

It is thus clear from the Records of Chancery Proceedings, and from the surviving ledgers of Backwell, that the most important goldsmith bankers of the post-Restoration era were of great assistance to the traders of the day in the business of exchange. But in addition to conducting big

---

[1] See Chap. IX, pp. 209-10, and Appendix 5, *infra*.
[2] P.R.O., Ch. P., Early (Reynardson), 97/19. *Ibid.*, 35/66, contains another illustration of a goldsmith banker financing trade.

transactions in bills of exchange, the goldsmith bankers were, as has already been stated, very much engaged with other important types of early English paper *media*, with promissory notes, with cheques, and with various kinds of Treasury-Exchequer payment orders, activities which are further proofs of the great development of English banking technique in the latter half of the seventeenth century.

Of these *media* the promissory note originated as a receipt given by the goldsmith for money, which he took charge of for a customer but was not allowed to use. Such a note was really a warehouse voucher which could not be assigned. When, however, it became a receipt for a money deposit, which the goldsmith was allowed by the depositor to use for the purpose of making advances to his customers, it developed into an assignable instrument. Ultimately such notes were issued by the goldsmiths in the form of loans and were not necessarily backed by coin and bullion. When this stage was reached the goldsmith had become a duly recognised purveyor of currency.[1]

A condensed form of the verbose mercantile bill of debt, the goldsmith's promissory note was the forerunner of the engraved bank note of which type the Bank of England note appears to have been the first example. When the goldsmith issued his notes on the strength of money deposits, which he was allowed to make use of, there emerged the practice of making part payments of the notes and indorsing such payments on the actual note.[2] Under the Law Merchant, the *Lex Mercatoria* or Custom of Merchants, the goldsmith's note was recognised, if made out to X or order, as transferable by indorsement.[3] The earliest known

---

[1] For a further discussion of the development of the goldsmith's promissory note see Chap. XI, Section iv, *infra*.

[2] *Cooksay* v. *Bouverie* (1682), 2 Show., p. 296, and *Ward* v. *Evans* (1702), 2 Ld. Raym., p. 928.

[3] P.R.O., Ch. P., before 1714 (Hamilton), 354/8, contains an interesting account of the circulation of a goldsmith banker's promissory note payable to order, dated 1667, which promised to pay £200 with interest on demand. It was made out by Sir Robert Vyner to N. Aske " or his assignes or order," was " delivered " by Aske to one Dr. Edward Bolnant, and by the latter " passed " to William Mellish, a London merchant. Mellish, " did assigne and deliver the said noat to one Barnwell," who " assigned and delivered " it to " Mr. Johnson and Mr. Kent," who presented it for payment in Vyner's shop.

specimens are made out to X or bearer,[1] and an example of this type in Messrs. Child's collection is thus worded : [2]

> *November 28th 1684.*
>
> *I promise to pay unto the Rt Honble Ye Lord North & Grey or bearer ninety pounds at demand.*
>
> > *for Mr Francis Child & myself*
> > *Jno Rogers.*

which may be compared with the following, the earliest surviving specimen of an engraved promissory note issued by Child's Bank :

> London, *Sept 5, 1729.*
>
> No. *366*
>
> I promise to pay *His Grace the Duke of Bedford* or *bearer* on demand *Forty Pounds* ....
>
> £40. 0. 0.   For Fra Child Esq
> 20. 0. 0.   J [remainder of signature missing]
> _____
>
> £20. 0. 0.

Reference must be made here to the promissory notes of the early English provincial bankers. The famous Smith family, mercers of Nottingham,[3] had undoubtedly originated an embryonic banking business in connection with their ordinary activities before the end of the seventeenth century, and these pioneers were followed in the eighteenth century by the Backhouses and Peases of Darlington,[4] worsted

---

[1] See *Walmsley* v. *Child* (1749), 1 Ves. sen., p. 341. "Charles Walmsley, in April 1742, lodged money in the shop of Mr. Child and Co., for which he took notes payable to himself or bearer."

[2] In this, and in all succeeding copies of notes, bills, or orders, the italics represent the written parts in the original specimens.

[3] For a detailed account of Smiths see H. T. Easton, *History of a Banking House (Smith, Payne and Smiths)*, (1903). See also F. G. Hilton Price, *A Handbook of London Bankers* (1876), pp. 123–24.

Thomas Smith of Nottingham appears to have been the only English provincial banker in the seventeenth century. He was the son of a farmer, and when a young man was apprenticed to a Nottingham mercer, ultimately developing a mercer's business of his own, in connection with which his banking transactions originated. He died in 1699, after which his eldest son Thomas conducted this dual business. Samuel and Abel Smith, the third and youngest sons, who succeeded Thomas, junior, in 1727, greatly extended the banking business.

[4] For the Backhouses and Peases see M. Phillips, *A History of Banks, Bankers and Banking in Northumberland, Durham and North Yorkshire* (1896), pp. 134 and 345–46; and P. W. Matthews and A. W. Tuke, *History of Barclays Bank, Limited* (1926), pp. 198–211.

manufacturers; the Gurneys of East Anglia,[1] who were also closely connected with the worsted trade; the Vaughans of Bristol,[2] goldsmiths; and the Woods of Gloucester,[3] grocers. Engraved promissory notes were issued by the Smiths in the first half of the eighteenth century, and the following is a copy of one of the earliest specimens :

No. *7346*. S.A.S.

I promise to pay *Evelin Chadwick Esq* or bearer *fifty pounds* .... at Nottingham on demand Value received. *December 22nd 1736.*

For *Bro Samuel & Self.*

£*50*——. *Abell Smith.*

This may be compared with the following engraved note issued by the same firm ten years later : [4]

No. *8195.*

I promise to pay *Mr. Wm. Elliot* or Bearer *Twenty Pounds* ....at Nottingham on Demand Value Received *Septemʳ 24th 1746.*

£*20. 0. 0.* For *Messrs. Samuel & Abell Smith & Co.*

& Self.

Abell Smith.

These early metropolitan and provincial engraved promissory notes do not appear to have been issued for small sums. The Bank of England, for instance, between 1696 and 1759, did not issue any such notes under the value of £20,[5] and in 1759 first issued engraved £10 notes. But during the

---

[1] For the Gurneys see W. Bidwell, *Annals of an East Anglian Bank* (1900); W. Howarth, *Barclay and Company* (1901), Chap. VI; and Matthews and Tuke, *op. cit.*, pp. 133–51.

[2] For the Vaughans see C. H. Cave, *A History of Banking in Bristol* (1899), p. 6.

[3] For the Woods see F. Martin, *Stories of Banks and Bankers* (1865), p. 138.

[4] These early Smith promissory notes were exhibited in the Royal Mint Annexe of the British Government Pavilion, British Empire Exhibition, Wembley, 1924–5.

Maberly Phillips, "Bank Note Collecting," *Connoisseur* 5, p. 38, gives an illustration of an engraved Smiths' promissory note, dated 1735, and states, p. 39, that there is a similar one in existence dated 26th August 1728, numbered 529, which he regards as the earliest known provincial bank note.

[5] The Bank, however, experimented unsuccessfully with an issue of "lettered notes indented on marbled paper," which included £5 notes, as early as 1695, while ordinary notes of small denominations also appear to have been issued prior to 1696. See Chap. VI, pp. 160–61 and 163–64, *infra*.

Napoleonic War, when large numbers of small country banks appeared, the issue of engraved promissory notes for small amounts increased rapidly in England.[1] Between 1797 and 1821, the period of cash suspension, the Bank of England issued £1 and £2 notes, while a great number of notes for both these values were at the same time circulated by provincial houses.

The development of the goldsmith's promissory note is closely connected with certain legal changes authorised during the seventeenth century with reference to the bill of exchange; but though the origin of the latter instrument has been discussed in numerous legal treatises,[2] its earliest history is still wrapped in obscurity.[3] We do not know when it was first introduced into England;[4] but we do know

---

[1] For excellent illustrations of the later eighteenth century provincial bank notes see H. L. Roth, *The Genesis of Banking in Halifax* (1914), supplement to Section XIV; S. Lloyd, *The Lloyds of Birmingham* (1907), pp. 62, 66; J. Hughes, *Liverpool Banks and Bankers* (1906), pp. 158, 160, 162; M. Phillips, *A History of Banks, Bankers and Banking*, etc., pp. 155, 292, 297, 404; and Cave, *op. cit., passim.*

Valuable information is contained in the Institute of Bankers *Catalogue of the " Maberly Phillips ".Collection of Old Bank Notes, Drafts, etc.* (1906), a collection preserved in this Institute.

See Chap. VIII, pp. 194–95, for further details about the notes of the country banks.

[2] See, for example, J. Chitty, *A Practical Treatise on Bills of Exchange, Promissory Notes and Bankers' Checks* (ed. 1834), p. 28; L. Nougier, *Des Lettres de Change* (1839), Chap. II; J. Reddie, *An Historical View of the Law of Maritime Commerce* (1841), Chap. VII; J. Story, *Commentaries on the Law of Bills of Exchange* (4th ed., 1860), Chap. I; H. D. Jencken, *A Compendium of the Laws on Bills of Exchange, Promissory Notes, Cheques, and other Commercial Negotiable Instruments in England* (1880), pp. 2–7; H. D. Chalmers, *A Digest of the Law of Bills of Exchange, Promissory Notes, and Cheques* (2nd ed., 1881), intro., p. xl; Sir John B. Byles, *A Treatise on the Law of Bills of Exchange, Promissory Notes, Bank-Notes, and Cheques* (18th ed., 1923), p. 4.

[3] See E. Jenks, " On the Early History of Negotiable Instruments," *Law Quarterly Review*, IX (1893), pp. 70–85; and A. P. Usher, "The Origin of the Bill of Exchange," *Journal of Political Economy*, XXII (1914), pp. 566–76.

[4] 3 Rich. II, c. 3 (1379), refers to the " lre deschange." A. H. Thomas, *op. cit.*, pp. 94 and 200–1, gives instances of early London Guildhall cases relating to bills of exchange dated 1300 and 1305. *Martin v. Boure* (1602) is the first case relating to a bill of exchange which appears in the printed Law Reports. 2 Croke, p. 6.

There are, however, records of still earlier cases among the manuscript reports of the Early Chancery Proceedings. *E.g.* P.R.O., Ch. Proc., Early, Bdle. 713/12, *Ardyson v. Mayor, Aldermen and Sheriffs of London, and Briard*; and *ibid.*, 725/7, *Barnes v. Mayor, Aldermen, and Sheriffs of London*; both cases during the Chancellorship of Sir Thomas Audley, 1533–38.

For examples of Tudor bills of exchange see *Select Pleas in the Court of Admiralty* (1894–97, ed. by R. G. Marsden for the Selden Society), II, pp. 68, 70, 71, 73.

that the recognition by the Common Law Courts of the assignability of the bill of exchange used in connection with overseas trade—the " outland " or foreign bill— payable to X or order, is the first legal step in the history of the bill of exchange as a negotiable instrument in England, an event of pre-eminent importance in the monetary economics of Stuart times.

Professor Holdsworth has recently described with great clearness the emergence of the quality of assignability in the English bill of exchange.[1] The curious reader may trace this interesting development in the various printed Law Reports relating to the seventeenth century. It is therefore only necessary to emphasise two important points here. The first is that the bill of exchange, originally regarded as valid when the parties concerned were actually merchants, was before the end of this century acknowledged by the Law Courts as a valid contract when neither of the parties concerned were merchants; [2] and the second is that the assignability of the bill of exchange was incorporated in the Common Law of England from the existing Law Merchant.

Malynes in his *Lex Mercatoria*,[3] which was originally published in 1622, has given us the first full account of the Law Merchant in English, but he does not refer in this important treatise to the assignability of the English bill of exchange, or to the terms " to order " or " to bearer." [4] Between 1622 and 1651, when John Marius, a London " pub- licke notary," first issued his interesting *Advice Concerning*

[1] *A History of English Law*, VIII (1925), Chap. IV.
[2] The various stages in this development can be followed in *Oaste* v. *Taylor* (1613), 2 Croke, p. 306; *Edgar* v. *Chut* (1663), 1 Keble, pp. 592 and 636; and *Sarsfield* v. *Witherby* (1686), Carth., p. 82. See Chief Justice Treby's remarks in *Bromwich* v. *Lloyd* (1696), Lutw, p. 1585, and Chitty, *op. cit.*, p. 28.
[3] For modern accounts of the Law Merchant see Sir John Comyns, *op. cit.*, 5; W. Mitchell, *An Essay on the Early History of the Law Merchant* (1904); T. E. Scrutton, " General Survey of the History of the Law Mer- chant," in *Select Essays in Anglo-American Legal History* (1909), III, pp. 7–15; W. Holdsworth, *op. cit.*, VIII (1925), chap. iv.
[4] There is, however, evidence which shows that the clause to order, or to assigns, appeared in bills of exchange before the time of Malynes. In I. B., *The Merchants Avizo*, for example, published in 1607, a specimen of a bill of exchange (p. 53), dated 1589, contains the clause " or his assigns."

Bills of Exchange,[1] it had apparently become common in England to transfer by indorsement bills of exchange payable to order.   In the first edition of his treatise Marius gives a specimen of a bill made payable to X or assigns,[2] and in his second edition, 1655, of bills payable to X or order, and to X or assigns, together with copies of actual assignments,[3] "which many times," he states, "especially in outland bills, are three and four upon a Bill."[4]

There are, also, some curious documents among the seventeenth-century Proceedings in Chancery which show that when Marius published the second edition of his valuable *Advice* it was customary to assign by repeated indorsements the outland bill of exchange payable to order. "Coniard did," states one of these documents [5] with reference to such a bill, "accordinge to the course and custom of merchants assigne the said bill . . . by indorsing said bill and subscribing his name thereunto." This particular bill was, two years later, taken by the holder as security for a loan to the shop of Sir Thomas Vyner who, "seeing the bill to be a lawful one . . . with several assignments and indorsements . . . did without further question " lend the sum desired.   It is also evident from these documents that loans were obtained by assigning bills of exchange to the "cashkeepers" of goldsmith bankers.

The increased importance of the bill of exchange during the next thirty years—a period which also witnessed a great development in the private banking of the goldsmiths—is clearly reflected by Scarlett in the first edition of his detailed *Stile of Exchanges*, published in 1682.   Scarlett devotes 25 chapters of nearly 200 pages entirely to bills of exchange. "When the Endorsement is made payable to order," he states, "he to whom it is endorsed as payable may again endorse it, and so may as often be endorsed as there is room on the Bill for endorsements."[6]

---

[1] "A very good book"—Chief Justice Holt in *Ward* v. *Evans* (1702), 2 Salk., p. 442.   [2] Pp. 44–45.
[3] Pp. 26–35.   Marius also refers, pp. 54–55, to bills of exchange payable to X or bearer.   [4] P. 45.
[5] P.R.O., Ch. P., before 1714 (Mitford), 64/81.
[6] P. 55.   In the preface of this book Scarlett gives some interesting details about the " mystery " or trade of banking.

It is thus evident from the *Advice* of Marius, from the *Stile* of Scarlett, from the contemporary Proceedings in Chancery, and also from the printed Law Reports, that, in the latter half of the seventeenth century the bill of exchange payable to order was freely transferred from one person to another by indorsement, and that the practice of repeated indorsements had become customary—that the quality of what jurists term complete assignability [1] had emerged—such assignments being recognised as legal by the Common Law Courts before the end of this century. [2]

Inland bills of exchange, [3] in connection with domestic trade, were increasingly used in England in the latter part of the seventeenth century. As in the outland variety, they were of three kinds, payable to X only, to X or order, and to X or bearer, and not long after their appearance it became customary under the Law Merchant, and shortly afterwards under the Common Law, to assign the second type by indorsement because they were regarded as the same class of instrument as the outland bills payable to X or order. [4] This development was followed by the promissory note payable to X or order also being recognised, first by the Law Merchant and then by the Common Law, as assignable by indorsement, [5] but there was a great deal of controversy in the Courts before all types of promissory notes were placed on a negotiable basis by Act of Parliament. [6] Thus when

---

C. Molloy, *De Jure Maritimo et Navali* (1676), devotes his tenth chapter to bills of exchange in which he deals with " bills assignable over according to the Customs of Merchants."

[1] Assignability is one of the three main characteristics of negotiability. For details of the emergence of the other two—consideration, and " the acquisition of a good title by a *bona-fide* holder for value, irrespective of any defects in or want of a title on the part of the assignor "—see Holdsworth, *op. cit.*, VIII, pp. 140–46.

[2] *Carter* v. *Downich* (1686), Carth., p. 83; *Jordan* v. *Barloe* (1701), 3 Salk., p. 67.

[3] Defined by Chief Justice Treby in *Bromwich* v. *Lloyd* (1696), 2 Lutw., p. 1585, as " bills between merchants trading one with another here in England."

[4] In *Carter* v. *Palmer* (1701), 12 Mod. p. 380, Chief Justice Holt declared that " inland bills were not known till trade grew to a height, and when they obtained, they received the same law with outlandish bills." See also *Marius*, *op. cit.* (2nd ed.), p. 45. For a clear ruling on the assignability of " bills of exchange " payable to X or order see *Jordan* v. *Barloe*.

[5] *Williams* v. *Williams* (1693), Carth., p. 269; *Nicholson* v. *Sedgwick* (1698), 3 Salk., p. 67 ; *Carter* v. *Palmer*; *Jordan* v. *Barloe*.

[6] 3 & 4 Anne, c. 8 (1704).

the goldsmith bankers were such important figures in the London money market there is, fortunately, a great deal of documentary evidence to show that they were big dealers in these three kinds of assignable instruments.

The outland and inland bills of exchange and promissory notes payable to X or bearer were not recognised as assignable by the Common Law Courts of Stuart England.[1] When inland bills were first used in England is not known, but they are referred to by Marius in the second edition of his *Advice*, which, he informs us, is " the Crop of foure and twenty years experience in my imployment in the Art of a Notary publicke, which I am, and do yet practice at the Royall Exchange in London both in Inland and Outland Instruments." [2]

.This statement of Marius seems to be evidence of the use of inland bills in England as early as 1631, eleven years before the outbreak of the Civil War. Their appearance in the Common Law Courts is shown by a declaration of Chief Justice Holt. " I remember," he states, " when actions on inland bills did first begin." [3] *Edgar* v. *Chut*, 1663,[4] is the first case in the Law Reports which clearly relates to an inland bill, and there is no doubt that both inland bills to bearer and to order were in frequent use in England in the years immediately following the Restoration,[5] an important factor in the expansion of goldsmith banking. [6]

Side by side with, even as it were under cover of, the inland bill of exchange, the promissory note developed into a negotiable instrument. The emergence of assignability in this instrument was apparently due to the confusion between these two forms by the later Stuart lawyers, for both notes and inland bills are frequently referred to as bills of exchange in the Law Reports of the period, a confusion which was dealt with by Lord Mansfield in *Grant* v. *Vaughan*, in 1764.[7] Therefore, as it was originally thought that there was no

[1] *Horton* v. *Coggs* (1691), 3 Lev., p. 299; *Hodges* v. *Steward*, 3 Salk., p. 68; *Bank of England* v. *Newman* (1699), 1 Ld. Raym., p. 42; *Carter* v. *Palmer*.

[2] Marius, *op. cit.*, preface. Malynes, *op. cit.*, makes no reference to inland bills.

[3] *Buller* v. *Crips* (1704), 1 Salk., p. 130. Holt was admitted to the Bar in 1663. [4] 1 Keble, p. 592. [5] See 9 & 10 Wm. III, c. 17.

[6] There are numerous entries in Backwell's ledgers relating to inland bills.

[7] 3 Burr., p. 1516.

real difference between the promissory note to order and the inland bill to order,[1] it is easy to understand why the former was regarded as negotiable under the Law Merchant. In 1704 Holt declared in *Buller* v. *Crips* that two of the most famous merchants in London had informed him that they looked upon promissory notes as bills of exchange, and that during the previous thirty years they not only frequently " transferred and indorsed " such notes as bills of exchange, but also " bonds for money." [2]

The promissory note was popularised during the last two decades of the Stuart period by the goldsmith and, in its engraved form, by the Bank of England. It is thus not surprising to find cases relating to this note becoming more frequent in the Courts in the closing years of the seventeenth century and the early years of the eighteenth; and in the 'nineties of the former century the promissory note to order was actually recognised by the Courts as assignable by indorsement. In *Williams* v. *Williams*, 1693,[3] it was held that a promissory note payable to order could be transferred by repeated indorsements, and that the " Custom of Merchants " concerning bills of exchange was but part of the Common Law of which the judges would take notice *ex officio*.

There was no ambiguity about this decision. Promissory notes were legally acknowledged to be bills of exchange, and, therefore, such notes payable to order were negotiable instruments. This held good until Holt, who was bitterly opposed to the goldsmith bankers, reversed it in *Clerke* v. *Martin* [4] in 1703 by declaring that a promissory note was

---

[1] See W. Cranch, " Promissory Notes before and after Lord Holt," *Select Essays A. A. L. H.*, III.

[2] 1 Salk., p. 130.　　　　[3] Carth., p. 269.

[4] 1 Salk., pp. 129-363.

Chief Justice Holt declared in this case that a promissory note payable to X or order or to X or bearer made by a goldsmith or other person was not a bill of exchange; " that the maintaining of actions upon such notes were innovations upon the rules of Common Law; that it amounted to the setting up of a new sort of speciality unknown to the Common Law, and invented in Lombard Street, which attempted in these matters of bills of exchange to give laws to Westminster Hall; and that the continuing to declare upon these notes upon the Custom of Merchants proceeded from obstinacy and opinionativeness." See Holdsworth, *op. cit.*, VIII, p. 175, upon the conclusions of Holt.

In the previous year 1702 in *Ward* v. *Evans*, Holt said, " I am of opinion and always was (notwithstanding the noise and cry that it is the use of Lombard Street, as if the contrary opinion would blow up Lombard

not a bill of exchange, a decision which undoubtedly resulted in the Act of the following year [1] which made all kinds of promissory notes negotiable. Within, however, three years of the decision of 1693 two new instruments appeared—the Bank of England sealed bill in 1694,[2] and the Exchequer bill in 1696.[3] These were from the outset legally assignable instruments, and there is a great deal of evidence which shows that the goldsmith bankers dealt largely in these new forms of paper credit in the closing years of the seventeenth century.[4]

Under the Law Merchant, cheques also, it would appear, were regarded from the outset as bills of exchange, and the earliest surviving specimens drawn on an English banker were used in connection with the private banking of the goldsmiths. These specimens are simply ordinary slips of paper containing a written order or demand addressed to the banker by a person having money in the banker's custody to pay the sum specified thereon to an individual only, to an individual or order, or to an individual or bearer. There is evidence to show that they were in use at least five years before the date of the earliest known specimen. In the Chancery documents relating to *Vyner* v. *Clipsham and Castle*,[5] Sir Robert Vyner, " knight and bart, cittizen and goldsmith of London," states in his " complaint " that Michael Clipsham and Robert Castle, " cittizens and merchants of London," " did upon a joint accompt pay into " his " shopp " " several sums of money all of which

---

Street) that the acceptance of such a note is not actual payment. . . . For when such a note is given in payment it is always intended to be taken under this condition, to be payment if the money be paid thereon in convenient time." See also *Anon* (1702), 12 Mod., p. 517.

[1] 3 & 4 Anne, c. 8.

[2] The sealed bill of the Bank of England is described in Chap. VI, pp. 156–57, *infra*.

[3] The Exchequer bill is described in Chap. V, pp. 141–43, *infra*.

[4] In, for example, one of Messrs. Hoare's earliest ledgers, commenced in 1694, there are many items in the various personal accounts of customers relating to the discounting of Bank of England sealed bills and of Exchequer bills; *e.g.* fol. 401, " By Bank Bill of £250 at 17½ p.c. discount—£206. 5. o." The goldsmith bankers also discounted Bank of England promissory notes, *e.g. ibid.*, fol. 208. " By a Bank note discounted at 15 p.c.—£80. 0. 0." For the Bank of England's relations with the goldsmith bankers see Chap. VI, pp. 171–72, *infra*.

[5] P.R.O., Ch. P., before 1714 (Reynardson), 35/66.

E

were repaid them at several times," and that about September 1665 the said Clipsham did " draw a note or bill upon Edward Backwell, Alderman, to pay £500 unto your orator [Sir Robert Vyner] upon the accompt of said Clipsham and Castle." This appears to have been a transfer of a deposit of £500 from the custody of Backwell to that of Vyner, for we are told that " Vyner or some of his servants did give a note unto Clipsham for the receipt of the said £500." But Clipsham, calling a little later at Vyner's shop, " to know if Vyner had received the £500 from Backwell," managed to obtain " another note signed to him for the receipt of the said £500," and " having got two notes " for this particular sum he " or Castle or some one on their order " did in December and January [1665–6] repair unto Vyner's shop, and, upon producing the said notes, " did receive from Vyner's servants at several times " £1,000 together with the interest due upon this sum.

These particular documents are striking contemporary evidence of some of the chief features of goldsmith banking : the keeping of, and payment of interest on, deposits; the withdrawal of deposits on demand; the issuing, and the assigning of, the banker's promissory notes; the drawing of " notes " or cheques on the banker by a customer.

The earliest known cheques [1] belong to the 'seventies of the seventeenth century,[2] and one of these, dated 1675, drawn on Thomas Fowles, a Fleet Street goldsmith, is worded thus : [3]

[1] The word cheque was not in use at this time. Such written orders from a customer to his banker were termed " drawn notes," and they are thus described in the earliest Court Minute Books of the Bank of England.

M. Phillips, " Bank Note Collecting," *Connoisseur*, v, p. 38, refers to a facsimile of a cheque drawn upon Smiths of Nottingham, dated 1705, which he regards as the earliest known provincial cheque.

For the evolution of the term cheque see *N. E. D.* For further details see R. D. Richards, " The Origin of the Cheque," in the *Banker*, IX (1929), pp. 29–36.

[2] All these have the name of the payee indorsed on- the back. An interesting indorsement of this nature in the possession of Messrs. Child is that of Titus Oates on the back of a cheque for £50 drawn by the Duke of Bolton " unto ye Reverend Doct^r Tytus Oates or his ord^r."

[3] Taken from a photograph published by the courtesy of the Institute of Bankers in *The Times*, dated 5th January 1915.

No cheque books were issued by the bankers at this time, therefore these early specimens do not possess counterfoils.

Mr Thomas ffowles.
>   *I desire you to pay unto Mr Samuel Howard or order upon receipt hereof the sum of nine pounds thirteen shillings and sixe pence and place it to the account of*

14 Augt 1675.   *yor servant*
                                    Edmond Warcupp.

£9. 13. 6.

>   *ffor Mr Thomas ffowles Gouldsmith*
>   *at his shop between the two*
>   *Temple gates ffleete streete.*

This may be compared with the following, which is a copy of the oldest of Messrs. Hoare's cheques :

June 11th 1676.

Mr. Hoare.
>   *pray pay to the bearer hereof Mr Will Morgan fifty four pounds ten shillings and ten pence and take his receipt for the same*

                          your loving friend
£54. 10. 10.   *Will Hale.*

>   *ffor Mr Richard Hoare*
>   *at the golden bottle in*
>   *Cheapside.*

Curious developments of the preceding forms are the sealed and the double cheque, both of which appeared before the end of the seventeenth century. The former was sealed by the drawer, usually in the lower right-hand corner, evidently as a precaution against forgery, while the latter has two cheques on one slip. The following are copies of the earliest specimens of each kind in Messrs. Child's collection :

Collonnell Childe & Partner.
>   *Pray pay to Sr Edward Cartarett or bearer the summe of two hundred pounds and place itt to my account. I will be with you this after noone.*

29 May 1689.

                          Rich Beauvoir. [Seal]

£200 : —: —

>   *For Collonnell Childe & Partners*
>   *Goldsmiths next to temple bar.*

Holland-house Kensington 6 Sep^tr
1688.

S^r

Pray pay to the bearer Henry Westenra Esq the sum of
seventy four pounds thirteen shillings and sixpence and putt
it to the account of

yr friend & serv^t
Ric Bridges.

For Mr Francis Childe
by Temple Barr.

12 Sep^tr 1688.

S^r

Pray pay to the bearer Henry Westenra Esq the sum of
thirty five pounds fifteen shillings and putt it to the account of
yr friend & servant
Ric Bridges.

For Mr Francis Childe
Temple Barr.

74–13–6.
35–15–0.
_____

110– 8–6.
_____

These early cheques drawn on goldsmith bankers resemble
the still earlier demand notes drawn on the Exchequer,
which were in frequent use throughout the seventeenth
century. The latter were notes made by persons such as
Government officials, or pensioners, who had claims on the
Exchequer, and who were paid by means of debentures,[1]
and, like the earliest cheques, begin with the name of a
person, an Exchequer official, usually a teller, followed by
the phrase " Pray pay," or a variant of this, such as " I
pray you deliver." The surviving specimens show that
sometimes they were simply notes by means of which
servants were able to draw money at the Exchequer on
behalf of their masters, that sometimes they were made out
to persons other than servants, and that sometimes they
were assigned by indorsement.[2] It is, of course, quite

[1] See pp. 56–57, *infra.*
[2] There are many surviving specimens of these demand notes, dated
1662 to 1665, addressed to " Mr Squibb," a teller of the Exchequer.
P.R.O., Recs. Ex. R., E. 407/123.

A specimen, dated 1674, addressed to " His Majesty's Tellers," contains
an indorsement in which the original payee has made out a fresh demand
note authorising payment to another person. *Ibid.*, E. 407/125.

possible, although there is no evidence to this effect among the surviving specimens, that such notes were sometimes assigned to a goldsmith banker as securities for loans. The following is an undated Jacobean specimen : [1]

Mr Bingley.
    I pray you deliver the bearer hereof Mrs Cisly Ryman one hundred pounds forth of my pencon w[ch] I am to receive from the king out of the Exchequer pray you let her have it as soon as you can and this my note shalbe for your sufficient discharge.
              your very friend
                 H. Notingham.

which may be compared with the following excellent example of a later date : [2]

                        The 29th June 1679.

Mr Thomas Vernon.
    I pray pay to Mr David Loggan the sum of
sixty two pounds tenn shillings due to me *lxij[li] x[s] sixty*
by Debentur directed upon you for the said *two pounds tenn*
sume and his discharge shall bee sufficient for *shillings.*
the same witness my hand.

Witness.   *Lucas.*
    Robert Squibb.

The debenture holder's note drawn upon the Exchequer must be distinguished from another Exchequer device, which from 1660 was regularly used until 1834. This was the auditor of the Receipt's note indorsed on payment orders issued by the Exchequer, orders which, as will be shown presently, were of great importance in the private banking of the goldsmiths. The said note gave a teller authority to pay or part pay the order, together with the interest due upon the sum which the order represented,[3] and unless the order contained this authority it could not be paid at the Exchequer.

Other specimens contain assignments of the following form on the back of the note : Y [the original payee] his Ass[nt] to Z [and the date]. *Ibid.,* E. 407/123.
  [1] P.R.O., Recs. Ex. R., E. 407/123. This specimen is receipted underneath the note thus : *I have resevid one hundred pounds accordingly this 22 of March Cisely Ryman.*   [2] *Ibid.,* E. 407/125.
  [3] Sometimes such notes authorising payment of interest only were written on the order. P.R.O., Recs. Ex. R., E. 404/619, contains several specimens of these.

Many seventeenth-century examples of these notes are still extant. They all commence with the name of a teller and the words " I pray pay," after which is specified the amount to be paid, and the branch of the revenue out of which the payment was to be made, followed by the *Recordatur*[1] and the signature of the auditor. The following is a copy of an example dated 1690 : [2]

Mr Villiers. I pray pay viij^l in full of the Princip and xviij^l ij^s xi^d for the interest thereof to the 13 of Nov 1690 in full 3 mo 27d out of 2s Aid.

14 Nov 1690.

Recordatur xiiij die November 1690 viij^l : Villiers in plen solutione mutui pred.
xviij^l ij^s xi^d

Exam. R. Howard.

Both these types of notes thus served to the tellers of the Exchequer of Receipt as cheques serve to a banker, and when paid and receipted, they were retained by these officials until their accounts were checked by the auditor of the Receipt, who afterwards took charge of them. The available contemporary evidence shows that they preceded the earliest cheques drawn on a banker. What appears to be the earliest proof among the Chancery Proceedings of the use of a cheque occurs, as we have just seen, in *Vyner* v. *Clipsham and Castle*; the earliest known English cheque is dated 1670.[3] The earliest surviving specimens of notes drawn upon the Exchequer by debenture holders[4] were in use at least forty years before the preceding Chancery case,

[1] The *Recordatur* had to be indorsed on the order before it could be paid. This was a note signifying that the order had been duly recorded in the Order Books of the Clerk of the Pells. The actual payment of the order had to be recorded in the Pells' Issue Books and Rolls. See *Reps. D.K.P.R.*, III, App. II, pp. 173–74, and VI, App. II, pp. 218–19.

[2] From P.R.O., Recs. Ex. R., E. 404/619. This specimen should be compared with the example which appears on the copy of Sir Thomas Player's repayment order, p. 62, *infra*.

[3] This is in Messrs. Child's possession and is dated 17th May, 1670.

[4] The demand note drawn upon the Exchequer must also be distinguished from the sealed letter or power of attorney, an instrument increasingly used in Stuart England, which gave authority to the maker's representative to receive money on behalf of the maker. The surviving seventeenth-century specimens show that these letters were frequently used in connection with payments by the Exchequer, and also in connection with payments made by merchants and others, while it is interesting to note that there are examples of such letters authorising goldsmiths to receive

and the auditor's notes indorsed on payment orders were in use five years before this case. Therefore, as there is no reason to think that the customers of the goldsmith bankers were not acquainted with both these Exchequer devices—in fact, there is a great deal of evidence to show that they were very well acquainted with the second one—it seems safe to conclude that these notes, particularly the one used by the Government debenture holders, were the immediate precursors of the modern cheque.

Though the transfer of money by means of cheques was thus functioning in the system of private banking conducted by the goldsmiths, the modern pass-book does not appear to have been used by these bankers in the seventeenth century.[1] There is no reference to these books among the documents appertaining to this century preserved in the strong-rooms of Messrs. Hoare and of Messrs. Child. The first record among the latter bank's early transactions relating to pass-books occurs in a letter written by Lady Carteret in 1715. " Mr Child," she states, " I desire you will send ye money I called ab^t t'other morning in 50 pound bills as far as 300 and ye other hundred in 5 twenty pound bills ye person I thought of sending to examine ye account is sick.[2] I shall be glad of a Book as I used to have at Mr Meade wth an account of all that you have received upon this article."

Finally, the third class of paper *media* of vital concern to the goldsmith bankers consisted of certain types of Government orders, which were of paramount importance in the public finance of the day, and which constitute a remarkable group of Treasury-Exchequer artifices meriting the closest attention.

The old English Exchequer had two important instruments of issue : the debenture, and the payment order.[3]

---

money in this way. P.R.O., Recs. Ex. R., E. 407/125, contains a large number of seventeenth-century sealed notes appointing " lawful Attorneys."

[1] Pass-books were, however, used by the Bank of England before the end of the seventeenth century. See Chap. VI, p. 169, *infra*.

[2] Personal accounts were often examined by the customer, and if in order were signed in the ledger as correct. See Appendix 3, *infra*.

[3] See *Parl.* P. (1797), XII, p. 425; *ibid.* (1831), X, 313; *Reps. D.K.P.R.*, V, App. II, pp. 295–99; *ibid.*, III, App. II, p. 174; Giuseppi, *op. cit.*, pp. 180–85.

The debenture, or " debentur," in its original form, was an instrument issued under the authority of Acts of Parliament, Royal Signs Manual, or Letters Patent Dormant, to Government officials, pensioners, or annuitants, to whom salaries, fees, pensions, or annuities were due at the Exchequer. It was always signed by the auditor of the Receipt, and was a written statement in Latin of the sum due, several of the words being invariably abbreviated by the writers, as is shown in the following specimen : [1]

| Debentur. | Georgio Neale falconar Dni R de Annuitate Sc ad l^{li} p Ann pro dio Ann fin ad fm Annun bte Marie Virg Anno Reg Caroli undecimo ———— | xxv^{li} sol p Savile |

Robert Pye

Recordatur xxiiijth Mai 1636.

and it was usually receipted thus : *Rec^d then the full contents of this debentur*—a form of receipt generally accompanied by the signature of a witness. Later specimens of this type have the receipts on attached slips, while on the debenture itself the particular branch of the revenue out of which it was to be paid is specified.

It does not appear to have been customary to assign this type of debenture. Among a large number preserved in the Public Record Office, which were issued between 1550 and 1834, not a single specimen has been assigned. Nor is there any evidence to show that the goldsmith banker made a practice of discounting these original debentures, or of accepting them as deposits. Such notes appear to have been presented at the Exchequer of Receipt for payment, and there are numerous examples of receipted specimens. Later in the seventeenth century, however, certain so-called " deben-

---

[1] One of a large number preserved in P.R.O., Recs. Ex. R., E. 407/79. This bundle contains about 100 debentures, dated 1636, all written and of the above form, and representing salaries to Court or Exchequer servants, or pensions, payable at the Exchequer of Receipt.

The above specimen would read thus *in extenso :*

| Debentur. | Georgio Neale falconario Domini Regis de Annuitate scilicet ad l^{li} per Annum pro dimidio Anni finito ad festum Annunciacionis beate Marie Virginis Anno Regis Caroli undecimo ———— | xxv^{li} sol per Savile. |

Robert Pye.

Recordatur xxiiijth Maii 1636.

tures " or " bills " were issued for special purposes. Such, for example, were the Transport Office debentures, the Ordnance debentures, the Nevis debentures, and the Navy and Victualling bills, which were usually printed orders of foolscap size.[1] These were frequently assigned, and in this way often got into the bankers' hands. In fact, they were simply interest-bearing assignable payment orders.

But the payment order, though often termed a debenture in Stuart times, was originally an order issued by the Lord Treasurer, and this official always signed it. When, however, the Treasury was put into Commission [2] it was signed by at least two of the Commissioners. Between 1660 and 1672, when the goldsmith bankers were so flourishing, the Treasury was vested in Commissioners for three periods : for three months in 1660 immediately after the accession of Charles II ; from 1667 to 1669 ; and from 1669 to December 1672 ; while from 1660 to May 1667 a Lord Treasurer in the person of Southampton functioned. Thus during the important twelve years which preceded the " Stop " of the Exchequer these orders were for seven years signed by the Lord Treasurer.

Payment orders were usually issued under the authority of Letters of Privy Seal addressed to the Lord Treasurer, or to the Treasury Commissioners, who, in turn, authorised the auditor of the Receipt to issue the orders from the Exchequer. They were, therefore, Treasurer's or Treasury orders issued by, and, when funds allowed, paid by the Exchequer of Receipt, and, as we have just seen, before they could be paid had to be indorsed with the auditor's special authority to the teller making the payment, together with the *Recordatur*.[3] In Tudor and early Stuart times the orders were usually written by the auditor, and even after the Restoration when the large printed order became so general they were also sometimes written. The printed orders had, like the

---

[1] Some excellent examples of indorsed Transport Office debentures and of Nevis debentures are contained in P.R.O., Recs. Ex. R, E. 407/79.

For details about Ordnance debentures see *Parl. P.* (1797), XII, p. 425; and *ibid.* (1792–93), XI, p. 7.

For Navy and Victualling bills see *ibid.* (1792–93), XI, App. 20.

[2] The office of Lord Treasurer was first vested in Commissioners by James I in 1612. See *Reps. D.K.P.R.*, VII, App. II, p. 9.

[3] See *Reps. D.K.P.R.*, VI, App. II, pp. 218–19; *ibid.*, VII, App. II, p. 9.

written orders, to be signed by the Lord Treasurer, or by at least two of the Treasury Lords Commissioners.

After the Restoration two new types of orders appeared. These were the repayment order issued with a tally, and that astonishing innovation the fiduciary order, both of which were invented by the Executive of Charles II. Thus in the years immediately preceding the " Stop " there were really three types of Treasury (or Treasurer's) orders : the common payment orders issued to Government creditors, the repayment order, and the fiduciary order; and the three, particularly the last named, are of the greatest importance in the remarkable development of goldsmith banking.

In order to understand more clearly the Exchequer system of money orders it is necessary to describe briefly the use made by this department of tallies, instruments which were still part of the mechanism of English national finance in the second decade of the nineteenth century.[1]

The working of the tally system in its original form was really quite simple. When loans were advanced to the Exchequer the tally,[2] a small stick, generally of hazel, on which was notched the amount advanced, was given to the lender as a receipt, a duplicate being kept by the chamberlains of the Exchequer of Receipt. [3] It was registered on a

---

[1] 23 Geo. III, c. 82 (1782), abolished the offices of the two chamberlains and authorised the substitution of indented receipts for the old wooden tallies. This substitution was not carried out until the death of the last of the chamberlains. See Chap. V, p. 138, *infra*.

[2] I am much indebted to Mr. C. Hilary Jenkinson, M.A., F.S.A., of the Public Record Office, for allowing me to examine a number of tallies in his custody, and for his revision of the section of this chapter relating to tallies.

I am also much indebted to Mr. Jenkinson and to Mr. D. L. Evans, M.A., for their assistance—so freely given on many occasions—in deciphering contemporary manuscripts.

[3] " On the Tally notches were cut indicating the sum in the Teller's Bill : a large notch for M($£1000$), a smaller notch for C(or $£100$), a smaller still for X(or $£10$), and so on for single pounds, shillings and pence . . . the Tally writer (who was afterwards the Auditor of the Receipt) wrote the sum on two sides of it, then it was cleft from the hand to the shaft through the notches, one part of which was called a Tally, the other a Counter Tally : one of the parts was retained by the Chamberlain, the other part was given to the party paying in the money." (F. S. Thomas, *op. cit.*, p. 26.)

For further details about the tally system see *Parl*. P. (1868–69), XXV, (366), pp. 334–49; H. Jenkinson, " Exchequer Tallies," *Archæologia*, LXII (1911), pp. 367–80; Giuseppi, *op. cit.*, I, pp. 183–84; H. de Fraine, " Tallies," *The Old Lady of Threadneedle Street* (the official magazine of the Bank of England), 2, No. 13 (March 1924).

branch of the public revenue and up to 1660 it does not appear to have borne interest. When the duration of the loan, which it represented, was completed it was presented for payment either to the receiver or " cashier " of the particular revenue upon which it was registered or to the Exchequer of Receipt. After the Restoration three important innovations were introduced : (1) the tally was authorised to bear interest,[1] (2) a repayment order, or " order of loan " as it was usually termed, was always to accompany it,[2] (3) the " orders of loan ' were, by an Act of Parliament made assignable by indorsement.[3]

The repayment orders or " orders of loan " were therefore negotiable interest-bearing securities. In the common parlance of the day it was customary to refer to these orders and the tallies which accompanied them simply as tallies. To the receiver of public revenue or the Exchequer official who cashed them, when the loan was due for repayment, both orders and tallies functioned as vouchers, which were carefully preserved until checked by the auditor of the Receipt. If, however, the lender was in need of ready money before the day of repayment, he might have his tally and order discounted by another person, usually a goldsmith banker, who ultimately presented it at the Exchequer for payment.

The " order of loan," which when issued represented an actual advance to the State, was soon developed by the hard-pressed Executive of Charles II into an order of an entirely different nature—the fiduciary order or " order of the Exchequer," which was issued in rapidly increasing numbers between 1667 and the end of 1671. " I think it is no exaggeration to say," writes Dr. Shaw,[4] " that this is the origin of official paper money in England."

The fiduciary orders when they were issued by the Exchequer did not represent any advances to the State. Like the " orders of loan " they were assignable interest-

---

[1] By 12 Chas. II, c. 9 (1660).   [2] By 17 Chas. II, c. 1 (1665).
[3] *Ibid.* This Act appears to be the first Parliamentary authority for the issue of negotiable interest-bearing public securities. See *Parl. P.* (1857–58), XXXIII (443), pp. 84–105.
[4] "The Treasury Order Book," *Economic Journal*, XVI (1906).

bearing instruments registered on branches of the public revenue, in the first instance on the Additional Aid of 1667, but they were used by the Exchequer officials for the paying of debts or for the raising of money. Their issue came to an end with the " Stop " of the Exchequer. Indeed, they were the direct cause of this dramatic event.

The circulation of the fiduciary orders was not a difficult matter. Large numbers were issued " by way of imprest " to various departmental treasurers, such as the Treasurers of the Navy, the Treasurer of Tangier, the Paymaster of Works, and the Cofferer of the Household, who either raised loans on their security, usually from goldsmith bankers, or gave them to Government creditors, who, in turn, almost invariably discounted them with the bankers. In fact, when the " Stop " was declared in 1672, practically all of these orders in circulation were in the hands of a number of goldsmith bankers who, in addition, held large numbers of individual tallies, and of tallies accompanied by repayment orders, which they had secured either through discounting or as securities for actual advances to the Government.

Striking evidence of the extensive issues of the various types of paper orders in the period between March 1667 and the end of 1671 will be found in a valuable series of Exchequer books known as the Registers of Orders for Repayment,[1] which contain copies of the original orders and of the assignments. Broadly speaking, the orders recorded in these registers fall into three classes : (1) repayment orders accompanying tallies, or " orders of loan," representing actual advances to the Exchequer ; (2) fiduciary orders, or " orders of the Exchequer," in the form of imprests to departmental treasurers ; (3) payment orders, or " debentures " to Government creditors, usually for " workmanship used upon several of his Ma[ties] shipps," or for naval or ordnance stores. Large numbers of the first and second classes were originally issued to such powerful goldsmith bankers as Sir Robert Vyner, Backwell, Colville, Whitehall, Snow and Portman ; and further large numbers of these classes, and also of the

---

[1] P.R.O., Recs. Ex. R., E. 403/2430–2435.

third class, were assigned to these bankers by the original holders or their assignees.

The fiduciary order was a fatal expedient. The financial mechanism of the day was too rudimentary to bear the burden of such worthless paper credit. But if the Exchequer had issued these orders in a strictly limited number, and in anticipation of a not too heavily mortgaged branch of the revenue, it is quite possible that this Government department would have functioned as a bank of issue, and, by anticipating in this way the most important of the original functions of the Bank of England, might have considerably delayed, if not completely dispensed with, the establishment of a great central bank of issue in England.[1] Later, however, two years after the foundation of the Bank, the Lords of the Treasury, under the guidance of the able and far-seeing Montague, launched with conspicuous success an issue of bills[2] which was in essence simply a repetition of the ill-fated fiduciary order experiment of Charles II.

The disastrous nature of the fiduciary order experiment was an important contributory factor towards the successful flotation of the Bank of England. Englishmen now began to realise more clearly the necessity of establishing a carefully organised institution, which could control the issue of paper money with much greater skill than an anæmic national Treasury dominated by an Executive which was in reality the King in person.

In view of the fact that the bankers were so seriously involved in these monetary devices, and as it does not appear to have been known hitherto that actual specimens of seventeenth-century " orders of loan," and of fiduciary orders still survive, copies of each kind are given herewith. The following is a copy of a printed repayment order for £2,450[3] issued with a tally to the Chamberlain, or City Treasurer, of London, who held large numbers of these orders, and of tallies, as receipts for the big advances made by the City to Charles II : [4]

[1] See *Cal. T. B.*, III, intro., p. xxxvii.
[2] Details of this are given in Chap. V, pp. 141–43, *infra.*
[3] P.R.O., Recs. Ex. R., E. 404/619.
[4] For further information about financial transactions of Sir Thomas Player see Chap. IV, pp. 108–109, *infra.*

74

Sr Thomas Player Knt Chamberlain of the Citty of London in repayment of Loane

Order is taken this *vijth* day of June 1678 By Virtue of His Majesties Letters of Privy Seal, dated the xxvij day of March last past That you Deliver and Pay of such of His Majesties Treasure as remains in your charge, arising by Virtue of an Act of Parliament lately passed for Raising Money by a Poll and otherwise, to enable His Majesty to enter into an Active War against the French King unto *Sr Tho Player knt Chamberlain of the Citty of London* .... or his Assigns, the sum of *Two Thousand ffour hundred & fifty pounds* in repayment of so much Money by him Lent unto his Majesty upon the Credit of the said Act and paid into the Receipt of His Majesty's Exchequer the said *vijth* day of *June* as by a Tally levied the same day appears; together with the Interest thereof at the rate of vij^l per Cent per Annum at the end of every three Months, until the Repayment of the Principal, And these, together with *his* or *his* Assigns Acquittance shall be your Discharge herein ——

mmiiij^{lti}
J. Ernle
Danby

Sr Tho Vernon.

I pray pay mmiiij^{lti} in full of the Principall money of this Ord^r and xxvj^{li} iij^s v^d for Interest from the date of the Ord^r to the xxiij day of August 1678 Inclusive out of Poll Money.
Recordatur xxvij die August 1678

mmiiij^{lti} Vernon in plena solutione mutui p^r dict et xxvj^{li} iij^s v^d pro Interesse eiusdem
            Exam R. Howard.

This particular repayment order was issued to Sir Thomas Player for a loan made directly to the Exchequer, and it therefore represented a sum of money actually received by

the State. The written fiduciary order for £5,500 which
follows [1] was issued to the Treasurers of the Navy, and did
not when it left the Exchequer represent any money paid in.
These Treasurers immediately assigned it to Bernard Turner,
goldsmith banker, of "The Fleece," Lombard Street, as
security for a loan of £5,000 at 6 per cent. interest plus
4 per cent. gratuity.[2]

179

Sr Thomas Osborne and Sr Thomas Littleton for the use and service of his Maties Navy.	*Order is taken this xxvjth day of June 1671 By vertue of his Maties L^{res} of privy Seale dated xxvjth day of May last in the xxiijth yeare of his Maties Reigne that you deliver and pay of such his Maties Treasure as is or shall be remayning in yor charge unto Sr Thomas Osborne and*	

Sr Thomas Osborne
and Sr Thomas
Littleton for the
use and service of
his Maties Navy.

To be regred &
paid out of the
London Excise

Order is taken this xxvjth day of
June 1671 By vertue of his Maties
L^{res} of privy Seale dated xxvjth day
of May last in the xxiijth yeare of
his Maties Reigne that you deliver
and pay of such his Maties Treasure
as is or shall be remayning in yor
charge unto Sr Thomas Osborne and
Sr Thomas Littleton, Bar^t Author-
ized by his Matie to execute the office
of Treasurer of the Navy during
his Maties pleasure or their As-
signes the sum of five thousand five
hundred pounds in part of the sum
of two hundred thousand pounds for
the use and service of his Maties
Navy by way of Imprest and upon
Account, And these together wth
their or their Assignes acquittance
shall be yor discharge herein ———

v^mv^c li
Ashley
J. Dun-
combe

The order is indorsed thus underneath the above:

We doe assign and transferre this ord^r and all our
interest and benefit therein unto Mr Bern^a Turner
or to his assigns for ye value rec^d of him witness
our hands ye 29th June 1671.

Thomas Osborne.
Thomas Littleton.

[1] From P.R.O., Recs. Ex. R, E. 407/120.
That the fiduciary orders issued to the Treasurers of the Navy were
usually printed is shown from an excellent example, in which even the
names of the Treasurers are printed, contained in *ibid.*, E. 404/619.

[2] P.R.O., Recs. Ex. R., E. 407/33. "A book for entringe the Accompts
of Goldsmiths and others." This order is one of the items in the accounts
of Turner which are entered in this Exchequer book. See p. 69, *infra.*
It will be observed that the order does not contain the usual subscribed
note from the auditor authorising a teller to pay the contents, nor is there
a *Recordatur* to indicate that it was recorded in the Order Books (Pells').

It is therefore clear that the bankers of the day had ample scope for carrying out big transactions in various types of assignable instruments.   But such goldsmith bankers as the Childs, Hoares, Heriots, Johnsons, Mawsons, Lambs, Sweetaples, Whites, Boltons, Kentons, Easts, Ballards, Pinckneys, Goslings, Stokeses, Wades, and Williamses of the reign of Charles II do not appear to have been very much concerned with the various types of Treasury-Exchequer payment orders.   They all seem to have pursued the even tenor of their way after Charles II, in January 1672, decided upon the artifice known as the " Stop " of the Exchequer, and they must be carefully distinguished from the group of bankers which advanced large sums to the King and of which the most powerful were, as we have seen, Sir Robert Vyner, Alderman Backwell, Isaac and Francis Meynell and Gilbert Whitehall.

With the exception of the Pinckneys and the Goslings, the names of the bankers in the first of these two groups appear in the list of forty-four goldsmiths which the *Little London Directory* published as keepers of " running cashes " in 1677.[1] It is interesting to note, however, that this list also contains the names of four goldsmiths of the second group,[2] which is further evidence of the fact that the bankers who financed Charles II were not all ruined by the " Stop " of the Exchequer, the results of which upon the private banking of the goldsmiths must next be examined.

[1] Reprinted in Price, *Handbook*, pp. 158–59.
[2] Joseph Hornby, " The Star "; Thomas Pardoe, " The Golden Anchor "; Thomas Rowe, " The George "; and Bernard Turner, " The Fleece "; all of Lombard Street.

CHAPTER III

THE GOLDSMITH BANKERS AND THEIR TRANS- ACTIONS WITH THE EXCHEQUER

" As soon as up I among my goldsmiths Sir Robert Viner and Colvill and there got £10,000 for my new tallies accepted."
The Diary of Samuel Pepys (Wheatley's ed.), 22nd July 1665.
" At noon Sir G. Carteret, Mr. Coventry and I by invitation to dinner to Sheriff Meynell's, the great money-man; he, and Alderman Backwell, and much noble and brave company, with the privilege of their rare discourse, which is great content to me above all other things in the world."
Ibid., 18th Sept. 1662.

THE transactions of the goldsmith bankers in the various types of paper orders were of a remarkable nature in the five years immediately preceding the " Stop " of the Exchequer. " I know and tell you," wrote Ashley, in October 1669, to Carteret, the Treasurer of the Navy, with reference to some of these transactions, " wee have often been forced to engage to them our personal credits. But I thinke wee shall all take care of that for the future. This cannot be strange to any that have been acquainted with the public affairs, neither can wee complain of the bankers for it, since I believe wee have owed some of them near a million at a time so frankly did they venture in the King's affairs when they could command money."[1]

[1] MSS. of the House of Lords, Bundle 213, document marked A 30.
The financial chaos which preceded the " Stop " of the Exchequer, and the extent to which certain prominent goldsmith bankers were involved, can be seen in the transactions of Carteret during his Treasurership of the Navy, and some astonishing information with reference to these is given in the Report of the Accounts Commission, dated 1669, *ibid.*, Bundle 213. Dr. Shaw regards the appointment of this Commission as one of the most important Parliamentary events of the reign of Charles II. See *Cal. T. B.*, II, intro., p. xxxvii.
There were ten charges against Carteret, the tenth referring to his transactions with the bankers, and it is stated that at one period he was allowing nearly £99,000 in interest to a small coterie of the bankers.
Striking evidence of the bankers' big transactions in fiduciary orders is contained in the accounts of Lord Anglesey, who followed Carteret as Treasurer of the Navy. These accounts show that Anglesey was charged with £480,000 ." by the imprest role " and that £426,893 was advanced upon the orders he issued, chiefly by the goldsmith bankers. B.M., Addit. MS., 28621, fols. 17–25.

F

There was, however, no possibility of averting a crisis. The suspension of cash payments to the bankers by the Exchequer of Receipt in January 1672 was fundamentally due to the fact that the annual sum of £1,200,000 granted by Parliament in 1660 for the expenses of the King was never reached through the sources available, and, even if this sum had been reached, it would have fallen short of the average annual expenditure between 1660 and 1671, which amounted to over £1,570,000.[1] Thus the process had been going on since 1660. The annual deficiencies accumulated, and in 1672 the actual amount of debt was approximately £2,250,000.

Of this enormous debt the greater part was due to the goldsmith bankers, and according to a special report presented to the King by Danby on 8th February 1677, this particular portion amounted on that date to £1,365,733 9s. 7¾d., which carried an annual interest at 6 per cent., of £81,944 0s. 2d. These totals were accepted by the King in Council, and an order was made authorising payment of the above interest out of the Hereditary Excise to commence from January 1st, 1677.[2]

Charles II duly paid this annual interest, but after his death no interest was paid until 1705, when the Government again, after having previously acknowledged the debt in 1701, commenced the payment of interest, at 3 per cent. This fresh acknowledgment was the result of prolonged litigation,[3] culminating in a statute in which it was enacted

[1] The sources of revenue never produced more than £900,000 in any of these years, and but for the fact that Parliament assisted with certain assessments, the total deficiency in 1672 would have been well over £4,000,000.

For a detailed examination of the financial position in the years preceding the " Stop " of the Exchequer see W. A. Shaw, " The Beginnings of the National Debt," *Historical Essays*, ed. T. F. Tout and J. Tait, pp. 391–422; and the same writer's introduction to *Cal. T. B.*, III.

[2] *Cal. T. B.*, V, pp. 542–46.

The total was arrived at by making "principal with interest every twelve months."

[3] For details of the litigation see T. B. Howell, *A Complete Collection of State Trials* (1812), 14, pp. 1–114; *The Argument of the Lord Keeper Somers on his giving Judgment in the Bankers' Case* (1733); H. Broom, *Constitutional Law viewed in relation to Common Law* (1866), I, pp. 373–75.

Among the Newcastle Papers, B.M., Addit. MS., 33038, fol. 100, is a curious scheme for the settlement of the bankers' debt in which it is proposed to issue " bills of credit " up to £2,500,000 secured on the surplus of a special Excise duty.

that; " in lieu of certain annual payments and of all arrears thereof " granted by Charles II, under Letters Patent, out of the Hereditary Excise in satisfaction of certain sums mentioned in the said Letters Patent as being due to the goldsmith bankers, the Hereditary Excise was, from 26th December 1705, to be charged " for ever " with the payment of annual interest on the said debt at 3 per cent. per annum, which was to be paid quarterly out of the Exchequer of Receipt to the bankers, their heirs and assigns without fee or charge, subject, nevertheless, to be redeemed upon payment of a moiety of the principal sum.[1]

In an Act of 1726[2] the moiety of the debt to the bankers is given as £664,263, the amount which was added to the English Funded Debt in 1705.[3]   In 1720 the bulk of this (£658,654 13s. 5¾d.) was added to the stock of the South Sea Company,[4] and the remainder was paid off in 1723.[5]

Careful analyses of this enormous debt to the goldsmith bankers are contained in two Exchequer books known as " The Bankers Booke of Interest "[6] and " A Booke for entringe of the Accompts of Goldsmiths and others,"[7] valuable records which hitherto appear to have escaped the notice of historians.   " It would," writes Dr. Shaw, referring to Charles II's debts to the individual bankers, in one of his lucid introductions to the *Calendar of Treasury Books,* " be of the highest value to the historian if they could be analysed."[8]   " The most interesting account of all," he adds, " if it could be recovered or reconstructed would be that of Alderman Backwell; such reconstruction is, however, hardly to be hoped for."[9]

---

[1] 12 & 13 Wm. III, c. 12, s. 15.   [2] 13 Geo. I, c. 3, s. 7.
[3] *Parl. P.,* (1898), LII, C.-9010, p. 16.   [4] Under 6 Geo. I, c. 4.
[5] *Parl. P.,* (1898), LII, C.-9010, pp. 4 and 21.
The unclaimed dividends of the bankers' debt which had accumulated between 26th December 1705 and 29th December 1717 amounted to £10,725 5s. 3¼d.   These dividends remained in the Exchequer until 1726, when by 13 Geo. I, c. 3, s. 7 they were made applicable for paying off debt as though they were monies of the Sinking Fund.   A provision was also made, *ibid.,* s. 8, for any future claims for principal and interest, such claims, if proved correct, to be paid up to a maximum of £10,725 5s. 3¼d., out of " the several surpluses, excesses or overplus monies, commonly called the Sinking Fund."
[6] P.R.O., Recs. Ex. R., E. 403/3019.
[7] *Ibid.,* E. 407/33-34, in two parts.
[8] *Cal. T. B.,* III, intro. p. xlix.   [9] *Ibid.,* III, intro.; p. 1.
Dr. Shaw states, *ibid.,* p. 1. that he has discovered two accounts relating

The account, or rather the accounts, of Alderman Backwell and of the other bankers who advanced money to the Exchequer, with one important exception—Gilbert Whitehall—and five minor exceptions, are contained in these valuable Exchequer books.   Commenced two years after the "Stop" of the Exchequer, they fill the breach which Dr. Shaw laments, and are striking documentary evidence of the care and labour expended by the officials of the Exchequer of Receipt in the collation and tabulation of the big transactions of the bankers with the Government.

Like the Registers of Orders for Repayment, already referrèd to,[1] these books reveal the overwhelming nature of the issue of fiduciary orders, and they also show that the most frequently anticipated branches of the public revenue, upon which such, and other, orders were registered, were the Excise, the Customs and the Hearthmoney.   The various accounts are presented in three ways : in the form of a number of statements with great wealth of detail; more concisely in tabulated form; or just a simple statement of the total debt and interest only.   There are many examples drawn out in each of the preceding ways, and the goldsmith bankers' debts analysed are those of Sir Robert Vyner,[2] Alderman Edward Backwell, Isaac Meynell, John Portman,[3] Joseph Hornby, Jeremiah Snow, Bernard Turner, Robert Welstead, Thomas Rowe, Robert Ryves, George Snell, Isaac Collier, Thomas Pardoe and Dorothea Colville, executrix of John Colville.

The first account in the Bankers Booke of Interest, that of Bernard Turner,[4] is an excellent example of the detailed

---

to these individual debts, those of John Lindsay, printed in *ibid.*, III, pp. 1335–6 from B.M. Addit. MS., 28074, and Jeremiah Snow's, printed in *ibid.*, III, intro., p. 1.   Lindsay's he regards as valueless for the " purpose of the statement of the bankers' debt in Jan. 1672 "; while Snow's, which he terms " the only other discoverable account," simply gives the amounts of four separate loans, the names of the borrowers, and the total, an account which is also valueless because it contains no details about the nature of the relations between the banker and the Exchequer with reference to securities, interest, gratuity and the dates when the advances were made.

[1] See Chap. II, p. 60, *supra*.

[2] For the life of Sir Robert Vyner see *D. N. B.*; and an anonymous work entitled, *Vyner, A Family History* (1885).

[3] For an Exchequer interest account attached to a Privy Seal and relating to one of Portman's loans to the State, see Appendix 10, *infra*.

[4] Fols. 1–9.

statement. Turner's debt was carefully examined by the
Exchequer officials in 1674. The principal sum amounted
to £14,200 13s. 8d., and the " interest and reward " on this
from January 1st, 1672, to January 1st, 1674, came to
£1,781 18s. 5d. Several sums had been advanced by this
goldsmith banker on fiduciary orders, or " orders of the
Exchequer " as they were termed, registered on the " Last
Wine Act," and the " Fourth Quarter of the Customs."
The following is a synopsis of a typical entry from Turner's
account : [1]

> " The said Bernard Turner craves allowance for interest
> and reward on 5,000 li " advanced to the Treasurers of the
> Navy " upon assignment to him of an order of the Exchequer
> for 5,500 li " on 29th June 1671, No. 179, registered upon
> the London Excise, interest at 6 per cent., and gratuity at
> 4 per cent., from 29th June 1671 to 1st January 1672,
> " the 5,000 li being then unpaid," amounting to ....
> £254 15s. 10d.

The analysis of Hornby's debt shows that Mr. Pepys was
an active intermediary in the circulation of the fiduciary
orders. Hornby claimed interest on two sums advanced to
Pepys, as Treasurer of Tangier, £4,000 on 22nd July 1671
and £6,500 on 30th August of the same year, " upon assignment " of several " orders of the Exchequer," six of which
for £1,000 each, numbered 39 to 44, were registered on the
" Fourth quarter of the Subsidies." In this transaction the
banker received orders amounting to a nominal value of
£12,500 for a total loan of £10,500 on which, in addition to
6 per cent. interest, he claimed 4 per cent. gratuity up to 1st
January 1672, after which date interest only.[2]

One of Sir Robert Vyner's accounts,[3] dated 15th September
1674, and signed by Sir Robert Howard, the auditor of the
Exchequer of Receipt, shows that some of this powerful
banker's loans were secured on the Hearthmoney, the

---

[1] A copy of the actual " Order of the Exchequer " referred to in this
entry is given in Chap. II, p. 63, supra.

[2] P.R.O., E. 403/3019, fol. 131.
For another of Hornby's accounts see Appendix 16, infra.

[3] Ibid., fols. 27–32.
For a list of tallies on the Hearthmoney held by Sir Robert Vyner see
Appendix 8, infra.

Customs, the Royal Aid and the Fee Farms. This particular account is headed, " Sir Robert Vyner Knt and Baronet and partners," and the total advanced is given as £98,714 19s. 10½d., with interest as £9,863 4s. 4d. This total, however, only represents a comparatively small portion of what was due to Vyner, for three years later his debt is given as £416,724 13s. 1½d.

The " accompts " of Isaac Meynell " and partners," [1] also signed by Howard, are big statements of dealings in fiduciary orders. One, dated 1st July 1674, shows a total debt of £216,379 14s. and that large sums had been advanced on the Hearthmoney, Customs, and Wines and Vinegars, including £15,000, upon several such orders to the Treasurers of the Navy.[2] Snow's account, a total debt of £51,218 5s., is a particularly valuable and interesting one.[3] It shows that between Michaelmas 1669 and Michaelmas 1671 this banker advanced £28,404 10s. 11d. to the Cofferer of His Majesty's Household upon two £10,000 " orders of the Exchequer," numbered 26 and 29, registered upon the Additional Excise, and two such orders of £5,000 each, numbered 512 and 513, registered upon the Country Excise; £1,000 on 8th August 1671 to Sir Dennis Gauden, Victualler of the Navy, upon one £1,000 " order of the Exchequer," numbered 142, and registered upon the " Act for imposition on Wines and Vinegars "; and £21,813 14s. 1d. between 22nd September and 15th December 1671 to Sir William Bucknell and " the rest of the farmers of the London Excise " upon eleven " orders of the Exchequer," including four of £5,000 each, registered on the London Excise. Another of Meynell's accounts deals with loans amounting to

[1] P.R.O., E. 403/3019, fols. 13–17, 92–115; and E. 407/33, fols. 55b–73.
[2] P.R.O., E. 407/33, fols. 55b–73b.
This loan of £15,000 was advanced upon the security of twenty " orders of the Exchequer " dated 27th February 1671, registered upon the Customs, three of which, each for £3,300, were " registered upon Customs in the quarter commencing Lady Day 1672," and were assigned to Meynell by the Treasurers of the Navy on 28th August 1671. This is only one instance of many in these accounts, which is evidence of the fact that public revenue was anticipated twelve months.
The total nominal value of these twenty orders was £17,594.
[3] P.R.O., E. 403/3019, fols. 121–24; and E. 407/33, fols. 33–36.
These accounts of Snow show that the bankers did not invariably claim both interest and gratuity.

£115,329 19s.;[1] one of Portman's refers to transactions in " orders of loans " registered on the Customs;[2] another of Vyner's reveals an advance of £30,000 upon fifteen such orders registered on the Hearthmoney;[3] and one of Hornby's made up to 1st July 1674 gives the debts due to this banker as £18,234 on that date.[4]

In these Exchequer of Receipt records the accounts of Backwell, who next to Sir Robert Vyner was the greatest of the Government's creditors, are examined in very great detail, and are striking testimony of the big transactions in paper orders of an individual banker.[5] Here will be found much interesting information about loans upon the security of tallies, tallies and repayment orders or " orders of loan," and fiduciary " orders of the Exchequer." No clearer evidence of the nature of the post-Restoration monetary artifices could be wished for; and there are significant entries relating to important transactions in foreign exchange, while Mr. Pepys, as a departmental treasurer, is again prominent in the circulation of fiduciary paper money. Loans to the Treasurers of the Navy, to the Duke of York, to the Prince of Orange, to the Cofferer of the Household, to the Exchequer of Receipt, and to other goldsmith bankers all figure in these accounts. There are even instances of payments of interest on loans by means of fiduciary orders.

Backwell's loans to the King are analysed in the Bankers Booke of Interest in three sections, and duplicates of these appear in the Booke for entringe of the Accompts of Goldsmiths and others. The accounts were prepared by the

---

[1] P.R.O., E. 403/3019, fols. 92–115.
[2] P.R.O., E. 407/33, fols. 17b–18b.   [3] *Ibid.*, fols. 7b–12b.
[4] P.R.O., E. 403/3019, fols. 129–33.
[5] Three of Backwell's accounts appear in P.R.O., E. 403/3019, fols. 58–68, 151–68, and 245–47; and three in P.R.O., E. 407/33 and 34, fols. 21–26b, 41a–55, and 35–38; the second of the latter group being a duplicate of the second account in the former. These accounts show that this banker made large advances upon the security of the Customs, the Country Excise, the Additional Excise, Wines and Vinegars, and the Exchequer in General.
One of these accounts, E. 403/3019, fols. 151–68, made up to 1st January 1674, gives a total debt of £229,845 4s. 0d.
For one of Backwell's accounts attached to a Privy Seal, see Appendix 9, *infra*.

Exchequer officials because Charles had, under Letters Patent dated 23rd July 1674, granted the sum of £140,000 as two years' interest on the total debt to the bankers,[1] a sum which was duly paid after a partial statement of the debt had been prepared by the Exchequer. But the loans of Backwell and of Vyner were on such a large scale that detailed examinations were not ready for presentation until 1677, when Charles commenced the regular payment of interest.

In these books, therefore, though all the loans and the total interest due to Backwell are examined, the amount investigated up to 21st April 1675, was £229,845 4s.[2] This was divided into £43,599 16s. 4d., " principal debt " due to Backwell on the 1st July 1674, upon " orders of loane at the Exchequer," and £186,245 7s. 8d., the " remainder of principal debt " owing to him on 1st January 1674, secured by " tallies and other orders of the Exchequer." The detailed statement of this particular debt of £229,845 4s. is signed by Richard Aldworth, and is preceded by a copy of Danby's warrant for the payment of interest, dated 23rd April 1675, stating that £4,525 7s. 4d. had already been paid as interest on the first part of the debt, and authorising the payment of £20,725 9s. 7d. (out of the £140,000 granted by the King) on the second part.[3] The details of the third part of the debt, referring to two loans of £1,000 and £10,663 4s. 9d.,[4] were not presented by the Exchequer officials until 22nd March 1677. In the meantime, interest, " reckoned and made principal every six months," on all Backwell's advances had been accumulating, and this explains how the total stood at £295,944 16s. 6d. when Danby presented his report on the bankers' debt to the King in Council.

Space will not allow a detailed examination of Backwell's

[1] P.R.O., Records of the Treasury, Miscellanea, T. 52/4, fols. 40–41. See also Cal. Treas. Books, IV, p. 540.

[2] P.R.O., Recs. Ex. R., E. 407/33, fols. 41a–55; and E. 403/3019, fols. 151–68.

[3] The total interest on the second part of the King's debt to Backwell amounted to £23,072 8s. 8d., but of this sum £2,346 19s. 1d. was deducted, " the same being already allowed and paid to the said Edward Backwell by bonds entered into by merchants for payment of the duty due from them upon the New Imposts and additional duty on Wine and Vinegar." P.R.O., Recs. Ex. R., E. 407/33, fol. 42.

[4] P.R.O., Recs. Ex. R., E. 407/34, fols. 37b–38.

loans to the Government.   A few selected examples, however, will show how they were recorded by the Exchequer officials, the nature of the securities and the amounts advanced.

The first account relating to Backwell in the Bankers Booke of Interest deals with a total of £43,599 16s. 9d.[1]   It was certified correct by Sir Robert Howard on 25th November 1674, and shows that large instalments of this loan were advanced on the security of the Customs, Wines and Vinegars, and the Country Excise.   Made up to 25th June 1674, it is of the tabulated variety, and is headed thus : " An Accompt of Monies due to Edward Backwell Esq. for Interest after the rate of six pounds p. cent p. annum (making the interest principal every six months) upon orders of loane registered upon severall Branches of his Maties Revenue according to the direction of his Maties Lres Patents under the Greate Seale of England bearing date the 23rd day of July in the 26th year of his Maties reign."   The following excerpt relating to a loan of £12,000 upon the security of the Customs illustrates this form of presentation and the official method of calculating the interest : [2]

ON THE CUSTOMS.

li.	s.	d.		li.	s.	d.
12,000	00	00	Upon an order No. 397 on the Customs in general from 25 Dec. 1672 to 25 Jan. 1673, being 6 months . . .	360	00	00
360	00	00				
12,360	00	00	from 25 June 1673 to 25 Dec. 1673, being 6 months . .	370	16	00
370	16	00				
12,730	16	00	from 25 Dec. 1673 to 25 June 1674, being 6 months . .	381	18	05
				1,112	14	05

[1] P.R.O., Recs. Ex. R., E. 403/3019, fols. 58–68; also in ibid., E. 407/33, fols. 21–6b.
[2] For further illustrations see Appendices 14 and 16, infra.

The order referred to in the preceding entry was a repayment order or " order of loan," and this was the customary method of recording loans " upon orders of loans."   But the details with reference to loans on fiduciary orders are invariably recorded by the Exchequer officials in the form of long statements containing full details about each order. There are excellent examples of these detailed statements in the second of the accounts dealing with the loans of Backwell recorded in the Bankers Booke of Interest.[1]   A large part of the total given in this account (£195,745 7s. 8d., afterwards reduced by repayments to £186,245 7s. 8d.) was advanced to various departmental treasurers on the security of fiduciary orders.   During 1671, for instance, the Treasurers of the Navy received from Backwell £27,800 on twenty-one " orders of the Exchequer purporting 30,000 li for the repayment of the said £27,800 out of the Customs upon the quarter ending Lady Day 1672," while Mr. Pepys as Treasurer of Tangier got £8,000 on four £2,000 " orders of the Exchequer registered on the Law Bill," and £9,000 on nine £1,000 similar orders " registered upon the 4th Quarter of the Subsidy." [2]

This account is remarkable testimony of the careful way in which the big debt to the bankers was examined and presented by the officials of the Exchequer of Receipt.   The following synopsis is given as an illustration of this particular method of presentation ; it deals with a total of £18,700, part of the £27,800 which Backwell advanced to the Treasurers of the Navy in 1671 : [3]

> £18,700 advanced thus: £5,000, 28th October; £1,800, 31st October; £900, 1st November; £1,000, 15th November; £3,500, 28th November; £500, 30th November; £6,000, 12th December; "by the hands of Mr. Anthony Stephens . . . as the said Mr. Stephens hath certified, and as it agrees with his books of Acc^t, But comparing the same with the said Edward Backwell's books I find the same to agree in every particular

[1] P.R.O., Recs. Ex. R., E. 403/3019, fols. 151–60.
[2] Ibid., fol. 156. Other examples from this statement of loans on fiduciary orders are : the Cofferer of the Household, £12,479 14s. 3d.; the Duke of York, £6,000. .   [3] Ibid., fols. 155–56.

save onely the sum of 900 li. which is entered therein as paid out viz. 610 li. the 31st October 1671 in part and the remainder the 7th November following, upon assignment to the said Edward Backwell of 21 orders of the Exchequer viz. 13 orders part thereof numbered 67, 68, 70, 71, 72, 73, 74, 77, 78, 79, 80, 81, 82 dated 20th May 1671 for the 13,500 li. charged on the Customes upon the quarter ended Midsummer 1672; seaven more orders in further part thereof viz. one order dated 14th August 1671 numbered 14, and six orders numbered 21, 23, 25, 27, 29, 31, dated the 19th September 1671 for 7,100 li. charged on the Customes upon the quarter ended at Christmas 1672, and one order more in full thereof dated 14th August 1671 for 900 li. charged on the Customes upon the quarter ended at Lady Day 1673 which compleat the said 21 orders purporting 21,500 li. the interest and reward thereon was allowed the said Edward Backwell to the 25th December 1671 being the day to which his last account of interest was made up, and the interest on the said 18,700 li. here stated for the said 25th December 1671 to the 25 December 1673 (being the day to which this interest account is made up) the said 18,700 li. being then unpaid as Sir Robert Howard hath certified amounts unto the sum of   .   .

li.   s.   d.

2,346. 19. 01.

Other interesting items in this second account show that Backwell carried out extensive exchange transactions by means of special "correspondents" overseas. £10,508 11s. 6d., for example, of a loan of £16,000 to the Treasurers of the Navy " was paid in Cadiz in peeces of eight to Sir Edward Spragg the 21st of February 1671 by John Mathew, Edward Backwell's correspondent there, and charged on him here by two bills of exchange dated the same day." [1]   And so, again, the £17,000, already referred to, advanced to Mr. Pepys upon the security of thirteen " orders of the Exchequer," " was supplyed in peeces of eight att Cadiz for the use of the garrison at Tangier as the said Mr. Pepys hath certified." [2]

It is quite clear from the details of Backwell's loans in

[1] P.R.O., Recs. Ex. R. E. 403/3019, fol. 154.   [2] *Ibid.*, fol. 156.

the Bankers Booke of Interest, and in the Booke for entringe of the Accompts of Goldsmiths and others, that advances on "orders of the Exchequer" were almost invariably for less than the orders "purported"; that loans were often paid in instalments over "severall days"; that the securities were usually the Customs, the London Excise, the Country Excise, and the Wines and Vinegars; that both the "orders of loan" and the "orders of the Exchequer" were often issued on the security of public revenue due twelve months after the date of their issue; that Backwell held a large number of both types of orders that had been assigned to him either by the original holders or by intermediate assignees; that he usually received 6 per cent. interest plus 4 per cent. gratuity on his loans to the Government; and that he received part payments of loans and of interest shortly after the "Stop,"[1] and before Charles granted in 1674 the payment of £140,000 as two years' interest on the total debt to the bankers.

Such are some of the remarkable transactions of Backwell as analysed in these valuable records. The numerous advances made to the Exchequer by the various goldsmith bankers are, of course, all carefully recorded in the Receipt Rolls and the Receipt Books (Pells'), and the interest payments and repayments which they received at the Exhequer of Receipt appear in the Issue Rolls and the Issue Books (Pells'). The Order Books (Pells') give the substance of the various types of Treasury-Exchequer payment orders which were issued,[2] and, like the Issue Rolls and Books, are evidence of actual payments made by the tellers of the Exchequer of Receipt, while copies of the original authorities for the issue of the payment orders will be found in the Privy Seal Books.[3] In addition, the various miscellaneous bundles of Exchequer papers contain many important documents relating to the transactions of the goldsmith bankers. In one of these bundles is an excellent specimen of a printed fiduciary order

---

[1] See also *Cal. T. B.*, III, intro. pp. xxvi–xxx.
Seven days after the "Stop" Backwell received £174 1s. 8½d. at the Exchequer of Receipt. P.R.O., Recs. Ex. R., E. 403/1779, fol. 233.
[2] See Appendix 12, *infra*.
[3] For copies of Privy Seals see Appendices 9, 11, and 15, *infra*.

for £100, dated 22nd August 1667, No. 376, registered on the
" Eleven Moneths Tax," and issued to the Earl of Anglesey,
the then Treasurer of the Navy, " for salaries and wages of
officers, seamen and marines." [1] This was assigned by
Anglesey to Backwell, who cashed the order at the Exchequer,
as is shown by the following curious receipt on the back :

1 die April 1669.

Rec^d then of Lawrence Squibb Esq. one of the four Tellers of his Maties Receipt of Excheq^r by me Edward Backwell Esq. assignee to the right Honble Arthur Earl of Anglesey the sum of one hundred pounds according to the order within menconed. I say rec^d by me ————	*li* *C one hundred* *pounds* *Edward* *Backwell*

This receipt is interesting for two reasons : (1) it proves that
the fiduciary orders were not invariably inconvertible, and
(2) it contains one of the few surviving specimens of this
great banker's signature, a bold modern business hand quite
different from the ordinary caligraphy of later Stuart times.

The payment of the £140,000 authorised by Charles II
in July 1674 as interest on the total debt to the bankers was
made between 15th March and 15th December 1675 to those
whose loans to the Exchequer are analysed in the Bankers
Booke of Interest and the Booke for entringe of the Accompts
of Goldsmiths and. others,[2] and also to six other bankers—
Gilbert Whitehall, John Grymes, Thomas Price, Richard
Stratford, Henry Lewis and Richard Temple—whose loans
do not appear in these Exchequer records.

But it was not until 1677, five years after the " Stop," that
Charles was able, by Letters Patent, to place this big debt
on a business footing by " granting unto ye said Goldsmiths
. . . and to their respective heires and assignes an annuall
sume of Payment answerable in value yearly to the Interest
of their respective debts at ye rate of Six pounds per centum
for all such moneys as are due to them." [3] This delay [4]

---

[1] P.R.O., Recs. Ex. R., E. 407/119.   [2] See Appendix 17, *infra.*
[3] P.R.O., Recs. Ex. R., E. 403/2510, fol. 129, from a copy of Sir Robert
Vyner's Letters Patent.
[4] See *Cal. S. P. Dom.*, 1676–77, p. 537. Memorial of the Goldsmiths to
Secretary Coventry.

was not due to any neglect on the part of the King, but simply to the fact that owing to the enormous and complicated nature of the debt it took the Exchequer officials all this time to collect, examine, verify and arrange the extra-ordinary material which appears in the Bankers Booke of Interest, and the Booke for entringe of the Accompts of Goldsmiths and others.

The following totals appear in the various Letters Patent granted by the King in 1677–78 : [1]

Date of Patent.	Banker.	Amount of Debt.			Annual Grant.		
30th April		£	s.	d.	£	s.	d.
1677	Sir Robert Vyner	416,734	13	1½	25,003	9	4
do.	Edward Backwell	295,994	16	6	17,759	13	9
do.	Joseph Hornby	22,546	5	6	1,352	17	10
do.	Gilbert Whitehall	248,866	3	6	14,931	19	4
3rd May 1677	John Lindsay, in right of his wife Dorothea, administratrix of her late husband John Colville	85,832	17	2	5,149	17	4
do.	Robert Welstead	11,307	12	1	678	9	0
do.	Thomas Rowe	17,615	17	8	1,056	19	0
do.	John Portman	76,760	18	2	4,605	13	0
do.	Jeremiah Snow	59,780	18	8	3,586	17	0
do.	George Snell	10,894	14	5	653	13	6
do.	Isaac Collier	1,784	6	4	107	1	1
do.	Bernard Turner	16,375	9	8	976	10	6
6th July 1678	Robert Ryves	16,368	4	4	982	1	8

These are astonishing figures with a debt total of £1,080,754 17s. 0½d. It will be observed that there are certain omissions. There is no reference to the big total due to Isaac Meynell and partners, nor do the names of Grymes, Stratford, Temple, Pardoe, Price and Lewis appear,

[1] P.R.O., Recs. Ex. R., E. 403/2510. This Exchequer book, dated 1673–78, contains copies of the Letters Patent of Sir Robert Vyner, Back-well, Portman, Lindsay, Snow, Snell, Whitehall, Collier, Turner and Rowe. See also *Cal. T. B.*, V, pp. 597–600.

all of which figure in the Letters Patent of 1674.[1] On the other hand, Whitehall, whose " accompts " do not appear in the Exchequer account books just described, has a total debt of nearly a quarter of a million.[2]

It was ordered that the interest on the debt was to be divided by the goldsmiths among their respective creditors, provided that the said creditors should within twelve months of the date of the Letters Patent deliver up their securities "and accept of Assignments of proportionable parts " of the yearly sum granted to each goldsmith. All such assignments had, within thirty days of the execution thereof, to be " inrolled before the Auditor and the Clerk of the Pells of the Exchequer of Receipt," and every assignment not so registered was to be void.[3]

The Exchequer books containing copies of these assignments are of two kinds—the Assignment Books (Goldsmiths') [4] and the Assignment Books (Pells').[5] They contain the names of the bankers' customers together with their professions, and the amounts of their individual deposits, and are therefore particularly valuable records. The information they reveal, added to the contents of the Bankers Booke of Interest and of the Booke for entringe of the Accompts of Goldsmiths and others, helps to fill to a large extent the breach caused by the missing personal ledgers.

In the second series [6] of the Assignment Books (Gold-

---

[1] Stratford and Lewis were partners of Vyner, and their debts are in all probability included under Vyner's total, for, as already noted, Vyner's accounts in the Bankers Booke of Interest are headed " Sir Robert Vyner and partners.".

[2] There is evidence to show that even after the " Stop," between 1672 and 1677, some of these bankers actually made further advances to the Exchequer. Backwell, for instance, on 29th October 1672, advanced £1,000 " upon an order of loane for the like sum, numbered 21, registered upon the Customs on the Quarter ended at Lady Day 1673." P.R.O., Recs. Ex. R., E. 407/34, fol. 36.

Such advances, together with the accumulating interest, account for the increased totals of the separate debts.

[3] P.R.O., Recs. Ex. R., E. 403/2510, fol. 129.

[4] Ibid., E. 406/1–26, First Series, dated 1678–1688[9], 15 volumes; Second Series dated 1676–1713, 11 volumes. For a brief description and inventory of the first series see Reps. D.K.P.R., IV, App. II, pp. 166–67, and V, App. II, pp. 245–46.

[5] Ibid., E. 406/27–44, dated 1677–1704, 18 volumes. For a brief description of these see Reps. D.K.P.R. VI, App. II, pp. 227–30.

[6] The first series of the Assignment Books (Goldsmiths'), E. 406/1–15, are in Latin, and the assignments, which are entered in chronological order,

smiths'), each of the eleven volumes deals with the assignments of a particular banker. The first four [1] are records of those of Sir Robert Vyner, the fifth and sixth of Backwell,[2] the seventh and eighth of Whitehall,[3] the ninth of Lindsay,[4] the tenth of Portman,[5] and the eleventh of Snell.[6] The first of the Vyner volumes, dated 1677–80, which is typical of the remainder of this series, contains 629 folios with a record of over 600 assignments, and the first folio has the following heading : " Assignments made by Sir Robert Vyner, Knight and Bart, upon the yearly Rent or Sume of Twenty-five thousand and three pounds nine shillings and four pence, and payable out of his Ma[ties] Revenue of Hereditary Excise by virtue of his Ma[ties] L[res] Patents under the Great Seal of England dated the 30th April last 1677 in satisfaction of the sum of four hundred and sixteen thousand seven hundred and twenty four pounds thirteen shillings and one penny halfpenny owing by his Ma[ty] to the said S[r] Robert the first of January 1676[7]."

William Newbold, " of the parish of St. Stephen, Coleman Street, London, gent," has the distinction of being the first of the Vyner assignees. The record of this assignment states that Newbold had " discharged " Sir Robert Vyner of his deposit of £359 2s. 9d., and " was content to accept of an assignment of a proporcionable part of the Rent or yearly sume of twenty five thousand and three pounds nine shillings and four pence [granted unto Vyner] . . . payable out of the Hereditary Revenue of Excise." Newbold was " granted and assigned " £21 10s. yearly.

These copies of the actual assignments made by the officials of the Exchequer of Receipt show that each assignment was signed and sealed by the banker in the presence of witnesses, usually three or four. The first three of the Vyner assignment volumes contain copies of over 1,200 assignments. The fourth Vyner volume, an exceptionally

---

are not, as in the second series, classified under the names of individual bankers. The first of the volumes, for example, contains a large number of mixed assignments of Backwell, Turner, Vyner and Snell.

Reps. D.K.P.R. do not contain either an inventory or a description of the second series of the Assignment Books (Goldsmiths') (E. 406/16–26).

[1] E. 406/16–19.   [2] E. 406/20–21.   [3] E. 406/22–23.
[4] E. 406/24.   [5] E. 406/25.   [6] E. 406/26.

important Exchequer record of 608 folios, contains the records of the re-assignments of Vyner's original assignees. One interesting specimen of these may be quoted in full, all the others having a similar phraseology :

> " By virtue of a deed of 14 Feb 167$\frac{8}{9}$ under the hand of Sir Robert Viner 6 l yearly was assigned to Christopher Wren in virtue of 100 l due from Sir Robert Vyner. Christopher Wren in consideration of a certain competent sum of money paid by E. B. citizen and apothecary of London hath bargained, sold, assigned and sett over unto the said E. B. his heirs and assigns said deed pole and said yearly sum of 6·l to said E. B. his heirs and assigns.
>
> Christopher Wren hath hereunto set his hand and seal 29 July 1703 ".   [In the presence of two witnesses.]

Thus originated that type of paper order termed in the records of the period " the bankers' annuity order," an Exchequer payment order on which was specified the sum assigned by a banker to one of his creditors. When each individual banker had, according to the covenant, duly assigned to his creditors their *pro rata* shares of the annual grant, which the said banker received as interest, these creditors obtained from the Exchequer an order, together with a tally, for the sum assigned which they presented for payment at the Excise Office.[1] The fourth of the Vyner assignment books shows that such " Exchequer orders commonly called bankers' annuity orders " were frequently assigned by indorsement in the presence of one or two witnesses. In fact, there are documents which prove that these orders were used as transferable instruments nearly forty years after the earliest of the bankers' assignments were made.[2] It was in this way that the creditors of the goldsmith bankers became the first investors in the English National Debt.[3]

[1] P.R.O., Recs. T., T. 29/5, fols. 267–8 and 297–8. See also *Cal. T. B.*, V, pp. 434 and 458–9.
A contemporary document points out that this arrangement considerably enhanced the credit of the Excise Office, which was thus able to fix the market rate of interest, " for no banker can lend money for more interest than that office usually takes, or, if they ask for more, the borrower leaves them and goes to the Excise Office so that the whole cash of Lombard Street is thereby reduced to the King's tearmes of interest." B.M., Addit. MS., 28078, fol. 438.   [2] P.R.O., Recs. Ex. R., E. 407/125.
[3] See *Cal. T. B.*, IV, intro., p. xv.

G

Among the hundreds of creditors in the Vyner books are a predominantly large number of minor London tradesmen— drapers, butchers, saddlers, chandlers, cooks, ironmongers, dyers, brewers, watchmakers, coachmakers, haberdashers, apothecaries, mercers, curriers and even goldsmiths. Vyner was evidently a ladies' banker, for in the second of these books there are many names of women depositors, particularly widows.[1] His customers, like Backwell's, were drawn from all parts of the country, and among them were many wealthy members of the old nobility and of the Anglican Church. Thus, for example, we find Sir John Brownlow of Belton near Grantham, whose deposits amounted to £4,880, receiving an assignment of £292 16s. per annum. Sir John Wynn of Wynnstay, Denbighshire, with an assignment of £207 per annum ; the Earl of Scarsdale £60 ; Lord Fauconberg £60 ; Sir Thomas Willis of Fen Ditton, Cambridgeshire, £63 ; and "the Reverend Father in God Seth, Bishop of Sarum," £99.[2]

The remainder of the second series of the Assignment Books (Goldsmiths'), appertaining to Backwell,[3] Whitehall, Lindsay, Portman and Snell, contain the names of large numbers of town and country depositors, and all include records of both assignments and re-assignments. London cordwainers, mercers and merchants, Nottinghamshire and Huntingdonshire gentlemen, and Hertfordshire widows patronised Whitehall, among whose assignments there is one particularly interesting example, that of £6, from Michael- mas, 1679, to the "Lord Mayor, Commonalty and Citizens of London, governors of the possession, revenue and goods of Christ's and St. Thomas' Hospitals" for a deposit of £100.[4] Similarly, John Lindsay, who took over Colville's business, and Portman had a large number of both town and country

[1] Typical examples of assignments to widows are : Susan Shaw of London, an assignment of £6 per annum, from Midsummer 1682, for a deposit of £100 ; Hester Trotter of London, £4 16s. per annum from the same date ; Elizabeth Sanders of Holborn, £12 18s. from Christmas 1686.   P.R.O., Recs. Ex. R., E. 406/17.

[2] All these are taken from *ibid.*, E. 406/16. They are among the very earliest of Sir Robert Vyner's assignments, and date from either Michaelmas or Christmas 1677.   [3] P.R.O., Recs. Ex. R., E. 406/20–21.

[4] *Ibid.*, E. 406/22, fol. 319.   This big brass-mounted volume relating to the assignments of Whitehall is the largest in the series. It contains 751 folios and an index.

depositors.   The. last-named was evidently well known as a
mariners' banker, for a large number of assignments to
sailors are recorded in the volume relating to his affairs.[1]
This may possibly indicate that Portman, in addition to
banking, conducted a marine insurance business.

The eighteen big books forming the Exchequer of Receipt
records known as the Assignment Books (Pells') contain to a
great extent duplicate copies made by the Pell of Receipt of
the various assignments recorded in the previous series.
The arrangement, however, is quite different from that of the
Assignment Books (Goldsmiths'), for in the Pells · series
separate books are not allotted to individual bankers.   The
first of these volumes, entitled " Liber Primus Banckers
Assignments, 1677," [2] contains records of the assignments
of Sir Robert Vyner, Lindsay, Backwell, Whitehall, Welstead,
Snell and Rowe.   Thus this particular series gives information about the depositors of two bankers not included in the
previous series.   The following brief list, compiled from the
" Liber Tertius Banckers Assignments, 1678," [3] gives
interesting details about some typical metropolitan and
provincial customers of the goldsmith bankers, together with
the amounts of their deposits, and of their assignments :

Banker.	Creditor.	Debt.			Annual Assign-ment.			Total Annual Grant to the Banker.		
		£	s.	d.	£	s.	d.	£	s.	d.
Sir Robert Vyner from Lady Day 1678.	Peter Hales, London, merchant.	530	0	0	31	16	0	25,003	9	4
	Thomas Peters, Lon-don, merchant.	220	0	0	13	4	0			
	Anne Hayes, Middle-sex, spinster.	500	0	0	30	0	0			
	John Fisher, Westmin-ster, gent.	400	0	0	24	0	0			
	W. Taylor, Caversham, Oxford.	200	0	0	12	0	0			
	John Overton, York-shire.	500	0	0	30	0	0			
	Dr. Samuel Parker, Archdeacon of Can-terbury.	1050	0	0	63	0	0			

[1] Some of Portman's sailor customers, with the amounts of their deposits,
were : William Osgodby of London, mariner (£986 12s. 6d.) ;   John Bugby,
of Stepney, mariner (£329 16s. 8d.) ; Anthony Archer, of Shadwell, mariner
(£86 17s. 5d.) ; Ellis Osborne, of London, mariner (£46 2s. 7d.). P.R.O.,
Recs. Ex. R., E. 406/25, fols. 21, 24, 29, 63.
[2] P.R.O., Recs. Ex. R., E. 406/27.   [3] *Ibid.*, E. 406/29.

Banker.	Creditor.	Debt.			Annual Assign- ment.			Total Annual Grant to the Banker.		
		£	s.	d.	£	s.	d.	£	s.	d.
	Humphrey Hyde, St. Martin's - in - the Fields.	800	0	0	48	0	0			
	John Cave, Great Milton, Oxford, clerk.	200	0	0	12	0	0			
	Rt. Hon. Henry Sidney.	1250	0	0	75	0	0			
	Michael Seller, London, cook.	420	0	0	24	10	0			
	Adam Harris, St. Clement's Dane, milliner.	200	0	0	12	0	0			
	Henry Martin, London, vintner.	400	0	0	24	0	0			
	Wm. Finney, London, chandler.	200	0	0	12	0	0			
	Elinor Wetherell, Middlesex, widow.	250	0	0	15	0	0			
	Frances Bansen, Herts, widow, executrix of W. Bansen.	800	0	0	48	0	0			
	Peter Gorray, London, merchant.	170	0	0	11	14	0			
John Portman from Christmas 1677.	Katherine Davidge, Somerset, widow.	685	5	10	39	19	0	4,605	13	0
	Wm. Cuthbert, London, goldsmith.	216	13	4	16	0	0			
	Sir Wm. Portman, Bart., Somerset.	236	6	8	14	0	0			
	Sir Wm. Farmer, Northants.	475	2	6	28	7	8			
	Robert Pierce, Middlesex, shipwright.	160	3	4	10	0	0			
	John Ballot, London, gent.	87	1	6	5	4	6			
	John Dryden, Chesterton, Hants.	776	5	0	46	11	6			
	Mary Hobby, executrix of J. Jarman, London.	279	0	10	16	14	0			
	Edward Bilton, Esq., London.	1210	11	4	12	12	8			
Gilbert Whitehall from Lady Day 1678.	Judith Gressam, London, widow.	260	0	0	15	12	0	14,931	19	4
	George Pitt, Esq., Stoatfield.	220	0	0	13	4	0			
	James Jacobs, London, merchant.	375	0	0	9	12	0			
	Thomas Townsend, Staple Inn, gent.	250	0	0	15	0	0			
	Mary Hobby, executrix of J. Jarman, London.	1050	0	0	63	0	0			
	Francis Morryson, Esq., Lincoln's Inn.	500	0	0	30	0	0			
	John Inwood, gent. Surrey.	1083	7	0	65	0	0			

Much interesting information about the customers of the goldsmith bankers is also contained among the contemporary Exchequer Bills and Answers,[1] and the Chancery Proceedings before 1714.[2] A curious instance in the former documents,[3] which throws a great deal of light upon the business methods of the most powerful of the ‚post-Restoration goldsmith bankers, is the " complaint " of " orators." John Waldren of Stokebliss, Hereford, and William Bray, of Upperton, Hereford, executors of one Mathew Pitts, which states that the last-named just before his death " left in the hands of Sir Robert Vyner, or paid unto one of his agents or partners," £300 of " good and lawful money," for which sum Vyner and his partners, Lewis and Stratford, " became bound unto the said Pitts by bond." Then follows the " joynt and several answers " of Vyner and his partners in which they admit that Pitts had deposited with them several sums of money on the security of " notes or other receipts or bonds for the repayment thereof," and that the issuing of these was duly registered in special books kept for that purpose. Stratford states that on 24th July 1671 Pitts visited Vyner's " shop " and " did settle the account between them," after which it was found that £300 of Pitts' money remained in the custody of Vyner and his partners, who " by bond became bound for this sum " to Pitts, or his executors, with interest at 6 per cent., one of the conditions being that twenty days' notice should be given when repayment was desired. This particular " bond," according to Stratford, was presented for payment on 31st August 1671 by two persons who stated that they were Pitts' representatives, and that, in spite of the fact that the twenty days' notice had not been given, he ordered the £300 to be paid together with £2 6s. 0d. as interest, while the " bond " made out to Pitts was cancelled. Stratford emphasises the fact that it was " very ordinary and

---

[1] The following all deal with the affairs of goldsmith bankers. P.R.O., Exchequer Bills and Answers, London and Middlesex, E. 112, Nos. 863, 931, 977, 982, 987, 1006, 1133, 1276, 1277, 1278, 1324, 1360, 1395, 1408, 1529, 1533, 1561, 1568, Charles II, and No. 28, James II.

[2] *E.g.* P.R.O., Ch. P. before 1714 (Hamilton), 224/83, and 354/12; *ibid.* (Mitford), 64/81 and 127/48; *ibid.* (Reynardson), 35/66 and 97/19.

[3] E. 112, No. 863, Charles II. For excerpts from two other examples, E. 112, No. 987, Charles II, and E. 112, No. 28, James II, see *Cal. T. B.,* III, intro., pp. lii–liv.

usual " for the bankers or their servants to pay such deposits
" without scruple " to the persons that presented the
bonds, and that Vyner and his representatives had done this
" many hundreds of times." The goldsmiths conclude by
offering to produce the cancelled bond, which they state was
still in their possession.

While the goldsmith bankers affected by the " Stop " were
busy with their assignments, new goldsmith bankers began
to appear. Two of the most prominent of these later bankers
between 1672 and the end of the seventeenth century were,
as has already been mentioned, Duncombe and Kent.

Charles Duncombe and Richard Kent [1] of " The Grasshopper," Lombard Street, conducted a very big banking
business which undoubtedly occupied a commanding position
in the London money market before the end of Charles II's
reign. Statements of their loans to the Government prepared by Richard Aldworth are of frequent occurrence in the
Treasury Books of the 'eighties of the seventeenth century.
One of these accounts, dated 24th June 1680, shows that the
balance due to this banking house was £123,465 17s. 3½d.; [2]
another, dated 30th December 1684, gives a balance of
£237,604 1s. 8d; [3] and another, dated 30th March 1685, a
balance of £227,700.[4] There are also numerous references
to Duncombe as an individual money-lender, and as a dealer
in bills of exchange, in the latter years of Charles II's reign,
and in the reign of James II he advanced large sums to
the State upon the security of the Linen and the Tobacco
Duty Acts.[5]

Duncombe was still a prominent City banker when the

---

[1] The names of Duncombe and Kent appear in the list of goldsmiths
keeping " running cashes " in 1677, printed in the *Little London Directory*
of that date. See F. G. Hilton Price, *Handbook, etc.*, p. 158.

For Duncombe's career see *D. N. B.* See also J. T. Thorold Rogers,
The First Nine Years of the Bank of England (1887), preface, pp. xi–xii;
Macaulay, *A History of England from the Accession of James the Second*
(1858–61 ed.) IV, p. 628.

For details of the charge made against Duncombe with reference to the
false indorsement of a number of Exchequer bills, see A. S. Turberville,
The House of Lords in the Reign of William III (1913), pp. 101–105.

[2] *Cal. T. B.*, VI, p. 594.   [3] *Ibid.*, VII, p. 1474.   [4] *Ibid.*, VIII, p. 93.

[5] For examples of Duncombe's financial activities see *Cal. T. B.*, VII,
pp. 1347 and 1350; VIII, pp. 148, 176, 302, 1621–24, 1687, 1981, 2183;
and B.M., Addit. MS., 17019, fol. 21, and 28075, fols. 346–47.

Bank of England was launched in 1694. This important event, as is evident from the contemporary Treasury Minute Books, the Bank's own Court Minute Books, and the early ledgers of Messrs. Child and of Messrs. Hoare, did not affect the financial activities of the goldsmiths before the close of the seventeenth century. The Treasury Minute Books give many details of Duncombe's loans to the Government in the years immediately following the Bank's flotation.[1] The Bank's Court Minute Books contain, as will be shown later,[2] a great deal of information relating to transactions with the goldsmith bankers, particularly during the first six years of the Bank's history. Indeed, much of the Bank's earliest business was concerned with the promissory notes of the goldsmiths, but there is no evidence to show that the Bank was used in these early years as a custodian of their reserves. Among Messrs. Child's earliest ledgers, one big book, labelled " William and Mary," contains numerous entries, which prove that, under the ægis of Sir Francis Child, they were particularly busy at " ye sign of ye Marygold" between 1694 and 1700; and a bulky ledger relating to the period 1698 to 1700 in Messrs. Hoare's possession shows that there was considerable activity at " The Golden Bottle " in the closing years of the seventeenth century.

It is thus evident that the goldsmith bankers of William III's reign were quite as important factors in the London money market as their forerunners were in the Cromwellian interregnum and in the early years of the post-Restoration period, and that neither the " Stop " of the Exchequer in 1672 nor the flotation of the Bank of England in 1694 prevented them from continuing their activities as keepers of demand and time deposits, purveyors of currency, discounters of bills of exchange, tallies and Treasury-Exchequer orders, money-changers and bullion merchants.

[1] *E.g.* P.R.O., Recs. T., T. 29/8, fols. 20 and 257, and T. 29/9, fols. 76–77. The latter of these minutes relates to an important meeting of the Lords of the Treasury at Kensington, on 10th February 1697, at which both William III and Duncombe were present, and to Sir Stephen Fox's proposition that Duncombe should advance £50,000 to the Government. A number of Duncombe's transactions appear in a special Treasury Book, dated 1690–1700, P.R.O., Recs. T., T. 29/627. See also *H.M.C.R.*, *MSS. of the Marquis of Downshire*, I, Pt. I (1924), p. 463.
[2] Chap. VI, pp. 154–55 and 171–72, *infra*.

Such was the banking system developed by the goldsmiths in the England of the Stuarts.   In conclusion it is interesting to note that more than one modern English bank can claim relationship with the shops of their seventeenth-century forerunners.   Child's Bank,[1] which was absorbed by Messrs. Glyn, Mills & Co., in 1923, and Hoare's Bank, which still preserves its separate identity, are very probably descended from the businesses of Elizabethan goldsmiths—those of John Wheeler and John Hoare respectively.   It is also quite possible that Martins [2] originated in the business of Gresham, who was associated with that prominent Elizabethan goldsmith, Master of the Mint, and Royal Exchanger, Sir Richard Martin, and that as a result of this the name of Martin first became connected with " Ye Grasshopper " in Lombard Street.[3]   Unfortunately there is no surviving evidence to prove the Elizabethan ancestry of Child's, Hoare's or Martins.

From the time of Charles II, however, we are on firmer ground, and there are many documents which prove the connection of modern English banking houses with the goldsmiths' shops of later Stuart times.   Messrs. Hoare's earliest surviving ledger, commenced in 1673, belonged to Richard Hoare of " The Golden Bottle,"[4] a prominent post-Restoration goldsmith banker.   Martins is directly connected with Duncombe and Kent,[5] the powerful goldsmith combination of the latter part of the seventeenth century. Messrs. Child's ledgers and documents relating to this century are remarkable evidence of the connection of this historic bank with the important business of Alderman

---

[1] The interesting story of Child's will be found in *Temple Bar, or Some Account of " Ye Marygold," No.* 1 *Fleet Street* (1875), by F. G. Hilton Price. Immortalised by Dickens as " Telson's " in the *Tale of Two Cities*, this famous bank is now officially known as Child's Branch of Messrs. Glyn, Mills & Co.
The old sign of " The Marygold " is still preserved in the present building.
[2] In 1918 Martins Bank of London amalgamated with the Bank of Liverpool under the title of the Bank of Liverpool and Martins, but in 1928 this was changed to Martins.
[3] J. B. Martin, " *The Grasshopper* " in *Lombard Street* (1892), p. 27.
[4] The sign of " The Golden Bottle " still appears above the main entrance to Hoare's Bank.   It is interesting to note that five of the present (1929) partners of this historic bank are direct descendants of Richard Hoare.
[5] See J. B. Martin, *op. cit.*, Chap. II.

Backwell. The famous firm of Coutts & Co., now affiliated with the National Provincial Bank, dates from 1692,[1] and is descended from the shop of George Middleton, which was situated near St. Martin's Church.[2]

Among the " Big Five " modern bank amalgamations there are several instances of indirect connections with the seventeenth-century goldsmith bankers.

Lloyds Bank is indirectly connected with the goldsmith banking business of Humphrey Stokes, Stocks, or Stoaks, Pepys' " little goldsmith," who kept " running cash " at " The Black Horse " in Lombard Street in 1677. The firm of Barnett, Hoare & Co., which became part of the modern Lloyds in 1884, was directly descended from the " shop " of Stokes.[3]

Barclays Bank was incorporated in 1896 by the amalgamation of twenty private banks, among which was Goslings and Sharpe,[4] an old foundation descended from the famous goldsmith's shop of " Ye Three Squirrels," which flourished under Major Henry Pinckney in Cromwellian times. The original " Three Squirrels " was burnt down in the Great Fire of 1666, but was soon rebuilt by another of the Pinckneys, William, who was succeeded by Abraham Chambers. In 1738 the house belonged to John Simpson and Thomas Wood, and four years later Wood took the first of the Goslings, Sir Francis, into partnership. Shortly after this " The Three Squirrels " passed into the hands of the Stanleys of Alderley, Cheshire, from whom it was ultimately purchased by the Goslings. In 1754 the firm was known as Gosling, Bennet and Gosling, and in 1794, after Benjamin Sharpe, one of the

---

[1] *The Bankers' Almanac and Year Book* (1925–26), p. 98. For the early history of Coutts see R. Richardson, *Coutts and Co., Bankers* (1902); E. H. Coleridge, *The Life of Thomas Coutts, Banker* (1920); and J. Ridley, " Thomas Coutts, Banker," in the *Banker*, II (1926).

[2] F. G. Hilton Price, *Handbook, etc.*, p. 42.

[3] This explains the modern Lloyds Bank crest—a black horse and the date 1677.
I am indebted to the Information Manager of Lloyds, Mr. W. F. Hughes, for his verification of the above account of the relationship of this great modern bank with the " shop " of Stocks.

[4] P. W. Mathews and A. W. Tuke, *op. cit.*, pp. 1–5. Three famous provincial firms included in this amalgamation were Backhouse of Darlington, Pease of Darlington and Gurneys of Norwich. ·
See also the *Banking Almanac, Directory, Year Book and Diary* for 1897, p. 82; and W. Howarth, *Barclay and Company Limited* (1901), pp. 2 and 21.

bank's faithful clerks, became a partner, the title was changed to Gosling and Sharpe, which was retained until 1896, when the modern Barclays was formed.[1]

Barclays is also—through Barclay, Bevan & Co., another of its constituent firms—directly connected with the business of John Freame, a Lombard Street goldsmith of the reign of William III.[2]　In 1698 this business was known as Freame and Gould, and was located at " The Three Anchors," Lombard Street, from whence it was transferred in 1728 to " The Black Spread Eagle " in the same street.　The first of the Barclays—a Quaker of Scottish descent—became a partner in the firm in 1736, and from 1759 to 1766 the house was known as Freame, Barclay and Freame.　The first of the Bevans was of Welsh extraction.　He joined the firm in 1776, when the title became Barclay, Bevan and Bening.[3]

The Westminster Bank, formerly the London, County, Westminster and Parrs, can claim relationship with that important Cromwellian and post-Restoration goldsmith's shop, " The Golden Anchor " of Jeremiah Snow.　It was of the Snow who presided over the destinies of " The Golden Anchor " during the terrible days of the South Sea crisis that Gay penned the following lines : [4]

> " When credit sank and commerce gasping lay,
> Thou stood'st ; nor sent'st one bill unpaid away ;
> When not a guinea clinked on Martin's boards,
> And Atwell's self was drain'd of all his hoards,
> Thou stood'st (an Indian king in size and hue)
> Thy unexhausted shop was our Peru."

In 1856 the old London and Westminster Bank, one of the constituent companies of the modern Westminster, took over the business of Strahan, Paul & Co., which traced its history back to the time of Jeremiah, the first of the banking Snows. The Westminster, also, by the amalgamation of the Consolidated Bank with Parr's in 1896,[5] is connected with

---

[1] See Mathews and Tuke, op. cit., pp. 79–89.
[2] Ibid., p. 32.
[3] Ibid., pp. 32–28.
[4] Poets of Great Britain (1795), ed. R. Anderson, VIII, p. 305, Epistle VIII, " To Mr. Thomas Snow, Goldsmith, near Temple Bar."
[5] The Banking Almanac, etc. (1897), p. 112.

Hankey & Co., originally a goldsmith firm in existence in the reign of William III, which the Consolidated absorbed in 1892.[1]

Finally, it must be noted that the National Provincial Bank has connections with those famous pioneers of provincial banking, the Smiths of Nottingham. By about 1759 Samuel Smith & Co. of Nottingham was part of the firm of Smith and Payne of Lothbury, London, which a little later became Smith, Payne and Smiths of Lombard Street, a firm which amalgamated with the Union Bank of London, which in turn was absorbed by the National Provincial.

---

[1] For further interesting details about the origin of London banks see F. G. Hilton Price, *Handbook of London Bankers, passim.*

CHAPTER IV

TUDOR AND STUART BANKING SCHEMES[1]

" The Banks that I should humbly propose may be thus established :
  1. That in every Shire there be a Bank erected by Act of Parliament.
  2. That the Fund of these Banks be Land and Money."
      SIR FRANCIS BREWSTER, *Essays on Trade and Navigation*
      (1695), p. 110.

" *Gentleman :* Your Bank Doctor, we hear that there are a Par-Royal of
  Land Banks setting up in London."
  Doctor : Those which you call Land Banks are not worth mentioning,
    mine is the only Bank of the World . . . whenever the Land
    Bank is mentioned you are to understand my Land Bank. . . ."
      A Bank Dialogue between Dr. H. C. and a Country Gentleman
      (1696).

THE petitions, propositions, " humble proposals " and
" seasonable observations " appertaining to banks and
banking, the earliest of which appeared in England during
the Tudor period, increased in number and in volume during
the Stuart régime, particularly during the two decades
preceding the foundation of the Bank of England. They
form an important field of economic literature from which
it is evident that a large number of Tudor and Stuart
writers fully realised the need of a well-organised credit
system. The great expansion of English domestic and overseas trade in the seventeenth century created big financial

---

[1] In July 1888 Professor Charles E. Dunbar contributed to the *Quarterly
Journal of Economics* (Vol. II) a brief article, reprinted in his *Economic
Essays* (1904), entitled " Notes on Early Banking Schemes." In 1901
another American economist, Mr. Andrew M. Davis, described some of
these schemes in more detail, and examined their effects on the genesis of
American banking, " Currency and Banking in the Province of Massa-
chusetts-Bay," *American Economic Association Publications*, Series 3,
Vol. II, No. 2. Later, Professor W. R. Scott, in his monumental *Constitution and Finance of English, Scottish and Irish Joint Stock Companies*
(1910–12), gave us new information relating to the activities of the various
English land bank promoters. The present chapter, while including in its
scope the schemes mentioned by these writers, is an attempt to throw
further light on this important phase of the economics of Stuart England,
a phase which Professor E. R. A. Seligman describes (*Curiosities of Early
Economic Literature* (1920), p. xi) as " one of the most interesting of
economic literature."

problems; the many banking schemes which accompanied this expansion give an excellent insight into the wide commercial activities of this important era.

The earliest English banking schemes belong to the reign of Elizabeth. Among these are : (1) the Bill of 1571 for the establishing of seven " principal banks or stocks of money," which were to be called " banks of relief of common necessity," in London, York, Norwich, Coventry, West Chester, Bristol and Exeter; [1] (2) the project of Stephen Parrott, probably in 1576, which appears to have been of the nature of a *Mont de Piété*, " a good, godly, and charrytable work "; [2] (3) Erasmus Vandepere's plan in 1580 [3] for the erection of an office in London out of which money was to be advanced on behalf of the Government to " collonels and captains " on active service for the payment of troops, and the purchase of supplies; and (4) the proposal of Christopher Hagenbuch,[4] which advocated the setting up of an institution in London " in which shall enter every year a large sum of money," and from which Elizabeth could obtain whatever " notable sum " she needed.

These were followed in James I's reign by the scheme of Paul Pindar [5] for " the erecting of a Bank for the Crowne upon occasion of ye King's demanding a loan from ye City," and a group of four schemes,[6] three of which—the first, second and fourth—appear to have been drawn out by Sir

[1] S.P. Dom., Eliz., 77, no. 55.
Each of these banks was to have seven " treasurers and wardens," and five " governors " appointed by the Queen. The governors were to receive from the treasurers and wardens a statement of accounts four times a year, which was to be presented to the Queen. Funds were to be obtained by persons bequeathing their "best garments " to the bank. Such garments were to be sold by the churchwardens in the bank's area, and the proceeds paid into the bank. Loans were to be allowed at 6 per cent. for a maximum period of one year.
Full details of this scheme are given in the *Journal of the Institute of Bankers,* Vol. 46 (1925), pp. 58–60.
[2] S.P. Dom., Eliz., 110, no. 51. See Tawney and Power, *Tudor Economic Documents* (1924), Vol. III, pp. 370–77.
[3] B.M., Lansd. M.S., 30, no. 37, entitled " Une Orddnance comodieus aux temps de guerre et necessaire pour Sa Mat^e et au Royaulme d'Angleterre c'est pour avoir argent a Interrest a Raysonnable pris."
[4] S.P. Dom., Eliz., 150, no. 73. Printed in F. G. Hilton Price, *Handbook of London Bankers* (1876), pp. 142–44.
[5] B.M., Lansd. M.S., 108, fol. 90.
[6] S.P. Dom., James I, 130, nos. 29–32.

Robert Heath. The first of these latter projects is entitled " ffor the Banke," and is a scheme for an establishment " wher all payments of 20 li or above shall be entred in ye Bank ther "; the second is contained in a document entitled " Merchaundising & Trade," which proposes the erection of a bank for the " assignation of debts " so that " he who hath not readye money to pay his dette at his day, if he hath dettes owing to him by others, may drive his trade and keep his credite as well as if he had money "; the third gives eleven suggestions dealing with commercial and financial matters, the first of which advocates the foundation of a " bancke " in imitation of that of Venice, all payments " exceeding v li or x li . . . to bee made at the bancke entred there "; the fourth, entitled " A means layd downe for the inlarging of trade," also urges the adoption of Venetian banking methods in England.

Early in Charles I's reign, the " gatheringe and raisinge of a Bancke or Treasure permanent " was proposed,[1] " which might ever be ready on all occurrences of occasions for ye supply of our soveraigns in their warrs," and enable " ye merchants to traffique, ye gentlemen, yeomen and husband-men to stock, store, and tyll their grounds, and ye artificers to worke and trade." Loans were to be advanced at 5 per cent., and the capital was to be obtained in four ways : (1) by declaring a weekly " official " one-meal day so that householders, " except ye poor and such as live onely by their labour or reliefe of ye towne," might be able to sub-scribe a halfpenny weekly on behalf of each member of the household to the bank, the subscriptions to be collected in every parish by the churchwardens and constables, and by these paid to specially appointed royal treasurers; (2) by compelling persons, whose " goods shall be of a clear value of an hundred pounds or assessed in lands in ye subsidie four pounds," to pay to the bank 10s. for a " mortuary " on " departing this life "; (3) by taxing " all such as be prac-tised in courts of law, clerks, officers in court, or attorneys at ye law," because as they " are seldom or never employed in military service," and " live safe and secure," daily

[1] S.P. Dom., Charles I, 89, no. 17.

attending to their " benefits and profits," each can easily afford " to give somewhat of his gettings every tearme " as a subscription to the bank, the annual scale suggested being " every philiser " 10s., " every cursitor " 20s., and " every attorney " 3s. 4d.; and that " for every sheete of paper in Chauncerie, Starr Chamber, Exchequer Chamber, Court of Wardes, and Court of Requests ye several clerks do alloue to ye. said Treasurers a halfpenny of what is taken for ye same "; (4) by a tax on the feasts of the London livery companies, and on the " sheriff's feasts in all cities."

Towards the end of Charles I's reign there appeared the elaborate plan of Benbrigge in 1646, and the brief proposal of Morrell [1] for " a bank in the cittie of London as is at Amsterdam," in 1647. Benbrigge's scheme, detailed in his *Usura Accommodata*, suggests the erection of two types of banks, the *Mont de Piété* or " Bank of Charity," for the use of those "whose only refuge is usury," and the *Mons Negotiationis*, or " Bank of Trade," for the needs of markets and traders.

Benbrigge defines the *Mont de Piété* as " a certain summe of money, or things estimable by money, which is laid up for the relief of the poore, either by one rich man, or by many, either by a Prince or Common-Wealth or some Company." [2] He deals in this treatise with : (1) the lawfulness of banks, (2) the " raising " of banks, (3) the government of banks, (4) the " benefits " of banks, and advocates the transference of the estates of rich men dying intestate to the *Monts de Piété*. [3] " The readiest way to suppresse unjust Usury," he states, " is to raise Bankes of Charity and Trade." [4]

The *Mont de Piété* was, as we have already seen, advocated in England many years before the publication of *Usura Accommodata*, by Huniman and Malynes, and by John Cooke and Sir Balthazar Gerbier, two of Benbrigge's immediate contemporaries. Cooke in his *Unum Necessarium* [5] urges the establishment of *Monts*, " to lend poore people small summes of money upon security without paying any

---

[1] *H.M.C.R., MSS. of the Duke of Portland*, Vol. II, (1893), pp. 405–6, Hugh Morrell to William Lenthall.
[2] *Usura Accommodata* (1646), p. 3.
[3] *Ibid.*, pp. 2–13.
[4] *Ibid.*, p. 36.
[5] Published in 1648.

interest." [1] He refers to the case of a small tradesman who is forced to borrow money from a money-lending broker. " The broker," Cooke states,[2] " will have 12d. a moneth for the 20s. and 6d. a yeare for the Bill, which comes to 18s. a yeare for 20s.," and he points out that " to prevent such like cruelties they have in many places banks of piety where the poor may bring a pledge or security and have 5 l or 10 l to begin a trade." [3] " Mounts," writes Gerbier, " will bring down the horrible usury practised by a contrary practice, for the brokers now take at least 40, 50, yea, in some cases 100 in 100." [4]

A lengthy residence in Holland had given Gerbier ample opportunity for studying continental banking methods. It is not surprising, therefore, to find him proposing in his *Some Considerations of the Two Grand Staple Commodities of England*, published in 1651, the erection of a " bank of payment " in London after the style of either the bank of Amsterdam or that of Venice.[5]

But the latter of Gerbier's projects was not the first of the Cromwellian banking schemes, for it was preceded in 1650 by those of Potter and of Robinson. The essence of Potter's plan, contained in two pamphlets, entitled *The Key of Wealth*,[6]

---

[1] P. 49.   [2] P. 49.

[3] Detailed information about *Monts de Piété* will be found in B.M., Lansd. MS., 351, fols. 18–40; Malynes, *Lex Mercatoria* (1622), Chap. 13; Cleriac, *Usance du Negoce* (1656), Chap. X; A. Henne, *Histoire du Regne de Charles-Quint en Belgique* (1858–65), Vol. V, pp. 220–23; P. H. Holzapfel, *Die Anfänge der Montes Pietatis*, p. 136.

Authority was actually given in 1662 for the establishment of a *Mont de Piété* in London, but advantage of this was not taken. S.P. Dom., Charles II, 68, no. 138.

The *Mont de Piété* must be distinguished from the so-called " Bank of Charity " authorised by a Treasury Warrant, dated 1st February 1687, which was a kind of superannuation fund for the support of old and disabled officials of the Excise Office. *Cal. T. B.*, Vol. VIII, p. 1173.

[4] S.P. Dom., Charles I, 478, no. 96.

[5] Ten years later Gerbier revived his banking schemes and presented them, among other propositions, for the consideration of the Privy Council. S.P. Dom., Charles II, 40, nos. 131–32.

Two years before the appearance of Gerbier's *Some Considerations*, Dr. Peter Chamberlen, father of the notorious " Dr." Hugh Chamberlen, published in 1649 *The Poore Mans Advocate*, in which he proposes the formation of a " joynt stock " out of which " twelve undertakings " were to be promoted, and one of these was " the erection of a publicke banck " (pp. 23–24).

[6] A plate of the title-page appears in Davis, *op. cit.*, and Seligman, *op. cit.*, gives the wording in full.

and *The Tradesman's Jewell*, both of which appeared in 1650, was that " Banks of Money " should be established in various towns, issue negotiable " bills " for deposits, and thus " quicken the revolution of money and credit." [1]   Robinson advocated the foundation of a bank in England with " agents," " banckers," or " public exchangers " in important continental towns such as Paris, Antwerp, Amsterdam and Rotterdam.   He published full details of the scheme in his *Certain Proposalls* [2] in 1652.   The " correspondent " or " agent of the Commonwealth " was to be provided with " a stock of money or credit " in order to " furnish all Passengers with the full value of their moneys in most principal places where they goe, as likewise all Merchants with whatsoever summes they desire."   "If all moneys," he adds,[3] " Delivered or Received by Exchange passe through this Publick Exchanger or Banckers hands, or be ordered to be paid in Bank, you may see who are Deliverers and who Takers, and to and from what parts moneys are remitted and received, and by whom."

This pamphlet shows that the study of the mechanism of exchange was well advanced in Cromwellian times.[4]   Robinson, however, had been in the field as an advocate of banks more than a decade before his scheme was elaborated in the *Certain Proposalls*.   In 1641 he had urged [5] " the erecting of a Bancke or Grand Cash on such foundation and security as all men may thinke their monies more sure there than in their houses, whereby they may bee induc'd to bring them in, and receive a certaine moderate interest of about 5 per 100 to keep them there till they shall have occasion to dispose of them, or pay them to another "; all payments to be made

---

[1] *The Key of Wealth*, pp. 71–72.
  In 1651, Potter published another pamphlet, entitled *Humble Proposals*, dealing with his banking schemes.
  [2] Pp. 14–19 and 22–23.   This pamphlet is reprinted in W. A. Shaw, *Select Tracts and Documents illustrative of English Monetary History, 1626–1730* (1896).   [3] P 17.
  [4] " But above all other Engines," writes Robinson in *Certain Proposalls* (p. 18), " the greatest pre-eminence is due unto a Banck. . . . In Briefe it is the Elixer or Philosophers Stone, to which all Nations, and every thing within these Nations must be subservient, either by faire means or by foule."
  [5] In *Englands Safety in Trades Encrease*.   Reprinted in Shaw, *op. cit.*
  H

by assignation. " Suppose," he continued, " I be the cash-keeper to ten wealthy men, that amongst them all for the most part have 10,000 li still lying dead, expecting a good opportunity and advantage to purchase Land, or otherwise : I that am Cashkeeper knowing there can be no occasion of these ten thousand pounds till such a time ; or if there should be sooner, know where to have as much to put i'th place of it, and withal having the owners consent, doe put these ten thousand pounds out at interest, or imploy it in one com-modity or other for my owne account and benefit, to the encrease of Trade, which is equally done as well with credit as ready money." [1]

Robinson's *Certain Proposalls* was followed by Samuel Hartlib's *Essay upon Master W. Potters Design,"* [2] in which is given what appears to be the first suggestion appertaining to the establishment of a land bank, a project which did not mature until the closing years of the seventeenth century. Hartlib states " that there be no way to raise credit in bank but by morgage of Land."

Perhaps, however, the most striking of the Cromwellian banking schemes is contained in the methodical pamphlet of a London merchant named Samuel Lambe, entitled *Seasonable Observations*,[3] which was presented for the Pro-tector's consideration. Lambe divides his essay into nine parts, five of which deal with banks and the remainder with English and Dutch trade and shipping. He proposes the establishment of a bank in London under the control of " good men or Governours " elected annually by the Merchant

---

[1] *Englands Safety*, pp. 34–35. In this treatise (pp. 43–44) Robinson also suggests the establishment of a " Bank or Mount of Charity " " to lend poore people upon pawnes."
  Another of Robinson's banking schemes, in which he advocates the establishment of a bank in England with " agents " in the chief conti-nental towns, is contained in his " Observations about Exchanges," S.P. Dom., Interregnum, 9, no. 64; and yet another appears among the Halifax Papers, Advocates' Library, Edinburgh, MSS., 31.1.17. In the latter he proposes that the King should appoint " receivers " in fifty or more towns to receive the King's " rents and dues," and that these officials should lend, at reasonable rates, the money that " lies dead " in their offices.
  For further reference to Robinson see *Cal. S.P. Dom., 1650*, pp. 182–83; *ibid., 1653–54*, p. 366; and *ibid.*, 1665–66, p. 344.
[2] Published in 1653.
[3] Published in 1657. Also in Somers' *Tracts*, Vol. II.

Adventurers, and the East India, Turkey, " East Country," Greenland, Muscovy and " Guynne " Companies; that such a bank should accept deposits, issue " imaginary money " or " credit upon ticket " at $2\frac{1}{2}$ or 3 per cent., and " furnish another Banke with a competent stock to let out any summe of money under five or ten l at reasonable rates upon pawns or other security."; and " that all bills of exchange be received and paid in Banke." " A Banke," he states, " is a certain number of sufficient Men of Estates and Credit joined together in a Joint Stock, being, as it were, the General Cashkeepers or Treasurers of that Place where they are settled, letting out imaginary Money at Interest 2 and $\frac{1}{2}$ or 3 l per cent. to Tradesmen or others that agree with them for the same, and making Payment thereof by Assignation, and passing each Man's account from one to another with much Facility and Ease, and saving much Trouble in receiving and paying of Money besides many suits in Law and other Losses and Inconveniences which do much hinder Trade." [1]

Lambe was followed three years afterwards by Francis Cradocke, the first of the post-Restoration advocates of English banks, who published in 1660 his *Expedient*, in which he discusses the " nature " of banks and the method of " erecting " them. In the following year he continued his argument in *Wealth Discovered*, a pamphlet which urges the establishment of banks upon securities other than money, such as jewels, " rich pictures or hangings," silks, iron, sugar, wines and tobacco, and also proposes the setting up of a land bank " wherein the security of Lands may pass and be held value or credit with any other species whatsoever."

Cradocke suggests the division of the kingdom into a hundred districts, and that in each district there should be erected " a standing and constant Bank or Registry " where all estates in " lands, houses or rents " should be registered, and where " land, goods or pawns " were to be the basis of

---

[1] Two years after the publication of Lambe's *Seasonable Observations*, Thomas Holmwood issued in 1659 his *Trade Revived*. He urges (p. 44) the raising of a " Publick Stock of Money " out of which merchants could be supplied with ready money at " easie rates " upon " the depository of their goods in custody for security thereof."

credit. He refers to the advantages of the continental banks; to the " shops " of Lombard Street, which he regards as " banks in effect "; and to the establishment of " petty banks," which he thinks would soon replace " the many Brokers, petty Goldsmiths and Scriveners who deal some in publique, others more private, in a kind of petty Usury (or . . . more properly . . . great Extortion)." He advocates a low rate of interest, a maximum of 3 per cent., and is particularly emphatic with reference to land as a basis of credit. " I shall now," he remarks after examining the " defects " of gold and silver as *media* of exchange, " offer to your consideration that such defects may be supplyed in this Kingdom by a Land Bank, or Bank wherein the security of Lands may pass and be held value or credit with any other species whatsoever . . . and when reduced into practice will be found to answer all those ends for which Money was first ordained." [1] Thus were the seeds of the disastrous land bank flotations of the last decade of the seventeenth century sown by Hartlib and by Cradocke many years before these extraordinary attempts to hoodwink the City of London were launched.

Five years after the publication of *Wealth Discovered*, " banks of loan upon pawns truly called mounts of piety " were again advocated, this time by Sir Edward Ford,[2] while in 1676 Robert Murray published a curious banking scheme

[1] Cradocke makes the following interesting suggestion (*Wealth Discovered*, p. 13), with reference to remittances and the settlement of accounts at great fairs : " That for the encouragement of Trade such as have Bank Credit in one place, and are desirous to have it in another (for their accommodation) may have it remitted, paying after the rate of 10s. for 100 l. to the Bank; and also that where there happens yearly to be a standing great Mart or Fair, (like that of Sturbridge or Way-hill) the Bank of that Division may be removed thither during the Fair time; which can easily be done, since nothing is required but the Books of Debitor and Creditor; so that whosoever shall have occasion to buy goods there need only to get his Bill of Credit allowed at the Bank, which may the next day pass for payment, and much trouble and danger of being robbed to such as live remote be prevented."
  Though his schemes were not accepted in England he was sent by Charles II to Barbados as " Provost-Marshal-General " with authority to establish a bank or banks in this island. Details of the Barbados scheme, which does not appear to have matured, are given in *Cal. S.P., Colonial Series, America and the West Indies, 1661–68*, nos. 183, 194, 266.
  [2] " Experimented Proposals how the King may have Money," *Harleian Miscellany*, Vol. IV, pp. 195–96 (dated 1666).

entitled *A Proposal for the Advancement of Trade*.[1]   In this pamphlet Murray urges the establishment of what he terms a " Bank and Lumbard united " where credit was to be " raised " by men depositing their " dead stock " in " magazines " at "Devonshire-house without Bishopsgate," London, the depositor to receive credit on the security of the goods deposited up to " two-thirds or three-fourths of their value according to the quality thereof."   " To the rendring this Credit Current," Murray declares, " no more is required than what is already practised in Banks here and abroad, where men deposite Money and obtain the Bank-Credit, which generally passeth in Receipts and Payments without the reall issuing of Money, the Money remaining as a Pawn or Ground of Security in the Cash-Chest, or else is imployed by the Banker to his own Benefit."

But the most elaborate of Murray's banking designs, *A Proposal for a National Bank*, appeared two years after the foundation of the Bank of England.   Much prominence is given in this pamphlet to Dutch banking methods, and the development of the Bank of Amsterdam, " incomparably the best and greatest in the World," is traced in some detail. He advocates the establishment of a bank which was " to consist of all things capable of being a Fund of Credit and convertible at any time as Land and Ground-Rents." " The Bank in this proposal," he states, " is to be under the Authority, Care, Inspection and Control of the known Legal and Publick Magistracy as most consonant to Reason, Nature and Publick Oeconomy "; and he suggests an initial " stock " of £1,000,000, part of which was to be deposited in the Chamber or City Treasury of London, and the remainder in other cities.[2]

[1] Murray's *Proposal* was preceded in 1674 by Thomas Newcome's " Humble Proposal whereby his Majesty may raise and extend his credit to the Annual Value of his Revenue without interest," *Cal. S.P. Dom.*, *1673-75*, p. 186, in which it is proposed that banks be erected in various parts of the kingdom where all receipts and payments by the Crown may be made, that persons having " running cash in bank " could assign over their credits, and that " bills of credit " as low as £5 be issued on the security of tallies struck at the Exchequer.   These " bills " were to be used to pay the King's debts, and were to be known as " check or bank money."

[2] Two more of Murray's schemes, entitled, " The Manner and Method of an Exchange Credit " and " A Proposal for payment of their present Ma[ties] Exchequer," appear among the Halifax Papers.   In both of these it is suggested that tallies should form a " fund " for the extension of credit.

Murray's *Proposal for the Advancement of Trade* was followed in 1678, the year after Charles II commenced the regular payment of interest on the goldsmith bankers' debt, by an important treatise by Dr. Mark Lewis entitled *Proposals to the King and Parliament, or a Large Model of a Bank*, in which it is suggested that the country should be divided into three or four hundred " precincts," each precinct to have a bank of deposit issuing transferable " bills of credit " to its depositors, and that no payment of £100 or above should be legal unless made through one of these banks. Lewis praises the Bank of Venice, the " perfect credit bank," and describes its origin; and he classifies the " benefits " of banks into : (1) those to the nation in general, (2) those to the Crown, and (3) those to the people, who are grouped into the poor, the middle " sort," the rich, the mariners, and the merchants.[1] " All men," he writes in this curious work,[2] " are satisfied a *Bank* is very advantageous to a Nation, especially to a Trading people, Situate as we are; but the great Question hath been how to make a Fund that shall be credited by all without vast quantities of ready Cash or bullion to ly dead, which we have not to spare for such a purpose."

Fifteen years before Dr. Lewis became prominent—he published four pamphlets dealing with his schemes—[3] as an

---

It may here be noted that the Halifax Papers comprise over seventy banking and revenue schemes, all of which were examined by Montague before the scheme which developed into the Bank of England was accepted. There are many " bills of credit " schemes in this collection, and in one of these, entitled " An Essay to Extend Credit " (undated), it is suggested that the King should annually extend his credit by " authorising and issuing out bills of credit " and making these " current for the public duties." In another curious scheme, entitled " A Speedy Way to Supply their Majesty's Occasions " (dated 1691), it is proposed that Parliamentary grants to the King should be issued in " bills of seal," which should function as " current money " until the sums granted were paid by the Exchequer.

I am much indebted to Mr. James Bell Richards for his assistance in the transcription of these schemes.

[1] *Proposals, etc.*, p. 27.   [2] *Ibid.*, p. 6.

[3] The other three are : *Proposals to the King and Parliament* (1677); *Proposals to increase Trade and to Advance His Majesty's Revenue* (1677); *A Short Model of a Bank* (1678).

The *Short Model* contains (p. 1) a synopsis of the scheme given in the *Large Model*. It reads thus :

" Divide the Nation into precincts.

Erect an Office in the most convenient places of each of these Precincts.

advocate of banks, that famous cameralistic writer, Sir William Petty, had emphasised the advantages of banking institutions in his *Treatise of Taxes and Contributions*.[1] " If public Loan Banks," he declares, in this interesting and important work,[2] " Lombards, or Banks of Credit upon deposited Plate, Jewels, Cloth, Wooll, Silke, Leather, Linnen, Mettals, and other durable Commodities were erected, I cannot apprehend how there could be above one tenth part of the Law-suits and Writings as now there are." Four years after the publication of Lewis's *Large Model of a Bank*, Petty, in his *Quantulumcumque concerning Money*,[3] strongly urged the establishment of a bank in England. " We must erect a Bank," he states, " which well computed doth almost double the Effect of our coined Money : and we have in England Materials for a Bank which shall furnish Stock enough to drive the Trade of the whole Commercial World." [4] He returned to the subject of banks in his *Political Arithmetic*,[5] published in 1690, where he emphasises the three great " policies " or " helps to trade " of the Dutch, and describes their banking methods, which he regards as their " third policy."

Of the preceding commercial writers, Potter, Cradocke, Lewis and Murray were advocates of numerous banks scattered all over the country, and so, also, in the last decade of the seventeenth century, were those lucid and vigorous economists, Cary and Defoe, and such lesser known writers as Beeckman,[6] Brewster [7] and Whately.[8] In his *Essay*

Order these Offices to be Cashierers to all persons, to keep any Money for safety they shall desire to deposit with them, and let the Office give the Depositor a Bill of credit for his money to repay it to him upon demand.
Let these bills be made transferable."

[1] Published in 1662. [2] P. 6.

[3] First published in 1682, and appears to have been written because the question of a recoinage was under consideration at the time. A second edition appeared in 1695, the year before the great recoinage of William III's reign was commenced.

[4] This is the answer given to the twenty-sixth question in this pamphlet of thirty-two questions and answers. [5] P. 28.

[6] In *Proposals . . . to raise Five Hundred Thousand Pounds per Annum to the Government* (1696). For Beeckman's scheme see Chap. IX, p. 237, *infra*.

[7] In *Essays on Trade and Navigation* (1695). See quotation at commencement of this chapter.

[8] Thomas Whately suggested the establishment, under the jurisdiction

towards the Settlement of a National Credit, published in 1696, Cary proposes the establishment of a bank " on the credit of Parliament " with a " Grand Chamber " in London, and " lesser Chambers " in other towns. These banks were to issue to depositors assignable interest-bearing notes payable to order, and advance money " upon reasonable security, either Rent, Personal or Goods,' while the " notes given in any one Chamber of the Bank" were to be " demandable in any other together with the interest due till payment." The accounts of each branch were to be submitted every three months to the " Grand Chamber " in London, and there to be examined by special commissioners.[1]

Defoe in his *Essay on Projects,* which appeared in 1697, refers to two banks then functioning in London; the Bank of England, the " Royal Bank " as he terms it, and " another with a large fund upon the Orphans' Stock," the Orphans' Bank of the City of London.[2] He both criticises and praises the " Royal Bank ";[3] suggests the subdivision of its business into six departments, the sixth to deal entirely with inland bills of exchange, " where a large Field of Business lies before them ";[4] and proposes the establishment of fifteen new banks in various important towns such as Bristol, Exeter, Shrewsbury, Manchester, Norwich, Newcastle and Canter-

---

of the Mayor and Aldermen, of a " Loan Office " or " Market Bank " in every market town. Details of this scheme are given in T. W., *Now is the Time* (1694); T. Whately, *The Loan Office* (1696); and T. Whately, " The Market Bank " in the Halifax Papers.

Another advocate of country banks was the anonymous writer of *Proposals for National Banks* (1695 ?), who suggests " one General truly National Bank" in London, and " that banks be erected in every Ward therein " and " in every other City and Market town in England and Wales."

[1] Pp. 3-5.

See also *An Essay on the State of England in Relation to its Trade, its Poor and its Taxes* (1695); *An Essay on the Coyn and Credit of England* (1696); and *Discourse on Trade* (2nd ed., 1745) by the same writer. In the last-named treatise, a revised and enlarged edition of the *Essay towards the Settlement of a National Credit,* Cary urges (pp. 29-30) the Bank of England to " appoint chambers " in the provinces.   [2] P. 40.

[3] *E.g.,* pp. 40 and 44. " I believe," he states (p. 44), " that the Bank of England has been very useful to the Exchequer, and to supply the King with Remittances for the Payment of the Army in Flanders; which has also, by the way, been very profitable to it self."

[4] Pp. 46-54. The other five departments were to be engaged in: " exchanges and foreign correspondence "; discounting of bills, tallies and notes; loans to traders; loans upon pledges; loans upon land securities.

bury, " some of which, tho' they are not the Capital Towns of the Counties, yet are more the Center of Trade, which in England runs in Veins, like Mines of Metal in the Earth." [1] " A bank," he explains, " is only a great stock of money put together for the benefit of the whole." [2]

But the schemes just discussed did not mature. Apart from the fact that they were sometimes too complicated, public opinion was not quite ripe enough to test them. There was, also, prior to the Revolution, the fear of Royal confiscation, a fear intensified by the Tower incident and the " Stop " of the Exchequer, while the prevalent passion for speculation was not conducive to the serious study of projects which did not fructify quickly. These schemes, however, show how the idea of a land bank originated, the idea that credit could be extended by mortgages on real estate; and they prove that Englishmen in pre-Bank of England days were well acquainted with the real essence of seventeenth-century continental banking practice. This was : the depositing of metallic money, usually debased or deteriorated in content, for safe custody in a bank; the granting of credit up to the face value of the coins deposited; and the adjusting of debts among the bank's customers by transfers of account. [3] " That admirable invention of a Bank," wrote Hartlib in 1653, [4] " is no other thing than the transmitting

---

[1] P 61.   [2] P. 64.

The famous author of *Robinson Crusoe* was also an advocate of land banks. " I had," he remarks in the *Essay on Projects* (pp. 66–67), " gone on with some sheets with my Notion of Land, being the best bottom for Publick Banks . . . but I find my self happily prevented by a Gentleman who has published the very same . . . Mr. John Asgill of Lincolns-Inn, in a small tract, entitled *Several Assertions proved in order to create another Species of Money than Gold or Silver.*"

For Asgill's scheme see pp. 117–120, *infra.*

[3] " The wise Senatours . . .," writes that keen observer Captain Lewes Roberts in describing the methods of the Bank of Venice in his *Merchants Mappe of Commerce* (1st ed., 1638), " set a distinction betweene the Monies payable for commodities, which they term their currant Monies and out of *banco*, and between their Monies paid by Bills of Exchange, which they term in *banco*, and by Bills of Exchange is accounted better by 21 per cent. than the payments made for commodities bought and sold between Merchant and Merchant."

See also C. F. Dunbar, " The Bank of Venice," *Quarterly Journal of Economics*, Vol. VI (1892), pp. 308–35, and *Economic Essays*, pp. 143–67; and Adam Smith's description of the Bank of Amsterdam, in *Wealth of Nations*, Bk. IV, Chap. III.

[4] *An Essay upon Master W. Potters Designe*, pp. 28–29.

of the Ownership of money . . . from hand to hand by assignation onely; without the danger and trouble of keeping, carrying or telling it." Hartlib, however, mentions three " inconveniences " of this method : (1) that hitherto it had been applied to the " despatch of business of payments " among merchants only; (2) that it was not a " new Medium of Commerce," but simply a better method of making payments than by means of gold and silver; and, (3) " that money deposited . . . in any one place proves not onely a temptation to the sword . . . but if once surprised becomes a certain loss to all the owners." The first two of these " inconveniences " were remedied when the goldsmith developed into a recognised keeper of deposits, for people who were not merchants became depositors in increasing numbers, and new *media* appeared in the form of goldsmiths' promissory notes and demand notes, or cheques, drawn on these bankers. The third " inconvenience " did not disappear until absolutism ceased to be an attribute of the English monarchy.

Thus was public opinion made to focus on the necessity of proper banking institutions, on various kinds of securities, on the great problems of organising and extending credit. It is therefore not surprising to find that, apart from the scheme which developed into the Bank of England, a number of English banking schemes did actually mature during the seventeenth century.[1] Such were the Orphans' Fund or Bank, referred to by Defoe; the ill-fated Bank of the City of London; the short-lived Million Bank; and the notorious land banks.

It is curious that the extraordinary story of the Orphans' Fund of the City of London has received singularly little attention from historians. By the last decade of the seventeenth century the mismanagement of this remarkable Fund had reduced the civic authorities of London to such a state of bankruptcy that Parliament was forced to intervene.

---

[1] What were termed " banks " were also created under certain lottery schemes.. In 1687, for example, James II granted Randolph Ashenhurst and his partners the sole use of the Royal Oak Lottery, and gave them power "to erect and have such bank-houses as shall be necessary." *Cal. T. B.*, Vol. VIII, p. 1422. See also *ibid.*, Vol. VIII, p. 2030.

Therefore, in 1694, an important legislative measure known as the Orphans' Act was passed, which completely reorganised the Orphans' Fund, a reorganisation which resulted in a large number of architectural developments in the rapidly expanding metropolitan area.[1]

Before the passing of the Orphans' Act it had been the custom to invest the Lord Mayor, Aldermen and Common Council of the City of London with the guardianship of the property of the orphan children of the City's freemen. The civic authorities could compel the executors of deceased freemen to submit to the Orphans' Court true inventories of bequeathed estates, and to invest the money of the orphans in the Chamber,[2] or City Treasury, the department presided over by the City Chamberlain.

Large sums of money were thus compulsorily paid into London's Chamber in Stuart times. In addition, it appears that voluntary deposits were accepted, usually at 4 or 5 per cent.[3] Benbrigge, writing in 1646, refers to the City Treasury as a place " whereinto men may put their moneys, for the Assurance whereof, and the payment of its Use (which is Five in the Hundred per annum), they have the security of the Chamber, which is accounted the best this day in England." [4]

According, however, to the Report of a special committee,[5] appointed in 1650 to examine the financial affairs of the Chamber of London, the City's debt in 1649 amounted

---

[1] There is preserved in the Records Department of the City of London a great deal of material relating to the Orphans' Fund, including some 350 ledgers and account books relating to Orphans' Stock, ten large books, dated 1694 to 1817, entitled Orphans' Ledgers, six Common Sergeant's books, dated 1598–1741, together with a large number of miscellaneous documents.

I am much indebted to Mr. A. H. Thomas, M.A., Clerk of the Records of the City of London, for his assistance during my visits to the City Records Department.

[2] A large number of details with reference to the estates of deceased freemen of the City are contained in the Common Sergeant's books.

Copies of the demands from the City magistrates to the executors of such estates are given in the Orphanage Book. There are many instances of demands for payments of money to the Chamber for the " use and behoof " of orphans.

[3] *Parl.* P. (1829), III (309), *Report from the Select Committee on the Orphans' Fund*, p. 20.

[4] Benbrigge, *Usura Accommodata*, p. 5.

[5] *London's Liberties* (1651).

to £246,066 14s. 9½d., of which £169,645 1s. 5½d. was orphans'
money, the remainder being described as " principal money "
belonging to other persons.   This Report also states that
out of a total expenditure of £455,148 11s. 2d. between 1630
and 1649, £180,000 [1] appertained to the banking operations
of the Chamber, i.e. loans, and the payment of interest on
deposits.   During the next four decades the City's debt
increased enormously; in 1676 that part of it due to the
orphans amounted to over £428,000,[2] an item which by 1694
had expanded into the huge total of £747,472 18s. 4½d.

In the meantime, the City Chamberlain, particularly
between the Restoration and the Revolution, was conspicu-
ously active as an agent for the collection of State loans
from the City Livery Companies and other lenders;[3] as a
distributor of the interest accruing on these advances to the
Exchequer; and as a receiver of various taxes, assessments,
aids and subsidies, out of which he was frequently authorised
to make direct payments on behalf of the Exchequer.[4]   He
was therefore a Government banker,[5] a characteristic which
is strikingly illustrated in the transactions of Sir Thomas
Player, the most prominent of the seventeenth-century City
Chamberlains, who presided over the civic finances of London
during an exceptionally critical period, which included the
second and third Dutch wars, the Plague, the Fire, and the
" Stop " of the Exchequer.

The various Treasury Books of the reign of Charles II
contain numerous details of Player's transactions, which are
remarkable evidence of the part played by London's Chamber
as a Government Treasury.   " All wee have to recommend
to you," states a letter from Lord Treasurer Southampton
and Lord Ashley to Player early in 1666, " is that as the
moneys shall be repaid unto the City or as you may have any

---

[1] Of this total, £120,000 represented " interest-money paid twenty years
at £6,000 per annum."
[2] A. F. W. Papillon, Memoirs of Thomas Papillon of London, Merchant,
1623–1702 (1887), p. 113.
[3] See R. R. Sharpe, London and the Kingdom (1894), Vol. II, pp. 543–44;
and Parl. P. (1852–53), XXII (916), Report from the Select Committee on
Coal Duties (Metropolis), p. 2.
[4] See, for example, Cal. T.B., Vol. I, p. 237; Vol. VI, pp. 157–58, 206,
402; Vol. VII, p. 1579.
[5] See Parl. P. (1852–53), XXII (916), p. 6.

other opportunity to make loans to His Majesty so you will continue your wonted diligence and good affection, and that you will receive those tallies which he hath lodged in your hands as your security." "You know," they continue, "how punctual His Majesty hath been with the City in point of repayment of principal [or] at least still to continue the due payment of interest. We may therefore reasonably expect a more considerable advance from the City than on other occasions he would press it to." [1]

The big extent of Player's loan operations is shown in a report, based on the City Chamberlain's petition, from the Lords of the Treasury to Charles II, dated 30th August 1668, which states that Player claimed that he had procured £350,000 for the King's use during a period of more than ordinary difficulty, and that for this purpose he was compelled to maintain out of his private purse several clerks and "other instruments" at a cost of £200 per annum. Upon examination the Treasury Lords found that Player had actually advanced up to the date of his petition over £340,000 on the security of various assessments and taxes, such as the "One Month's Assessment" and the Hearth-money.[2] Thus was the money of the orphans, of the freemen who had deposits in the Chamber of London, and of the various subscribers to the State loans raised by the City Chamberlain placed at the disposal of the Exchequer, and thus, also, was this official overwhelmed, in the same way as the goldsmith bankers were, with tallies and repayment orders which ultimately proved worthless.

Several schemes were suggested during the seventeenth century for strengthening the City's finances, and two of these, an insurance project [3] and a banking scheme, were actually floated but survived for a brief period only. Even so early as 1665 an "Office of Credit" had been proposed in London,[4] but it was not until 1682 that the Lord Mayor, Aldermen and Common Council referred the state of the

---

[1] *Cal. T. B.*, Vol. I, pp. 717–18.
[2] P.R.O., Recs. T., Miscellanea, T. 51/15, Vols. 74–75; and *Cal. T. B.*, Vol. II, p. 613.
[3] B.M., 816.m.10(69).
[4] *A Description of the Office of Credit* (1665), Chaps. I–III.

City Chamber for the consideration of a select committee with power to receive and examine propositions for increasing the revenue of the Chamber.   It was this committee that recommended for the approval of the civic authorities a number of proposals for the immediate establishment of a " Bank of Credit " in London, with " books of accompts, books of register, journals and other books " under the inspection of the Common Council.   These proposals were accepted by the Lord Mayor and Corporation, and the City's seal affixed to them on 29th August 1682.[1]   Thus was launched the so-called " General Bank of Credit," or " Bank of the City of London."

This bank appears to have been primarily a " lumbard," an institution where " goods and merchandise " could be deposited, and credit obtained on such deposits.[2]   Money subscriptions were also taken; subscription books were opened at various coffee-houses such as Garroway's, Jonathan's and the Amsterdam;[3] and it was definitely stated in the bank's constitution that the profits were to be chiefly devoted to the reduction of the big debt due to the City's orphans.[4]

But the experiment was a diastrous one.   The bank suddenly collapsed, leaving the City's finances in a still more parlous state.   Finally, after a number of petitions to Parliament, and the drafting of two Bills,[5] the Orphans' Act of 1694 [6] was passed.   This measure created a " perpetual fund " for discharging the interest upon the debt to the orphans; it authorised that the contributions to this fund were to be certain " rents " chargeable upon the estates and revenues of the City, certain profits and impositions within the City, and the duties upon coal and wine imported into the port of London; and it forbade the old type of

---

[1] Corporation Credit (1682), pp. 3–4.
[2] Ibid., p. 5; and Bank-Credit (1683), pp. 10–15.   [3] Ibid., p. 6.
[4] See The Many Advantages the Bank of the City of London will afford to the Public, and to all sorts of Traders (1684 ?); An Account of the Constitution and Security of the General Bank of Credit (1683); Several Objections sometimes made Against the Office of Credit fully answered (1683); England's Interest (1682).
[5] See C. J.,Vol. XI, pp. 14, 28; H.M.C.R., 13, App. V. Nos. 329, 434; Parl. P. (1812), III (268), Report from the Select Committee on the Orphans' Fund ; and J. Strype, Stow's Survey of the Cities of London and Westminster (1720 ed.), Vol. V. p. 324.   [6] 5 & 6 Wm. & M., c. 10.

compulsory contribution to the Chamber. Thus was the original Orphans' Fund replaced by the new " perpetual fund," which was also known as the Orphans' Fund, though its revenues were derived from sources other than the estates of deceased freemen, and its functions were quite different from those of the old Fund.

The new Orphans' Fund was of paramount importance in the development of Hanoverian London. By 1714 its yield was equal to the charge upon it for interest, and after this date it produced surpluses. In 1766 Parliament commenced to make use of the fund for public improvements. It thus became the Orphans' and Improvement Fund, and finally the London Bridge Approaches Fund, which supplied the money for many striking and necessary changes in London's streets, buildings and bridges.[1]

The immediate effects of the Orphans Act are noticeable in the early transactions of the Bank of England. On 16th January 1695, for example, the directors of the Bank decided to advance money at 5 per cent. for three months on the security of the Orphans' Fund.[2] In May of the same year, however, the Bank refused to take the notes of the trustees of the Orphans' Fund,[3] but in the following August, such a note for £12,400 was accepted from one of the Bank's customers, who was given in return a " running cash note " for this sum.[4] On 4th March 1696 the Bank authorised one of its directors, Mr. Abraham Houblon, to take Orphans' Fund notes " in his own name " for £10,000 or £12,000,[5] and on the next day a special sub-committee of the directors was authorised to issue Bank bills for Orphans' Fund notes up to a total of £10,000.[6]

---

[1] See *Parl.* P. (1812), III (268), *op. cit.*; *Parl.* P. (1822), IV (481), *Report from the Select Committee on the Orphans' Fund of the City of London*; and *Parl.* P. (1829), III, 309, *op. cit.*, for the later history of the Orphans' Fund. Before the debt of £747,472 18s. 2¼d. provided for by the Orphans Act of 1694 had been finally discharged in 1820, £3,079,432 17s. 2¼d. had been paid in interest.

[2] The Court Minute Books of the Bank of England, Lib. A. fols. 138–39.

[3] *Ibid.*, Lib. B. fols. 35–36.   [4] *Ibid.*, Lib. B. fol. 60.

[5] *Ibid.*, Lib. B. fol. 111.

[6] Court Minute Books of the Bank of England, Lib. B. fol. 113.

It is interesting to note that when the Bank of England's directors discovered that one member of the directorate, William Paterson, held £4,000 of Orphans' stock, they passed a strong resolution of protest in which it is stated that this was a " breach of Paterson's trust." *Ibid.*, Lib. A. fol. 164.

We know also from the newspapers of the day that in the closing years of the seventeenth century the Orphans' Fund issued " bills " or notes payable to bearer; [1] that " Orphans' Money " was given " in the Chamber of London every day from one o'clock to four in the afternoon " in exchange for Million Lottery tickets; [2] and that Orphans' Fund Stock, which on 22nd February 1695 stood at 63 and on 5th March 1697 at 37,[3] was regularly quoted.[4] L'Hermitage, the representative of the States-General in London, referring in one of his despatches dated $\frac{19}{20}$ January 1696 [5] to what he terms *la banque des orphelins*, gives the stock quotation as 65, and adds that after the Bank of England, *la banque royale*, it possessed " the greatest reputation " among the English banks of the day.

Not long after the Orphans' Fund had been placed on a sound basis by Act of Parliament, and within twelve months after the establishment of the Bank of England, the City of London witnessed the flotation of the Million Bank, or " Bank on the Tickets of the Million Adventure." This institution, noteworthy because of its connection with the early history of the English Funded Debt, was a curious result of the Million Act of 1693,[6] a supplementary Act of the following Parliamentary session but of the same year,[7] and a second Million Act of 1694.[8]

The third of the preceding Acts, a measure for the raising of £1,000,000 upon the security of the duties on salt, beer, ale " and other liquors," originated the " Million Adventure " or Lottery Loan of 1694, a scheme in which 100,000 lottery tickets were issued for sale at £10 each.[9] This " Adventure,"

---

[1] *E.g. The London Gazette*, No. 3,120, dated 3rd–7th October 1695. " Lost six notes of the Orphans' Fund Nos. 415–420 payable to Mr. John Fenner or bearer. . . ."
See also *ibid.*, No. 3,197, dated 29th June–2nd July 1696.
[2] John Houghton's weekly periodical entitled *A Collection for Improvement of Husbandry and Trade*, No. 161, dated 30th August 1695; and No. 162, dated 6th September 1695.
[3] *Ibid.*, Nos. 134 and 240.
[4] *E.g. ibid.*, in each issue from Nos. 134 to 240.
[5] Transcript in B.M., Addit. MS., 17677, QQ.   [6] 4 Wm. & M., c. 3.
[7] 5 Wm. & M., c. 5.   [8] 5 and 6 Wm. & M., c. 7.
[9] Of these 97,500 " blank " or " unbenefited " tickets entitled the holders to an annual interest of £1 for sixteen years. The remaining 2,500, the " fortunate " or " benefit " tickets, would in addition to the said interest entitle the holders to certain sums of money according to the luck

which produced the required £1,000,000, is the first of a remarkable series of English public loans raised by means of lotteries. The tickets, at their market price, were accepted as subscriptions by the proprietors of the Million Bank up to two-fifths of the amount promised by the subscriber.[1]

A loan of £1,000,000, in this case upon the security of beer, ale " and other liquors," was also the object of the first Million Act; but as the required amount was not obtained under this measure, the deficiency of £118,506 5s. 10d. was made up under the special supplementary Act of the following session. This loan, raised in two ways, the greater part by means of life annuities and the remainder by a " tontine," [2] is of pre-eminent importance in the history of English national finance. It was the first sum to be acknowledged as part of the English National Debt, the earlier debt to the goldsmith bankers remaining, as we have seen, unacknowledged by the Government of the day until 1701.

Speculations in the life annuities soon made the Million Bank conspicuous in the City. Not long after commencing operations it announced in the press that it had " amalgamated " with the " Fund for Annuities." The latter is described in three announcements, which appeared in the Post Boy during October 1695,[3] as " a fund for granting annuities " and advancing money at 3 per cent., towards which any person might subscribe either " money or land," those that subscribed money " to have in the first place 6 per cent. for their money and afterwards the profits to be divided between the land and the money." The third of these announcements states that £130,000 in " land and money " had been subscribed to this " fund " by 19th October 1695. Early in the following month it was advertised that the said " fund " was " joyned " to the Million

---

of the draw, the principal prize being £1,000. See the *London Gazette*, No. 2968, dated 19th–23rd April 1694, for a striking announcement relating to the Million Adventure.

[1] The *Post Boy*, No. 79, dated 7th–9th November 1695. The market quotations of the tickets are regularly given in the newspapers of the period.

[2] £773,393 14s. 2d. was raised under the life annuity scheme. *Parl.* P. (1898), LII (C.–9010), p. 3.

[3] No. 68, dated 12th–15th October; No. 69, 15th–17th October; No. 70, 17th–19th October.

I

Bank by the consent of the general meetings of the " sub-scribers to the fund " and of the " proprietors " of the bank.[1]

Strengthened by this amalgamation the Million Bank commenced to speculate in the life annuities, which, in the first instance, were granted to the subscribers to the Million Loan of 1693 at the rate of 14 per cent. upon a single life. Under subsequent legislation[2] these annuities were granted on one, two or three lives—the 14 per cent., 12 per cent. and 10 per cent. annuities—at the option of the purchaser, and the single life 14 per cents. were converted into " long " annuities of 96 years' duration from the year 1695, upon payment of £63, *i.e.* 4½ years' purchase. But if the original annuitants did not convert, any other persons upon payment of £70, *i.e.* 5 years' purchase, were allowed to invest in the " long " annuities. Under this scheme the Million Bank acquired a large number of reversions of the 14 per cents.,[3] and after a brief attempt at actual banking it confined its attentions, under the title of the Million Bank Society, for nearly a hundred years to dealings in these " long " annuities, and in other types such as South Sea and Consolidated.[4]

Thus the story of the Million Bank *qua* bank is quickly told. A copy of its curious prospectus is preserved in the British Museum.[5] It reads thus :

AN ABSTRACT OF THE PROPOSALS FOR THE BANK ON THE TICKETS OF THE MILLION ADVENTURE.

The Subscription-Book lies open at the Outropers-Office on the West Side of the Royal Exchange up two Pair of Stairs, from 11 of the Clock in the Forenoon till 6 in the Afternoon.

[1] Houghton, *A Collection for Improvement of Husbandry and Trade*, No. 171, dated 8th November 1695, advertisement headed : " 1st November 1695, Million Bank and Fund for Annuities."
The *Post Boy*, No. 76, dated 31st October–2nd November, also contains an advertisement headed : " Million Bank and Fund for Annuities " in which the " directors " give notice of " the said fund being joined to the said bank."
[2] 5 and 6 Wm. & M. c. 20 (1694) ; and 6 and 7 Wm. III, c. 5 (1695).
[3] *A List of the several Annuities to which the Million Bank are intituled* (1695) ; *The Scheme for the proposals for making a fund for granting Annuities for Lives* (1695 ?) ; W. Fairman, *The Stocks examined and compared* (1795) ; Parl. P. (1792–93), XXVIII (780, 3).
[4] For details of the history of the Million Bank Society see W. R. Scott, *Joint Stock Companies*, Vol. III, pp. 279–87.
[5] B.M., 816.m.10(8), (1695). Another copy appears in Houghton, *Collection*, etc., No. 144, dated 2nd May 1695.

Any Person may subscribe in Money or in Tickets.

Those that subscribe in Money may pay in Ticket if they please.

Seven unbenefited Tickets are taken at 50*l.* besides 10*s.* per ticket for prompt Paiment : Benefited Tickets are taken at half a Year's Purchase more than unbenefited.

300*l.* makes a Vote, and none to have more than one Vote.

500*l.* qualifies Persons of any Nation whatsoever to be of the Committee.

10*l.* per cent. to be paid at subscribing; 15*l.* per cent. more either at subscribing, or ten Days after the Election of the first Committee; 25 per cent. in full at Christmas next, unless any Paiments be deferred by a General Meeting.

A Discount of 3*l.* per cent. besides the 10*s.* per ticket will be allowed on what shall be subscribed and paid by the 30th March ; 2*l.* per cent. till the 13th of April; 1*l.* per cent. till the 27th April, and 10*s.* per cent. till the 10th of May next.

A Committee of 24 Managers is to be chosen by the General Meeting within five Days after closing the Books, and then the present Trustees to deliver the Tickets and Money to the said Committee, and to be discharged of their Trust.

The Committee and a General Meeting may inlarge the Fund as they think most advantageous to the Proprietors.

For the Encouragement of the Subscribers the Proposers are contented to take 10*s.* per cent. on what the Fund shall be.

If 100,000*l.* be not subscribed before five Days after the 10th of May next, the Subscription to be void, and the Money and Tickets to be returned.

Note, the Settlement will be so made, that no Person shall be further answerable than his Stock, and that one shall not be answerable for another.

A Dividend must be made at least once a Year, and yet the Capital may be kept entire to purchase a Fund of a much larger Continuance as the General Meeting shall think fit.

The *Post Boy* dated 12th–15th October 1695 advertised that the Million Bank, " which opened with a fund of £200,000," of which £100,000 was " paid," [1] had " declared a dividend of £4,000, being 2 per cent. on the capital, to be paid on 8th November," therefore all the " proprietors " were invited " to come to the said bank to receive the warrants for the same." A later advertisement in the *Post Boy*, dated 31st October–2nd November, which was inserted after the bank had amalgamated with the " Fund for Annuities," states that the subscriptions amounted to

---

[1] According to Houghton's periodical, No. 144, dated 2nd May 1695, the £100,000 had been subscribed by this date.

" near 200,000*l.* in money, almost 7,000*l.* per annum in land, and several thousand pounds for purchasing annuities." L'Hermitage, writing in January 1696, remarks in a despatch to the States-General that *la banque des billets de la lotterie* was " commencing to decline." [1]   On 23rd June, 1696, it was reported in a general meeting of the subscribers that the banking department was not a success,[2] and it apparently ceased to function on this date.   The institution, however, continued to be called the Million Bank for some years afterwards,[3] though its business was confined to lottery tickets and annuities.   Early in the eighteenth century the title Million Bank Society was adopted and was used until 1796, when the company's activities came to an end.

While the Million Bank was attempting to obtain subscriptions the promoters of the land banks were particularly active, and after much advertising, pamphleteering and discussion they managed, during 1695 and 1696, to launch in London four separate land bank schemes.   These were " The Land Bank," or " Lincoln's Inn Land Bank," or " Exeter Exchange Land Bank," founded by John Asgill and Dr. Nicholas Barbon; " The National Land Bank," founded by John Briscoe; " The Office of Land Credit," or " The Bank of Credit on Land Rents," founded by " Dr." Hugh Chamberlen; and " The National Land Bank " established by Parliament, a flotation which must be carefully distinguished from Briscoe's venture.

The originators of the first three of these banking projects were, apart from their faith in the possibilities of land as a basis of note issue, men of different outlook.   Barbon, for instance, was, as is evident from his refutation of the prevailing " balance of trade " theory,[4] more modern in his

---

[1] B.M., Addit. MS., 17677, QQ, despatch dated $\frac{13}{23}$ January.
[2] *Parl. P.* (1792–93), XXXVIII, 780(3).
[3] The *Flying Post*, No. 737, dated 27th–30th January 1700, states in an advertisement that the " Million Bank " had in its possession at this time a great number of reversions of 14 per cent. annuities.
[4] The writer of the article entitled " Balance of Trade (History of the Theory)," in *D. P. E.*, states that this was " the first thorough refutation " of the balance of trade theory.   In another article (" Nicholas Barbon, M.D.," *ibid.*) the same writer remarks that Barbon's *Discourse of Trade* contains " the ablest refutation " of this theory " previous to Hume and Adam Smith."   Sir William Ashley, " The Tory Origin of Free Trade," *Quarterly Journal of Economics*, Vol. XI (1897), pp. 335–71, regards these statements as " somewhat excessive praise."

views than the majority of his contemporaries. An able economist, his *Discourse of Trade*, published in 1690, is a notable contribution to the economic thought of the seventeenth century. In this interesting little book he discusses money, credit, " public Banks of Credit," interest, rent and trade.[1] " It is much to be wondered at," he declares,[2] " that since the City of London is the Largest, Richest and Chiefest City in the World of Trade; since there is so much Ease, Dispatch and Safety in a Publick Bank; and since such vast losses have happened for want of it; that the Merchants and Traders of London have not long before this time Addressed themselves to the Government for the Establishing of a Public Bank."

Barbon was a keen and enterprising City man,[3] and had been concerned in several important undertakings before he was attracted to the idea of a land bank. It is therefore not easy to understand why such an experienced man of affairs decided to become one of the promoters of the land bank, which commenced its short-lived activities in Lincoln's Inn Fields. Asgill,[4] on the other hand, does not appear to have been connected with any City enterprise previous to his association with Barbon as a land bank promoter. He was, however, obsessed with the idea of creating a new type of currency, an obsession which is reflected in the pages of his *Several Assertions proved in order to create another Species of Money than Gold or Silver*,[5] in which he ingeniously leads the reader to his main theme—the flotation of a land bank. " Securities on lands," he emphasises in this treatise,[6] " are capable of being made money."

---

[1] For Barbon's monetary views see A. E. Monroe, *Monetary Theory before Adam Smith* (1923), *passim*.

[2] *Discourse of Trade*, p. 29.

[3] Barbon studied medicine at Leyden, graduated M.D. at Utrecht in 1661, and became a Fellow of the College of Physicians in 1664.

For details of his career see *D. P. E.*; *D. N. B.*; and S. Bauer, " Nicholas Barbon," in *Jahrbücher für Nationalökonomie und Statistik*, Vol. XXI (1890), pp. 561–90.

[4] Asgill was a Worcestershire man who became a student in the Middle Temple, and was called to the Bar in 1692. Author and politician, he acquired much notoriety because of his eccentric writings, and his expulsion from the Irish House of Commons in 1703 and from the English Parliament in 1707. See *D. P. E.* and *D. N. B.*   [5] Published in 1696.

[6] P. 18. A criticism of Asgill's *Several Assertions*, etc., appears in *Mr. J. Asgill, his Plagiarism detected* (1696).

Asgill and Barbon's Land Bank was enrolled in Chancery in 1695, and the trustees declared that, on or before 30th August 1695, they would establish in or near the City of London " an office for auditing the values and registering and assigning the titles of Lands in order to raise a current credit thereon "; and that the office was to possess an " auditor," with a " surveyor " as his assistant, and a " registrer," with " examiners," " accountants " and " entering clerks " as his assistants. Those that " settled their lands " in the bank were termed the " holders of the Equitable Interests," and each " interest " was divided into : (1) " the Value of the Register," equivalent to three-fourths of the total value of the land subscribed, and (2) " the Equity of Redemption," equivalent to the remaining quarter. The auditor's duty was " to adjust the valuation of the land," which was officially termed the " value of the auditor," the " registrer " reducing this to " the value of the register "; and paper notes termed " bills of charge," of various face values up to £1,000, were to be issued to subscribers and also as loans at $3\frac{1}{2}$ per cent., up to this reduced valuation of the estates " settled " on the bank.[1]

The bank started operations just a year after the establishment of the Bank of England, and was in the first instance divided into two offices : the " Register Office " for entering the estates, situated " over the Stamp Office in Lincoln's Inn "; and the " Bank Office, for " paying and taking in money " and issuing the bank's bills," in the " upper part of Exeter Exchange."[2] " Dr. Barbon's and Mr. Briscoe's land banks go on very successfully," wrote Luttrell

---

[1] *The Monthly Account of the Land-Bank*, dated 7th January 1696; and Somers, *Tracts*, Vol. XI, pp. 16–34.

An Account of the Land Bank (1695 ?) preserved in the Burney Collection of early English newspapers, B.M., 113a, states that " the Bills of Credit charged on the Land and given out by the Governors for the taking in of Money shall be paid on demand with interest after the rate of 2l. per cent. per annum. For which purpose One Hundred Thousand Pounds is subscribing. That there may be a sufficient cash lye ready to answer such bills."

[2] *An Account of the Land Bank.*

In the pamphlets and newspapers of the period this land bank is variously referred to as ' The Exeter Exchange Land Bank," " The Land Bank at Exeter Exchange," " The Lincoln's Inn Land Bank," " Asgill and Barbon's Bank," " Asgill's Bank," " Barbon's Bank," " Dr. Barbon's Bank " and " The Land Bank."

on 15th August 1695,[1] "and so does the orphans bank, to which last the lord Godolphin has removed his effects out of the Bank of England, which has raised the orphans bank 10*l.* per cent." " The Lincoln's Inn Bank," states a contemporary pamphleteer,[2] "assumes the name Land Bank improperly, for Money is their Fund, the society Monied-Men, who appoint Trustees,[3] Directors, etc., wherein the Landed-Men have no vote, not so much as for a Doorkeeper."

The bank's notices appear fairly regularly in the columns of the *Post Boy*.[4] One of these, in No. 21, dated 25th–27th June 1695, states that £50,200 had been subscribed towards the proposed stock of £100,000; a second, in No. 33, dated 23rd–25th July 1695, that the £100,000 had been oversubscribed to the extent of £10,000; a third, in No. 38, dated 3rd–6th August 1695, that it had been decided to take in additional subscriptions up to £500,000; a fourth, in No. 44, dated 17th–20th August 1695, that a total of £350,000 had been subscribed; a fifth, in No. 70, dated 17th–19th October 1695, that on and after 24th October the bank would commence to lend money, and issue interest-bearing " bills," payable on demand, " charged on lands and the stock of moneys and funds of ensurance annexed to the said bank," the " bills " to be " given out for running cash to any persons bringing in the same "; and a sixth, in No. 72, dated 22nd–24th October 1695, that the bank was "proceeding" to make advances " on lands " and to "issue out" its "bills."[5]

---

[1] *A Brief Historical Relation of State Affairs* (1857), Vol. III, pp. 512–13.
[2] *Mr. J. Asgill his Plagiarism detected*, p. 42.
[3] A copy of *The Monthly Account of the Land Bank*, " published in August 1695," Burney Collection, B.M., 113*a*, gives the names of twenty-one " Trustees and Managers " who were appointed on 30th July 1695 " to continue to 21st November." These include Sir Leonard Robinson, the London City Chamberlain; Mordecai Abbot, a commissioner of the Bank of England; Edward Harley; Philip Foley; the Rt. Hon. Thomas, Lord Jermyn; Barbon, and Asgill. [4] Burney Collection.
[5] That the bank's " bills " were actually issued is proved by an announcement in *The Monthly Account of the Land Bank*, dated 5th November 1695, which requests the return of ten £20 " bills " to the bank for cancellation.

Asgill, *Several Assertions*, which is dated Lincoln's Inn, September 1696, states (p. 46) that the first issue of " bills " took place on 26th October 1695. He also states (p. 47) that " bills " to the value of £45,000 were issued, " all which have been paid and repaid as Money," and that though the Bank " had valued estates for issuing " a further total of £100,000, the directors " foreseeing the impossibility of maintaining a Credit in their Infancy during the Regulation of the Coin they stopt their hands and content themselves at present in paying their Bills already issued."

But the £500,000 was never obtained.   Before the end of
1695 the promoters announced that they had " already lent
out considerable sums of money at 3*l.* 10*s.* per cent. on real
securities," and that they would " receive all Moneys on
Bills or Notes for such persons as should lodge their cash "
in the bank.[1]   What happened afterwards is not clear.
Luttrell states, under 4th February 1696, that this bank and
Briscoe's were " both united " for the purpose of advancing
the loan of £2,564,000 needed for the establishment of the
National Land Bank authorised by Parliament in March
1696.   The newspapers of the day, however, show that
Asgill and Barbon's Bank did not wind up its affairs until
about four years after the Parliamentary attempt to establish a land bank.   Early in December 1696, according to the
Post Boy,[2] the " Land Bank in Exeter Exchange " desired
the return of all " bills on lands or notes issued by their
cashier."   In September 1697 the *Post Man*[3] announced
that the trustees intended " with all convenient speed to
make a dividend," and the subscribers were invited to Exeter
Exchange to discuss the proposed method.   A little later it
was advertised in both the *Post Boy*[4] and the *Post Man*[5]
that the " Land Bank late of Exeter Exchange " had
removed its office to " Mr. Springfield's apothecary, against
Salisbury Court in Fleet Street," and persons having claims
on the bank were asked " to come and receive their money "
at this address.   What appears to be the final reference
to this bank occurs in the *Flying Post*[6] dated 5th–7th
January 1700, in which it is stated that the trustees
hoped to divide " the remaining effects " of the bank, and
persons " with just demands " were requested to acquaint
Mr. Chambers at " The Mermaid " before 1st February
1700.

The banking project of Briscoe[7] possessed similar features
to that of Asgill and Barbon.   Details of the scheme will be

[1] The *Post Boy*, No. 81, dated 12th–14th November 1695.
[2] No. 250, dated 10th–12th December 1696.
[3] No. 366, dated 2nd–4th September 1696, B.M., Burney Collection.
[4] No. 378, dated 5th–7th October 1697.
[5] No. 391, dated 2nd–4th November 1697.
[6] No. 571, B.M., Burney Collection.
[7] For a brief account of Briscoe see *D. P. E.*

found in the two treatises,[1] and the numerous pamphlets,[2] which this promoter published. One of the treatises[3] contains twenty-nine proposals[4] appertaining to the establishment of a land bank in England, the first of which reads thus : " That it be enacted that any person who' hath an Estate in Fee, of Freehold, or Cop$_y$-hold Land, may settle such their Estate upon twenty Commissioners . . . in Trust for a Security to make good all Bills as shall be issued upon the Credit of such their Estates to be settled for such Purposes."

These twenty-nine proposals appear to have been Briscoe's original scheme under which " bills of Credit " " not exceeding the value of the twenty years' purchase " of the "settled" estates were to be issued to the subscribers and advanced to " their Majesties " at 3 per cent.[5] " That any Person or Persons," states the twenty-second proposal,[6] " (after their Estate or Estates shall be settled six Months) may have the Bills of Credit they please to their proper Use or Uses ... . paying the Commissioners and Directors for each 100*l*. value in Bills of Credit to be kept for their own proper Use or Uses 10*s*. per annum for the Charges which the said Commissioners and Directors must necessarily be at in issuing out, and renewing the Bills of Credit . . . and to all other their Charges whatsoever."

A little later, however, this proposal was changed, apparently after Briscoe had decided, as a result of being " earnestly importuned by divers persons," to accept money subscriptions " in lieu of land," up to a maximum of £1,000,000, every £1,500 to be regarded as equivalent to " £2,000 in land." [7] It was now announced that those who mortgaged their estates were to be allowed, upon payment

[1] *A Discourse on the Late Funds of the Million-Act, Lottery-Act and Bank of England* (1st ed., 1694) ; and *An Explanatory Dialogue of a late Treatise, intituled, A Discourse on the Late Funds, etc.* (1694).

[2] The B.M. General Catalogue contains a list of thirteen of Briscoe's pamphlets dealing with this project. Among these are : *An Account of the National Land Bank* (1695 ?); *An Answer to a late pamphlet intituled Reasons offer'd against the intended project commonly called the National Land Bank* (1696); *To the Lords Spiritual and Temporal and Commons in Parliament assembled* (1696).

[3] *A Discourse, etc.*   [4] *Ibid.*, pp. 23–30.

[5] *Ibid.*, p. 26.   [6] *Ibid.*, p. 28.

[7] *Proposals for raising Money for the National Land-Bank* (1695).

of £3 0s. 10d. per cent. interest, to obtain advances in " money or bills of credit " up to any amount not exceeding three-fourths of the value of the estates thus " settled," but " no man's estate " was " to stand or be engaged for any other or greater Sum than what he himself shall actually receive and be indebted for." [1]

Briscoe's National Land Bank was situated in Exchange Alley, and eight representatives were appointed to receive subscriptions in various parts of London.[2] Wide publicity was given to the project; several of the promoter's descriptive pamphlets published in London were reprinted in Edinburgh for distribution in the northern counties.[3] The subscription books were first opened on 11th June 1695,[4] and, according to a report issued by Briscoe, the " yearly value of the estates subscribed " in various counties on the first two days amounted to £29,466,[5] which another report states was increased to £60,270 10s. per annum by 3rd August.[6] Before the end of October the directors appear to have been appointed, for a notice in the *Post Boy*, dated 22nd–24th October, states that the bank's directors attended daily at " their office in Exchange Alley " for the purpose of receiving the first instalment of " money " subscriptions due on or before the 30th October. Another announcement in the *Post Boy* [7] shows that a " general assembly " of the subscribers was summoned for 23rd January 1696 in order to elect thirty-six directors for the ensuing year; and that the notes of the bank were being issued in return for " any money that hath a currency," and " for the value of any other money that is not passable whether Crowns, Half-Crowns, Shillings or Six-Pences."

[1] *The following Proposals for, and Accounts of, a National Land Bank have been printed at London . . .* (1695).
[2] *An Account of the Value of the Estates in the Several Counties subscribed towards the Fund for a National Land Bank.* This was a periodical issued by Briscoe. Three copies, dated 11th–13th June, 11th June–27th July, 11th June–3rd August 1695, still survive. B.M., 712.m.1(51); 8223.e.7(5); 712.m.1(43).
[3] *E.g., An Account of the National Land Bank ; Advice to the Freeholder* (1696).
[4] *An Account of the Value of the Estates, etc.*
[5] *Ibid.*   [6] *Ibid.*
[7] No. 104, dated 4th–7th January 1696. Reprinted in No. 109, dated 16th–18th January 1696.

The last of the preceding announcements shows that there were difficulties in obtaining cash subscriptions, for subscribers were informed that unless their second instalments were paid on or before 15th January 1696 " all the benefits . . . of their first payment " would be lost; while there is no evidence to show that the directors for 1696 were appointed. Two later announcements, however, appeared in the *Post Boy*, dated 15th–18th and 20th–22nd February 1696. Both are simply brief invitations to the subscribers to meet, first of all on 20th February, and again on the 25th, at ." their office in Exchange Alley." No further notices were inserted by Briscoe in the newspapers of the day, therefore in the absence of other evidence it would appear that the project collapsed early in 1696.[1]

In the meantine Chamberlen had commenced to take subscriptions for his Office of Land Credit, a scheme which was undoubtedly the most brazen attempt to hoodwink the public that the City of London had yet witnessed. Hugh Chamberlen,[2] senior, " M.D.,"[3] " F.R.S.,"[4] " Doctor in Physick,"[5] " Physician in Ordinary " and ".Doctor in

[1] For a criticism of Briscoe's project by a shrewd contemporary " person of honour " see *Angliæ Tutamen* (1695), pp. 9–10.

[2] For details of Chamberlen's career see H. D. MacLeod, *Dictionary of Political Economy* (1863); J. H. Aveling, *The Chamberlens and the Midwifery Forceps* (1882); *D. N. B.*, and *D. P. E.*

The writer of the article in *D. P. E.* makes no reference to the "Office of Land Credit," and associates Chamberlen with the National Land Bank established by Parliament in March 1696 for the raising of a loan of £2,564,000, a scheme which had no connection with Chamberlen's " office."

There appears to be some misunderstanding among economic historians with reference to the various land banks. See, for example, J. E. T. Rogers, *The First Nine Years of the Bank of England* (1887), pp. 50–88; E. von Philippovich, *History of Bank of England* (1911), pp. 281–84; and A. Andréadès, *History of the Bank of England* (1909), pp. 103–107.

[3] The letters M.D. appear after Chamberlen's name on the title-page of *The Constitution of the Office of Land Credit* (1696). There is, however, no record to show that he qualified for the degree of M.D. When fined £10 by the College of Physicians on 11th May 1668 for " *mala praxis* in a high degree " he is referred to as ' Mr. Hugh Chamberlen of the Parish of St. Clements Dane, Westminster, practicer in midwifery." Aveling, *op. cit.*, p. 139.

[4] " Fellow of the Royal Society" appears on the title-page of *Manuale Medicum* (1685). Aveling, *op. cit.*, p. 138, states that he was elected F.R.S. on 2nd November 1681.

[5] *Dr. Chamberlen's Petition and Proposals for a Land Bank to increase Trade* (1693). This pamphlet gives details of ' the humble petition of Hugh Chamberlen, Doctor in Physick, and others.'

Ordinary " to Charles II,[1] obstetrician or " man mid-wife," [2] and land bank promoter, had already been connected with at least one City banking scheme [3] before he published " from his house in Essex Street near Temple Bar " the first of his own projects in 1690. This is entitled *Dr. Hugh Chamberlen's Proposal to make England rich and happy*,[4] and is described as " a scheme ready to be offered at a Million clear per annum . . . but for one hundred years as a secure Fund after the Nature of Banks, and enable the Undertaker to provide Tickets of Credit or Bills of Exchange thereupon not exceeding the Value of the said Fund, which Bills will in no respect be inferior to Money, and are to be controuled by Commissioners, appointed by and accomptable to Parliament from time to time." But though the proposer offered " to provide for ever much better for all the Poor," to repair " effectually " the King's highways, to " enrich " the nation " by means of trade," " to encourage soldiers and seamen with a donative of six months' pay," " to pay the London Orphans their full debts," and " to plainly demonstrate with rational arguments " the advantages of the scheme to a Parliamentary committee, he does not appear to have proceeded further with this particular " proposal."

Within the next three years, however, Chamberlen

[1] Appointed to these offices in 1673.
A Few Proposals humbly recommending . . . the establishment of a Land Bank in this Kingdom (1700) was written by " Hugh Chamberlen formerly Physician in Ordinary to King Charles II."

[2] *A Hue and Cry after a Man Mid-Wife who has lately deliver'd the Land Bank of their Money* (1699) ; G. Burnet, *History of My Own Times* (1724–34), Vol. I, p. 752; Luttrell, *op. cit.*, Vol. IV, p. 496.
" The Chamberlens," writes Aveling, *op. cit.* (p. 3), " have for many years been to the medical profession a source of interest and mystery. It has been known there were several generations of them, and that one of their number had invented the midwifery forceps, but to which generation each member of the family belonged, and to whom the honour of the invention was due, were problems no one took the trouble to solve. For ten years I have been collecting materials relating to the Chamberlens, but it was only quite recently that I have mastered the subject and dispelled from my mind the confusion caused by there being three Peters and two Hughs."

[3] *The Bank of Credit*, a pamphlet published in 1683, states (p. 4) that Chamberlen and Murray had been associated in a banking scheme, but " they found themselves necessitated to quit the Design by reason of the City's not encouraging their Proceedings as was expected."

[4] The British Museum does not possess this pamphlet, a copy of which is given in Aveling, *op. cit.*, pp. 154–56.

published, both in England and Scotland,[1] several new, revised and highly-coloured descriptions of his " design of a land bank." His English " design " of 1693, presented to, and considered by, Parliament on 7th December of that year,[2] he describes as a " Bank of Credit " for " raising a stock " for the formation of a fishing company, a " stock " which was to be obtained by " the freeholders of England " subscribing " their lands into the bank "; and he vaguely proposes " that for every 150l. per annum secured for 150 years for but 100 yearly payments of 100l. per annum free from all manner of taxes and deductions," every subscribing freeholder should receive £4,000 in " bills of credit," and £2,000 in " the fishery stock," while for each such investment £2,000 was to be placed at the Government's disposal for financing the war with France. These proposals [3] were referred by Parliament " for examination and consideration " to a large special committee, which, early in February 1694, reported that this scheme was practicable and would be beneficial to the country.[4]

In the next five years, during which the Office of Land Credit appears to have functioned for a brief period, Chamberlen was particularly active with his English and Scottish schemes, circularising members of the English Parliament, and publishing many explanatory pamphlets and advertisements. In its final form the scheme appears in *The Constitution of the Office of Land Credit*,[5] which thus states the essence of the various proposals : " A. settles £150 per annum on the trustees for a year and a half to secure the payment of £100 (above all reprises) at the end of one year. The trustees do therefore issue their bills of credit of £100 chargeable upon such land and payable at a year. . . . At the end of the year the bill is either brought to the trustees to be exchanged for money and so cancelled or

---

[1] The first of his Scottish schemes is contained in *Papers relating to a Bank of Credit upon Land Security proposed to the Parliament of Scotland by Dr. Hugh Chamberlen* (1693).
For details of Chamberlen's Scottish projects see *The Acts of the Parliament of Scotland*, Vol. IX, App., p. 91 ; Vol. XI, App., p. 64 ; Vol. X, p. 213.
[2] C. J., Vol. XI, p. 22.
[3] *Dr. Chamberlen's Petition and Proposals for a Land Bank to increase Trade.* [4] C. J., Vol. XI, pp. 22 and 80.
[5] It contains 65 clauses in 17 pages.

(which is the same thing) it comes to the hands of one that owes £100 to the trustees, who therefore accept it in lieu of their debt and cancel it." [1] A pamphlet published just before the *Constitution* describes the scheme as the issue of " 8,000*l.* in credit for every 100*l.* a year in land, the annual payments to continue for 100 years "; [2] while two other pamphlets [3] state that each land subscriber was allowed to deposit in the " office " £1,000 in " current coin," and that for every such deposit " bills of credit " for £7,000 would be issued.

The Office of Land Credit was located in No. 6 New Buildings, Lincoln's Inn, where subscriptions, which were also accepted at " Dr. Chamberlen's house in Essex Street " and " Mr. Puckle's at the Outropers Office in the Royal Exchange," [4] were taken on Mondays, Wednesdays and Fridays. The *Constitution* states [5] that it possessed three " branches " : (1) " the Settled Lords and Noble Visitors," chosen from " the nobility and great officers of State," who exercised a general supervision over the " office " by means of frequent personal visits; (2) " the Land Subscribers and Proprietors," *i.e.* those who mortgaged their estates to the bank; and (3) " the Undertakers and Managers." There were also three " chambers " : (1) " the Chamber of Comptrol," for the regulation of the bank's credit; (2) " the Chamber of Trade," for managing " the joint stock in trade," and (3) " the Chamber of Trustees," which was responsible for the " regular execution and economy " of the bank, and composed of " certain persons on whom the estates subscribed . . . are to be equally settled in trust for the due payment of the annuities for one hundred years." [6]

[1] *The Constitution, etc.*, p. 6.
[2] *A Bank Dialogue, or Doctor Chamberlen's Land-Bank explained by way of Question and Answer* (1695).
[3] *A brief narrative of the nature and advantages of the Land Bank as proposed by Dr. Hugh Chamberlen* (1695).
A proposal by Dr. Hugh Chamberlen in Essex Street for a Bank of Secure Current Credit to be found upon Land (1695).
An amusing description of the Office of Land Credit is given in *A Bank Dialogue between Dr. H. C. and a Country Gentleman* (1696).
[4] *A Bank Dialogue, or Dr. Chamberlen's Land-Bank explained by way of Question and Answer.*   [5] Pp. 8–10.
[6] The members of the first and third " branches," and of the first and second " chambers," were all appointed and their names published.

Thus was launched the most notorious and the most fantastic of the land banks. According to an advertisement which appeared in Houghton's periodical,[1] £50,000 " in land " had been subscribed by 29th November 1695. Later advertisements in this paper and in the *Old Postmaster* show that this total had not been increased by 20th December 1695, when subscriptions in specie and coin were invited up to a maximum of £50,000, and every depositor of £1,000 was offered an annuity of £350 for four years; [2] that by the end of February 1696 the total " in land " had increased to £70,000; [3] that it was not until 8th May that a general meeting of the subscribers was summoned for 9th June in order to consider " the speedy opening and setting on foot of the said undertaking; " [4] that after 12th June clipped money, guineas and plate could be disposed of " to much better advantage than elsewhere at the Office of Land Credit "; [5] and that " with great industry and pains and not without smart opposition " Chamberlen had " prevailed upon persons to subscribe to near 100,000*l.* per annum Land-Estates for to be a fund " for " a secure and useful Land-Credit." [6]

Despite, however, such numerous and regular advertisements—at least thirty-eight of which appeared in Houghton's paper—in the press of the day, Chamberlen's project soon came to an end. Its advertisements do not appear in any contemporary newspaper after July 1696, and not long afterwards this audacious, scurrilous and persistent promoter mysteriously disappeared from England, a disappearance which is thus described by a contemporary pasquinader : [7]

Among the members of the first " branch " were the Earls of Monmouth, Torrington, Romney and Arran; Lords Wentworth, Allington and de Courcy; and William Bridgeman, Secretary to the Admiralty. *The Constitution, etc.,* p. 1.

For the names of the " undertakers and managers " see *ibid.,* p. 1.

The members of the second and third " chambers " were elected at a general meeting held on 9th June 1696, and their names, together with the number of votes they obtained, published in the *Old Postmaster,* No. 1, dated 20th–23rd June 1696.

[1] *A Collection, etc.,* No. 174.
[2] *Ibid.,* No. 177.   [3] *Ibid.,* No. 185.
[4] *Ibid.,* No. 197.   [5] *Ibid.,* No. 202.
[6] The *Old Postmaster,* No. 1, dated 20th–23rd June 1696.
[7] *A Hue and Cry after a Man Mid-Wife.*

" By common Report unto Holland he's fled.
If so, the Land Bank is brought finely to bed,
For if to the old place of Refuge he's run,
Adzooks, you're all cozened as sure as a Gun,
And you that are chous'd for your money may mourn,
For Holland, like Hell, never makes a return."

While Chamberlen was busy advertising his Office of Land Credit, Parliament decided, on 6th March 1696, to establish a land bank for raising a loan of £2,564,000. On this date Sir Thomas Littleton submitted to Parliament, from a committee of the whole House, five resolutions appertaining to the flotation of this bank.[1] These were accepted, and an Act[2] was immediately passed which included a number of sections[3] authorising the establishment of a National Land Bank. The King was empowered under the Great Seal to appoint commissioners to receive voluntary subscriptions, " as shall be made in land," from subscribers " other than the Governor and Company of the Bank of England "; interest on the loan was fixed at 7 per cent.; the contributors were to be incorporated under the title of " the Governor and Company of the National Land Bank "; the loan, " or one moiety thereof," had to be subscribed before 1st August 1696, otherwise the " powers and authorities " for " erecting the corporation " were to cease. It was also enacted that the subscribers were to be incorporated " in order to enable them to lend monies on securities of lands at low interest," and at least £500,000 per annum was to be loaned in this way at rates not exceeding 3½ per cent. if paid quarterly or 4 per cent. if paid half-yearly.

Subscription books were opened on 4th June 1696 at the Hall of the Company of Grocers, and at Exeter Exchange;[4] but only a very small amount was subscribed,[5] and the project collapsed. Luttrell, Kennet and Burnet all refer to

---

[1] C. J., Vol. XI, pp. 494–95.
[2] 7 & 8 Wm. c. 31.
[3] Nos. 11–26, and 30–38.
[4] The London Gazette, No. 3,188, dated 28th May–1st June 1696, and the two next issues, Nos. 3,189 and 3,190.
[5] £1,775 according to B.M., Harl. MS., 1282, which also states that £560,000 was transferred to the " Land Bank " from the " Coles, Glass, etc. loan " of £564,700.

this unfortunate Parliamentary banking scheme. " The land bank makes but little progress," wrote the first-named on 11th June.[1] " The unhappy project of the Land Bank," remarks Kennet,[2] not quite accurately, however, with reference to the subscriptions, " proved wholly abortive and did not produce one penny of above two millions and a half with which it was charged." " There was a set of under-takers," declares the famous bishop of Salisbury,[3] " who engaged that it should prove effectual for the money for which it was given : this was chiefly managed by Foley, Harley and the tories; it was much laboured by the earl of Sunderland, and the King was prevailed to consent to it, or rather to desire it, though he was told by many of what ill consequence it would prove to his affairs." " I believe," wrote Montague, just after the scheme collapsed, to Blath-wayt, the Secretary at War,[4] there never was any transaction in any place or in any age wherein there was more artifice and less sincerity shewed than has appear'd in this affair of the Land Bank."

In a number of earlier letters Montague had regularly informed Blathwayt, who was at the time on active service in Flanders, of, the preparation for, and the disastrous flotation of this land bank. It is revealed in this corre-spondence that the promoters brought a first draft of their scheme to the Treasury on 30th April 1696; that this was signed by the King before the Act establishing the bank had been printed; that early in June the promoters proposed to the Government that they should be allowed to send clipped money to the Exchequer, and receive Exchequer bills in exchange, a proposal which was not entertained; that on 5th June not a single subscription had been received; that after the promoters " had put off one of their Houses in despair " they asked the Government to reduce the total (£2,564,000) to be subscribed, a request which was refused; and that the failure of the scheme was a great shock to English credit; in fact, Montague goes so far as to state that

[1] *Brief Historial Relation*, Vol. IV, p. 71.
[2] *A Complete History of England* (1706), Vol. III, p. 723.
[3] *History of My Own Times*, Vol. IV, p. 301.
[4] B.M., Addit. MS., 34355, letter dated $\frac{17}{27}$ June 1696.

K

the credit of the country was " entirely destroyed " by this
" fatal project." [1]

Several references to this ill-fated flotation are also
contained in the minutes of the Treasury for 1696.[2]   One of
these minutes, dated 29th May,[3] gives a lengthy account of a
discussion between the bank's commissioners—the chief of
whom appear to have been Sir Joseph Herne, Sir Thomas
Meere and Sir Thomas Cook—and the Lords of the Treasury
about the clipped money proposal.   Another minute, dated
3rd June,[4] states that the " Naconell Land Bank come in "
and " put their Memoriall " announcing that their subscriptions books were to be opened on 4th June.   A later
minute [5] shows that the bank's commissioners visited the
Treasury Chambers on 3rd July, reported that they had
received no subscriptions since 19th June, and appealed
for an allowance of £300,000, an appeal which was not
entertained.

Such were the land bank schemes of Asgill and Barbon,
of Briscoe, of Chamberlen, and of Sunderland, Harley, Foley,
Herne, Meere and Cook.   The displacement of the old
landed gentry by prosperous commercial men had reduced
the numbers of their potential supporters; the bitter
antagonism some of them manifested towards the Bank of
England greatly weakened their cause.[6]   Any attempt to
issue inconvertible " bills of Credit " based on variable land
securities in an age of financial instability when the negotiability of various other forms of paper credit already in use
had not yet been settled by Act of Parliament was fore-
doomed to failure.   Nor is it surprising to find the Parliamentary National Land Bank with its 7 per cent. interest
failing to compete with the Bank of England's 8 per cent.
Asgill has described some of the causes of the failure of this
bank : [7] the indifference of Englishmen to land bank schemes,

---

[1] B.M., Addit. M.S., various letters between May and July 1696.
[2] P.R.O., Recs. T., T. 29/8.   [3] *Ibid.*, fols. 311–14.
[4] *Ibid.*, fol. 315.   [5] *Ibid.*, fol. 327.
[6] This antagonism is illustrated in a merciless pamphlet entitled *The
Tryal and Condemnation of the Trustees of the Land Bank at Exeter Exchange
for murdering the Bank of England at Grocers Hall* (1696 ?).
[7] *Remarks on the Proceedings of the Commission for putting in Execution
the Act passed last Session for establishing a Land-Bank* (1696), pp. 15–24.

and their confidence in the Bank of England, which was generally referred to as *The* Bank; the competition of the goldsmith bankers, whose credit at this time was sound; the impossibility of raising such a big sum as £2,564,000 during a period of currency difficulties, difficulties which were increased by the great recoinage of 1696–99; and the partial suspension of cash payments by the Bank of England in May 1696. " It is," he laments,[1] " the most unreasonable thing in Nature to make the particle *The* such a Monster as to carry in its belly all the cash in the Kingdom and to be destructive to all future Corporations and Bodies Politic."

But the third of the financial schemes of William Paterson developed into a far bigger " monster " than Asgill ever dreamed of. The foundation of the Bank of England was, through the courage and integrity of its earliest directors, well and truly laid in 1694, and of all the great banking schemes of Stuart England it alone survived.

[1] *Remarks on the Proceedings of the Commission for putting in Execution the Act passed last Session for establishing a Land-Bank* (1696), p. 15.

CHAPTER V

THE FOUNDATION OF THE BANK OF ENGLAND [1]

" I believe it [the Bank of England] is a very good fund, a very useful one, and a very profitable one. It has been useful to the Government, and it is profitable to the proprietors; and the establishing it at such a juncture, when our enemies were making great boasts of our poverty and want, was a particular glory to our nation and the City in particular."

DANIEL DEFOE, *An Essay on Projects* (1697), p. 43.

AN influx of continental traders and financiers in the latter half of the seventeenth century undoubtedly gave a stimulus to large-scale financial transactions in the Lombard Street of later Stuart times. Pre-eminent among these immigrants were many wealthy Jewish merchants who settled in England during the Cromwellian régime, in the early part of Charles II's reign, and in the years immediately following the " glorious Revolution." [2] The influence of these merchants rapidly increased during the Commonwealth period, and in this interregnum the Jew, hitherto rigidly excluded,

[1] The account of the early history of the Bank of England in this and the next two chapters is, as already stated, based to a large extent upon hitherto unpublished material collected by permission of the Governor and Company of the Bank of England from the valuable records preserved in the Bank, particularly the earliest Court Minute Books.

I am very much indebted to the Secretary of the Bank of England, Mr. R. C. G. Dale, and to his predecessor, Mr. H. Tilden, for the expert assistance so freely given me during the many visits I made to the Bank, and for their kindness in revising the manuscript copy of this chapter and the two succeeding ones.

[2] See T. Violet, *Petition against the Jews* (1660); G. Leti, *Historia, e Memorie recondite sopra alla vita di Oliviero Cromvele* (1692), II, pp. 442–49; W. Godwin, *History of the Commonwealth of England*, IV, Chap. XVII; F. P. G. Guizot, *Histoire de la République d'Angletere* (1850–54), II, pp. 154–57; S. R. Gardiner, *History of the Commonwealth and Protectorate* (1894–1901), II, pp. 30–31; A. M. Hyamson, *A History of the Jews in England* (2nd ed. 1928), Chaps. XVII–XXI; J. Picciotto, *Sketches of Anglo-Jewish History* (1875), pp. 25–27, 43–44, 58–59; L. Wolf, *The First English Jew* (undated); L. Wolf, *The Re-Settlement of the Jews in England* (1888); L. Wolf, *Crypto-Jews under the Commonwealth* (1894); W. Sombart, *The Jews and Modern Capitalism* (1913), *passim*; J. Jacobs, " Banking," in the *Jewish Encyclopædia* (1925 ed.); A. H. Valentine, " Brokers, Jew," *ibid.*.

was officially admitted to the Royal Exchange,[1] an important concession which resulted in a sudden increase of Jewish brokers in London, particularly the unofficial ones. Before the end of the century a fifth of the "sworn" brokers in Lombard Street and its vicinity were either " Jews or foreigners,"[2] who possessed their own pitches or " walks " in the Royal Exchange.

There is evidence to show that Cromwell employed important members of the Hebrew race domiciled in England not only as army contractors and " political intelligencers," but also as money-lenders. Among those active in one or more of these capacities were Antonio Fernandez Carvajal,[3] who annually imported into England large sums of Spanish money and great quantities of bar silver; Rodriguez Marques, who at the time of his death had gold and silver to the value of 1,000,545 milreis on its way from Portugal to England;[4] Simon de Caceres, who submitted for the Protector's consideration a remarkable scheme appertaining to the conquest of Chile;[5] and Henrique Mendes da Costa, who was connected with the important Jewish banking firm of Mendes, which had agencies at Antwerp and Lisbon.[6] Members of the da Costa family assisted both Cromwell and Charles II financially,[7] while, later, Solomon de Medina,[8] the first professed Jew to be knighted in England and a commissariat contractor to Marlborough, advanced money both to William III and this famous general. Antonio (Isaac) Lopez Suasso, Baron d'Avernas

---

[1] Valentine, *op. cit.* See also Stow, *Survey*, Strype's ed. (1720), II, p. 243. [2] The *Post Boy*, No. 308, dated 24th–27th April 1697.

[3] See S. P. Dom., Interregnum, 102, no. 27; 124, no. 20; 129, no. 75; and L. Wolf, *The First English Jew*.

[4] L. Wolf, *Cromwell's Jewish Intelligencers* (1891), p. 14.

[5] L. Wolf, *The Re-Settlement of the Jews in England*, pp. 5 and 6.

[6] *Ibid.*, p. 5; Hyamson, *op. cit.*, p. 137.

[7] L. Wolf, *Crypto-Jews under the Commonwealth*, pp. 13–14; Picciotto, *op. cit.*, p. 44; *Thurloe Papers*, V, p. 572.

Sombart, *op. cit.*, p. 89, states that Moses (or Anthony) da Costa became a director of the Bank of England at the end of the seventeenth century. This is inaccurate. No such name appears among the lists of directors during the seventeenth and eighteenth centuries contained in the Book of Directors preserved in the Bank.

[8] See *D. N. B.*, under John Churchill, Duke of Marlborough; Jacobs, *op. cit.*; Hyamson, *op. cit.*, p. 269; Picciotto, *op. cit.*, p. 58; G. Lipkind, " Medina, Sir Solomon de," in the *Jewish Encyclopædia*; and Chap. VII, p. 179, *infra*.

le Gras, of The Hague, a powerful supporter of the House of Orange who migrated to England, is said to have loaned 2,000,000 guilders free of interest to William III for his English invasion.[1] It has been remarked that " Ramillies, Oudenarde and Blenheim contributed as much to the wealth of the Hebrew as to the glory of England." [2]

But the financial transactions of these Jewish merchant princes in England were eclipsed by those of the goldsmith bankers of the type of the Meynells, the Vyners, Backwell, Duncombe and Evans,[3] and though we are told that the Jews thronged Exchange Alley,[4] there is a great deal of contemporary evidence which shows that the Englishman at this time was also predominant in the sphere of exchange.[5]

Nor do these Jewish immigrants, or the Dutch financiers who migrated to England in the train of William of Orange, appear to have influenced English banking technique.[6] It is true that some of them subscribed to the earliest English funded State loans, the Million Loan of 1693, the Million Lottery Loan of 1694, and the original capital of the Bank of England, but the great majority of the subscribers to these historic flotations were Englishmen, metropolitan and provincial.

This alien immigration, however, was one of the factors which helped to focus English public opinion on the problems of currency and of banking. These problems, as we have seen, had also been brought to the front by the rapid expansion

---

[1] M. Kayserling, " Suasso," in the *Jewish Encyclopædia* ; Jacobs, *op. cit.* No authority, however, is given for this statement.

[2] Picciotto, *op. cit.*, p. 59.

[3] Sir Stephen Evans, a powerful Lombard Street goldsmith of William III's reign, advanced large sums to the Government. P.R.O., Recs. T., T. 29/627, *passim*.

[4] *The Anatomy of Exchange Alley* (1719), reprinted in J. Francis, *Chronicles and Characters of the Stock Exchange* (1849), pp. 359–83 : " The Alley throngs with Jews, jobbers and brokers " (p. 378).

[5] Many proofs of this predominance will be found among the various Records of the Exchequer and the Treasury Books of the period.

[6] There does not appear to be any evidence to show that any members of the Jewish or Dutch colonies in England made a practice of acting as custodians of deposits and issuing such deposits as loans. The most important members of these colonies during the latter half of the seventeenth century deposited large sums of money with Backwell, Sir Robert Vyner and Sir Francis Child. See Chap. II, p. 28, *supra*.

The part played by Dutchmen and Jews as capitalists in Stuart England is examined in Chap. IX, Section iii, *infra*.

of English overseas trade, by the ill-fated fiduciary paper money experiment of Charles II, by the publication of numerous banking schemes, and by the commercial writers of the day with their glowing accounts of the continental banking methods.

Indeed, the commercial treatises of the second half of the seventeenth century had sung the praises of the continental banks with such emphasis, and on so many occasions, that the bankers and traders of later Stuart times had obtained from this source alone much detailed information about the practices of these institutions. And in 1697 Sir Theodore Janssen, one of the original directors of the Bank of England, had informed the City that they were already thirty in number.[1]

The most important of the banks of the Continent as far as England's mercantile and financial interests were concerned was the Bank of Amsterdam,[2] which, like the older *Banco* of Venice [3] and the still older *Banco* of Genoa,[4] was a powerful and well-conducted institution.[5] It had been in existence for eighty-three years before the English Lords of the Treasury decided to experiment with the third of Paterson's financial schemes, and was followed within the five decades succeeding its foundation by the establishment of important banks at Hamburg,[6] Middleburg,[7] Rotterdam [8] and Stockholm,[9] all of which [10] had functioned for many years before

---

[1] *A Discourse concerning Banks* (1697), p. 1.

[2] Established in 1609. See foot-note 1, p. 136, *infra*.

[3] The *Banco di Rialto* of Venice was founded in 1587. This was followed by the *Banco del Giro* in 1619. The latter absorbed the former in 1637, became known as the Bank of Venice, and continued to function until 1806. [4] The Bank of St. George, Genoa, dates from 1407.

[5] For details of the early history of banking in Genoa and Venice see R. Cleriac, *Usance du Negoce ou Commerce de la Banque des Lettres de Change* (1656), Chap. IX; C. Cuneo, *Memorie sopra l'antico Debito Publico Mutui, Compere e Banca di S. Giorgio in Genova* (1844); Prince Adam Wiszniewski, *Histoire de la Banque de Saint-George de Gênes* (1865); E. Lattes, *La Libertà delle banche a Venezia dal secolo XIII al XVII secondo i documenti inediti del R. Archivo dei Frari* (1869); F. Ferrara, " Gli antichi banchi di Venezia," in *Nuova Antologia*, XVI (1871); E. Nasse, " Das venetianische Bankwesen im 14. 15. und 16. Jahrhundert," in *Jahrbücher für National-ökonomie und Statisik*, 34 (1879); C. F. Dunbar, " The Bank of Venice," *Quarterly Journal of Economics*, VI (1892); P. des Essars, " A History of Banking in Latin Nations," in *A History of Banking in all Nations*, III (1896), pp. 1–379; C. A. Conant, *A History of Modern Banks of Issue* (5th ed., 1908), p. 10. [6] 1619. [7] 1616. [8] 1635. [9] 1656.

[10] See J. K. Ingram, " Early European Banks," *D. P. E.*; Sir R. H. Inglis Palgrave, " Banks and Banking," *Enc. Brit.* (11th ed., 1910–11).

the Tunnage Act, which established the Bank of England, became law.

The Bank of Amsterdam appears to have been the only overseas bank with which the Bank of England transacted any business during its earliest years.   Primarily a deposit and exchange bank (*wisselbank*), it was originally established for the express purpose of monopolising the Amsterdam exchange business conducted in registered offices by private money-changers.[1]   The city of Amsterdam paid the salaries of its officials and was its security.   Similarly, in Venice the Republic was the *Banco del Giro's* security, and paid the salaries of this bank's officials.[2]

Such methods did not prevail in England.   The infant Bank of England was not a copy of a continental model. Its chief original function was that of a bank of issue, whereas the banks of the Continent were essentially banks of deposit and of exchange.   It did not monopolise the London exchange business, for the goldsmith bankers or any other financiers, alien or native, were allowed to engage in such transactions.[3]

[1] See R. van der Borght, " A History of Banking in the Netherlands," in *A History of Banking in all Nations*, IV, pp. 191–98, for the establishment of the Amsterdam *Wisselbank*, and the era of exchange banks in the Netherlands.
For other descriptions of the Bank of Amsterdam see Cleriac, *op. cit.*, Chap. XI ; Sir William Temple, *Observations upon the United Provinces of the Netherlands* (1676), pp. 99–100–101 ; W. Carr, *The Traveller's Guide* (1690), pp. 84–91 ; S. Ricard, *Traité Général du Commerce* (1705), pp. 170–79 ; J. Wagenaar, *Amsterdam* (1760–77), III, Bk. II, V, pp. 401–7 ; W. C. Mees, *Proeve eener Geschiedenis van het Bankwezen in Nederland, gedurende den tijd der Republiek* (1838), Chaps. II–V ; A. Smith, *The Wealth of Nations*, Cannan's edition, I, pp. 443–52 ; and H. Sée, *Modern Capitalism* (English trans. by H. B. Vanderblue and G. F. Doriot, 1928), pp. 63–66.

[2] Janssen, *op. cit.*, pp. 1–4, classifies the banks of the day into three types : (1) " some for safety and convenience," (2) " others for the benefit of the income only," (3) " others for safety and convenience and likewise for benefit and advantage " [of the promoters].   In the first class he places the banks of Amsterdam, Rotterdam, Hamburg and Stockholm ; in the second those of Rome, Bologna, Milan and Paris ; and in the third " the several banks of Naples, one of the banks of Bolonia and the Bank of St. George at Genoa," together with the Bank of England.

[3] In Amsterdam it was originally provided that all bills of exchange of 600 guilders and over, drawn on or negotiated in this city, were payable in the bank unless otherwise specifically stated on the bill, and the payments were strictly regulated.   Bills had to be paid within six days after they were due, and when they became due, with the exception stated, the bearers thereof took them to the persons making the payments, each bill bearing the following order :   " Write the contents of the other side upon my account in Bank at Amsterdam the ... day of ..." [Signature].
Alexander Justice, *A General Treatise on Moneys and Exchange*, p. 355. See Robert H. Inglis Palgrave's article on " Banks and Banking," *Enc. Brit.*

There was no guarantee for its security from the State or even from the City of London. City magistrates, as in the Bank of Amsterdam, had no controlling interest in its affairs. Nor did it in the first three years of its existence possess a monopoly of joint-stock banking. A comparison of its constitution with, for instance, that of the *Banco del Giro* will show how different it was from one of the great Italian banks of the day.

Moreover, while the continental banks, especially that of Amsterdam, appear to have been established under propitious circumstances, the Bank of England was founded under the most distressing of conditions, so distressing, in fact, that it was miraculous that the project survived. " All sorts of Paper creditt in Orders, Bills, Noats, Bonds, Assignments, etc.," writes a contemporary official of the Mint, " overflowed the Kingdom. All our wealth seem'd to consist in a little Gold and adulterated Silver ; a world of wooden scores and paper sums. Never was there known before such vast debts owing for Excise and Customs, upon Bills and Bonds unsatisfyed. All sorts of provisions grew to an extravagant price. . . . Wee had all the symptoms upon us of a Bankrupt State and an undone people." [1] " From 1690 to 1699," declares Lecky,[2] " there was hardly a single year of average prosperity. The loaf which in the previous reign cost threepence rose to ninepence." " The vessel of our commonwealth," remarks Hallam,[3] " has never been so close to shipwreck as in this period."

The nation, as a result of the terrible struggle with France, was in a precarious condition ; the Treasury-Exchequer mechanism was as rudimentary as in the days of the second Charles ; the Government raised loans in the same old mischievous way ;[4] the financial devices so prominent between the " happy " Restoration and the " glorious " Revolution became even more firmly entrenched under the ægis of

[1] B.M., Lansd. MS., 801 ; H. Haynes, "Brief Memoirs relating to the Silver and Gold Coins of England," fol. 49.
[2] *A History of England in the Eighteenth Century* (1892), I, p. 21.
[3] *The Constitutional History of England* (1854), III, p. 134.
[4] See the " Account of Tallies struck upon Parliamentary Funds," *C.J.*, XI, under 1st December 1696.

William of Orange.[1]   There was, with the exception of the abolition of the wooden tallies in 1826,[2] hardly any change in the Exchequer methods of the receipt and issue of public revenue until the reign of the fourth William in 1834.   The old methods survived for nearly a century and a half after the coming of the third William in 1688.

Like the other money-lenders of the day, the infant Bank was immediately drawn into this financial maelstrom, and during its earliest years it advanced very large sums of money to the Government on the security of tallies struck on various branches of the revenue.[3]   As early as 8th August 1694, only twelve days after the Bank's Charter had been sealed, the court of directors decided to discount talhes registered on the following funds : the Land Tax, not exceeding £1,200,000; the " two-thirds Excise," not exceeding £500,000; " East India Goods," not exceeding £460,000; " Wines and Tobacco," not exceeding £660,000 ; and " Paper and Parchment," not exceeding £30,000.[4]   The first four

[1] See, for example, 7 & 8 Wm. III, c. 30 (1696); 8 Wm. III, c. 3 (1696); 8 & 9 Wm. III, c. 28 (1697); 9 Wm. III, c. 3 (1697); 9 & 10 Wm. III, c. 44 (1698); 10 Wm. III, c. 1 (1698); 10 & 11 Wm. III, c. 22 (1699); 12 & 13 Wm. III, c. 11 (1700).

[2] 23 Geo. III, c. 82 (1782) abolished the offices of the two chamberlains, the tally cutter, and the usher of the Exchequer, and authorised the substitution of written indented receipts for the old wooden tallies.   This substitution, however, was not carried out until the death of the last of the chamberlains in 1826.   The duties of these officers were then transferred to the auditor, and the tally system came to an end.   When the last auditor, Lord Grenville, died in 1834, a Comptroller General of the Exchequer, together with an assistant comptroller, were appointed under 4 & 5 Wm. IV, c. 15; and the powers formerly exercised by the auditor, the tellers and the clerk of the Pells were transferred to the Comptroller General, while a new official termed the Paymaster of the Civil Services was appointed to make all the detailed payments previously made at the Exchequer with the exception of certain life annuities, which were taken over by the National Debt Office.   In 1836, under 5 & 6 Wm. IV, c. 35, the office of Paymaster General, which still exists, was established.   See Parl. P., 1868-69, XXXV (366), Pt. II, pp. 338-47.

[3] The Bank's initial capital of £1,200,000 was advanced to the Government upon such securities.   See p. 149, infra.   The Bank remitted large sums to Holland, for financing William III's campaign, on the security of tallies deposited by the Earl of Ranelagh, the Army Paymaster.   See Chap. VII, p. 187, infra.

[4] The Court Minute Books of the Bank of England, Lib. A, fol. 25.

These books are the most valuable of the carefully treasured and excellently preserved records among the archives of the Bank.   They are a complete record of the resolutions passed at, and the routine business of, the various meetings of the directors; and as in the earliest years of the Bank's history the court of directors usually met daily, except Sunday, the information they contain, as will be seen from this and the two succeeding chapters, is of great interest and of exceptional value.

of the Bank's Court Minute Books [1] contain numerous details of such transactions,[2] while the surviving Treasury Books and Papers of the period testify to the serious depreciation of tallies, and even contain many references to their " worthlessness " owing to the remoteness of the revenue upon which they were registered.[3]

Such financial instability was, during the first eight years of the post-Revolution period, accompanied by the chaos caused by the deplorable state of the coinage. " England hath been more grieved with Clip'd and Counterfeit Money than any other Country," declared Chaloner [4] in the year the Bank of England was established. " The Current Coin of this Kingdom," observed a thoughtful Bristol merchant [5] in the following year, " is now so debased that Men rather truck than sell for Money." " We had little or no Silver Coin from about Midsummer till after Christmas last," wrote the critical author of *Decus and Tutamen* [6] a little later. Clipping and counterfeiting were rampant. The severest laws [7] do not appear to have interfered in the slightest with the work of the " clippers." [8] " They cannot see . . . the wickedness of these Practices," remarked a popular contemporary ecclesiastic [9] in a sermon at the London Guild-

---

[1] The first four Court Minute Books, which cover the period 1694–1705, are known as : Lib. A, dated 27th July–20th March 1695; Lib. B, dated 27th March 1695–14th July 1697; Lib. C, dated 26th July 1697–10th April 1700; Lib. D, dated 12th April 1700–28th March 1705. In succeeding footnotes they will be referred to as C.M.B., Lib. A, etc.

[2] The directors gave notice in the *London Gazette*, No. 3,006, dated 30th August–3rd September 1694, that they were prepared to discount tallies and orders on funds on which there was " a credit of loan by Act of Parliament," and which were not remote. A minute of the Commissioners of Public Accounts, dated 18th October 1694, states that the Commissioners for taking subscriptions to the Bank brought to one of the meetings of the Accounts Commissioners " a great bundle of tallies," which they stated were struck at the Exchequer upon payment of the first £300,000 to the Government. B.M., Harl. MS., 1492, fol. 97. See also C. J., XI, p. 614.

[3] See, for example, *Cal. T. P., 1557–1696*, pp. 289, 397, 424.

[4] *Proposals humbly offered for Passing an Act to prevent Clipping and Counterfeiting of Money* (1694), p. 1.

[5] John Cary, *An Essay on the State of England in Relation to its Trade, its Poor, and its Taxes* (1695), p. 32.

[6] P. 63.　　[7] See 6 & 7 Wm. III, c. 17, 1695.

[8] Between 17th January 1696 and 24th March 1697 the new milled money amounted to £2,458,882 10s. 3d. The enormous extent of the evil of clipping is shown by the fact that this was obtained from a total of clipped money nominally amounting to £4,875,920 1s. 4d. B.M., Harl. MS., 1282, fols. 33–34.　　[9] William Fleetwood, *A Sermon against Clipping* (1694), p. 25.

hall Chapel, " they know not how to repent." Rogers has described the serious state of affairs in an unforgettable passage; " The Old Bailey," he states, " witnessed the sentence of death on clippers by the dozen as Tyburn did their execution." [1]

Reform of the coinage was therefore imperative, and as a result of the activities of Montague, Locke, Newton and Somers,[2] particularly the first named, a great recoinage, which lasted over three years and cost over £2,700,000, was commenced in 1696,[3] two years after the Bank's foundation. " Never," writes Macaulay,[4] " had the world seen the highest practical and the highest speculative abilities united in an alliance so close, so harmonious and so honourable as that which bound Somers and Montague to Locke and Newton."

The recoinage was preceded by a flood of polemical literature ; [5] by many parliamentary debates ; by a panic among the people ; and by remarkable fluctuations in the market prices of gold and silver, in the value of guineas, and in the foreign exchanges. " I cannot but believe," declares Rogers, " that this terrible condition of the foreign exchanges must have precipitated the conclusion at which Montague and Somers arrived that the currency must be reformed at all hazards." [6]

Operations were commenced early in 1696,[7] and though

---

[1] *The First Nine Years of the Bank of England*, p. 30. See also *H.M.C.R.*, *MSS. House of Lords*, I, New Series, Nos, 831, 833, 908, 912.

[2] Charles Montagu (1661–1715), afterwards Chancellor of the Exchequer and Earl of Halifax; John Locke (1632–1704), famous philosopher and economist; Sir Isaac Newton (1662–1727), became Master of the Mint in 1699; John Somers (Lord Somers), (1651–1716), Lord Keeper of the Great Seal, afterwards Lord Chancellor.

[3] Under 7 Wm. III, c. 1, to which additions were made by 7 & 8 Wm. III, c. 10 and c. 19; and 8 Wm. III, c. 1 and c. 7.

[4] *Op. cit.*, IV, p. 630.

[5] The outstanding feature of the preliminary polemics was the well-known Locke-Lowndes controversy.

[6] *First Nine Years of the Bank of England*, p. 42.

[7] Contemporary accounts of the recoinage are given in the despatches of N. de l'Hermitage, the Dutch envoy in London. According to his despatch dated 21st January 1696, preparations were made early in this month by the construction of ten furnaces in the garden of the Exchequer. Another despatch dated 7th February states that melting had been commenced a few days previously. Transcripts of these despatches are in B.M., Addit. MS., 17677, volume marked QQ, and dated 1696.

For accounts of the recoinage by modern writers see Ruding, *Annals of the Coinage*, II, pp. 29–60; Macaulay, *op. cit.*, IV, pp. 630–43; E. Hawkins, *The Silver Coins of England* (1876), pp. 388–93; Rogers, *op. cit.*, pp. 29–60; C. D. Horton, *The Silver Pound* (1887), pp. 64–69; H. D. Macleod, *The*

six mints were soon functioning there was in the initial stages a very serious monetary stringency. In order to ease the situation the Lords of the Treasury under the guidance of the able and far-seeing Montague decided to issue Exchequer bills, "indented bills of credit," as they were originally termed,[1] thus repeating what was in essence the fiduciary order expedient of Charles II.[2] One of the earliest warrants for the issue of these bills states that they were to be signed by Sir Robert Howard, auditor of the Exchequer of Receipt, "sealed with a publique seal," and issued to the tellers of the Exchequer, who were authorised upon money being advanced " to their hands by any person or persons upon ye credit of any such bills . . to deliver to such person or persons respectively such bill or bills for ye same to the amount of the moneys so advanced in principall."[3] The first issue to a member of the public was made by Thomas Howard, first teller of the Exchequer, on 14th July 1696,[4] and from this date they became a regular and permanent feature of English public finance.

Specimens of some of the original issues still survive. The earliest of those preserved in the Public Record Office [5] are narrow printed slips of the following form : [6]

Theory and Practice of Banking (5th ed., 1892), pp. 452–73; A. Andréadès, *History of the Bank of England*, pp. 90–102; Cunningham, *Growth of English Industry and Commerce, Modern Times*, I, pp. 431–39.

[1] P.R.O., Recs. Ex. R., Exchequer Bills, Warrants and Contracts. E. 406/207, dated 1696–98, fol. 1.

[2] Exchequer bills were issued in anticipation of public revenue such as the land tax.

[3] P.R.O., Recs. Ex. R., E. 406/207, fol. 1. Copy of Warrant for issuing Exchequer Bills of Credit, dated 16th July 1696, addressed to Sir Robert Howard, and authorising him " to make and prepare " bills to the value of £40,000; to take care " that the counterpart of the said bills . . . do remain for trying the truth of the original bills "; and " to deliver forthwith " £10,000 in bills to each of the four tellers, " taking their receipts for the same." The original warrant is signed by Godolphin, Montague, Smith and Littleton.

[4] On this day a total of £5,250 was issued in Exchequer bills to Edward Pauncefort " for so much money advanced by him on credit thereof." P.R.O., Recs. Ex. R., Certificates of Exchequer Bills, E. 406/89.

[5] P.R.O., Recs. Ex. R., Miscellanea, E. 407/134 (2). This parcel of documents contains about three dozen of the earliest Exchequer bills of various forms and sizes. The three earliest are dated 26th April 1697, and they were " cancelled on the 2, 3s. Ayd " on 15th February 1703. Two of these for £10 carried ½d. a day interest, the other is for £5 and carried ¼d. a day interest. Each has several indorsements.

[6] This may be compared with the wording given by the diarist of the day, Narcissus Luttrell, in *A Brief Historical Relation, etc.*, who states under

Exchequer
No. *8961.*   2^d *August* 1697.
   Pursuant to an Act of Parliament Authorizing Bills to be
issued for 1,200,000 li This Bill entitles the Bearer to Five
Pounds to pass in all Paym^{ts} to Receiv^{rs} or Collect^{rs} of
Supplys for ye Warr Anno 1697 Except ye III Shill^g Ayd.
                                  A farthing a day Interest.
   Ro. Howard.

   As there was more than one issue of Exchequer bills
between 1696 and 1700, and as certain additions were made
to the law relating to them, the earliest specimens are of
various forms and sizes. Another 1697 specimen,[1] for
example, reads thus :

Exchequer.
No. *188.*   26 *Aprill* 1697.
   By Virtue of an Act of Parliament passed in the VIII
year of his Maties Reign, THIS BILL entitles the bearer
to ffive......Pounds to pass in all payments to Receiv^{rs} or
Collectors of any Ayd Taxes or Supplys for the service of
the War for the Year 1697 (Except ye III shilling Ayd) to
be Recd and satisfied by ye said Receiv^{rs} or Collect^{rs} under
ye Penalties in ye Act Contained
                                  A farthing a day Interest.
   R. Howard.

   The above specimen contains several indorsements which
show that the bill passed frequently from hand to hand.
Rapidity of circulation can also be seen from indorsements
on several of the other surviving early specimens.[2] It is

23rd July 1696, that the " form of the bill is as followeth : num. 411.
exchequer July 18. 96.   By vertue of an act of parliament past in the 8th
of his majesties reign this bill entitles the bearer to 10 l. with interest at
the rate of 3d. per cent per diem, payable at the receipt of the exchequer
on demand. Entred Robert Howard."   Luttrell, however, does not
describe the bill.
   [1] Taken from B.M., Addit. MS., 31025, Exchequer Bills 1697–1700.
   [2] The first issue of Exchequer bills was made in 1696 under the authority
of a section of 7 & 8 Wm. III., c. 31 (1696), the Act which established the
ill-fated National Land Bank. New duties were imposed on salt, and
borrowing on these was authorised up to £2,564,000, either by tallies and
orders of repayment at 7 per cent., or by " bills of credit " up to £1,500,000
—the bills to bear interest up to a maximum of 3 pence per cent. per diem,
and to be payable on demand at the Exchequer.   There was, however,
no provision in this particular Act that the bills were to pass as legal
payments for taxes.   8 Wm. III., c. 6 (1696), rectified this omission, and
though this Act contained no provision for any interest on the bills it authorised a second issue of £1,500,000. 8 & 9 Wm. III., c. 20 (1697)—the

thus evident that these bills were popular with the general public,[1] and that they were invaluable negotiable instruments during the trying period of currency stringency. It is true that they competed to some extent with the Bank's paper money, but it was not, however, until the early years of the eighteenth century that the Bank was officially concerned with their issue,[2] though before this it had assisted in their circulation.[3] Indeed, some of the Bank's first directors were among the earliest " trustees for managing the moneys advanced or to be advanced for exchanging and circulating " these " indented bills of credit." [4]

During the four years which preceded the first issue of Exchequer bills the strain on the Lords of the Treasury was an extraordinarily heavy one. The large sums outstanding on, and the serious depreciation of, tallies, the enormous charges on the public revenue, and the drain of the war with France compelled these harassed guardians of the public purse to consider many new devices for increasing the revenue. One

second Bank Act—authorised interest at 5 per cent. per diem, and under section 66 of this Act the Commissioners of the Treasury were allowed to " covenant with any person or persons " for exchanging and circulating the bills, and to offer 10 per cent. on any sums advanced for this purpose.

The whole of the second £1,500,000 was circulated—commencing on 26th April 1697—chiefly in £5 and £10 bills, but the first issue—commenced on 14th July 1696—only amounted to £159,169. The above specimens, therefore, belong to the second issue. There do not appear to be any surviving examples of the first issue.

[1] See Macaulay, *op. cit.*, IV, p. 700.
[2] See 5 Anne, c. 13 (1707); 7 Anne, c. 7 (1708); 7 Anne, c. 8 (1708); 9 Anne, c. 7 (1710); 12 Anne, c. 11 (1713). See also *Parl.* P. (1898), LII, C.-9010, pp. 69–70.
[3] P.R.O., Recs. T., Treasury Minute Books, T. 29/9, fol. 123, minute dated 19th April 1697. Here it is recorded that the Governor, Deputy Governor and other directors of the Bank attended the Treasury, and Sir John Houblon stated that the Directors were " froward to promote " the Exchequer bills. William III, who was present at this meeting of the Lords of the Treasury, requested the directors to assist "by their subscriptions to give a credit to the Exchequer bills," and this they agreed to do.

On 11th August 1697 Exchequer bills were accepted by the Bank " for the payment of a bill of exchange of £8,315, 3s. 2d. drawn by Mr Hill on the Lord Ranelagh payable to Mr Abraham Houblon for the use of the Bank." C. M. B., Lib. C, fol. 8.

On 11th December 1700 it was ordered " that Bank sealed bills to any sum not exceeding 20,000 li be delivered to the Trustees for circulating Exchequer Bills on a deposit by them to be made of the value thereof in Exchequer specie notes." *Ibid.*, Lib. D, fol. 40.

[4] P.R.O., Recs. Ex. R., E. 406/207, gives a list of these trustees, which includes the names of five of the Bank's directors.

of these, copied from the Continent, was the expedient of distributing over a period of many years " the excessive taxation which was made necessary by one year of war." [1] This device was first legalised in England by the Million Act of January 1693 [2] with its 14 per cent. single life annuities, an Act which, as we have already seen,[3] was the real beginning of " the greatest prodigy that ever perplexed the sagacity and confounded the pride of statesmen and philosophers," [4] the English Funded Debt.[5]

In the following year the system of annuities was extended by the Act which set up the Bank of England, which authorised the granting of further annuities on one, two or three lives at the option of the purchaser,[6] and a sum of £300,000 was thus obtained,[7] while in the same year, also, the Million Lottery Loan produced another £1,000,000.[8]

These expedients figure in the annual Parliamentary grants of the years 1693 and 1694, grants which are a striking index of the extraordinary increase in public expenditure during the years following the Revolution. In 1689 the total of the first post-Revolution Parliamentary grant was £1,184,786 16s. 4d.; in the fifth session of William III's second Parliament in 1694 the annual grant amounted to £5,030,581 9s. 9d., and in the first session of the third Parliament in 1696 to £7,961,469.[9] The total for 1694

[1] Macaulay, *op. cit.*, IV, p. 325.   [2] 4 Wm. & M, c. 3.
[3] Chap. IV, p. 114, *supra*.   [4] Macaulay, *op. cit.*, IV, p. 327.
[5] The sum due to the goldsmith bankers was not at this time acknowledged by the Government.
   For a useful condensed account of the origin and development of the English National Debt see T. P. Taswell-Langmead, *English Constitutional History* (8th ed., 1919), pp. 593–95.
[6] 5 and 6 Wm. & M., c. 20, ss. 34–38.
[7] See *Parl.* P. (1898), LII (C.-9010), p. 3.
[8] Under 5 and 6 Wm. & M., c. 7.
[9] These totals are taken from B.M., Harl. MS., 1282, fols. 1, 11, 15. Similar totals are given in B.M., Addit. MS., 20721, fol. 11.
   Compare F. Bonnet's report, dated April $\frac{20}{30}$ 1694, printed in L. von Ranke, *A History of England principally during the Seventeenth Century* (English trans., Oxford, 1875), VI, p. 246; and J. Postlethwayt, *The History of the English Revenue from the Revolution in 1688 to Christmas 1753* (1759), pp. 9–10.
   After the Revolution direct taxation became the usual means of obtaining annual increases of revenue, and new taxes were introduced in order to meet the rapidly increasing public expenditure. In the period immediately preceding the Revolution the only direct tax which formed part of the ordinary annual public revenue was the Hearthmoney. For further details

includes the proceeds of the Million Lottery, minus discount and expenses of management; and of the Tunnage Act, which includes £1,200,000 from the Bank of England together with £300,000 under the second of the annuity schemes. Thus the Bank was responsible for nearly one-fourth of the estimates for this particular year.

Such were the exceptional circumstances under which the Bank's history commenced.   That the Lords of the Treasury avoided national bankruptcy was a remarkable achievement; that the Bank did not immediately collapse was even still more remarkable.   "This Bank," declared a critical " person of honour " shortly after its establishment, "was to the Amazement of our selves, as well as the Astonishment of our Enemies (the French), completed in less time than could have been imagin'd." [1]   Its establishment under such extraordinary financial conditions was, as that able economist of the day, Daniel Defoe, has truly stated, a " particular glory " to the English nation.[2]

Before, however, Montague, with the unanimous approval of the other Lords of the Treasury, decided to experiment with the third of the financial schemes submitted for his consideration by William Paterson,[3] he had carefully examined many other similar proposals.[4]   The essence of the one adopted, was, as is well known, a loan of £1,200,000 to the Government at 8 per cent., the scheme which developed into the Bank of England.   It must, however, be remembered that, including this loan—the original " capital stock " of

---

with reference to taxation during the Bank of England's early years, see Sir John Sinclair, *The History of the Public Revenue of the British Empire* (1785–90); S. Dowell, *History of Taxation and Taxes in England* (2nd ed., 1888); W. Kennedy, *English Taxation 1640–1799* (1896); A. L. Smith, " Taxation and Finance, 1689–1714," in *Social England*, ed. H. D. Traill and J. S. Mann, IV (1901).

 [1] *Angliæ Tutamen* (1695), p. 5.
 [2] *Essays on Projects*, p. 43.
 [3] William Paterson (1658–1719), was a native of Dumfriesshire.   For details of his extraordinary career see *D. N. B.*; *D. P. E.*; S. Bannister, *The Writings of William Paterson* (1859); H. Warren, *The Story of the Bank of England* (1903), pp. 1–5; A. Andréadès, *op. cit.*, pp. 60–71.
The first of Paterson's schemes, which appeared in 1691, was a plan to lend the Government £1,000,000 for a yearly payment of £65,000.   The second was a project to raise £2,000,000 at 7 per cent.

 [4] *E.g.* those contained among the Halifax Papers.   See Chap. IV, p. 102, *supra*.

the Bank—the Government created between 1693 and the close of the seventeenth century new stock to the extent of £5,418,801 10s.[1]

The Bank was established, under the authority of sixteen sections of the Tunnage Act of 1694,[2] for " the better raising and paying into the Receipt of the Exchequer the sum of Twelve hundred thousand Pounds, Part of the sum of Fifteen hundred thousand Pounds." [3]   Their Majesties were authorised to appoint Commissioners to receive subscriptions on, or before, 1st August 1694, by " any person or persons, natives or foreigners, bodies politic or corporate," who, provided the full loan or " a moiety thereof " was subscribed before 1st August 1694, were to be incorporated under the title of " The Governor and Company of the Bank of England."   No person was allowed to subscribe more than £20,000, and the £1,200,000 was to be redeemable after 1705 upon one year's notice being given to the company. The Bank was not allowed to borrow above its original capital except under special Parliamentary authority, to oppress any subjects by " monopolising or ingrossing any sort of goods, wares or merchandizes," or to trade with its own securities.   It was permitted to deal in bills of exchange, to buy and sell bullion, to sell any commodities deposited as securities for loans which were not redeemed at the date agreed upon or within three months afterwards, and to issue assignable sealed bills.

Three years later the second Bank Act [4] augmented the Bank's original capital by £1,001,171 10s.,[5] and is noteworthy because it contains the first of a series of prohibitory

---

[1] It will thus be noted that in six years the debt created exceeded the annual revenue in the year the Bank was established.

By the end of the financial year (29th September) in 1700, £671,868 12s. 6d. had been paid off, thus leaving the amount of Funded Debt on this date as £4,746,932 17s. 6d.   This reduction was accomplished by means of tallies subscribed for by the proprietors of the Bank of England, and Malt Lottery Tickets issued under the Malt Lottery Loan of 8 & 9 Wm. III, c. 22 (1696).

[2] 5 and 6 Wm. & M., c. 20 (1694), ss. 18–33.   See L. J., XV, under 23rd, 24th, and 25th April 1694.

[3] " The Bank was cradled in a Ways and Means Act."   H. S. Foxwell, intro. to E. von Philippovich, History of the Bank of England (1911), p. 5.

[4] 8 & 9 Wm. III, c. 20.

[5] This increase of capital also meant that the Bank could increase its issue of sealed bills to the extent of the new capital, but the new bills had to possess a distinguishing mark.   Ibid., s. 30.

enactments, a section which attempted to give the corporation a monopoly of banking. "That," it reads, "during
the continuance of the corporation of the Governor and
Company of the Bank of England no other bank, or any
corporation, society, fellowship, company or constitution
in the nature of a bank shall be erected or established, permitted, suffered, countenanced or allowed by Act of Parliament within this kingdom." [1]

Nevertheless, this enactment did not prevent corporations
other than those specifically stated to be " in the nature of
a bank " from issuing promissory notes and sealed bills, and
in 1704 a company of mining adventurers proceeded to do
this. Therefore, in 1707, the Bank's partial monopoly was
made more rigid, and it was declared illegal for " any body
politic or corporate whatsoever, erected or to be erected
(other than the said Governor and Company of the Bank of
England), or for any other persons whatsoever united or to
be united in covenants or partnerships exceeding the number
of six persons, in that part of Great Britain called England,
to borrow, owe, or take up any sum or sums of money on
their bills or notes, payable at demand, or at any less time
than six months from the borrowing thereof." [2]

It was authorised in the Act of 1697 that the subscriptions
to the new capital, or " engrafted stock " as it was termed,
could be paid up to four-fifths of the amount in tallies,[3] upon
which the Government allowed the Bank 8 per cent., and up
to one-fifth in bank bills or notes,[4] which had " so much
money bona fide resting due thereon as the said one-fifth
part of the said respective subscriptions shall fully amount
to;" and additional sealed bills bearing a distinguishing mark
could be issued up to the total of the new capital. The
existence of the corporation was prolonged, for it was agreed
that the original capital would not be redeemed by the Govern-

---

[1] 8 & 9 Wm. III, c. 20, s. 28.
[2] 6 Anne, c. 22, s. 9. This was repeated the next year, 1708, in 7 Anne,
c. 7, s. 61.
[3] See *The Arguments and Reasons for and against Engrafting the Bank
of England with Tallies* (1697).
[4] When the second Bank Act became law, tallies were at 40 per cent.
discount, and bank bills and notes about 16 per cent. B.M. Addit. MS.,
20721, fol. 35, and Rogers, *op. cit.*, Table IV.

ment until one year's notice was given after 1st August 1710 ; the stock of the Bank was exempted from taxation; and not more than two-thirds of the directors retiring in one year could be re-elected in the next year.[1]

The " engrafted stock " had to be paid off by the Bank itself, and as the tallies received as subscriptions were met by the Government, the Bank was authorised to distribute among the subscribers at the end of each quarter the sums thus received.[2] These quarterly payments, however, caused much inconvenience to the ordinary business of the Bank, therefore it was enacted that, after 20th March 1698, the payments should be made every six months;[3] and later, in 1701,[4] that they should be made when most convenient to the directors. In this way the new capital of £1,001,171 10s. was paid back to the subscribers between 31st August 1698, and 10th July 1707,[5] and while this operation was in progress the nominal capital was not altered; but this was done upon completion of the payments when the Bank's capital again became £1,200,000.

Almost immediately after the passing of the Act which augmented the Bank's capital, fresh stock to the extent of £1,217,630 was raised by the Malt Lottery Loan,[6] and in 1698 the New East India Company was responsible for another £2,000,000.[7] It was thus that over £4,000,000 was added to the Funded Debt between 1697 and 1700.[8]

The Bank's original capital of £1,200,000 was quickly subscribed. Narcissus Luttrell, the diarist of the day, states that the subscription lists were opened in " the Mercers Chappel " on 21st June 1694;[9] that the Lords of the

---

[1] See Professor F. S. Foxwell's introduction to Philippovich, *History of the Bank of England*, p. 19, for a criticism of this provision.
[2] 8 & 9 Wm. III, c. 20, s. 45.
[3] 9 Wm. III, c. 3.   [4] 12 & 13 Wm. III, c. 12, s. 14.
[5] See *Parl.* P. (1898), LII (C.-9010), p. 68.
[6] Under 8 & 9 Wm. III, c. 22.   [7] Under 9 & 10 Wm. III, c. 44.
[8] For fuller details see *Parl.* P. (1898), LII (C.-9010), p. 14.
[9] *Brief Historical Relation*, III, pp. 331–32.   There is no record either in the records of the Bank or of the Mercers' Company of banking business being transacted in the Mercers' Chapel. Sir Robert H. Inglis Palgrave, " Banks and Banking," *Enc. Brit.*, states, without giving any authority, that " the business of the bank was first carried on in Mercers' Chapel," and that " it continued there " until 28th September 1694, when operations were commenced at Grocers' Hall, which the Bank occupied until 1732.

Treasury "came themselves and subscribed £10,000 for the Queen "; [1] that Sir Robert Howard, the auditor of the Exchequer of Receipt, and his son were responsible for £18,000 and Sir John Houblon for £10,000; that the total of subscriptions for the first day amounted to £300,000, and for the first three days to £600,000, which meant that the subscribers became a corporation, and that by noon on 2nd July the total of £1,200,000 had been completed. [2]

Luttrell's totals may be compared with those announced in the *London Gazette*. The issue dated 21st–25th June states that the Commissioners for taking subscriptions first met on 21st June, and that £736,000 had been subscribed up to 23rd June. The next number gives the total as £996,350 on 27th June, the next announces that it was £1,181,925 on the night of Saturday, 30th June, and the next, dated 2nd–5th July, that the £1,200,000 had been completely subscribed.

But these were promises. Only 60 per cent., *i.e.* £720,000, of the capital had been actually paid up by December 1694. Yet before the end of the same year the Bank had advanced to the Government the whole of the £1,200,000 : £300,000 in various instalments on or before 1st September; [3] £300,000 in various instalments on or before 9th October; [4] and the balance in various instalments on or before 22nd December. [5] This remarkable transaction was carried out by advancing the greater part of the loan in sealed bills, usually of the value of £100, and "running cash notes," [6] tallies being given by the Government as receipts. [7] In fact, the sum of £44,335 18s. 9d., the very last instalment, was ordered by the court of directors, on 19th December, to be paid to the Exchequer in "running cash notes." [8]

---

[1] In the earliest subscription book preserved among the archives of the Bank this appears as a joint subscription of the King and Queen.
[2] *Brief Historical Relation*, III, pp. 332, 333, 338.
[3] C. M. B., Lib. A, fols. 48–49.
The very first instalment of £4,000 was received at the Exchequer on the 4th August 1694. P.R.O., Recs. Ex. R., E. 401/1994, fol. 386.
[4] C. M. B., Lib. A, fol. 75.
[5] *Ibid.*, Lib. A, fol. 117; and P.R.O., Rec. Ex. R., E. 401/1995, fol. 221.
[6] See Chap. VI, p. 158, *infra*.
[7] A Court minute of 22nd December 1694 reads thus :—" Mr. Malborne is ordered to cast up the Tallys for the severall payments of the 1,200,000 li. into the Exchequer and to see what they amount to in the whole." C. M. B., Lib. A, fol. 122.   [8] *Ibid.*, Lib. A, fol. 117.

In addition, within eleven weeks of the completion of this transaction the Bank had advanced to the Government a further £644,408 7s., a sum equal to more than half of the original loan. Of this total £300,000 was paid into the Exchequer on 5th February 1695,[1] and £344,408 7s.,[2] the first instalment of another loan of £514,000,[3] on 8th March. These later transactions were even still more remarkable, for it was not until the latter part of July 1697 that another 20 per cent. of the Bank's original capital was paid up. Indeed, a period of three years elapsed before the whole of the capital was paid up, and this was done in five instalments : 25 per cent. between 21st June and 2nd July 1694, 25 per cent. by 27th September 1694, 10 per cent. by 27th November 1694, 20 per cent. by 24th July 1697, and 20 per cent. out of the profits about 24th July 1697.[4] Thus when the Act of 1697, which increased the Bank's capital, became law, only 80 per cent. of the original capital had been called up.

Immediately the original capital had been guaranteed, notice was given to each subscriber of £500 [5] and upwards to meet at Mercers' Hall on Tuesday, 10th July 1694, at 8 p.m., to take the following oath : [6]

"I, A. B., do swear that the sum of £500 by me subscribed (or the sum of £500 at least of the money by me subscribed) is my own proper money, for my own use and is my own right and not in trust whatsoever."

After taking this oath, such subscribers had " to give in writing, rolled up," the names of two persons whom they thought " fit and proper " to hold the offices of Governor and Deputy Governor; and the next day they had in the

[1] P.R.O., Recs. Ex. R., E. 401/1995, fol. 488.
[2] *Ibid.*, E. 401/1995, fol. 532.
[3] The Court Minutes show that the directors decided to advance this sum on 6th March 1695. C. M. B., Lib. A, fol. 175. See Chap. VII, p. 184, *infra.*   [4] See *Parl.* P. (1898), LII (C.-9010), p. 67.
[5] " The Book Conteyning the Subscriptions," preserved in the Bank, contains the names of over 1,200 subscribers, 63 of whom, including the Duke of Devonshire, the Earl of Portland, the Duke of Leeds, Sir Stephen Fox, Lord Godolphin, and the Countess of Carlisle subscribed £4,000 or more, thus qualifying to act as Governors.
I am much indebted to the Chief Accountant of the Bank of England, Mr. F. S. Arnold, for his assistance in examining this well-preserved book.
[6] The *London Gazette*, No. 2,989, dated 2nd–5th July 1694. Repeated in No. 2,990.

same way to nominate twenty-four persons to act as directors.

Thus were elected the first Governor, Sir John Houblon; [1] the first Deputy Governor, Michael Godfrey; and the first directors, Sir John Huband, Sir James Houblon, Sir William Gore, Sir William Scawen, Sir Henry Furnese, Sir Thomas Abney, Sir William Hedges, Brooke Bridges, James Bateman, George Boddington, Thomas Goddard, Abraham Houblon, Gilbert Heathcott, Theodore Janssen, John Lordell, Robert Raworth, John Smith, John Ward, Edward Clerke, James Denew, Samuel Lethieullier, William Paterson, Obadiah Sedgwick and Nathaniel Tench. [2]

Seventeen days after the election of the first directors the charter establishing the " Corporation of the Governor and Company of the Bank of England " was sealed; and the Court Minute Books show that the first court of directors met at Mercers' Hall on the afternoon of the day the charter was granted—Friday, 27th July—" at ye opening of ye Charter." The very first matter discussed was " the method of giving receipts for running cash." Three methods were proposed : (1) " by keeping accounts with the creditors in books," (2) " by endorsing notes given," (3) " by charging notes on the bank; " and after a lengthy debate it was resolved to observe the following three methods : (1) " to give out Running-Cash-Notes and to endorse on them what is paid off in part," (2) " to keep an Account with ye Creditor in a Book or Paper of his owne," (3) " to accept Notes drawn on ye Bank." [3]

At the meeting of the third court on 30th July 1694 the first officials of the Bank were appointed. They numbered nineteen, and, with the exception of two doorkeepers, each had to produce a security of from £500 to £5000, according to the importance of his position, the latter sum being required from the " First Cashier." John Ince was appointed " Secre-

---

[1] For the history of the Houblons see Lady Alice Archer, *The Houblon Family, its Story and Times* (1907).

[2] The first twenty persons in this list were all qualified to act as Governors. Edward Clerke did not serve; he was replaced by John Knight on 10th August, 1694.

[3] C. M. B., Lib. A, fols. 2–3. A full copy of the minutes of the first court of directors together with the names of those present is given in Appendix 21, *infra*.

tary and Sollicitor " at a salary of £200 per annum; Thomas Mercer " First Accomptant," at £200; John Monteage, " Second Accomptant," at £100; Abraham Wright, " Third Accomptant," at £100; John Kenrick, " First Cashier," at £200; Robert Hedges,. " Second Cashier," at £100; Thomas Maddocks, " Third Cashier," at £80; ten tellers, Joshua Odams, Richard Meverelle, Joshua Willet, George Hindley, Thomas Morris, William Ayleworth, John Wase, James Watkins, John Malborne and Edward Miller, at £50; and two doorkeepers, who also acted as messengers, at £25.[1]

Thus the Bank commenced its eventful history with nineteen officials;[2] with a " Secretary and Sollicitor," a " First Accomptant " and a " First Cashier " as its departmental heads; and with its business clearly defined in its own minutes as that of issuing " running cash notes," of posting up its customers' private books, and of cashing its customers' " drawn " notes; and by Act of Parliament as that of dealing in bills of exchange, buying and selling bullion, lending money on securities including merchandise, issuing assignable sealed bills, and borrowing " sums of money " up to a maximum of £1,200,000.[3]

How this business was transacted during the Bank's earliest years, and the changes in organisation that were necessary to cope with its increase, will be next described.

[1] C. M. B., Lib. A, fol. 7.
[2] The salaries of these nineteen officials amounted to £1,530. Sir Robert H. Inglis Palgrave, " Banks and Banking," *Enc. Brit.*, states that " the Bank commenced business with 54 assistants whose salaries amounted to £4,350." Macaulay also states, *op. cit.*, IV, p. 504, that the persons originally employed by the Bank were 54 in number.
The Court Minute Books show that these statements are inaccurate.
[3] For a description of the Bank's business by its first Deputy Governor see M. Godfrey, *A Short Account of the Bank of England* (1695). Reprinted in J. Francis, *History of the Bank of England* (1848), App. I.
The writer of *Reasons for Encouraging the Bank of England* (1695), pp. 3–4, thus sums up the " usefulness " of the Bank of England to private persons " :—(1) " lending money on mortgages at 5 per cent. without any Procuration or Continuation "; (2) " discounting foreign and inland bills of exchange some at 3 per cent. and others at 4½ per cent." ; (3) " lending money on Pawns at 5 per cent. whereas some in their necessities have heretofore paid above 100 per cent. for money lent them on pawns "; (4) " lending money on the Orphans' Fund at 5 per cent., which has relieved divers Orphans "; (5) " lending money at 5 per cent. on the Benefitted and Blank Million Lottery Tickets, whereby the necessities of many have been relieved and the credit of the publick funds preserved."

CHAPTER VI

THE EARLY TRANSACTIONS OF THE BANK OF ENGLAND

" L'etablisement de cette banque paroist une tres bonne chose, et l'on tien qu'on ne sauroit mieux placer son argent."

L'Hermitage to the States-General, despatch dated $\frac{18}{20}$ January 1696, B.M., Addit. M.S., 17677, QQ.

" The advantages that the King and all concerned in tallies had from the Bank were soon so sensibly felt that all people saw into the secret reasons that made the enemies of the constitution set themselves with so much earnestness against it."

G. BURNET, *History of My Own Times*, II, p. 125.

THE three resolutions relating to the Bank's methods of conducting business with its customers, passed at the first court of directors on Friday, 27th July 1694, were again considered at the court's fourth meeting on the following Tuesday. " The question being putt," the minutes of this meeting state, " whether the former of the three methods in keeping running cash, viz.—

1. Notes payable to bearer to be endorsed,
2. Books or Sheets of Paper wherein their Acco^{ts} to be entered,
3. Notes to persons to be accomptable,

should be confirmed or not the same was pass^d in ye affirmative." [1]

It will be observed that running cash notes are now referred to as notes payable to bearer, and that the third resolution appears to be quite different from the original third resolution. But, as will be explained in more detail later, a customer who held the Bank's " accomptable note " was empowered to draw notes—they were not yet termed cheques—on the Bank, and for the guidance of the officials these particular.

[1] C. M. B., Lib. A, fols. 12–13. These minutes contain the first reference to the " accomptable notes."

minutes give the form in which accomptable notes were to be made, thus :

> " Rec^d the .... of .... 1694 of .... the
> sume of .... for which I promise to be
> accomptable on demand.
> For the Govr and Compa of
> the Bank of England." [1]
> [signature of cashier]

Two important decisions with regard to the Bank's paper money were also made at this meeting : (1) that all running cash notes " being first entered " were to be " signed and countersigned " by two of the cashiers; and, (2) that one accountant, Monteage, and two cashiers, Kenrick and Hedges were to sign all sealed bills in the presence of at least three directors. Thus the minutes relating to the first four business days of the Bank's history contain references to three types of paper credit, the running cash note, the accomptable note, and the sealed bill.

Such are the earliest references in the Court Minute Books to the Bank's paper credit. The first reference to tallies is contained in the minutes dated 1st August,[2] the directors resolving that " the five tallies amounting to 112,000 li. be locked up in the new iron chest for the present," an important minute which, in view of the fact that the first instalment (£4,000) of the original loan of £1,200,000 was not received at the Exchequer of Receipt until 4th August,[3] appears to indicate that within a week of its establishment the Bank had either discounted these tallies or accepted them as deposits. Six days later the directors discussed for the first time the important problem of goldsmiths' notes, and decided : (1) that all subscribers who paid their second quarterly subscriptions in such notes must indorse them payable to the Governor and Company of the Bank of England, and, (2) that all the goldsmiths' notes thus paid could only be accepted on condition that they were immediately cashed by the original issuers, the Bank's tellers

---

[1] " And," it is added, " ye particulars of the bills drawn are to be entered on ye side."   [2] C. M. B., Lib. A, fol. 13.
[3] P.R.O., Recs. Ex. R., E. 401/1994, fol. 386.

to receive the metallic money which the notes represented at the shops of the said issuers.[1]

It is evident from the minutes dated 9th August,[2] that the Bank began to specialise almost from the outset, for on this date the duties of each cashier were carefully defined; the first cashier was made responsible for " the generall cash," the second for goldsmiths' notes, and the third for bills of exchange. This specialisation became more marked a little later when various departments began to develop. A minute dated 12th August 1697 shows that in three years some striking changes had taken place in the Bank's internal departmental organisation, which is thus described : the " Accomptant's Office," six " accomptants " and seven " sub-accomptants," with Mercer still " first accomptant " but with his salary increased to £250 per annum; the " Cash Office," two cashiers and six sub-cashiers, the two former being the original second and third cashiers, Hedges and Maddocks, each now receiving £180 per annum; the " Discount Office," three; the " Tellers' Office," twenty-one; the " Tally Office," one; the " Secretary's Office," two, with Ince still " Secretary and Sollicitor," enjoying an enhanced salary of £250, assisted by Thomas Baines, who was officially known as the " Assistant Secretary "; " to attend ye Exchequer," two; " to attend ye Sub-committee," one.[3]

By May 1700 this arrangement had developed into the following : the " Accomptant's Office," thirteen, of which Mercer was still the head at a salary of £250; the " Cashier's Office," sixteen, Maddocks being chief cashier with a like salary; the " Discount Office," three; the " Teller's Office," twenty-four; the " Secretary's Office," three—Ince, Baines, and Dyer; " to attend ye Exchequer," three; " to attend ye Sub-Committee," one.[4]

The running cash note, the accomptable note and the sealed bill referred to in the minutes of July were supplemented a little later by two other types, the " lettered note indented on marbled paper " and the specie note. It will, however, be recalled that the Act which established the Bank

[1] C. M. B., Lib. A., fol 24, 7th August 1694.   [2] *Ibid.*, Lib. A, fol. 27.
[3] *Ibid.*, Lib. C, fols. 9–13.   [4] *Ibid.*, Lib. D, fols. 4–6.

makes no reference to the issue of different types of notes. The only authority granted was that of giving securities " by bill, bond, covenant or agreement or other writing . . . made, sealed or given under the common seal of the said corporation " up to the amount of the original capital of £1,200,000,[1] securities which are referred to in another section of the Act as " bills obligatory and of credit under the seal of the said corporation." [2]

" Bank bills, sealed," which were printed,[3] assignable by indorsement and delivery,[4] interest-bearing,[5] and payable to bearer,[6] were used in the transactions with the Exchequer, particularly in connection with the loan of £1,200,000 to the Government, whose creditors received these bills after they were sent by the Bank to the Exchequer, and either deposited them in the Bank as cash or presented them for payment. In the latter case, metallic money was not invariably given in exchange, as the Bank frequently gave its customers running cash notes or even new sealed bills when the old sealed bills were presented for payment.

The earliest Court Minute Books contain numerous references to these bills. " That soe many Bank Bills," reads, for example, a minute dated 22nd August 1694,[7] " be made as with those paid will make up the sum of 300,000 li. to be paid into the Exchequer each of them to be for 100 li," a minute which is typical of many relating to £100 sealed bills being " made " for the various instalments of the £1,200,000. In fact, it is quite clear from the minutes that the greater part of this loan was advanced to the Government by means of these bills.

The first evidence of the issuing of sealed bills to private

---

[1] 5 and 6 W. & M., c. 20, s. 25.
[2] *Ibid.*, s. 28.
[3] " That Mr. Staresmore print 1500 Bank-bills more." C. M. B., Lib. A, 8th August 1694.
[4] 5 and 6 W. & M., c. 20, s. 28.
[5] Originally twopence per cent. per diem. Later, as the Bank gained in strength, they were issued without interest. " That 200 Bank-bills without interest made out and dated 12th September last be sealed by the Committee in waiting," states a minute dated 19th October 1698. C. M. B., Lib. C, fol. 121. No specimen survives.
[6] See *Anonymous* (1698), 1 Ld. Raym., p. 738; and *Anonymous* (1699), Holt, p. 118.
[7] C. M. B., Lib. A, fol. 43.

customers in return for deposits of money is contained in a minute dated 2nd August 1694,[1] which states " that every person shall have Bank-bills in course as he has paid money to the Bank and enters his name in a Book for that purpose." An increase in the issue of these bills to the Bank's private customers during the next few weeks is reflected in a minute dated 19th September 1694,[2] which authorises the making of sealed bills amounting to £20,000 " for the use of the House to be delivered out to such as bring money for them "; and at the same time it was decided with reference to lost bills that " the party making cash thereof and giving security to indemnifie the Bank and bringing the number of the bill shall be paid the money." [3] During the next two years the issue of sealed bills grew enormously, as is shown in the Bank's balance sheet signed by Mercer, and submitted to Parliament on 4th December 1696,[4] which contains as the first item on the Dr. side the following : " To sundry persons for sealed bank bills standing out—£893,800 0s. 0d."

Not one of these bills appears to have been sent to the Exchequer in connection with the loan of £1,200,000 unless an official request for an instalment was forwarded to the Bank by the Lords of the Treasury. Sometimes bills were made by the Bank in expectation of such a request; sometimes they were prepared after the request was received. A large number of these requests are entered in the early minutes. On 19th September 1694, for instance, a letter was read from Henry Guy, the Secretary of the Treasury, containing a request for the payment of £54,738 4s. 7d. into the Exchequer on the following Friday, whereupon the court ordered bills amounting to this sum to be prepared, and decided that if there was any money due to the Bank from the Exchequer, " so many Bank bills " were to be brought back as amounted to the sum due.[5]

---

[1] C. M. B., Lib. A. fol. 20.   [2] *Ibid.*, Lib. A, fol. 62.
[3] *Ibid.*, Lib. A, fol. 58.
For legal discussions with reference to lost Bank bills see *Anonymous* (1698), 1 Ld. Raym., p. 738; *Anonymous* (1699), Holt, p. 118; *Ford* v. *Hopkins* (1701), Holt, p. 119; *Glynn* v. *Bank of England* (1750), 2 Vesey, sen., p. 38.
[4] *C. J., XI*, p. 614.
This balance sheet is given in full in Appendix 23, *infra*.
[5] C. M. B., Lib. A, fols. 61–62.

Until 28th November 1694 the only form of paper credit used by the Bank for these loan instalments to the Government was the sealed bill. On this date, however, the directors resolved that the next instalment of £50,000 was to be paid in running cash notes or sealed bills at the discretion of a special sub-committee of the directors.[1] Early in the following month it was decided that the remainder of the loan (£250,000) was to be paid in notes, bills or " in money."[2] These decisions prove that running cash notes were issued in large numbers on a fiduciary basis within four months of the Bank's foundation.

The Bank's running cash note resembled the goldsmiths' note. Like the latter it was originally a deposit receipt in the form of a promissory note upon which part payments were indorsed; and was, in the first instance, made payable to an individual or bearer on demand. It appears to have been the forerunner of the modern bank note; for two brief periods it carried interest;[3] and with the exception of a few weeks in 1695, when the " lettered notes indented on marbled paper " were circulated, it was issued in its original form until about 1730.

It is probable that the very earliest promissory notes issued by the Bank were entirely written. On 31st July 1694, however, it was decided that they were to be printed and made payable to bearer; on 14th August 1695 it was ordered that they were to be written " and no more printed." There does not appear to be any record in the early Court Minutes stating when the printed notes were again resumed. But the two earliest specimens in the Bank's remarkable collection of paper money are printed, and dated 1699. Even, however, after this date written promissory notes were again issued, for a minute dated 21st August 1700 [4] states

---

[1] C. M. B., Lib. A, fol. 108.
[2] Ibid., Lib. A, fol. 114, 12th December 1694.
As already stated, see Chap. V, p. 149, supra, the very last instalment of the £1,200,000 (£44,335 18s. 9d.) was paid into the Exchequer of Receipt in running cash notes on 19th December 1694.
[3] " Running cash notes with 2d. a day interest to be given in exchange for Bank bills in certain cases." C. M. B., Lib. A, dated 31st July 1695. " All persons who have Running Notes with interest may change the same for Bank bills." Ibid., Lib. B, 24th September 1695. " No interest to be allowed on Running Cash Notes." Ibid., 29th September 1696.
[4] Ibid., Lib. D, fol. 21.

that the cashiers were authorised " to make Bank notes of
their own handwriting on Bank paper payable to order for
any sums and to such known persons as shall desire the same."
It is quite possible, however, as this appears to be the first
reference to such notes payable to order, that up to 1700 only
notes to bearer had been issued, and that, as at this time these
were all printed, the first notes to order were written.

The following is a copy of the better preserved of the two
1699 promissory notes :

[Britannia   *27 Aprill*
  Medallion.]   *J.V.*
No. 104.

    I promise to pay to *Mr Daniell Denny* or Bearer on
demand the Summe of *One hundred and fifty pounds eight
shill and 8d* .... London the *24* day of *January
1699.*

£130. 16. 8. pt £180. 16. 8 Atwill. For the Govr & Comp^a
  19. 12. –   ——————— Slone. of the Bank of England
                                            John [Wase]
  150. 8. 8.

This specimen contains many interesting features. The
entry on the top right-hand corner is probably the date when
the note was finally paid, together with the initials of the
official who made the final payment. The £130 16s. 8d. and
£19 12s. appear to be part payments to persons of the
names of Atwill and Slone. There are no indorsements on
the back of the note. The medallion is of crude design and
was altered on at least three occasions between 1694 and
1702.[1] The sign £ is engraved. In fact, the stages in the
development of the engraving on this part of the bank note
are of peculiar interest. At first only the sign £ was engraved
with no indication of the amount. About 1730 £ with one
figure limited by hyphens appeared, *e.g.* £5=, for £50 to £59
notes. Sum blocks were not introduced until about 1743,

---

[1] A note in the Bank's collection dated 14th May 1700 shows a second
type of medallion containing a figure of Britannia with only three toes.
A third type of medallion appears on a note for £100 dated 17th July
1702.
    The development of the medallion from the earliest type is not clear.
It would, for instance, be interesting to know how the leopard's head, the
crown, and the beehive originated.

and cashiers could still add to the amount in the block until 1809, when the complete note was engraved except the signature.[1]

Another early specimen in the Bank's collection is for £555, dated 19th October 1699, and numbered 47. It shows £131 10s. 1d. paid off four days after it was issued, leaving a balance of £423 9s. 11d. ; a further payment of £360 leaving a balance of £63 9s. 11d. ; and, finally, that also paid. The part payments are all indorsed crosswise on this note, and also on two other early specimens for £63 15s. dated 14th May 1700, and for £239 5s., dated 8th October 1712.

In the earliest days promissory notes [2] were only issued to " known persons," and, as already mentioned,[3] from 1696 to 1759 the minimum value of what appear to have been engraved notes payable to X or bearer was £20. Engraved £10 notes payable to X or bearer became a regular feature of the Bank's issues in 1759, and engraved £5 notes payable to X or bearer in 1793, while from 1797 to 1821, during the period of suspension of cash payments, engraved £1 and £2 notes payable to X or bearer were issued. The Court Minute Books show that the directors decided on 14th August 1696 to fix £20 as the minimum, " no note," it is stated, " to be given under £20 ";[4] but a little later a temporary minimum of £50 was authorised.[5]

It is clear, however, from the minutes that previous to 1696 notes for even less than £5 were issued, and these were probably promissory notes payable to X or bearer. A minute dated 21st October 1696 [6] states that " all notes of £5 and under " were to be " paid off in full every Wednesday beginning with those payable to names of A and B and so on alphabetically." It is, as we have just seen, also clear that

[1] I am much indebted to Mr. T. Zswinger of the Accountant's Bank Note Office, the Bank of England, for his assistance in examining the early forms of paper money preserved in the Bank.
[2] The ordinary promissory note as distinguished from the " lettered note indented on marbled paper." £5 and £10 varieties of the latter were circulated for a short period in 1695. See pp. 163–64, infra.
[3] Chap. II, p. 42, supra.
[4] C. M. B., Lib. B, fol. 155.
[5] Ibid., Lib. B, fol. 168, 23rd Sept. 1696.
[6] Ibid., Lib. B, fol. 172.

even so early as 1700 cashiers had authority to issue written promissory notes payable to order for sums less than £5, and though there is no documentary evidence to show that this was done, it is very probable that such notes were actually issued.

The "accomptable note" was really a type of deposit receipt. The only specimen preserved in the Bank is damaged and worded thus :

London ye 10th June 1697.

Received of *Capt Bas Percy*
forty seaven pounds five shillings
current money
for which I promise to be accountable.
li   For the   [This part and   ]
47 [*5s.* obliterated]   of the   [signature missing.]

On 12th October 1697 it was decided that " Bank notes to be accomptable " issued after this date were to state that the Bank would be " accomptable " for deposits which were to be returnable in the same kind of coin as received.[1] Previous to this these notes were used not only as receipts for deposits of coin but also for tallies,[2] and for " any notes on either of the other banks," [3] while in 1701 they were given for the Bank's own sealed bills.[4]

Early in the eighteenth century a new type was introduced, a note of the following form, " made on Bank paper," in which the Bank promised to be "accomptable " to an individual or bearer.[5]

" Received of .... for which I promise
to be accomptable to him or Bearer on demand
For the Governor and
Comp^a of the Bank of England "
[signature of cashier]

[1] G. M. B.. Lib. C, fol. 34.
[2] *Ibid.*, Lib. B, dated 3rd February 1695. " Bank Notes to be Accomptable to be signed by any 2 cashiers and to be given for tallies discounted up to £10,000 at Mr. Speed's discretion."
[3] *Ibid.*, Lib. B, dated 17th February 1695. The minute referring to this concludes thus : " but that such notes be forthwith sent for and rec^d either in notes of this Comp^a or otherwise."
[4] *Ibid.*, Lib. D, fol. 51, 12th February 1701.
[5] *Ibid.*, Lib. D, fol. 90, 20th August 1701. No specimen survives.

M

The accomptable note was thus a counter receipt for a deposit which might be coin, tallies, goldsmiths' notes or even the Bank's own sealed bills.   When the holder of such a note wished to withdraw a portion of his deposit he drew a demand note or cheque on the bank, and presented this, together with his accomptable note, to one of the cashiers, who indorsed the amount withdrawn on the accomptable note.   But though a new form of this note was decided upon in 1701, its use seems to have declined after the introduction of the Bank's official pass-book in 1696.[1]

The Bank's promissory note payable to X or order was a legally recognised assignable instrument.   The mercantile custom of assigning such promissory notes had, as we have seen, been recognised in the Courts of Common Law in the year preceding the Bank's foundation.   The Bank's promissory note payable to X or bearer, however, was the same type of instrument as the mercantile or goldsmith's note payable to X or bearer, and was, therefore, not legally recognised as assignable until the Act of 1704 [2] made all kinds of promissory notes negotiable.

But it must be remembered that neither cheque nor note was regarded as absolute payment of a debt until honoured,[3] unless, of course, definitely accepted as such.   Moreover, bank notes were not legal tender at this time, and they did not become legal tender, except when offered as payment by the Bank itself, until the reign of William IV.[4]   There is, however, a great deal of evidence which shows that both varieties of bank notes and of the other bankers' notes were regarded by contemporary merchants as cash.   " The notes of goldsmiths," declared Chief Justice Holt in 1698, " whether they be payable to order or bearer, are always accounted by merchants as ready cash and not as bills of exchange " ; [5] and in 1758 Lord Mansfield stated in an important judgment [6] that it had been, and was, the custom to treat " bank notes " as " money, as cash, in the ordinary course and transactions

---

[1] See pp. 168–69, infra.   [2] 3 & 4 Anne, c. 9.

[3] *Vernon* v. *Bouverie* (1682), 2 Show., p. 296; *Cooksay* v. *Bouverie* (1682), ibid., p. 296; *Ward* v. *Evans* (1704), 1 Ld. Raym., p. 928.

[4] 3 & 4 Wm. IV, c. 98, s. 6 (1833).

[5] *Taswell and Lee* v. *Lewis* (1696), 1 Ld. Raym., p. 744.   See also *Ford* v. *Hopkins* (1701), Holt, p. 119.

[6] *Miller* v. *Race*, 1 Burr., p. 452.

of business by the general consent of mankind, which gives them the credit and currency of money to all intents and purposes." "They are," he added, "as much money as guineas themselves are, or any other current coin that is used in common payment as money or cash."

In 1695 the "lettered note indented on marbled paper" was introduced. This innovation, as the early Court Minute Books show, was not only an attempt to improve the running cash note, but was also a deliberate scheme to evade that section of the Act which authorised the issue of sealed bills up to a maximum value of £1,200,000. On 22nd April 1695 a special committee of the directors [1] was appointed to obtain legal advice on the question of borrowing "on their common seale or notes at interest more than £1,200,000 notwithstanding the Act of Parliament." No details of the report of this committee are given in the minutes, but after considering the opinion of the legal advisers the issue of lettered notes was authorised by the directors. A new type of promissory note was thus circulated on a fiduciary basis, and the Bank's paper credit was increased by means of an instrument which was not a sealed bill.

This experiment, however, was not a success. The lettered notes were printed in various denominations ranging from £5 to £100, were made payable to bearer, and were issued from 13th June [2] to 14th August 1695,[3] when, upon notice being given to the directors of a counterfeit specimen, the issue was stopped. On May 1st 1695 [4] it was resolved that these notes, signed by two of the cashiers, were to be of the following form :

We promise to pay to the Bearer of this Indented note the summe of .... pounds on demand. London the .... day of .... 169...
[Signatures of two cashiers] for the Governor and
Company of the Bank of England.[5]

and it was authorised that they were to be issued in the following quantities; 2,000 £5 notes lettered A; 2,000 £10 notes lettered B; 1,000 £20 notes lettered C; 1,000 £30 notes lettered D; 1,000 £40 notes lettered E; 1,000 £50 notes lettered F; and 1,000 £100 notes lettered G.   Six days later it was decided to issue 1,000 £15 notes to be marked with the letter C,[1] the letters of the higher denominations being changed accordingly.   On 5th June [2] the £5 and £10 notes were increased to 3,000 each, and those of £20 to £100 to 1,200 each; and on 13th June [3] a committee was appointed to " deliver out " the notes twice weekly.

Although these totals were printed the actual number issued appears to have been a small one.   This is proved by a special report of Abraham Houblon and Peter Godfrey " touching their proceedings in the business of the Lettered Notes," which was considered by the directors on 19th May 1697.[4]   A large number described as " not delivered into cash " were burnt by Houblon and Godfrey. Those circulated were chiefly £5 notes, and of these 1,800 were issued, together with 700 at £10, 700 at £20, 700 at £50 and 600 at £100, all of which, except three lost ones, were cancelled before the date of this report.

As a result of the monetary stringency caused by the recoinage in 1696 specie notes were issued, and there are many references to these notes in the early Court Minute Books, but, unfortunately, no specimen survives.   They are first mentioned on 23rd June 1696.[5]   " Whoever," states a minute of this date, " shall bring in Guineas or milled money shall have a Note to have the same repaid on demand in the same specie in the following form, viz. :

> Received of A. B., the .... day of .... the sume of .... in milled money (or in Guineas, as the case is) which I promise to repay on demand in the same specie.

Specie notes were thus both receipts and promissory notes. There is no record of their initial minimum value, but very

---

[1] C. M. B., Lib. B, fol. 22.   [2] *Ibid.*, Lib. B, fol. 39.
[3] *Ibid.*, Lib. B, fol. 44.   [4] *Ibid.*, Lib. B, fol. 227.
[5] *Ibid.*, Lib. B, fol. 42.

shortly after they were first issued they were authorised to bear interest at 6 per cent., and to be of a minimum value of £50.[1] Later, however, they were issued for lesser sums, and also with lesser rates of interest, for on 7th July 1697 the following sliding scale of rates was decided upon : £25 to £50 notes $\frac{3}{4}d$. per cent per diem; £50 to £75, $1\frac{1}{2}d$.; £75 to £100, $2\frac{1}{2}d$.; and £100 and upwards, 3d.[2]

The preceding form shows that they were in the first instance gold or silver certificates issued on a 100 per cent. metallic basis. But in 1697 they were given for tallies.[3] and for bills of exchange,[4] and were also issued temporarily without interest[5] in 1698 for " good " goldsmiths' notes.[6] There is evidence to show that in 1701 some were even issued on a fiduciary basis. A minute dated 7th February of that year[7] states that no specie notes were henceforth to be issued unless " money in specie " was actually deposited in the Bank " to answer ye same," but, despite this resolution, five days later the " committee in waiting " was empowered to issue these notes to " such who demand any money of them," and Maddocks, one of the two chief cashiers, was authorised to give them to " any person to whom he directs any money to be paid."[8]

It is interesting to trace in the Court Minutes the various changes in the regulations governing the issue of specie notes. They were, as we have just seen, first discussed by the directors on 23rd June 1696 when the form of the note was decided upon. It appears that between this date and the following 10th November the cashiers were in the habit of making part payments to known holders of specie notes although the actual notes were not presented at the Bank for this purpose. Therefore, on the latter date, the directors decided that " no money be paid hereafter by the Cashiers on Specie Notes without the said notes be first actually brought to the Bank and either delivered up or indorsed upon for what is paid in part."[9] On 2nd December 1696[10]

---

[1] C. M. B., Lib. B., fol. 146.
[2] *Ibid.*, Lib. B, fol. 249.
[3] *Ibid.*, Lib. B, fol. 220, 19th April 1697.
[4] *Ibid.*, Lib. C, fol. 21, 8th September 1697.
[5] *Ibid.*, Lib. B, fol. 250, 14th July 1697.
[6] *Ibid.*, Lib. C, fol. 69, 16th February 1698.
[7] *Ibid.*, Lib. D, fol. 49.
[8] *Ibid.*, Lib. D, fol. 51, 12th February 1701.
[9] *Ibid.*, Lib. B, fol. 178.
[10] *Ibid.*, Lib. B, fol. 188.

" the Proposal to give Specie Notes to such who will give two sufficient securities to repay the same in six months " was " respited to a further time," a proposal which, however, was not again discussed. In April 1697 it was decided that " Specie Notes without interest " were to be issued for " the Tallies on the Annuities transferred to the Land Tax for the present year as far as £300,000; the notes for the first and second £100,000 to be payable at the end of two months commencing from the time the Tallies are brought to the Bank; the notes for the third £100,000 to be payable at the end of three months commencing as aforesaid; and that the same be published in the Hall and in the Gazette." [1]

On 14th July 1697 the court resolved that the sliding scale of interest, which was adopted a week earlier, was only to apply to notes of " the said sums of 25, 50, 75 and 100 li. or upwards," and that no specie notes carrying interest were to be issued for sums " between the said sums " or " under 25 li." On 18th August 1697 [2] it was ordered that after this date holders of notes bearing 6 per cent. interest could not demand separate payment of the interest, and that after the following 1st September the sliding scale of interest was to be replaced by a flat rate of 2d. per cent. per diem, an order which was altered before the end of this month, when only notes " above 100 li." were allowed the 2d. interest.[3] An important minute dated 1st September 1697 [4] shows that on this date it was decided to make these notes " payable at any time not exceeding one year " from the date the note was originally issued. How this rule was enforced is shown in a minute of 15th February 1698,[5] which states that " Mr. Wallinger having kept a Bank Specie note with interest longer than the time limited, viz. from 15th December to 10 February, ordered he be paid interest for the said time at 2d. per diem."

There are a number of curious minutes relating to specie notes which show the progress of the recoinage of 1696–99.

---

[1] C. M. B., Lib. B, fol. 220, 17th April 1697.   [2] Ibid., Lib. C, fol. 15.
[3] Ibid., Lib. C, fol. 29.   [4] Ibid., Lib. C, fol. 19.
[5] Ibid., Lib. C, fol. 152.

On 8th September 1697 [1] the cashiers were forbidden to give specie notes for " new money "; on 22nd December of the same year [2] they were authorised " to continue to take in old money, giving notes to repay it in the same specie at 5s. 2d. per ounce "; and from 19th January 1698 they were to pay, " in new money at demand," all notes " given out for old money." [3]

On 23rd March 1698 Abraham Houblon proposed at the meeting of the court that all specie notes bearing 6 per cent. interest be " paid off." [4]   This proposal was submitted for the consideration of the Bank's legal adviser,[5] who was evidently of opinion that this could safely be done, for on 14th September 1698 it was decided that " persons possessed of notes at 6 per cent. dated on or before 31 May 1697 " must " bring them in and receive their money before 15 December, or else exchange them for Bank Sealed Bills at 2d. per diem interest payable on demand, for after 15 December interest is to cease on such Bank notes." [6]

The calling in of the notes continued throughout 1699. On 22nd February it was " ordered that all persons possessed of the remainder of the Bank Specie Notes with interest, which are dated July, August, and September 1697, bring in the said Notes into the Bank and receive their money on or before the tenth day of May next or exchange them for Bank Sealed Bills at 2d. per diem interest payable at demand, for after the said tenth May interest is to cease on the said Notes." [7]   This order shows that the twelve months rule did not apply to these particular issues.

The original issues appear to have all been called in and cancelled during 1699, for there is no further reference to specie notes in the minutes after 22nd November of this year until 5th February 1701, when they were again issued on a 100 per cent. metallic basis, each £100 note to carry interest at 3d. per cent. per diem " for any time not exceeding six months." [8]   Before the end of this month, however, they were, as already stated, issued on a fiduciary basis.   The

[1] C. M. B., *Ibid.*, Lib. C, fol. 21.   [2] *Ibid.*, Lib. C, fol. 55.
[3] *Ibid.*, Lib. C, fol. 63.   [4] *Ibid.*, Lib. C, fol. 76.
[5] *Ibid.*, Lib. C, fol. 76.   [6] *Ibid.*, Lib. C, fol. 119.
[7] *Ibid.*, Lib. C, fol. 153.   [8] *Ibid.*, Lib. D, fols. 48–49.

interest-bearing notes thus issued for a maximum period of six months were accepted in August 1701, and sealed bills bearing 2d. per cent. per diem interest were given in exchange.[1] After 1701 no further issues of specie notes were made.

It is thus evident that specie notes when presented for payment were, like the ordinary running cash or promissory notes, often paid in part, and that in the first instance the interest was paid separately. The Bank kept " a considerable sum constantly in cash to answer ye specie notes ";[2] and as they were frequently given for deposits of guineas, and therefore in such cases only payable in guineas, they were sometimes termed " guinea notes." Although made payable to an individual only, specie notes appear to have been transferable, apparently by indorsement. This is shown in a curious minute dated 11th August 1697 [3] in which it is stated that three specie and a number of running cash notes held by a person named Smee were burnt in a baker's furnace, the holder petitioning the Bank to have them replaced.[4] The burnt specie notes were for £195 17s., payable to Smee; £107 10s. payable to William Smaldridge; and £30 payable to Jonathan Smart. Large numbers of specie notes were called in during the year 1698, and when presented, either both principal and interest were paid in full, or sealed bills bearing 2d. per cent. per diem interest were given in exchange.[5]

It will be remembered that in the very first meeting of the directors the second method of " giving receipts for running cash " decided upon was the keeping of " an Accompt with ye creditor in a Book or Paper of his owne," which, however, appears to have been supplied originally by the customer himself, for it was not until November 1696 that the Bank

[1] C. M. B., Lib. D, fol. 87.
[2] Ibid., Lib. B, fol. 160.
  According to the report of Sir John Bolles presented to Parliament on 10th December 1696, the Bank on 10th November of the same year had £68,669 6s. 1d. outstanding on specie notes, which carried interest " if for 20 l. or upwards " at 6 per cent., about one-third of this total representing notes of less than £20 in value.   C. J., XI., p. 621.
[3] C. M. B., Lib. C, fol. 7.
[4] Smee was given new notes " upon his giving two sufficient securities to indemnifie the Bank." Ibid., Lib. C, fol. 7.
[5] Ibid., Lib. C, fols. 76, 112, 119, 135, 146 and 153.

offered to provide its customers with what were termed " private " books.[1] This innovation was the result òf complaints made about the " inconveniences happening to Trade by the want of small bank notes to pass in ordinary payments," and of the " mischiefes occasioned by counterfeit notes." [2] . Therefore the directors authorised that those who kept their " Acco^{ts} with the Bank " should " have liberty to transfer any sums from one Acco^t to another not under 5 li. ; " that the person so transferring must keep ". a private Book of his own wherein the cashier from time to time shall write down the sums so written off from one Acco^t and carried to another ; " and " that both sides of the said Book be cast up and sett downe at every payment and receipt." A few days later it was announced that these books were " ready to be delivered at the Bank to all persons desiring the same." [3]

The Bank's desire to remedy these " inconveniences happening to trade ." [4] is also clearly reflected in a number of interesting minutes of December 1697 and January 1698,[5] a series of minutes which throws a great deal òf light on the Bank's early cheque system. On the 9th of the former month the directors referred the question of " a drawing account for the accommodation of merchants " for the consideration of a special committee. This committee sent in its report on the 29th of the same month, but as "; several gentlemen

[1] C. M. B., Lib. B, fol. 183, 20th November 1696.
[2] Ibid.   [3] Ibid., Lib. B, fol. 183, 25th November 1696.
[4] Some of the pamphleteers of the day were severe critics of the Bank from the standpoint of its relations with traders. " A merchant of London," who gives details of the establishment, the constitution, the privileges and the restrictions of the Bank in his Remarks upon the Bank of England with regard more especially to our Trade and Government (1705), concludes that the Bank was injurious to trade. . The anonymous writers of A Short View of the apparent Dangers and Mischiefs from the Bank of England (1707); Arguments against Prolonging the Bank (1708); and Some Considerations ordered against the continuance of the Bank of England (undated), also arrive at the same conclusion, which was based on the fallacy that because money was deposited in the Bank it was withdrawn from trade. " Money'd men," writes the author of Arguments against Prolonging the Bank, " who used to employ their spare Money in Home Traffic and in carrying on Manufactures . . . throw most of their cash into the Bank." For lists of contemporary pamphlets relating to the Bank see T. A. Stephens, A Contribution to the Bibliography of the Bank of England (1897); and H. D. Macleod, A Dictionary of Political Economy (1863), pp. 152–57.
[5] C. M. B., Lib. C, fols. 56, 59, 61, 62, 63.

of the court " were absent on this day, no resolution concerning it was passed by the directors present. On 12th January 1698 the report was again considered, and it was unanimously decided to appoint a special cashier for entering in " a distinct cash book " the transactions of " all persons that shall keep a drawing account."   A " particular ledger " and a " waste ledger " were also to be kept for the accounts of such customers, and the cashiers were authorised " to pay or discharge " the customer's " drawn note at the sight thereof (so far as the drawer has creditt) and not suffer any person to carry away such note with a promise of payment."

When a customer began to " draw on the Bank " he was required " to enter his name and sett his seale in an Alphabet for that purpose with his additions and habitacon," and all notes drawn were to be " numbered, signed and sealed by y[e] Drawer."   As an additional attraction it was also decided in the same meeting to discount at $4\frac{1}{2}$ per cent. foreign bills up to a maximum of £5,000 to each customer ; to accept as cash sealed bills up to £1,000 from each customer ; and that the regulations with reference to " the drawing account " were " to be put in practise and observed for the accommodation of those who by approbacon in writing of the 3 Directors in Waiting, or any 3 other Directors, should keep their cash with the Bank by a Drawing Acco[t]." [1]

It will thus be seen that though originally intended for the " accommodation " of merchants, customers other than merchants were allowed to make use of " drawn notes, sealed " as they are termed in the Court Minutes.   At first the sealing of these demand notes, or cheques, was rigidly enforced, for just a week after the preceding regulations were authorised " the question was putt whether ye drawer should putt his seale to the notes drawn," and this " passed in ye affirmative." [2]   After a few weeks, however, the rule with reference to sealing was relaxed.   A minute dated 16th February 1698 [3] states that the directors, having considered a recommendation for the abolition of the sealing of " drawn notes " from a special committee, which they had appointed

[1] For a full copy of these resolutions see Appendix 22, *infra.*
[2] C. M. B., Lib. C, fol. 63, 19th January 1698.
[3] *Ibid.*, Lib. C, fol. 69.

to " treat " with merchants [1] about keeping accounts with the Bank, decided that the sealing of these notes be dispensed with as regards " such as are not willing to seal the same."

While the Bank was thus regularly issuing its sealed bills and promissory notes, experimenting with other types of notes, transferring accounts, and cashing its customers' " drawn notes," it was also conducting fairly extensive transactions in goldsmiths' notes; and, as we have seen, one of its cashiers had, within twelve days of the sealing of the charter, been made responsible for this side of the Bank's business. Early in 1695, the directors decided that " the receiving of goldsmiths' notes proceed on the same method as is now used," the Bank only accepting them at " the hazard " of the persons who offered them; that all such notes thus offered were to be sent out each day to be cashed by the bankers who had issued them; that the Bank's tellers were to supply the cashier responsible with a daily list of the issuers who had refused or even delayed payment; and that " if there be more notes on any goldsmith than any one teller can receive," two or more of these officials were to act as collectors,[2] a decision which shows that within seven months of the Bank's foundation there was a brisk business in these notes. Further evidence of the extent of these transactions is shown by the appointment, a fortnight after the preceding resolutions were passed, of a special committee to draw up an account of " the goldsmiths' notes standing out on cash." [3]

Owing to the general antagonism of the goldsmith bankers, of whom Duncombe was the most vindictive, the attitude

[1] That the directors fully realised the importance of encouraging trade is also shown in their relations with the new East India Company. On more than one occasion this company was given permission to overdraw—once up to a maximum of £30,000—and it secured several large loans usually on the joint securities of three or four of the Bank's directors. *Ibid.*, Lib. D, fols. 97 and 112.

A quaint minute with reference to overdrafts is worth quoting in full. It reads thus : " Ordered that if any person keeping his Cash in the Bank shall hereafter chance to overdraw, the Directors in waiting shall be made acquainted therewith by the Cashiers and their advice taken before the Bill of such person be refused. And in case the Committee [in waiting] be not present the Cashiers are to desire the person privately to have a little patience till the Committee come." *Ibid.*, Lib. C, fol. 119. 13th September 1699. [2] C. M. B., Lib. A, fol. 136, 12th January 1695.
[3] *Ibid.*, Lib. A, fol. 147, 26th January 1695.

of the Bank with reference to these notes was a cautious one. It is true that, like the goldsmith banker, the Bank was in its early days a keeper of pawns,[1] but there is no evidence to show that previous to 1700 it functioned as a special bank to the other bankers of the day. On the other hand, it does not appear to have made any deliberate attempt to injure the private banking of the goldsmiths. Indeed, there is a great deal of evidence which shows its tolerance in this respect. From the outset it accepted goldsmiths' notes that were immediately met by their issuers,[2] and during its first seven years it allowed its cashiers to give accomptable notes, specie notes without interest, and even ready money for " good " goldsmiths' notes. Apparently the Bank had also occasionally paid such notes to the Exchequer, for a minute dated 10th May 1699 states that the tellers of the Exchequer of Receipt were forbidden from this date to receive any goldsmiths' notes " among the money they received from the Bank." [3]

The Bank's connection with the other bankers was in this way a close one. Its tellers were constantly visiting the shops of the goldsmiths for the purpose of presenting the notes accepted by the Bank and collecting the cash. But there were also other connections. The surviving ledgers of the Child and the Hoare of the day show that these two goldsmith bankers were frequently discounting the Bank's sealed bills and promissory notes.[4] Furthermore, the Bank as a keeper of pawns, sometimes accepted as securities for loans jewels in the custody of a goldsmith banker. An instance of this is revealed in a minute of December 1694, which shows that on the 12th of this month the Bank advanced £4,000 on two " parcels " of jewels, one of which was allowed to remain in the custody of Sir Francis Child.[5]

---

[1] The credit side of the statement presented by Mercer to Parliament on 4th December 1696 shows on the preceding 10th November £266,610 17s. 0d. " by Mortgages, Pawns, other securities and Cash." C. J., XI, p. 614.

[2] Later, however, the Bank appears in certain instances to have relaxed this rule. Mercer's statement shows that on 10th November 1696 the Bank held £5,636 14s. 1d. in goldsmiths' notes. Ibid.

[3] C. M. B., Lib. C, fol. 74.

[4] E.g. from one of Messrs. Hoare's early ledgers : " December 24th 1696, By Bank Bill of £250 at 17½ per cent. discount.........£206 5s.," " June 24th 1697, By a Bank note discounted at 15 per cent..........£85."

[5] C. M. B., Lib. A, fols. 114-15.

Although the Bank in its very early days functioned as a pawnbroker,[1] it does not appear to have been very active in this respect. There are, however, in the earliest Court Minute Books several references to pawnbroking transactions. The first of these occurs in a minute dated 24th October 1694,[2] which shows that £4,000 was advanced to a customer for three months at 5 per cent. on " a pawne of coffee to the reall value of 6,000 li." Between this date and the end of the year there are further instances of such loans, the securities being tin, iron, copper and jewels.

Pawnbroking, as a regular feature of the Bank's business, appears to have been soon discontinued. A minute dated 9th January 1695[3] states that the directors decided to establish a " lumbard " for lending money on small pawns, and that they appointed a sub-committee[4] to prepare the necessary details. These details were duly placed before the court a week later, but there is no record to show that the project was carried out.

While the Bank's pawnbroking business thus declined and its transactions with the goldsmith bankers increased in volume, an important administrative feature was gradually developed. This was the delegation of certain responsibilities to special court committees, of which the most important was the " committee in waiting," or weekly committee. This committee commenced to function as soon as the Bank did; it exercised a general responsibility over the whole of the Bank's business; it was always available; its personnel was changed each week; and it was a valuable medium through which all the directors acquired first-hand experience of the Bank's transactions.

The committee in waiting was directly responsible for the issues of the various kinds of paper money; for the safe custody of tallies and other securities; for the various advances made to the Exchequer; and for the discounting of both inland and foreign bills of exchange. Its importance

[1] It is interesting to note that under its by-laws the Bank can still, if it so desires, take pawns.
[2] C. M. B., Lib. A, fol. 84.
[3] *Ibid.*, Lib. A, fol. 134.
[4] The members were Sir William Scawen, Sir Thomas Abney, Sir James Houblon, and Messrs Tench, Janssen and Goddard.

is shown by the fact that after it had functioned for three months the court decided that no customer should be allowed to receive from the Bank a running cash note, a sealed bill, or a bill of exchange except by its order.[1]   A little later it was decided that " tallies, bills and notes " could only be discounted before twelve noon, and after they had been submitted for the consideration of this committee.

For dealing with special transactions other committees were set up.   Such were the " committee of remittances," the " committee to attend ye Treasury or Exchequer," and the committee for supervising the transactions with the goldsmith bankers.   The first-named, whose major operations will be dealt with in detail a little later,[2] is first mentioned in a minute of 29th September 1694,[3] which shows that on this date it was empowered to negotiate with the Lords of the Treasury about the financing of the campaign in Flanders.

These committees soon increased in number, and, like the development of the various departments, are cogent proof of the rapid growth of the Bank's business.   Evidence of the great importance attached by the directors to this system of administrative committees is contained in the minutes of 27th October 1697.[4]   On this date the court " took into its consideration the severall committees formerly appointed " for the purpose of " making a new establishment thereof." As a result the following regular committees, in addition to the committee in waiting, were decided upon, together with their times of meeting : the " Committee of Accompts " (8), Friday, 9 a.m.; the " Committee for the Cash and Tallies " (9), Wednesday, 4 p.m.; the " Committee for the House and Servants " (6), Thursday, 9 a.m.; the " Committee to attend ye Treasury or Exchequer " (14), Wednesday, one hour before the meeting of the court; the " Committee for Bullion " (9), Wednesday, 4 p.m.; the " Committee to consult Councill " (5), Wednesday, one hour before the meeting of the court.   It was also ordered that the proceedings of these committees be entered " into a fair book to be laid on the table every Wednesday morning " for the inspection of the members of the court.

[1] C. M. B., Lib. A, fol. 129, 2nd January 1695.
[2] See Chap. VII, pp. 182–87, infra.
[3] C. M. B., Lib. A, fol. 71.   [4] Ibid., Lib. C, fols. 41–43.

Thus did the early directors of the Bank of England receive valuable experience in the hard school of banking technique. Mistakes, due mainly to the prevailing evil methods of public finance, were, of course, made, but the courage, integrity and sense of responsibility of the directors outweighed these natural initial errors. " The Bank," declares a shrewd contemporary critic,[1] " was esteem'd a secure Repository not only upon account of the Credit it had always had and preserv'd from its first Opening but also for the great Reputation of the Managers of it." " I think," writes Rogers,[2] " Macaulay over-rated the political genius of William the Third, great as it was. I think he over-rated the financial genius of Montague, great as it was. I think he might have given greater credit to those honest, God-fearing, patriotic men who really founded the Bank of England, watched over its early troubles, relieved it, by the highest shrewdness and fidelity, from the perils it incurred, and established the reputation of British integrity."

It was under such guardianship that the Bank survived, despite the fact that it was launched in an age of financial chaos, of war, of bad harvests, of deplorable coinage conditions, of " golden " lotteries, of rival banking projects, of " bubble " companies, of Tory antagonism, and of Jacobite " art and artifice." By the end of its sixth year it was quite evident that its foundation was well and truly laid. Its notes, though now largely issued on a fiduciary basis, passed freely from hand to hand as cash ; its business had increased enormously ; its departments and committees of management had been properly established and were functioning smoothly ; its official pass-books, the system of transferring accounts, and its customers' demand notes were in common use ; in short, it had become indispensable to the Government, to the City, and to the traders of the day.

In the meantime it had also more than justified its establishment by carrying out, in connection with the war against France, financial operations of the first magnitude, and to these we must next turn.

---

[1] *The Arguments and Reasons for and against Engrafting upon the Bank of England with Tallies* (1697), p.6.
[2] *First Nine Years of the Bank of England*, preface, p. xii.

CHAPTER VII

THE EARLY TRANSACTIONS OF THE BANK OF ENGLAND (*continued*)

" For as to the credit in the Exchequer, how that will succeed no man can answer, only I assure you no pains shall be wanting to establish it. And to show the King that though these gentlemen [of the National Land Bank] have failed him, there is yet some hope, and that the Bank of England is still devoted to him under all the discouragement they have met with, they do by this post give Mr. Hill credit for one million florins."

Montague, Chancellor of the Exchequer, to Blathwayt, Secretary at War, dated 5th June 1696. B.M., Addit. MS., 34355.

THE surviving Treasury Minute Books of the last six years of the seventeenth century [1] show that there was, during this period, a particularly close personal relationship between the Lords of the Treasury and the directors of the Bank of England. There were many important consultations with reference to the problems of national finance, the directors making frequent visits, either of their own accord or by special request, to the Treasury Chambers in Whitehall, and to the Cockpit where the new Treasury Office was established after the original headquarters were destroyed by fire early in January 1697.

Some curious and interesting information is to be found among these valuable records. A minute, for instance, dated 17th April 1695 [2] shows that the Lords of the Treasury resolved on this day to invite " the Gentlemen of the Bank " to visit the Treasury on the following day in order to inform

---

[1] P.R.O., Recs. T., T. 29/8–11, dated 1695–1700; and T. 29/627, which contains excerpts relating to the period 1694–1700 taken from the actual minute books.

The Treasury Minute Books from 1690 to 1694 are missing. The first of the surviving books (T. 29/8) appertaining to the last decade of the seventeenth century was commenced on 12th April 1695 and finished on 11th September 1696. Thus there is no Treasury record of the Bank's relations with the Lords of the Treasury for the period 27th July 1694 to 12th April 1695. At the time of writing (1929) these books are not calendared.

[2] *Ibid.*, Recs. T., T. 29/8, fols. 5–6.

them that the King was " extremely dissatisfied " that their bills, " to the great Hazard of the Army," were " not answered " in Holland. This, of course, is a reference to the remittances for carrying on the war against France, and was the result of a special report from Hill, the Deputy Paymaster of the army in the Low Countries. In response to this invitation the Governor, Deputy Governor, and a number of the directors visited the Treasury on 18th April, when Hill's report was discussed; but they had every confidence in their bills, and reassured the Lords of the Treasury that " the next post " would bring " a better account of the answering their bills in Holland." [1] A minute dated 11th June 1695 [2] throws new light on the expeditious way in which the Bank paid into the Exchequer the initial loan of £1,200,000. It states that Sir John Houblon and " some of the directors " were " called in " to be informed that the Lords of the Treasury had decided to pay the Bank £6,876 15s. 4d. " for advancing and paying the Exchequer 900,000 li., being the last part of their Subscription Money, sooner than the days that were prescribed for the payment thereof by the Commissioners of the Bank." A minute dated 28th October 1696 [3] shows that in response to a special invitation from the Lords of the Treasury Sir William Scawen and " other gentlemen of the Bank " visited the Treasury on this date, and that Sir William, on behalf of his fellow directors, suggested the following " methods of raising the credit " : (1) " Increasing the species," (2) " Hastening the Coinage," (3) " The Parliament going on vigorously towards making good the deficiencies," (4) " Lessening the discount of Talleys." Three days later another delegation from the Bank to the Treasury, headed by Sir William Scawen, added three further proposals to the preceding : (1) " That there be no other Bank but the Bank of England," (2) " That ye said Bank be continued for four years beyond ye present time (about nine years to come) but redeemable by Parliament," (3) " That some way

---

[1] P.R.O., Recs. T., T. 29/9, fol. 7.
[2] *Ibid.*, T. 29/627, fol. 11.
[3] *Ibid.*, T. 29/9, fol. 29.

N

be found out to supply the Bank speedily with a considerable sum of present money." [1]

These minutes are also evidence of the use made of both Bank and Exchequer bills in financing the war. On 18th December 1696,[2] for example, it was ordered by the Lords of the Treasury that all Bank bills in the Exchequer of Receipt were to be immediately issued to the Earl of Ranelagh, the Army Paymaster, for raising money thereon in order to pay " Mr. Eyles in discharge of Mons. Schulenburgh's bills for subsistence in Flanders." A later minute [3] shows that on 11th May 1697 the Treasury issued £4,500 in Exchequer bills to Ranelagh " to be by him paid over to Mr. Francis Eyles in satisfaction of the loss or discount at the Rate of £15 p. cent. on tallies and orders for £30,000 charged on the Ayd of 3s. p. £. which he accepted for Bills of Exchange to Flanders at 11 guilders to the £. for subsistence there."

Francis Eyles,[4] referred to in the preceding minutes, whose transactions are sometimes referred to as " Eyles & Compa," appears to have been heavily concerned in the business of remittances to Flanders. " Mr. Eyles," states a minute of 5th July 1696, " will immediately give bills for £30,000 to Lord Ranelagh to send to Holland by this night's post . . . and he is to have a tally . . . transferable to ye next ayd for ye 30 m[li]." [5]   Other Englishmen also figure very prominently in these transactions, particularly Sir Joseph Herne, but for whose credit to the Ordnance Department the soldiers of the English ammunition train in Flanders would have received no rations, stores, or ammunition during the winter which preceded the successful siege of Namur,[6] Sir Stephen Evans, and Duncombe. Evans and Herne also remitted large sums to Leghorn and Genoa for the operations in Savoy,[7] and, like Duncombe, made many direct loans to the Government at home.[8]   The Treasury

[1] P.R.O., Recs. T., T. 29/9, fol. 31.
[2] Ibid., T. 29/627, fol. 17.   [3] Ibid., T. 29/627, fol. 20.
[4] Afterwards Sir Francis. He was elected a director of the Bank of England in 1697. See J. Francis, History of the Bank of England, II, p. 362.
[5] P.R.O., Recs. T., T. 29/9, fol. 54.
[6] Cal. T.P., 1557–1696, p. 424.
[7] P.R.O., Recs. T., T. 29/627, fols. 2, 8; T. 29/9, fol. 1.
[8] Ibid., T. 29/627, passim.

Minute Books show that the part played by Solomon de Medina, and other foreign merchants resident in England, in financing William III's campaign was not an important one. Most of the exchange operations in this connection were carried out by the Bank of England, and by private English financiers; and the Bank's Court Minute Books prove that the directors also remitted large sums to Savoy,[1] and to the English fleet, particularly that part under the command of Admiral Russell.[2]

Indeed, the Bank was so heavily involved in the " business of remises," as it is usually termed in the Court Minutes, that the directors reported to the Treasury in 1696 that they had " extreamly strained themselves."[3] These transactions were, as we have seen, carried out under the personal supervision of a special committee of the directors, " the committee of remittances," some of whose members were sent overseas to manage " ye House at Antwerp," the Bank's headquarters in the Low Countries.

Even, however, before the arrival in Antwerp of these specially selected members of the directorate the Bank had, as early as October 1694, employed in this city a special exchange agent, Jacobus de Koning. A minute dated 8th of this month [4] states that credit for £84,188 was given to Ranelagh together with " a bill of £64,000 at 25 days sight," and that de Koning was " the person employed therein." Continental business, however, had increased so much during the next seven months that a most important development occurred, interesting particulars of which are given in an unusually detailed court minute, dated 15th May 1695.[5] Six of the directors—" the gentlemen who are to go over "— were " nominated, constituted, and appointed to be a sub-committee in any of the Territories of the Allies of the King of Great Britain"; and were authorised " to performe and

---

[1] C. M. B., Lib. A, fol. 175; Lib. B, fol. 4.
[2] *Ibid.*, Lib. A, fol. 175, 6th March 1695—" 80,000 l. to be furnished to Admiral Russell 40,000 l. presently and 40,000 l. soon after . . ., the 80,000 l. to Russell at 4 shillings and 9 pence and the Savoy Money if it be on the 2nd years Customs to be remitted at 64 pence and if on the 3rd years Customs at 65 pence."
[3] P.R.O., Recs. T., T. 29/8, fol. 375.
[4] C. M. B., Lib. A, fol. 76.
[5] *Ibid.*, Lib. B, fols. 25–27.

execute in those parts the affairs and business of the Governor and Company, and to transact and negotiate Bills of Exchange, and to receive and pay monies and to give notes for the same, and there to trade and deal in Bullion, Gold and Silver, and to constitute and appoint Correspondents and Factors, Officers, and Servants, and generally to doe, fulfill and performe all and every other matters and things in the name and for and on behalfe of the said Governor and Company."

Thus was established " ye House at Antwerp," an agency, which, as some of the directors announced later, cost nearly £16,000 per annum to maintain.[1] The "gentlemen in charge " were changed from time to time, and there were frequently at least four directors in residence there. Those first appointed claimed " one third of all clear profits of all the Remittances for all places and also of the bullion besides the ½ per cent. to De Koning." The court, however, refused to grant this, and directed that they should receive " one per cent. on the remises for such moneys only as are for the supply of the army in Flanders upon which amount they to beare all charges and the Bank to allow them over and above the same moneys ½ per cent. as they did to Mr. de Koning." [2]

The establishment of a similar agency in Amsterdam was contemplated in the early part of 1695. But on the 26th June of that year the court rejected the proposition to establish in this town " a Bank for current money," [3] because, among other things, it was not satisfied that the directors in Holland, " being but four persons," could carry on " soe weighty a concerne in two distant places at one time," or that it could safely employ any persons in Amsterdam " to deliver out notes."

The Bank, however, had agents in various other European towns, and though the first of its continental representatives was an Antwerpian broker, there is, with the exception of the two Italian mercantile houses which were its agents at Genoa, no further reference in the Court Minutes relating to the period 1694–1700 to the appointment of any foreigner

[1] B.M., Harl. M.S., 7421, fol. 15.
[2] C. M. B., Lib. B, fol. 25–27.
[3] C. M. B., Lib. B, fol. 47.

or foreign firm as an overseas agent. In addition to Antwerp and Genoa the chief continental centres of the day, such as Cadiz, Madrid, Lisbon, Oporto, Venice, Leghorn, Hamburg, Rotterdam and Amsterdam possessed Bank of England " correspondents beyond the sea," [1] as these representatives were usually termed; and there is a great deal of evidence to show that they were selected by the directors with the greatest care.

Thus, after the establishment of " ye House at Antwerp," with the exception of the Genoese firms of Battista and Richieri & Co. and Gasper and Bussiere & Co.,[2] all the Bank's continental agents during the earliest and most momentous years of its history were either individual Englishmen or English commercial firms established over-seas; [3] and it is definitely laid down in the minutes that Englishmen were in this respect "to be preferred to strangers." [4] A minute dated 27th March 1695 illustrates the method of selection. It shows that new " correspondents " at Leghorn, Messrs. Rigby and Sheppard & Co., were on this date elected at a court meeting by ballot, and that before this firm was formally appointed it had to guarantee a security amounting to £20,000. " Alexander Rigby," we are told, " being called in delivers in the names of his security. And the same were approved by the Court to the sums following : Thomas Coulson for £3,000; Thomas Sheppard £3,000; Fra. Baynton £2,000; Richard Blacken £2,000; Gab. Roberts £2,000; William Cony £2,000; Rog. Drake £2,000; Rich. Rigby £2,000; Maj. Long £2,000. Ordered that Mr. Rigby give his bond with each of the said persons to the several sums aforesaid." [5]

There are many references in the early minutes to the most important of the Bank's continental agencies, the " weighty

[1] *Eg.* C. M. B., Lib. A, fol. 165; Lib. B, fol. 10; Lib. B, fol. 150.
[2] *Ibid.*, Lib. B, fol. 10.
[3] At Venice, for example, the agents between 1694 and 1700 were Messrs. Thomas Williams & Co.; at Madrid, Messrs. Ballard, Stone & Co.; at Lisbon, Messrs. James and Josiah Milner; at Cadiz, Messrs. Hodges, Haines and Terrill; at Leghorn, Messrs. Western, Burdett & Co., who were succeeded by Messrs. Rigby and Sheppard & Co.; at Oporto, Messrs. Houblon, Harris and Pile; at Hamburg, Mr. Francis Stratford. C. M. B., Lib. A, fols. 177–178.
[4] *Ibid.*, Lib. A, fol. 165.   [5] *Ibid.*, Lib. B, fol. 2.

concerne " at Antwerp, which throw a great deal of light on
the financial activities of the Bank's representatives in the
Low Countries. A minute of June 1695 [1] states that the
" directors att Antwerpe " proposed " to lay out 8 or 10,000
li. for the raising of guineas beyond sea "; but the court was
of opinion that this would not be " for the service of the
Bank." Evidence of the heavy expenses of " ye House at
Antwerp " is contained in a minute dated 18th September
1695,[2] which shows that the directors considered the problem
of continuing " the correspondence concerning Remises "
at Antwerp and at Amsterdam " without the continuance
of ye Directors at Antwerp." It was, however, regarded
as unsafe to withdraw all the directors, for it was decided
that Sir James Houblon should remain at Antwerp until
" some other directors go over."

The procedure with reference to the remittances to
Holland and the raising of loans overseas is of much interest.
Several sums appear to have been borrowed in Holland which
were included under the title of " remises," [3] tallies being
deposited as securities for the money thus raised with the
Dutch ambassador in London.[4] Metallic money and bullion
were also sent over. " Mr. Deputy," states a minute of
21st November 1694,[5] " reports the shipping of 7,000 odd
hundreds pounds to Holland by the Committee of Remittances on board the Province of Utrecht." The greater
part, however, of the transactions were carried out by
means of bills of exchange.[6]

Indeed, a great deal of the Bank's earliest business was

[1] C. M. B., Lib. B, fol. 46–47.   [2] Ibid., Lib. B, fol. 69.
[3] B.M., Harl. MS., 7421, " A Copy of ye Earl of Ranelagh's Report."
[4] C. M. B., Lib. B, fol. 74, dated 11th October 1695. '. Ordered that
this Court do conclude to deposit Tallys with the Dutch Ambassador for
whatsoever monies the Directors shall take up at Interest in Holland and
that Sir James Houblon be acquainted therewith." See C. J., XI, p. 614.
[5] C. M. B., Lib. A, fol. 102.
On 2nd February 1695 the directors were allowed to export silver to
Holland " not exceeding 10,000 l. in any one man of war." Ibid., Lib. A,
fol. 152.
[6] A frequent method was the granting of credit to Ranelagh up to a
certain maximum, and allowing him to draw bills on the Bank up to the
total granted. Bills were also drawn in this way by Hill up to a specified
sum. Eg. " several bills being drawn on the Bank by Mr. Hill to value of
£1,700 the court approve of their acceptance." C. M. B., Lib. A, fols.
65–66, dated 21st November 1694.

concerned with the "remises." The Court Minute Books show that as early as 29th September 1694 a "message" from the Treasury requesting the directors to undertake the remittance of "the money for the Army in Flanders" was considered by the court, "which message being debated" a special committee was appointed "to consider the same and report their opinion to the court." [1] On 2nd October this committee presented a report, which recommended that "the Bank may safely make the Lords [of the Treasury] a proposall to remit the money for Flanders without any hazard from the Act of Parliament or otherwise." [2]

At the next meeting of the directors the special "committee of remittances," whose members were Sir John Houblon, Sir John Huband, and Messrs Ward, Bateman, Knight, Sedgwick and Janssen,[3] was authorised "to treat with the Lords of the Treasury about supplying the Land Forces in Flanders for six weekes with any sum not exceeding £200,000 in the best manner they could for the advantage of the Bank." [4] On 8th October the Deputy Governor, Godfrey, reported to the court that the committee had agreed with the Treasury Lords to remit "the money for the use of the army so far as £200,000 at 10 Gilders 6 S$_{tiv}$ers, for part of which credit is to be furnished to-morrow." [5] Two days later the committee was allowed "to call such of the directors to their assistance as they think fit and to use their names if they see cause "; to have "money or Bank bills to answer the value of the sum remitted"; and "to have power to buy Bullion for the account of the Compa, and to export the same at the Compa's hazard." [6]

Thus within ten weeks of its foundation, and before it had paid to the Government the final instalments of its original loan of £1,200,000, the Bank had commenced to remit large sums overseas. On 14th November the maximum

[1] C. M. B., Lib. A, fol. 71.　　　　[2] Ibid., Lib. A, fol. 73.
[3] Ibid., Lib. A, fol. 74.　　　　　[4] Ibid., Lib. A, fol. 74.
[5] Ibid., Lib. A, fol. 75.
　A credit of £84,188 was, as already stated, given Ranelagh on 8th October together with "a bill of 64,000 li. at 25 days sight." This is the first reference to the Army Paymaster in the Low Countries in the Court Minute Books. Ibid., Lib. A, fol. 76.
[6] Ibid., Lib. A, fol. 78, 10th October 1694.

of £200,000 was increased to £250,000, the committee responsible being empowered " to remit over and above ye sum formerly agreed to the value of £50,000." [1]

Between 14th November and the end of the year 1694 there were several other big transactions in the " business of remises." On 21st November another £94,000 was authorised to be remitted " at the same rate as the other money "; [2] and on the same date the Deputy Governor reported the shipping of the " 7,000 odd hundreds pounds to Holland " by the " Province of Utrecht." A little later the committee of remittances was allowed to import from Calais, " on board any of the Men of Warr," foreign silver " not exceeding 50,000 li. in the whole and not exceeding 8,000 li. in any one ship." On 26th December it was allowed " to proceed further in remitting the King's money not exceeding 100,000 li." [3]; and on 2nd February 1695, although Ranelagh had been granted credit " over and above the sum limited by the court to the value of 20,000 li.," it was " approved and ordered " by the court that the committee " have liberty to give Ranelagh further credit up to 40,000 li." [4]

When it is recalled that at the time the last of these grants of credit was made the Bank had not completed its first seven months, and that it had advanced to the Government before 6th February 1695 not only the whole of its original capital of £1,200,000, but also a further sum of £300,000, these early remittances overseas were remarkable transactions. But there were even bigger remittances to follow within the next eighteen months, and four of these, all of which were remittances to Holland, are examined in great detail in a special report prepared by Ranelagh [5] at the request of the Lords of the Treasury.[6] Meanwhile, however, as already stated, large sums were also remitted by the Bank to Savoy, and for the use of the fleet.[7]

---

[1] C. M. B., Lib. A, fol. 99.   [2] *Ibid.*, Lib. A, fol. 65.
[3] *Ibid.*, Lib. A, fol. 125.   [4] *Ibid,.* Lib. A, fol. 151.
[5] B. M., Harl. MS., 7421.   [6] P.R.O., Recs. T., T. 29/9, fol. 5.
[7] These remittances were part of the loan of £514,000 on the security of the Land Tax and the Customs granted by the Bank to the Treasury on 6th March 1695.   C. M. B., Lib. A., fol. 175.

In his report Ranelagh states that the first of these later operations was the remitting of £536,744, between 24th May and 20th December 1695, in twenty-one instalments varying from £4,000 on 19th November to £97,674 on 14th June. The Bank alleged that the provision made in Holland to answer this credit cost £634,794 2s. 2d., so that there was lost by exchange a sum of £98,050 2s. 2d. To this was added £12,695 16s. 9d., commission at 2 per cent. at Antwerp and Amsterdam, plus other expenses, which brought the total loss to £110,745 18s. 11d.[1]

Ranelagh's criticisms of this operation are of peculiar interest. He states that the directors had, in error, overestimated their loss by £49,806 16s.; that they had made an overcharge for commission of at least £8,789 9s. 3d. because the Bank's charge was 2 per cent., whereas the highest rate among " sworn " brokers at this time was ½ per cent.; that they had received an extra allowance amounting to £5,859 12s. 6d. which was deducted " on ye exchange for differences of sight "; and that £200,000 had been borrowed in Holland, therefore there was no loss by exchange on this item, " since that sum was not remitted hence." [2]

The second operation was carried out in eight instalments between the last day of 1695 and 21st April 1696. The directors announced that this transaction resulted in a loss of £12,814 2s. 10d.; that the total of the credits supplied amounted to £337,886; and that the cost of remitting came to £350,700 2s. 10d., which did not include a sum of £21,857 11s. 2d. demanded for " commission, brokerage, interest and expenses of management." In dealing with this account Ranelagh lays special [3] stress on the charge for interest, amounting to £3,378 17s. 2d., and, incidentally, gives some important information relating to the Bank's methods of business.[4]

[1] B.M., Harl. M.S., 7421, fol. 2.

[2] *Ibid.*, fol. 2b–3b. When this operation—the remittance of £536,744—was in progress Sir John Houblon (the Governor), Michael Godfrey (the Deputy Governor), and Sir William Scawen visited, in July 1695, the King's headquarters outside Namur in order to discuss the " business of remises " and the rating of guineas (then at 26s.). Godfrey was killed on 17th July while talking with William III during the attack on Namur. See Horton, *op. cit.*, pp. 241–43, and Macaulay, *op. cit.*, III, pp. 363–64.

[3] *Ibid.*, fols. 4–4b.   [4] *Ibid.*, fols. 5, 5b, and 6.

It appears that the interest arising out of this transaction was paid in London " within the time of this account untill the bills were comply'd with wch was for 2 months at 6 p. cent. p. annum," and that it was claimed by the directors because the Lords of the Treasury had no other way of paying the Bank except by tallies on the Exchequer in general, which the Bank accepted despite the fact that they were worthless until their securities were announced by the Treasury. Ranelagh, however, frankly admits that in this particular operation the Bank was paid for its credits in clipped money, goldsmiths' notes, and, to a great extent, in its own notes. This, he adds, was not an unusual procedure in the first half of 1696, for " there was little other payments anywhere." Even the Bank itself at this time gave its notes for clipped money, and " the bills of ye gentlemen of the Bank " sent to Flanders " to answer the credits " which he received for the army " were very probably paid for by them with the same money or notes for which they charged the King with this interest," a charge which he thinks excessive.[1]

The third operation was the remittance to Hill, the Deputy Paymaster in Flanders, of one million florins during the latter part of May 1696. This was done in two instalments— 600,000 florins on the 19th and 400,000 on the 26th— equivalent to a total of £104,956 11s. 1d., which with broker-age at 2s. per cent., commission at 1½ per cent., and sundry expenses, brought " the total for ye first million " to £106,638 18s. 10d.[2] The fourth operation was the remittance of another million florins to Hill on 15th June 1696, the total for which, including brokerage and commission, at the same rates as in the previous transaction, and sundry expenses, amounted to £106,880 4s.[3]

Ranelagh states that as securities for " ye said two millions of florins" he had delivered to the Bank the following tallies and orders : [4]

[1] B.M., Harl. MS., 7421, fol. 6.
[2] *Ibid.*, fol. 7.
[3] *Ibid.*, fol. 7.
[4] *Ibid.*, fol. 7b.

"On the continued impositions on Wines,
  Vinegars and Tobacco struck ye 11th of
  March last and bearing interest at 5 per
  cent. . . . . £61,000. 0. 0.
On same funds struck same day bearing
  interest at 6 per cent.. . . . £41,000. 0. 0.
On same funds struck 7th May bearing
  interest at 7 per cent. . . . . £17,823. 18. 3.
On the Act for enlarging the times for
  purchasing annuities struck 11th April
  1696 bearing interest at 6 per cent. . £100,000. 0. 0."

representing a nominal value of £219,823 18s. 3d., which,
despite the serious depreciation of tallies, he thinks was
ample security for the sum of £213,519 2s. 10d., the equivalent of the two million florins. He points out that the
directors had charged £4,270 7s. 7d. for "management,"
and £27,759 9s. 5d. for "loss by exchange for want of new
money which the Bank was to receive for ye above credits
at 13 per cent."

These additions brought the total cost of the third and
fourth operations to £245,548 19s. 10d., which meant that the
nominal amount of the security was insufficient to the extent
of £25,725 1s. 7d. Ranelagh, however, declares that the
Bank made "a considerable profit" on these last two
transactions because the exchange with Holland when they
were carried out was "about 30s. 6d., whereas the directors
allowed 29s. 6d. and 29s. 3d. respectively." Moreover, the
tallies delivered to the Bank as securities produced interest
for quite two months before the money was supplied by the
Bank in Flanders. He therefore objects to the directors'
charges for "commission and management." [1]

But the directors had another tale to tell, a tale revealed
in the Court Minute Books, which throws a different light
on these big operations, and shows that they resulted
in serious losses. Even before the first remittance of
£536,744 was completed, the directors foresaw that the
Bank would be a heavy loser. This is evident from a
Treasury Minute dated 19th November 1695,[2] which states

[1] B.M., Harl. MS., 7421, fol. 8.
[2] P.R.O., Recs. T., T. 29/9, fol. 106.

that on this day Sir William Scawen and other directors visited the Treasury for the purpose of supporting an important letter sent the previous day from the court to the Treasury Lords. This letter stated that, owing to the monetary stringency caused by the coinage—" as matters stand now with regard to the coynes "—the court had resolved to discontinue the remittances to Holland, after having come to the conclusion that the borrowing of another £200,000 in Holland would not " keep them in the business," because it would have to be repaid under great disadvantages, the money already raised there costing 7½ per cent.

Despite this decision the King ordered them to continue the remittances, but later in the same month Sir William Scawen told the Lords of the Treasury that the Bank had already lost £50,000 over the " remises," and at the same time Sir James Houblon proposed that dollars of the same weight and fineness as the Dutch dollars should be coined in England for the use of the army overseas, a proposition which was not entertained by the Treasury.[1] No attempt, however, appears to have been made to recoup the directors until February 1697, when the King agreed to a Treasury grant of £75,000 " in full of their account of losses by remittances."[2]

According to the Bank's minutes this sum was " allowed " in tallies,[3] but though it did not cover the total loss, the court resolved to thank the King for his consideration, and five of the directors were appointed " to attend his Majestie " at 6 p.m. on 31st March 1697 " to offer him the most humble thanks of this Comp[a] for the 75,000 li allowed the Bank for the loss on Remittances."[4]

[1] P.R.O., Recs. T., T. 29/8, fol. 114, dated 27th November 1695.
[2] Ibid., T. 29/9, fol. 77.
[3] C. M. B., Lib. B, fol. 209.
[4] Ibid., Lib. B, fol. 216.

CHAPTER VIII

THE SALIENT FEATURES OF ENGLISH BANKING HISTORY IN THE EIGHTEENTH AND EARLY NINETEENTH CENTURIES

" After so many Difficulties, and so much Opposition from Malice and Ignorance, we see the Bank of England not only brought to some degree of Perfection but crowned with so glorious Success, and under such Advantageous Circumstances, as are not only surprising at home, but sufficient to amaze all Europe."—*Observations upon the Bank of England* (1695), p. 1.

THE war with France was concluded in October 1697 by the Treaty of Ryswick, and the Bank entered an important period in its history, a period in which it was able to consolidate its position before the outbreak of the War of the Spanish Succession in 1702. During these five years the directors commenced the repayment of the "engrafted capital stock" of 1697, an operation which, as we have seen, was completed in 1707, six years before the Treaty of Utrecht brought the War of the Spanish Succession to an end. The year 1699 saw the completion of the recoinage, which had, particularly in its earlier stages, been a serious strain on the Bank in its position as a Government agent for calling in the old coin and distributing the new; and as it did not receive the new coin from the Mint in sufficient quantities, the shortage of cash was intensified. This, together with the over issue of sealed bills and notes,[1] was common knowledge and resulted in a " run " in May 1696,[2] with a consequent partial suspension of cash payment, which, however, does not appear to have been a serious matter, as it is not recorded in the Court Minute Books.

---

[1] According to the report of Sir John Bolles presented to Parliament on 10th December 1696, a total of £1,657,996 10s. 6d. outstanding in sealed bills, promissory notes and specie notes on the previous 10th November was backed by cash in hand amounting to £35,664 1s. 10d. C. J., XI, p. 622.

[2] The " run " is mentioned, p. 62, by the writer of *Decus and Tutamen* (1696), and by N. de l'Hermitage, the Dutch envoy in London, in his despatch of $\frac{8}{18}$ May 1696, B.M., Addit. MS., 17677, QQ. Macaulay's description of this " run " is based on the latter authority.

Three months before the "run," Bank stock commenced to depreciate in price, a depreciation which caused much anxiety until September 1697.[1] In 1696 the quotations were low because of the Government's attempt in April to establish a National Land Bank; the recoinage, which was in full operation after March; the introduction of what was originally a rival paper currency in the form of Exchequer bills in July; and the increasing strain of the war. The price fell from 107 on 31st January 1696 to 83 on 14th February. This was followed by a gradual rise to 91 on 27th November, and the last quotation for the year, on 25th December, is 73. In the following year there was still more serious depreciation due to the continuance of the war, to the initial effects of the second Bank Act, and to the calling up of the fourth instalment of the original capital to be paid on or before 24th July 1697.

Some of the subscribers who could not pay the call had to sell Bank stock, and this, together with the accepting of subscriptions of tallies at 40 per cent. discount towards the augmented capital authorised under the second Bank Act, resulted in a big drop in the price of Bank stock. From 5th February to 28th May 1697 it fluctuated between 51 and 56, and it was not until September of the same year, as a result of the negotiations at Ryswick, that it was quoted in the 'nineties. On 17th September 1697 it stood at 98, and between this date and the end of the seventeenth century it never dropped below 86. On 22nd December 1699 it was $117\frac{1}{2}$; on 27th December 1700, $124\frac{1}{2}$; between these two dates it had even reached $148\frac{1}{4}$.

In addition, the Bank's sealed bills,[2] and notes, were very much depreciated in the latter part of 1696, and in the first half of 1697. On 16th December 1696 the discount of bills was $16\frac{1}{4}$; on 29th January 1697, 17; on 9th April, 19; and throughout May, 21. On 17th September they were at par; and from that date to the end of 1697 the discount was 1.

It is thus clear that from January 1696 to September

[1] For the early prices of Bank stock see Rogers, *First Nine Years of the Bank of England*, pp. xxiii–xxvii; Scott, *Joint Stock Companies*, III, p. 244. For later quotations see J. Francis, *op. cit.*, App. 3.

[2] For a full list of the early quotations see Rogers, *op. cit.*, Table IV.

1697 was a period of great anxiety to the directors, an anxiety which was intensified by the effects of the drain of the " remises " to Flanders, to Savoy, and to the fleet. Therefore it is not surprising to find that no dividends were paid from profits in 1696, but in 1697 the total for the year amounted to £27 10s. per cent. in three payments. In 1698 a total of £6 3s. 2½d. per cent. was paid; in 1699, £9 10s.; in 1700, £10; and it is interesting to note that during the War of the Spanish Succession £12 10s. per cent. was paid in 1708, and £16 in 1709.[1]

This is evidence of the Bank's sound position in the first decade of the eighteenth century.[2] The augmented capital, and the banking privileges, authorised under the second Bank Act in 1697, had strengthened the Governor and Company's position, which was made still stronger when the Act of 1707[3] forbade banking partnerships of more than six persons, a prohibitory enactment which, as we have seen, was confirmed in the Act of 1708.[4] The latter statute also enacted that the charter was not to be redeemed until twelve months after 1st August 1732, and gave the Bank authority to double its capital, which at the passing of this Act stood at £2,201,171 10s., an increase brought about by a call of 50 per cent. on the total of the original plus the " engrafted " capital.[5]

Even, however, before the Act of 1707 became law the Bank had commenced its official connection with the circulation of Exchequer bills,[6] and under the Act of 1708 it was given authority to circulate £1,500,000, receiving from the Government 4½ per cent. for so doing.[7] Many of these bills

---

[1] Scott, op. cit., III, p. 245.

[2] For details of the prices of Bank stock between 1700 and 1720 see Scott, op. cit., III, pp. 215–240.

[3] 6 Anne, c. 22, s. 9.   [4] 7 Anne, c. 7, s. 61.

[5] By 5 Anne c. 13, the Bank was empowered to call in any sum of money for the circulating of Exchequer bills as should be thought necessary by the Governor and Company in a general court meeting. Accordingly a call of £1,100,585 15s. was made on the proprietors, and this amounted to 50 per cent. of the capital as it stood between 1697 and 1707 (i.e. 50 per cent. of £2,201,171 10s.). At the same time, however, the sum of £99,414 5s. was divided out to the proprietors, thus restoring the capital to the total of £2,201,171 10s. As a result, therefore, of the Act of 1708, the Bank's capital was increased to £4,402,343. Parl. P. (1898), LII, C.-9010, pp. 68–69.   [6] 5 Anne, c. 13 (1707).

[7] See also 7 Anne, c. 8 (1708); 9 Anne, c. 7 (1710); 12 Anne, c. 11 (1713).

were used by the Bank for remitting the " Equivalent money" to Edinburgh in accordance with the Act of Union of 1707.[1] The bonds between the State and the Bank were further strengthened in 1715, when, under two Acts of this year,[2] the Bank began its management of the National Debt; in 1717 under an Act [3] which confirmed the provisions relating to this management; and in 1722 when it took over £4,000,000 of the stock of the South Sea Company.[4]

Thus the first decade of the eighteenth century witnessed the granting and confirming of a banking monopoly which was to last for over a hundred years. In 1742 [5] the Bank's monopoly was renewed by a clause [6] in which it is defined as " the privileges or power given by former Acts of Parliament to the . . . Governor and Company of exclusive banking." It was in virtue of this clause, which within the next sixty years was confirmed in two other Acts,[7] that the Bank of England continued to function until 1826 as the only English joint-stock banking company.

In the meantime both the country and the London private banks, particularly the former, had greatly increased in number, and the London Clearing House [8] had been established by the London bankers, an innovation which greatly facilitated their transactions with one another. The increased use of cheques is a striking feature of London private banking in the latter half of the eighteenth century. During this period the notes of the metropolitan private bankers decreased in number, whereas the notes of the Bank of England, and of the country bankers, became much more

[1] 6 Anne, c. 6.   [2] 1 Geo. I, c. 19 and 20.   [3] 3 Geo. I, c. 7.
[4] See J. W. Gilbart, *The History and Principles of Banking* (3rd. ed., 1837), Section III; Francis, *op. cit.*, Chaps. VII–VIII; J. W. Lawson, *History of Banking* (1855), pp. 77–84; H. D. Macleod, *Theory and Practice of Banking* (5th ed., 1892), pp. 486–540; W. R. Bisschop, *The Rise of the London Money Market* (1910), pp. 132–38; *Parl. P.*, 1898, LII, C.-9010, p. 71.
[5] The Bank's charter had been renewed to 1742 by the Act of 1713, 12 Anne, c. 11.
[6] 16 Geo. II, c. 13, s. 5.
[7] 21 Geo. III, c. 60, s. 12 (1781); and 39 and 40 Geo. III, c. 28, s. 15 (1800)..
[8] For its early history see P. W. Matthews, *The Bankers' Clearing House* (1921), Chap. I; H. T. Easton, *History and Principles of Banks and Banking* (3rd ed., 1924), p. 178; E. T. Powell, *The Evolution of the Money Market*, p. 305; and *D. P. E.*

numerous.[1] There is, as we have seen,[2] evidence to show that at least two private bankers, one provincial and one metropolitan, were issuing engraved promissory notes prior to 1750. After this date the country banks rapidly increased, and by 1820 they numbered over 780,[3] most of which possessed London agents.

There were, however, two types of London agents for the country banks, the bill-broker and the banker, and though the country banker usually used a London bank to draw upon, it was not the general custom to possess both types of agents. A London bill-broker told the Select Committee on the High Price of Bullion in 1810 that the nature of his particular type of agency for country bankers was twofold : " in the first place to procure money for country bankers on bills when they have occasion to borrow on discount, which is not often the case, and in the next place to lend the money for the country bankers on bills on discount." [4] The London banker agents of the country bankers kept their reserve deposits,[5] cashed their drafts and bank post bills,[6] and in some cases cashed their notes.[7] The drafts were usually for 30, 60, and 90 days, and the bank post bills at 7 days,[8] and, except during the Napoleonic War, interest was allowed by the London agent on these reserve deposits.[9] " The

---

[1] See E. Cannan, *The Paper Pound of 1797–1821* (1919), intro., p. viii; and E. Sykes, *Banking and Currency* (6th ed., 1925), pp. 87–88.

[2] See Chap. III, pp. 41–42, *supra*.

[3] For details about the country banks during this period see Sir Francis Baring, *Observations on the Establishment of the Bank of England and on the Paper Circulation of the Country* (1797), pp. 13–20; E. Thornton, *An Enquiry into the Nature and Effects of the Paper Credit of Great Britain* (1802), Chap. VII; J. Wheatley, *An Essay on the Theory of Money and the Principles of Commerce* (1807), I, pp. 336–39 and 372–76; T. Joplin, *An Analysis and History of the Currency Question* (1832), pp. 89–101; Gilbart, *op. cit.*, Section V; T. Tooke, *A History of Prices and of the State of the Circulation from 1793 to 1837* (1838), pp. 146–52; Lawson, *op. cit.*, Chap. VIII; Bisschop, *op. cit.*, pp. 145–57; A. Andréadès, *op. cit.*, pp. 170–72; J. F. Rees, *Fiscal and Financial History of England* (1921), pp. 18–19. See also *Parl. P.* (1810), III (349), *Report from the Select Committee on the High Price of Bullion*, pp. 122–25; and *ibid.*, (1831–32), VI (722), *Report from the Committee of Secrecy on the Bank of England Charter*.

[4] *Parl.* P. (1810), III (349), p. 122.

[5] *Parl.* P. (1831–32), VI (722), Q. 2898, evidence of George Carr Glyn.

[6] *Ibid.*, Q. 4124, evidence of Joseph C. Dyer.

[7] *Ibid.*, Q. 961, evidence of Vincent Stuckey.

[8] *Ibid.*, Q. 4124.

[9] *Ibid.*, Q. 2934, evidence of Glyn.

O

Welsh cattle trade," states Professor Fay,[1] " supplies a quaint example of the orientation on London. The Black Ox Bank of Llandovery was founded by a drover, David Jones, in 1799, and was called locally the Black Ox Bank [2] because its notes were engraved with a Black Ox. At Aberystwyth there was the Bank of the Black Sheep : each sheep on the note represented a pound, each lamb ten shillings. For generations the Welsh had been receiving money from persons who had payments to make in London and elsewhere. This money they left at home and paid the creditors out of the proceeds of their sales in London, thus avoiding the risk of loss through accident or robbery. When this custom was formalised the drover became a country banker."

John Parry Wilkins of the Brecon and Merthyr banking house of Wilkins & Co. told the Committee of Secrecy on the Bank of England Charter in 1832 that it was the practice of his bank to allow interest of 3 per cent. on time deposits of over six months.[3]   This appears to have been the general practice of the country bankers. No interest was given on demand deposits or those under six months. The country bank notes were issued in discounting good trade bills or as loans upon the security of the borrower's promissory notes.[4] Attempts at forgery were, curiously enough, few in number. " We have," Vincent Stuckey, the famous West Country banker, told the Committee of Secrecy,[5] " never lost 100 l. by forgeries since we have been bankers, and we have been bankers upwards of sixty years." Stuckey's figures with reference to his note issues given to this Committee show that in June 1830 the total amount in circulation was £155,000, and in June 1832, £170,000.[6] Wilkins and Co.'s total circulation in September 1818 amounted to £89,000, in September 1823 to £83,000, in September 1827 to £124,000, and in September 1831 to £52,000.[7]

The amount of the notes circulated by the private bankers

---

[1] *Great Britain from Adam Smith to the Present Day* (1928), p. 109.
[2] Banc yr Eidion Du.   Absorbed by Lloyds in 1909.
[3] *Parl.* P. (1831–32), VI (722), Q. 1593.
[4] *Ibid.*, Q. 1582, evidence of Wilkins.   [5] *Ibid.*, Q. 1156.
[6] *Ibid.*, Q. 1006.   [7] *Ibid.*, Q. 1599.

was not regulated by Parliament. The 780 private country banks and the 60 private London banks, which were functioning round about 1820, were subject to three regulations only : the lowest denomination of their notes was fixed by law; a stamp duty on notes had been introduced in 1804; after 1808 all note-issuing banks had to obtain a licence. Prior to 1775 the private banks were allowed to issue notes for less than £1, but a law of that year [1] made the lowest denomination £1. This remained operative until 1777, when notes under £5 in value were forbidden.[2] In 1797, when cash payments were suspended at the Bank of England, all banks were allowed to issue notes for less than £5, with £1 again as the minimum value. In 1822 authority was given for continuing the circulation of notes under £5 in value until 1833. This decision, however, was cancelled in 1826, when Parliament once more decided to make £5 the minimum value of both Bank of England and country bank notes.[3]

The country notes filled a breach in the currency.[4] Bank of England notes in the eighteenth century did not circulate very much outside a radius of sixty miles from Charing Cross, and even when they did the provincial farmers and traders, except in Lancashire, usually preferred the notes of a country banker.[5] " The Bank of England," wrote that assiduous student of contemporary banking, Thomas Joplin of Newcastle in 1824,[6] " having no means of issuing notes out of London, the country banks entirely possess the country circulation. Independent of this, Bank of England notes would not pass in most parts of the kingdom, as, where local notes can be had, no person in the more northern counties will take a Bank of England note if he can help it." No attempt was made by the Bank to establish country branches

---

[1] 15 Geo. III, c. 51.   [2] By 17 Geo. III, c. 30.   [3] 7 Geo. IV, c. 6.

[4] See W. Graham, *The One Pound Note in the History of Banking in Great Britain* (2nd ed., 1911), Chap. XVII.

[5] It must be remembered that there was no legal tender paper until Bank of England notes were placed in this category in 1833 by 3 & 4 Wm. IV, c. 98, s. 6.

J. W. Angell, *The Theory of International Prices* (Harvard Economic Studies, XXVIII, 1926), gives, App. A. p. 496, a valuable table of statistics relating to the circulation of Bank of England and country bank notes between 1791 and 1821.

[6] " On the General Principles and Present Practice of Banking in England and Scotland," in the *Pamphleteer*, XXIV (1824), p. 17.

during the eighteenth century, a serious omission which retarded the provision of credit facilities in provincial England; and it was not until the Act of 1826 [1] gave the Bank power to establish branch banks that the first three of its branches were opened at Gloucester, Swansea, and Birmingham.

By 1831 eight more Bank of England branches had appeared : Liverpool, Bristol, Leeds, Exeter, Newcastle, Hull, Manchester and Norwich.[2] They provided the local gold supplies, discounted bills of exchange at London rates, which were less than country rates, took " drawing accounts " on which no commission was charged, granted letters of credit, and accepted deposits on which no interest was payable.[3]

Though at first the country bankers offered a great deal of opposition to the Bank's branches, they appear to have realised before 1832 that these branches were a convenience. Vincent Stuckey told the Committee of Secrecy in 1832 that the Bank's branches were appreciated because they took " the expense and risk of sending down gold and of keeping up a supply in the country," and thus relieved the strain on the country bankers.[4] And the head of the well-known London banking house of Glyn & Co.—George Carr Glyn— informed this Committee that, as a result of the " opinion of his correspondents," he had come to the conclusion that the branches were " rather useful than otherwise to them," and that there had been " no material interference as yet with the business of the private bankers." [5]

The Bank's branches, however, should have appeared in provincial England much earlier than 1826. There were, it is true, strong reasons for their absence prior to 1760. The towns were in a very backward state and were not easy of access; the roads were, as Arthur Young emphasised,

---

[1] 7 Geo. IV, c. 46, s. 15.

[2] For important statistics relating to the Bank's branches between 1828 and 1831, see *Parl. P.* (1831–32), VI (722), App. 37–54.

[3] J. W. Gilbart, *A Practical Treatise on Banking* (6th ed., 1856), II pp. 361–67, gives details about the early branches of the Bank of England, including an interesting account of their methods of business taken from a contemporary issue of the *Cambrian*.

See also T. Hankey, *Banking : Its Utility and Economy* (1860), p. 109, and J. H. Clapham, *Economic History of Modern Britain* (1926), pp. 276–78.   [4] *Parl. P.* (1831–32), VI (722), Q. 1135.   [5] *Ibid.*, Q. 3078.

" execrable "; there were no large scale provincial industries. Moreover, the inland bill was very popular with provincial traders, and, after 1738; much use was made of the
bank post bill [1] for the transmission of money. But in the
last four decades of the eighteenth century the midlands and
the north rapidly increased their industrial activities, and
sound provincial banks became indispensable. The breach
was partly filled by the country bankers, but not without
many casualties.

It is strange, therefore, that this rapid increase of industrial
activities in the provinces, accompanied as it was by many
failures among the provincial private banks, did not affect
the Bank's monopoly of joint-stock banking before 1826,
when the " Act for the better regulating Co-partnerships of
certain Bankers " became law, not, however, without a great
deal of controversy, in which Joplin played a prominent part.
Joplin appears to have been the first writer to point out
that owing to the popularity of the country notes, and the
scarcity of Bank of England notes outside London, the
establishment in provincial England of joint-stock banks
with more than six proprietors and with note-issuing powers
would not have an adverse effect upon the Bank. " The
charter of the Bank," he states, " does not expressly confer a
monopoly, nor could it be discovered from the charter itself
that the monopoly of a circulation of notes was intended." [2]

The Act of 1826 allowed the establishment of note-issuing
banking corporations—" co-partnerships of bankers "—with
an unlimited number of partners at any place outside a
radius of sixty-five miles from London, a radius which Carr
Glyn wished to reduce to twenty-five miles. [3] The first three
provincial joint-stock banks to be established under this Act
were the Huddersfield Banking Company, the Bradford
Banking Company, and the Lancaster Banking Company
in 1827. [4] These were immediately followed by the Bank

[1] The bank post bill was introduced by the Bank of England in 1738.
It may be described as a bill of exchange, payable at seven days' sight,
drawn and accepted by a bank. For the form of this bill see W. Thomson,
Dictionary of Banking (6th ed., 1926).
[2] " On the General Principles and Present Practice of Banking in
England and Scotland," *Pamphleteer*, XIV, p. 23.
[3] *Parl.* P. (1831–32), VI (722), Q. 2956.   [4] *Ibid.*, p. 323.

of Manchester, with 600 proprietors and a capital of £2,000,000,[1] which was established in 1828 but did not commence to operate until March 1829. "I am aware," remarked Carr Glyn to the Committee of Secrecy when discussing the activities of this bank, " the Company carries on its business remarkably well and under excellent management; it is constituted in such a way that it was enabled to get together a great deal of business. They have a very large list of subscribers, and in that list, I believe, some of the principal people in the town and neighbourhood of Manchester."[2]

The early business of the Bank of Manchester was described in detail to the Committee of Secrecy by three of its directors. Singularly enough it did not issue its own notes, but made use of a type of bank post bill, usually in denominations of from £50 to £100, payable seven days after date.[3] Discounting was generally done by means of Bank of England notes obtained from the Bank's branch at Manchester, a custom which helped to increase the popularity of Bank of England paper money in Lancashire. Money was remitted to London by means of drafts on Glyn & Co. at 30, 60, and 90 days, and by bank post bills.[4]

Between the Bank Act of 1826 and the end of 1830 fourteen joint-stock banks had appeared in the provinces outside the sixty-five miles radius.[5] The Bank of Liverpool was established in 1830, and so also were the York City and County and the Whitehaven Banks. When the Bank of England Act of 1833 was passed the number had more than doubled.[6]

In 1833 the Bank's charter was considered for renewal. The Government's legal advisers were of the opinion that the " exclusive banking " clause of 1742, or any confirmation of this clause, did not prevent the establishment of joint-stock banking companies of more than six persons in London, and the sixty-five miles radius area, provided that such corporations did not issue notes. As a result the Bank Act of 1833[7] allowed such banks to be established in this area.

[1] *Parl.* P. (1831–32), VI (722), Q. 4120, evidence of Joseph C. Dyer.
[2] *Ibid.*, Q. 3119.   [3] *Ibid.*, Qs. 4124, 4125.
[4] *Ibid.*, Q. 4124.   [5] *Ibid.*, p. 323.
[6] See Clapham, *op. cit.*, pp. 278–79, for an interesting account of early provincial joint-stock banking.   [7] 3 & 4 Wm. IV, c. 98.

This legislative measure was immediately followed by the establishment of the London and Westminster Bank,[1] under the management of J. W. Gilbart, an event which inaugurated a new epoch in the history of English banking.[2] " And after joint-stock banking was permitted in the country," writes Bagehot, describing this great development in the most famous of his works,[3] " people began to inquire why it should not exist in the Metropolis too. And then it was seen that the words [of the Act of 1742] only forbid the issue of negotiable instruments, and not the receiving of money when no such instrument is given. Upon this construction the London and Westminster Bank and all our older joint-stock banks were founded. But till they began the Bank of England . . . was in every sense the only banking company in London."

It is therefore evident that throughout the eighteenth century and the early years of the nineteenth the Bank of England's first interests were the guarding of its monopoly, the issuing of notes, and the strengthening of the bonds which united it to the State by taking every advantage of the financial weakness of the Treasury. Indeed, the period under review falls into two great epochs. The first was initiated in 1697 by the Second Bank Act, with its objects of increasing " the credit of the Bank " by augmenting its capital, and of preventing other joint-stock banking corporations from functioning. The second commenced in 1742, with the Act which gave it the ." exclusive privilege " of joint-stock banking, and ended in 1833 with the Act which allowed the establishment of "co-partnerships of bankers" of more than six persons within the metropolitan area.

The last forty years of the second of these epochs are of outstanding importance in the Bank's history. In 1793 the struggle with France commenced and was to continue until

---

[1] Established in 1834, followed in 1836 by the London Joint Stock Bank and in 1839 by the Union Bank and the London and County Bank. .

[2] For the beginnings of joint-stock banking in England see Gilbart, *History and Principles of Banking* (3rd ed.), Section VI; Lawson, *op. cit.*, Chap. VIII; McLeod, *op. cit.*, II, Chap. XVII; Bisschop, *op. cit.*, pp. 198–200; E. T. Powell, *op. cit.*, Chap. X; Andréadès, *op. cit.*, pp. 258–59; H. E. Fisk, *English Public Finance from the Revolution of 1688* (1921), pp. 166–68; Clapham, *op. cit.*, pp. 278–79 and 509–12; J. Sykes, *The Amalgamation Movement in English Banking, 1825–1924* (1926), pp. 1–17.

[3] *Lombard Street* (Withers' edition), pp. 96–97:

1815, a period during which the National Debt increased from £240,000,000 to £876,000,000, and national expenditure from about £19,000,000 to nearly £100,000,000.   From 1797 to 1821 [1] cash payments were suspended at the Bank, and as a result of the depreciation of the Bank note the Government in 1810 appointed the famous Select Committee on the High Price of Bullion, whose remarkable Report [2] was issued in the same year.   In 1816 a Coinage Act [3] authorised the free coinage of gold at the Mint price of £3 17s. 10½d. per ounce.   In 1819 the Resumption Act [4] authorised the Bank to exchange its notes for bullion, as from 1st May 1821, at the Mint price, and to resume cash payments of all its notes not later than 1st May 1823, a resumption which the Bank actually commenced nearly two years earlier.   The failure in 1825 of several country banks and of two prominent London houses [5]—Pole, Thornton & Co. and Williams, Burgess & Co.—caused the Government in 1826 to consider the Bank's privileged position.

Of this position the Bank had made excellent use in the eighteenth century, and had steadily built up a big business, described by Thomson Hankey, one of its Governors in the middle of the following century, as " of a threefold nature " : the management of the National Debt, the issuing of notes, and Government and private banking.[6]   Possessing so many advantages the Bank easily overshadowed its competitors, and, as Bagehot has stated,[7] " it inevitably became *the* bank in London ; all the other bankers grouped themselves round it, and lodged their reserve with it."

[1] For a detailed study of the position of the Bank of England and of the country banks during this period see N. J. Silberling, " Financial and Monetary Policy of Great Britain during the Napoleonic Wars," *Quarterly Journal of Economics*, XXXVIII, (1923–24), pp. 214–33, and 397–439.

See also Tooke, *op. cit.*, pp. 146–70 ; Cannan, *op. cit.*, intro., pp. xiii–xiv ; Fisk, *op. cit.*, pp. 162–65 ; R. G. Hawtrey, *Currency and Credit* (2nd ed., 1923), Chap. XVI ; Andréadès, *op. cit.*, pp. 187–242 ; Clapham, *op. cit.*, pp. 263–64 ; and Fay, *op. cit.*, pp. 94–95.

[2] *Parl.* P. (1810), III (349).   [3] 56 Geo. III, c. 68.

[4] 59 Geo. III, c. 49.   The suspension was authorised by 37 Geo. III, c. 34.

[5] For details of this crisis see Andréadès, *op. cit.*, pp. 248–53.

The number of commissions of bankruptcy issued against country banks in 1824 was 10 ; in 1825, 37 ; and in 1826, 43.   In 1827 there were only 8 ; in 1828, 3 ; and in 1829, 3.   *Parl.* P. (1831–32), App. 101.

[6] Hankey, *op. cit.*, p. 13.   [7] *Lombard Street*, p. 97.

Such are the salient features of English banking history in the eighteenth century and the early part of the nineteenth, a period of great wars, of rapid National Debt expansion, of big State lotteries, of remarkable progress in scientific agriculture, of striking commercial and industrial developments, a period in which England became the workshop of the world.

But the history of the Bank of England in these eventful years, as recorded in its own Court Minute Books and in the Records of the Treasury and of the Exchequer, has not yet been written.

CHAPTER IX

CONCLUSION

(i) The Economic Background.
(ii) The Political Background.
(iii) The Religious Background.
(iv) The Evolution of Banking Theory and Practice.

(i) *The Economic Background.*

THE remarkable economic expansion of the seventeenth century conduced to the accumulation of capital and to its greater fluidity. As a result there emerged in England a specialised technique in the supply of loanable capital; the crude money-lending transactions of an earlier age gave way to the economic institution of banking. Before the end of this century Englishmen were well versed in the essentials of the banker's trade, a trade which, originating in England as a graft on another type of business, rapidly developed into an independent profession.

With economic advancement banking emerged as an indispensable and highly specialised business. Specialisation in trade during the Elizabethan and Stuart periods, accompanied by an increase in the scale of enterprises, of " adventures," of risks, and of trading responsibilities, and in the number of individual traders and of combinations of traders, created a big demand for capital. Funds had to be always easily accessible; the money power had to be mobilised; immobilised capital in such a dynamic age was a serious impediment to economic progress. With the shifting of the economic centre from the Mediterranean to the North Atlantic a new economic organisation appeared, which during the seventeenth century was to be dominated first by Holland and then by England.

The seventeenth century was an epoch of economic nationalism, of intensive mobilisation of economic power, and of fierce international rivalry. " States," as Dr. Gooch emphasises,[1] " became the forcing houses for the rearing of industries." The régime of economic nationalism was fundamentally concerned with the favourable " balance of trade," with " well-ordered " commerce, with great privileged merchanting combinations, with colonial expansion, with the strict regulation of colonial intercourse, with rapidly expanding businesses, with the extension of markets, with sources of supply, with new trade routes, with sea power, with increasing public expenditure, with the sinews of economic warfare. It was under such economic conditions that banking was born in England and rapidly reached its adolescence.

In pre-Tudor times English commerce was largely in the hands of aliens, but by the spacious days of Elizabeth the régime of the Merchant Adventurer was supreme. England's overseas trade was managed by Englishmen by means of numerous continental business connections, which they personally supervised. Under the early Stuarts trade was extended further afield. The first English settlement in Virginia in 1606 was soon followed by others on the eastern seaboard of America—Maine in 1615, Massachusetts in 1629, Maryland in 1632, Connecticut in 1633, New Hampshire in 1635, and by settlements in the West Indies such as Barbados in 1627.[2]

By 1660 the trade with the American colonies was an important one, and it was rapidly developed during the post-Restoration era, an era of remarkable economic expansion in which the private banking of the goldsmiths reached its apogee. The importance of this trade was fully realised in England, as is evidenced by the numerous councils and committees of trade and of the plantations, but much

---

[1] *Political Thought in England from Bacon to Halifax* (1914), p. 230.

[2] For an interesting survey of British colonisation under the Stuarts see Basil Williams, *The British Empire* (1928), Chap. II. For more detailed accounts see G. L. Beer, *The Origins of the British Colonial System* (1908), and *The Old Colonial System* (1912); and *The Cambridge History of the British Empire*, Vol. I (1929), edited by J. Holland Rose, A. P. Newton and E. A. Benians.

friction was caused by the attempts to regulate it in the interests of the mother country by means of the Navigation laws.

This economic nationalism found able practitioners in Cromwell and Charles II. Cromwell's famous Navigation Act of 1651, though ostensibly aimed at the carrying trade of the Dutch, was nevertheless a deliberate attempt to regulate the trade of the colonies in favour of England. Its fundamental purpose was the fostering of national strength by an increase of sea power and of trade. Under this historic Cromwellian ordinance no goods could be imported into England from the colonies or from any non-European countries in ships other than English ones, nor could any commodities be shipped from European countries to England or any of the plantations except in English ships or the ships of the countries from which the goods emanated.

This restrictive policy was further developed in 1660 by the Navigation Act of Charles II,[1] which introduced the principle of " enumeration," a novel feature not included in the original draft of this Act, but which appears to have been incorporated under the influence of Downing as an addendum. No sugar, tobacco, cotton-wool, indigo, ginger, fustic or other dyeing-woods produced in the colonies could be shipped to any country except England, Ireland or another colony. These were the " enumerated articles," and this was the policy of enumeration under which the trade of the colonies was strictly regulated in the interests of England.

The Act of 1660 was followed by the Staple Act of 1663, under which no European merchandise could be imported into the colonies unless it had been laden and shipped in England, and by the Plantation Duties Act of 1673, which taxed the enumerated products when exported to another colony.

These four Acts were the economic framework of what has been termed the old colonial system,[2] a system which had as its object " the maintaining a greater correspondence and

[1] 12 Chas. II, c. 18.
[2] For full details of this system see G. L. Beer, *The Old Colonial System* (1912).

kindnesse " between England and the colonies, and keeping the latter " in a firmer dependance " upon the former.[1] " In the beginning,". remarks a well-known authority,[2] " the colonial system contributed powerfully to the development of capitalism, and it is one of the ironies of history that the development of capitalism in turn brought about the overturn of the trade monopolies set up in the interest of the mother country."

In addition, trade with India and with the Levant and with northern and western Africa was rapidly developing. East India and Turkey merchants and traders to Barbary and Guinea flourished.   Their wares were sold in the London exchanges, which, before the end of the seventeenth century, were, as we have seen, four in number—the Royal Exchange, the New Exchange, the Middle Exchange and Exeter Exchange.   " The Merchants meeting-place, which the common people call the Burse and Queen Elizabeth with a solemn ceremony named The Royal Exchange," wrote Leigh in 1659,[3] " was set up by Sir Thomas Gresham, Citizen and Knight; a magnificent work, whether you respect the model of the building or the store of the wares there."   In the 360 years of its remarkable history the Royal Exchange has functioned as a home for most of the London exchanges of to-day.[4]

But though these early exchanges were primarily produce exchanges where mercer and merchant were predominant, a trade in securities arose and the stock-jobber emerged as a new type of dealer. Before the end of the seventeenth century stock-jobbing was an important business.   Regular quotations were given of prices of shares in the great trading companies, of Bank of England stock, and of Orphans' Bank stock, and there were many transactions in the buying and selling of the Government's floating debt represented by tallies, navy bills, and Exchequer orders and bills.   The traffic in negotiable securities and speculative operations in

---

[1] 15 Chas. II, c. 7 (1663), s. 1.
[2] H. Sée, *Modern Capitalism,* p. 183.
[3] *England Described*, p. 132.
[4] For the story of the London Exchanges see W. S. Dowling, *The Exchanges of London* (1929).

capital had commenced under the ægis of " tally-jobber "
and " Exchequer-broker." [1]   " For Trade being obstructed
at Sea," wrote Houghton in June 1694 in his curious newspaper,[2] " few that had Money were willing it should be idle,
and a great many that wanted Employments studied how
to dispose of their Money, that they might be able to command it whensoever they had occasion, which they found
they could more easily do in Joint-Stock, than in laying out
the same in Land, Houses, or Commodities, these being
more easily shifted from Hand to Hand.   This put them
upon Contrivances, whereby some were encouraged to buy,
others to sell, and this is what is called Stock Jobbing."
Houghton divided the brokers of the day into six classes : [3]
(1) Corn, (2) Dyer's Wares, (3) Exchange, (4) Grocery, (5)
Hemp, (6) Silk.   Hatton, a contemporary of Houghton,
classified them into : (1) Brokers " who are a kind of Factors,
there being Brokers for almost all kinds of trades," (2)
Exchange brokers, and (3) " Brokers of Stock." [4]

Even, however, after the foundation of the Bank of England large dealings in pepper, corn, silk, coffee, spice, hemp
and indigo were carried out at the " candle auctions " [5]
in the Metropolitan exchanges, and before the end of the
seventeenth century Exeter Exchange in the Strand had
witnessed the disastrous flotation of Asgill and Barbon's
Land Bank.   " In the reign of King James," Leigh tells
us with reference to this famous exchange,[6] " Robert, Earl
of Salisbury caused to be erected a stately building in the
Strand which upon Tuesday the tenth of April in the year
1609 was begun to be richly furnished with wares, and the
next day the King, the Queen and Princes with many great
Lords and Ladies came to see, and the King gave it the name
of Britain's Burse."

The trading operations in these exchanges resulted in big

---

[1] *Angliæ Tutamen*, p. 6.
[2] *A Collection for Improvement of Husbandry and Trade*, B.M., Burney
Collection, 105 A, No. 98, dated 15th June 1694.
[3] *Ibid.*, No. 121, dated 23rd November 1694.
[4] *The Merchant's Magazine* (4th ed., 1701), p. 208.
[5] For a description of the " candle auctions " see Malynes, *Lex Mercatoria*, pp. 201–3, " Of the Buying and Selling of Commodities by Brokers
and by the Candle."   [6] *England Described*, p. 133.

profits. It is therefore not surprising to find under the later Stuarts a rapid increase in the deposits of the goldsmith bankers, and in the discounting of commercial bills. The ledgers of an outstanding banker like Backwell are striking proof of the increase in deposits derived from mercantile profits, and of the expanding bill market of the London of post-Restoration times. The wealthiest customers of the bankers were the great traders of the day, who flourished in an age in which commercial capitalism was predominant, and in which loanable capital was mobilised for the use of trade by great banker capitalists such as the Vyners, the Meynells, the Hornbys and the Snows, and Backwell, Whitehall, Portman and Colville.

That the profits of trade were considerable long before the post-Restoration period is shown by the many loans made by the Merchant Adventurers and by individual metropolitan merchants to Elizabeth and James I, and by the remarkable activity of the wealthier merchants in the business of exchange. Government borrowings absorbed a great deal of the traders' savings. In the reign of Elizabeth and in the earlier half of the seventeenth century loans were made directly to the sovereign, that is to say, the Exchequer of Receipt actually received the money from the lender or his personal representative, or through an agent of the Exchequer or of the sovereign, the tally functioning as a receipt when the money was handed in at the Exchequer. All part payments and repayments of the loan and payments of interest were made directly by officials of the Exchequer of Receipt. A Pell Office entry dated 31st December 1608 shows, for example, that an Exchequer payment order for £24,580 7s. 8d. was made out in part payment of a loan of £120,000 advanced to James I on 23rd October 1607 by a number of London merchants.[1] In the second half of the seventeenth century these loans to the State were usually made through the City Chamberlain of London, as is shown

[1] P.R.O., Recs. Ex. R., E. 403/2728.
Another striking illustration will be found in B.M., Addit. M.S., 5755, fol. 6, which shows that John Eldred, clothworker, and W. Ferris, mercer, of London, were appointed to receive £10,000 from the Exchequer in part payment of loan of £60,000 plus £3,000 interest, the said £10,000 to be distributed by the two receivers among the various lenders.

by the numerous advances to Charles II made by Sir Thomas Player, or from the deposits held by the goldsmith bankers, which had greatly increased between 1650 and 1672. Even during this latter period, however, large sums for the use of the Government were advanced by merchants to the Exchequer of Receipt. Thus not only did the profits of traders result in a big accumulation of loanable capital, but the increasing need of money by the State led to further accumulation from the interest payments. Between 1650 and 1672 very large sums were advanced to the Government from the deposits held by the bankers, and during these years very large sums were paid to the bankers as interest. The private banking of the goldsmiths was linked up with the fiscal needs of the State; there was a close association between the bankers and the Exchequer, between banking and public finance.

Under these conditions goldsmith banking rapidly matured into a powerful factor in the economic development of the nation. The bankers became the specialists who mobilised capital for trade and for the Exchequer. With the expansion of overseas trade, the increase of internal joint-stock enterprise, and the growth of public expenditure there was a big demand for mobilised capital, for a service by means of which funds could be obtained quickly and at a reasonable rate of interest. Such a service was provided by the goldsmith who developed into a banker.

Despite, however, the important service rendered by the private banking of the goldsmiths, some of the writers of the day opposed the establishment of the Bank of England on economic grounds. A big banking corporation, it was argued, would have adverse effects on trade by attracting money which would otherwise be invested in business enterprise. " Trade," states one of these writers,[1] " is like a coy Mistress and must be earnestly and warmly courted . . . and that which hinders the courting and following this coy Dame is that the thoughts of our Merchants and Traders instead of being employ'd about the improving of trade are diverted into the Bank."

[1] *Arguments against Prolonging the Bank* (1708).

(ii) *The Political Background.*

The seventeenth century, the age of Bacon and Hobbes, of Milton and Harrington, of Locke and Halifax, is a period of stimulating political thinkers, of eloquent philosophers, of novel democratic ideas, and of striking constitutional changes. English political theorists in this century gave much attention to new schemes of human association, to the rights of sovereigns, to the rights of the Church, and to the rights of the people.

The political thought of Stuart England, from the rigid constitutionalism of the first two Stuarts—the absolute monarchism championed by Bacon and Raleigh—to the communism expounded by Winstanley, is kaleidoscopic in its variations. It was not until the system of Parliamentary control of expenditure was initiated at the accession of the third William that the Stuart theory of undefiled absolutism, of divine right and its corollary of non-resistance, finally disappeared. "The Divinity of Kings which had entered England with James I left it for ever in the baggage of his grandson." [1]

In this atmosphere of divine right and monarchical absolutism the risks of the financier were enormous. Yet even when Hobbes was writing his *Leviathan* [2] with its gospel of the indivisibility of sovereignty, Filmer his *Patriarcha* [3] with its paternal basis of absolute monarchism, and Harrington his *Commonwealth of Oceana,* [4] "the least Utopian of Utopias," [5] with its "idea of a perfect Commonwealth," and when Leveller and Independent, Presbyterian and Fifth Monarchy Man were engaged in the bitter political polemics of the day, and the fundamental principles of "life, liberty and property" were not securely established, the first of the banking Vyners and the younger and ever active Backwell were bankers of repute in Lombard Street. Both Sir Thomas Vyner and Backwell were always ready to advance large sums to the Protector on much less security than the

[1] Gooch, *op. cit.,* p. 181.　　[2] First published in 1651.
[3] First published in 1680 but written between 1651 and 1653.
[4] First published in 1656.　　[5] Gooch, *op. cit.,* p. 117.

P

"Spanish plate" or the "coine of Mexico lately brought from Portugal." "That Sir Thomas Vyner and Alderman Riccards," states an order of the Lord Protector, dated 9th August 1655,[1] with reference to one of Sir Thomas Vyner's monetary transactions during the Interregnum, "doe forthwth pay unto ye Receipt of his Highness Excheq^r the sum of fifty thousand pounds of the 85,000 l. by them received by order of his Highness from ye Dutch Ambassad^r and that a warr^t doe issue to them for that purpose." "Of Edward Backwell, cittizen and goldsmith of London," reads an entry dated 9th May 1656, in a Cromwellian Receipt Book of the Exchequer of Receipt,[2] "in part of twenty thousand ffoure hundred pounds for a certain quantity of the coine of Mexico and Chile lately brought from Portugal, 6,000 l., 5,400 l., 6,000 l.," items which comprise the total receipts— "the sume of the day"—at the Exchequer of Receipt on this particular date.[3]

But though the individual banker capitalist boldly faced the unstable political conditions of the day and took many risks, the establishment of a great joint-stock banking corporation, even for the express purpose of floating a big State loan, was obviously too dangerous an experiment during the absolute monarchism of the Stuarts or the autocracy of the Interregnum. The deposits of such an institution might be commandeered by king or protector in the same way that the second of the Stuarts commandeered the money deposited by London merchants for safe custody in the Mint. If the Mint was not a safe depository, then a big bank holding large deposits of money and of plate would be far too tempting an institution for an absolute ruler worried with the balancing of budgets and the increasing complexity of national finance, for, as Hartlib had emphasised during the Cromwellian period, "money deposited . . . in any one place proves . . . a temptation to the sword."[4]

Even the Exchequer under such conditions was not

---

[1] S.P. Dom., Interregnum, 25, no. 101.
[2] P.R.O., Recs. Ex. R., E. 401/1930, fol. 199.
[3] For details of a similar transaction see Appendix 5. *infra*.
[4] *An Essay upon Master W. Potters Designe.* Quoted in Chap. IV, p. 106, *supra*.

immune. Under the Privy Seal and Letters Patent the King could immediately obtain from this great Department of State any sum he desired for his personal use, for his Cofferer or his Jewel House. And did not Charles II attempt, with disastrous results, to convert the Exchequer into a bank of issue by circulating fiduciary paper money through this department? Experiments of this nature would inevitably be applied to a joint-stock banking corporation established under a régime of absolutism. That Backwell's bank at the sign of " The Unicorn " anticipated one of the functions of the Bank of England, by keeping the reserves of the other goldsmith bankers, is remarkable testimony of the rapid development of banking under the most adverse conditions of governmental instability.

Neither the setback of 1672—the so-called " Stop " of the Exchequer, when the fiduciary paper money issued by the Exchequer became worthless—nor the shock of three wars with the Dutch checked the progress of the private banking of the goldsmiths. After the " Stop," some of the bankers, it is true, fell by the way, though not without a gallant struggle to keep going, and large numbers of their depositors were crippled. But the system was firmly established, and such a system was very necessary with trade expanding so rapidly; the bill market had to keep pace with the produce market. New goldsmith bankers filled the breach made by the " Stop," and like their predecessors faced one political shock after another until the " Glorious Revolution " of 1688 ushered in an era of governmental stability.

With the accession of William III Parliament obtained control of public revenue and expenditure and of the defence of the realm. The Exchequer was no longer subservient to the sovereign; the navy and the army were made dependent on the decisions of Parliament. Under such conditions of political stability, schemes for the establishment of a great central joint-stock bank soon came to the forefront of political discussion. Many were carefully considered, and within six years of the initiation of the rule of Parliament and of the disappearance of the figment of divine right, Montague had launched the Bank of England as a " Whig finance company," [1] with Sir John Houblon and Michael Godfrey at the helm.

(iii) The Religious Background.

The connection of social facts with ethical and religious principles is of paramount importance in the evolution of large-scale financial transactions.   In mediæval times the Church was antagonistic to the money trade.   Mediæval theologians frowned upon the money-lender, upon the pursuit of wealth, upon " eagerness for gain," and regarded avarice as one of the seven deadly sins.   Mediæval moralists based their theories on the Canon Law, the central feature of which was the prohibition of usury.   The Church enforced a moral code with the strictest of discipline; social morality was rigidly regulated through the agency of a powerful theocracy.

A momentous change in the old scheme of Christian ethics was soon to take place.   The precepts of the mediæval schoolmen were swept away with the growth of foreign trade and the rise of a new plutocracy.   The social ethics of mediævalism gave way to a new economic radicalism. Ecclesiastical pretensions were pruned with the growth of the City interest;   the old religious theories could not withstand the new economic realities;   the canonist ethics of money-lending broke down with the rise of a monied class in a new world of business enterprise.

This great change from the ethical and religious theories of an earlier age to the hard realities of a new economic régime was not a sudden one.   Even the break with Rome in 1535, though undermining the influence of the canonist doctrine, did not make any sudden change in English economic thought.   A new version of Christian ethics was gradually formulated under the wing of the reformed faith.

[1] Bagehot, *Lombard Street*, p. 90.
" The Bank," states Professor Foxwell in his Introduction to Phillippovich, *History of the Bank of England and its Financial Services to the State*, " was at its origin rather an incident of State finance than the foundation of a national banking system."

Business enterprise became the star to which Protestantism hitched its economic waggon.

Several breaches had already been made in the ethical standards of the earlier age before the last of the Tudors ceased to reign. After a set back the taking of interest had been finally legalised during the Elizabethan period, and under the Stuarts the problem of interest developed into a question of high rates and low rates. Wilson had noted in the " Merchant's Oracion " in his *Discourse uppon Usurye* that traders " lend not for usurie but for interest and by exchange," that " hope of gayne maketh new industries, and where no gayne ys to bee had men will not take paynes," and that " merchants doings must not thus be overthwarted by preachers and others that can not skill of their dealings." [1] And two decades before the publication of Wilson's famous treatise the *Market or Fayre of Usurers,* which in 1550 was translated from the " high Almaigne " by William Harrys, had declared to Englishmen that if a person " ask and receive amendes " for " losse or hinderance " as a result of his loans he sins not, because such " amendes " constitute interest, not usury; [2] while Bullinger in his *Decades,* which appeared in England in 1577, stated that " Usury is forbidden in the Word of God so far forth as it *biteth,*" [3] and " so far as it is joined with iniquity and the destruction of our brother or neighbour." [4]

Before the end of the Elizabethan period most of the clergy appear to have accepted the explanation of Miles Mosse, " Minister of the Worde and Bachelor of Divinitie," in his *Arraignment and Conviction of Usury.* [5] Mosse justifies interest on investments of the nature of partnerships which necessitated a share in the risk of the " adventure." " Interest," he states, " is justly due not only when a man hath lent and for want of receiving againe of his own in appointed time he suffereth damage, but also when wanting

[1] *Discourse uppon Usurye,* fol. 72 *b.*
[2] *The Market or Fayre of Usurers* has no pagination. The declaration with reference to interest is in the section marked H. II.
[3] English translation (1850), edited by T. Harding for the Parker Society, Vol. II, p. 42.
[4] *Ibid.,* Vol. II, p. 41.
[5] Published in 1595.

his own to employ for his best advantage his gaine and increase is hindered." [1] Once these principles were laid down the taking of a pre-arranged payment for the use of money was ably defended by later ecclesiastics. Thus we find Dr. William Ames, "sometime of Christ's College, Cambridge," [2] in his *Conscience*, an outstanding early Stuart theological treatise, boldly asserting that "the Scripture doth not take away altogether Usury," [3] and clearly explaining "what things are to be observed in the putting out of money that sinne may be avoided." [4]

Mosse and Ames were undoubtedly influenced by the teaching of Calvin and his school. The Calvinist doctrine with reference to interest was antagonistic to the doctrine of the Catholic Church. In his famous letter to Œcolampadius, Calvin is quite clear with reference to the taking of interest. It was not to be condemned any more than the profits of trade or the payment of rent for land were to be condemned. There were, however, certain limitations. Calvin forbade the taking of interest from the needy; interest must not be forced from a borrower in times of calamity and distress; the taking of excessive security was not allowed; the advantage obtained by the borrower must not be more than that obtained by the lender. In other words, the creditor was not to exploit the debtor; the lender was to be just; he was not to thrive by the sweat of the borrower. "Calvinism and its offshoots," writes a recent historian of capitalism,[5] "took their stand on the sides of the activities which were to be the most characteristic of the future, and insisted that it was not by renouncing them, but by untiring concentration on the task of using for the glory of God the opportunities which they offered, that the Christian life could and must be lived."

The decision of Calvin is undoubtedly a landmark in the history of European religious thought, and in the evolution of modern capitalism. But it must not be forgotten that a

[1] *Arraignment and Conviction of Usury*, p. 25.
[2] Ames was Professor of Divinity in the University of Franeker, Friesland, from 1622 to 1632.
[3] *Conscience with the Power and Cases thereof* (English trans., 1639), p. 241. [4] *Ibid.*, p. 243.
[5] Tawney, *Religion and the Rise of Capitalism*, p. 108.

definite decision with reference to the taking of interest had been made in England nearly three decades before Calvin's opinion was announced. The Act of Henry VIII in 1545, which authorised payment. for the use of money up to a maximum of 10 per cent., was operative for seven years, and though cancelled in 1552, was again made operative under the Elizabethan Act of 1571.

But Calvinism as expounded by the English Protestants soon developed an economic individualism, and the battle-ground was shifted from the field of usury to that of liberty in business. Despite the prevailing economic paternalism of the State, a philosophy of *laissez-faire* gained ground in England after the Civil War, though its heralds had already appeared earlier in the seventeenth century in the persons of Malynes and Sandys.[1] The Puritans urged that commercial enterprise should be free, that economic energies should not be bridled, that the business man should be unfettered in his actions, that personal responsibility and initiative should be encouraged.

Regardless of the mercantilistic policy of a central government, which was fully alive to the potentialities of commercial expansion, this economic individualism was undoubtedly a prominent characteristic of the post-Restoration period. The various Puritan sects of the day were exponents of both religious and economic toleration. The field of trade had been evacuated by the old type of Christian moralist and was now invaded by strictly disciplined moralists with new ethical ideas, moralists who, in an age of economic action, applied to their economic activities the fundamental virtues of prudence and diligence. " Their *moral* virtues," as Professor Sée emphasises,[2] " were often transformed into *economic* virtues." It was in this atmosphere of religious radicalism and mundane materialism that the private banking of the goldsmiths, unregulated by a paternally inclined State, matured with such rapidity.

The influence of Calvinism upon the evolution of capital-

---

[1] Malynes published his *Maintenance of Free Trade* in 1601, and Sir Edwin Sandys introduced his two " Bills for Free Trade " in 1604.
[2] *Modern Capitalism*, p. 40.

ism has been discussed with some emphasis by more than one recent writer.[1] Another religious theory with reference to the capitalistic movement has been advocated by Professor Sombart,[2] who states that capitalism developed in Holland and England during the seventeenth century through the activities of the Jews, who possessed the same type of religious morale.as the Calvinists.

These two theories have been examined by Professor Sée, who, while admitting that the disciplined and simple life of the Puritans was an important factor in the accumulation of wealth, is careful to point out that " capitalism had obtained a vigour " in England before the influx of Jewish traders in the seventeenth century.[3]

But in addition to Calvinists and Jews we must also consider another important religious body—the Anglicans—as a factor in the capitalistic movement of Stuart England. Singularly enough, however, the part played by Anglicanism in this movement has been neglected by the historians of capitalism. That Laud and the Puritans were incessantly at war on points of religion does not mean that English Churchmen in the early half of the seventeenth century failed to realise the possibilities of economic enterprise. Later in this century, under Taylor and Stillingfleet, Anglicanism in England developed a generous spirit of toleration, a toleration which was accompanied by intensive commercial activity.

In assessing the parts played in Stuart England by Calvinist, Jew and Anglican in the rise of capitalism, the assessor must be particularly cautious in his study of the polemic literature of the day. Among the economic tracts and pamphlets of Stuart England the pitfalls are many. A

---

[1] *E.g.* R. H. Tawney, in *Religion and the Rise of Capitalism* and M. Weber, " Die protestantische Ethik und der Geist des Kapitalismus," in *Archiv für Sozialwissenschaft und Sozialpolitik Statistik*, Bd. 20 (1905).
   On this subject see the following interesting articles: M. M. Knight, " Recent Literature on the Origins of Modern Capitalism," *Quarterly Journal of Economics*, Vol. XLI (1927), pp. 520–33; O. H. Taylor, " Tawney's Religion and Capitalism and Eighteenth Century Liberalism," *ibid.*, Vol. XLI, pp. 718–31; and F. H. Knight, " Historical and Theoretical Issues in the Problem of Modern Capitalism," *Journal of Economic and Business History*, Vol. I (1928–29), pp. 119–36.
[2] In *The Jews and Modern Capitalism*.
[3] *Modern Capitalism*, p. 96.

single instance, with reference to the Hebrew race, taken from Thomas Violet's *Petition against the Jews*, which appeared in 1661, will suffice. Cromwell's design, we are told in this vituperative pamphlet,[1] was to bring the Jews to England in order to make them farmers of the Customs and the Excise, and " by that means to have drawn into this nation the principal Jews of the World with their estate and credit."

This was certainly not the Protector's design. Prior to the Cromwellian period a number of Crypto-Jews had already settled in England under the guise of Catholicism. They formed an active trading colony whose numbers increased in the early years of the Protectorate. Cromwell had duly noted their great energy in the commercial life of the nation. He had also, as we have seen, received assistance both financially and politically from more than one member of this prosperous little colony. Therefore, fully recognising the importance of these settlers in the expansion of England's trade, and in a spirit of economic toleration, he invited the most distinguished of the Amsterdam Jews, Menasseh ben Israel, to London in order to present to the English Council a petition for the re-admission of the Jews to England. Menasseh duly visited England and presented his petition, which the Council referred to a special committee, which, in turn, referred it to a public conference. The conference proved unfavourable to admitting any further Jews, and was dissolved by Cromwell, who thereupon gave an assurance to the Jewish colony of his personal protection, and allowed the members to worship in accordance with the Jewish faith. Consequently these Crypto-Jews threw off the guise of Catholicism, and until Cromwell's death they carried out their transactions with other London merchants without interference.[2] This is the real beginning of Jewish prosperity in England during the seventeenth century.[3]

[1] P. 7.
[2] For full details of the Crypto-Jews and the re-settlement of the Jews in England see A. M. Hyamson, *A History of the Jews in England* (2nd ed., 1928), Chaps. XVII–XX.
[3] For the denization and naturalisation of Jews in England during the seventeenth century see Huguenot Society of London Publications, XVIII (1891), *Denizations and Naturalisations of Aliens in England and Ireland*.

The Jews who had settled in London during the Cromwellian period and the preceding decade were undoubtedly a valuable factor in the mercantile life of the City, but there is no evidence among the surviving Cromwellian Records of the Exchequer of Receipt to show that any member of the Jewish colony in London functioned as a Revenue official of the Protector. The Cromwellian officials of the Exchequer were Englishmen. Nor is there any evidence among these records to show that the Jew was a conspicuous figure in the State finance of Cromwellian England. In the flotation of State loans Cromwell relied primarily on Englishmen. The financial assistance he received from two of the goldsmith bankers has already been mentioned.

We must now briefly consider the latter part of the seventeenth century. Happily, the documentary material appertaining to the finances of the later Stuarts preserved in the archives of England is of excellent quality. What evidence do the Records of the English Treasury, of the English Exchequer of Receipt, of the Chancery Proceedings, of the Bank of England, and of the historic English banking houses directly descended from the goldsmith bankers contain with reference to Calvinists, Jews and Anglicans as factors in the growth of the capitalistic movement in the England of Charles II, James II and William III?

It has already been shown in an earlier chapter that these records prove quite definitely that both Jews and Dutch Calvinists, though active as traders and financiers in the England of the later Stuarts, were easily overshadowed by Englishmen in both these capacities. And while several Englishmen developed into wealthy private bankers during the latter half of the seventeenth century, there is no record of either Hebrew or Hollander functioning in this respect in England during this period.

So far, therefore, as England is concerned the rôle of the Englishman is overwhelmingly more important than that of Jew or Dutch Calvinist in the capitalistic movement of the seventeenth century. In, for example, one of the valuable Treasury Books of the period—the special minute book containing extracts from the Treasury Minute Books, dated

1690–97 [1]—only one Jewish name appears in the records of exchange transactions, that of Solomon de Medina, who, as we have seen, became one of the food contractors to Marlborough's victorious army. Almost without exception the most important exchange specialists of the England of the Stuarts were Englishmen.

Further interesting proofs of the capacity of Englishmen as capitalists in the late seventeenth century will be found among the names of the investors in the 14 per cent. annuities initiated in the reign of William III. These names are duly recorded in a special series of Exchequer Issue Rolls, and the two earliest Rolls,[2] dated 1696 and 1697, show a large proportion of English investors, such names as Smith, Robinson and Williamson being of frequent occurrence. Indeed, in the first two Rolls of this remarkable series of records foreign names are comparatively few in number.

And so, also, in the list of the subscribers to the original capital—the first twelve hundred thousand pounds—of the Bank of England,[3] which is carefully preserved in the Bank's archives, few Dutch and other foreign names occur. The numerous subscribers to the Bank's first " capital stock " in 1694 were, as were the numerous subscribers to the Bank's "enlarged capital stock" in 1697, almost entirely Englishmen —City mercers and haberdashers, merchants and mariners, salters and saddlers, vintners and brewers, coopers and dyers, chandlers and grocers, and even goldsmiths and money scriveners.

The contemporary documentary evidence thus shows that it is inaccurate to say that the Jews had " a very great share in the establishment of the Bank of England," [4] that English finance in the seventeenth century was " very extensively controlled by Jews," [5] that Jews were " the principal participants in the first English loan," [6] and " that a large part of the capital of the Bank of England came from the Dutch." [7] Nor is there any evidence to prove that " the

[1] P.R.O., Recs. T., T. 29/627.
[2] P.R.O., Recs. Ex. R., E. 403/1330–1331.
[3] " The Book conteyning the Subscriptions."
[4] Sombart, *The Jews and Modern Capitalism*, p. 373.
[5] *Ibid.*, p. 54. [6] *Ibid.*, p. 88.
[7] Clive Day, *History of Commerce*, p. 156.

business of stock-jobbing as a specialised profession was introduced into the London Exchange by Jews." [1]

It is, however, interesting to note that among the 176 commissioners appointed "to take and receive all such voluntary subscriptions as should be made " to the first " capital stock " of the Bank of England, on or before 1st August 1694, were certain important members of French and Dutch families settled in London, such as Sir James and Sir John Houblon and Peter and Abraham Houblon, Thomas and Philip Papillon, Sir Peter Vandeputt, Jasper Vandebush and Gerard Vanhuitsen. But no Jewish name figures in this list.[2]

The first fact, therefore, of outstanding importance that emerges from this mass of unimpeachable documentary evidence is that in Stuart England, Englishmen were predominant as traders, as middlemen, as " factors " and commercial agents, as financiers, as bill brokers, as company promoters, and as bankers. The remarkable ledgers of Backwell's bank, which was England's great monetary pool during the two decades which followed the Navigation Ordinance of Cromwell, contain ample evidence of the supremacy of Englishmen in all fields of economic activity during the Cromwellian and post-Restoration periods. Moreover, there is a great deal of documentary evidence of this supremacy during these decades, and also during the other decades of the seventeenth century, among the various Records of the Exchequer, which contain countless proofs of the predominance of Englishmen in the capitalistic movement of seventeenth century England.

The next important fact that emerges is with reference to the creed of the Englishmen engaged in capitalistic enterprise during the Stuart period. We are certainly not justified in concluding from the available documentary evidence that the Calvinists were either the wealthiest or the more numerous capitalists of this great epoch of commercial expansion. During the years when the private banking of the goldsmiths was of such paramount importance in English govern-

---

[1] Sombart, *op. cit.*, p. 90.
[2] *The Schedule containing the Draught of the Charter* (1698).

ment finance and in the development of English trade, the
wealthiest of the great bankers were Anglicans who wor-
shipped God in the Church of St. Mary Woolnoth and
mammon in its immediate vicinity. The parish registers of
this famous City church show that such prominent " keepers
of running cashes " as Sir Thomas Vyner, John Portman,
John Colville, Peter White and Bernard Eales functioned as
its churchwardens, Portman acting in this capacity in the
year of the " happy Restoration." These registers also show
that the most powerful of the goldsmith bankers, Sir Robert
Vyner [1] and Backwell,[2] were Anglicans. In addition, these
two wealthy bankers were strong supporters of the throne,
despite the fact that they had assisted in financing the
Exchequer during the Cromwellian régime—Sir Robert
as the partner of his uncle Sir Thomas, and Backwell both
independently and in conjunction with Sir Thomas. Sir
Robert made the regalia for Charles II's coronation at a cost
of over £31,000, and in 1661 he was appointed to the office
of " King's Goldsmith." [3] " And whereas the said Edward
Backwell," states a warrant of Lord Treasurer Southampton,[4]
with reference to one of this faithful Royal banker's outstanding services to Charles II, " did by His Ma[ties] Comands
transport himselfe with his servants into ffraunce to count
and receive ye sume of ffour Millions and five hundred
thousand Livres agreed to be paid to His Ma[tie] by the ffrench
king upon the rendring of Dunkirke His Ma[tie] for the great
paines and charge in that service and likewise in respect of

[1] Sir Robert Vyner was responsible for the expenses incurred in building
the north side of the Church of St. Mary Woolnoth. His brother, Dr.
Thomas Vyner, was Dean of Gloucester.
[2] " Went to church," wrote Mr. Pepys on 11th January 1668, " where
first I saw Alderman Backwell and his lady come to our church, they living
in Mark Lane."
All Backwell's children were christened in the Church of St. Mary
Woolnoth. And so, also, were the children of the following seventeenth-
century goldsmith bankers : Sir Thomas Vyner, Portman, Colville, Francis
Meynell, Robert Welstead, Bernard Turner, Henry Lewis, Thomas Williams,
Thomas Price, John Snell, Henry Lamb, Peter Wade, Peter White, John
Thursby, John Temple, Bernard Eales, Richard Snagg and John Tassell.
[3] *Vyner: a Family History* (1885), pp. 55–56. It is also stated in this
book (p. 70) that Sir Robert presented to Charles II a statue " intended
to represent his Majesty on horseback trampling underfoot an enemy
supposed to represent Oliver Cromwell."
[4] P.R.O., Recs. Ex. R., E. 403/3032, fol. 12. See Appendix 7, *infra*.

the hazard in securing it against all false counting and false monies hath determined to make him an allowance in grosse of the sume of 1500 li and by his Lres of Privie Seale hath directed the same to be paid without accompt."

We know also from those valuable Exchequer records, the Assignment Books (Goldsmiths'), that when the Exchequer partially suspended payment in 1672, some of Sir Robert Vyner's wealthiest depositors were prominent members of the Anglican Church, such as the " Reverend Father in God Seth Bishop of Sarum," [1] Dr. Samuel Parker, Archdeacon of Canterbury, and Dr. George Beaumont, Prebendary of Winchester, while a little later another, and more famous, Bishop of Sarum, the great Burnet, was a wealthy customer of Child's.

These Assignment Books also show that a large number of Sir Robert Vyner's depositors were members of well-known Anglican families, and the names of a large number of other prominent Anglicans are to be seen in the old ledgers of Richard Hoare and of Backwell. Many of the wealthy depositors at " The Golden Bottle " and " The Unicorn " were members of the Anglican nobility, and many were Anglican knights who were heads of City trading companies. It is, of course, true that among the merchant capitalists of the post-Restoration era there were prominent Puritans representing the " ultra-Protestantism of the City," [2] such as Sir Patience Ward and Michael Godfrey, members of French Huguenot families like Thomas Papillon and the Houblons, and Dutchmen like Vandeputt. There were also wealthy Jewish merchants such as Henry and Isaac Alvarez, Ferdinand Mendes da Costa, the two de Silvas, and Alfonzo Rodriquez, who, like Godfrey, Papillon, Vandeputt and the Houblons, had accounts at Backwell's. But there appears to be no ground for concluding that the rôle of Puritan or of Jew was greater than that of Churchman in the evolution of capitalism in the England of the Stuarts.

[1] Dr. Seth Ward, Bishop of Salisbury, was one of the founders of the Royal Society of London.
[2] Tawney, *Religion and the Rise of Capitalism*, p. 252.

(iv) *The Evolution of Banking Theory and Practice.*

The scrivener was the first financial intermediary in England to make a regular practice of keeping money deposits for the express purpose of lending such deposits to customers at high rates of interest. It is not known when the scrivener commenced this practice, but he certainly functioned in this capacity as early as the reign of James I. The shop of the scrivener was the first English bank of deposit.

There is no evidence to show that any goldsmith's shop was a recognised bank of deposit in Jacobean times. It is true that the wealthiest goldsmiths of the reign of James I, and also of Elizabeth's reign, advanced money to the Government and to their private customers, but such advances were made out of their profits as craftsmen, jewellers and bullion merchants.

The first stage in the evolution of the goldsmith into a banker in the modern sense was the accepting of money deposits in trust, the custody of money which the custodian was not allowed to use. Money thus deposited was, for a small payment, kept in chests or sealed bags, and was returnable on demand, while the receipts given were simply warehouse dockets. The goldsmith was the trustee or bailee, and the depositor the bailor.[1] The records of the Goldsmiths Company of London show that a number of metropolitan goldsmiths functioned as bailees of valuables and of money during the reigns of James I and Charles I.

The next stage was reached when the deposit keeper was allowed to make whatever use he liked of the money deposited, provided that an equivalent sum was returnable to the depositor on demand. Thus the goldsmith bailee developed into the debtor of the depositor; and the depositor became an investor who loaned his money to the goldsmith for a " consideration."

This transition was accelerated by an increasing flow of foreign coins into England. The goldsmiths were recognised

---

[1] For further information about the goldsmith bailee see E. T. Powell, *The Evolution of the Money Market*, pp. 64–68.

money-changers, and with the expansion of trade under the Stuarts large quantities of foreign coins, particularly those of Holland, of France, and of Portugal, found their way into their hands. These coins were melted into bullion for the manufacture of jewellery—" they culled the weighty shillings and sixpences to make into plate and silver ware," [1] or the bullion itself was sold to the Mint for coining. But the goldsmiths always took the precaution to keep back large reserves for the use of merchants travelling overseas, and they found this a very profitable business.

In addition, however, to functioning as money-changers the goldsmiths were big speculators in foreign monies. "Hambrough merchants," states a contemporary "working" goldsmith,[2] " bring great quantities of Rix-dollars from Hambrough and other parts of Germany and pay no Custome . . . which the merchants usually sell to the goldsmiths, and the goldsmiths for the most part sell to the merchants that trade in Norway and Denmark, which dollars are closely packed in some part of the ship and so no Custome is paid." Thus vast quantities of both English and foreign coins were accumulated by the goldsmiths as a result of their money-changing transactions, and their speculations in foreign currencies. The goldsmiths' shops became recognised cash depositories, where a " great Stock of Treasure," " of gold, forraign coines and silver," was always to be found.

This business in foreign coins greatly stimulated the goldsmiths as dealers in bills of exchange, and also enabled them to carry out big transactions on behalf of both English and foreign merchants in the remittance of money overseas, either by receiving money shipped direct to themselves on behalf of a customer or by shipping it to an agent in a foreign country. Hence we find the term " casheer " or " cash-keeper " applied to those goldsmiths who by specialising in money-changing surmounted the difficulty of differences in currency systems.

The goldsmith was undoubtedly prominent as a bill broker before he developed into an actual purveyor of

---

[1] T. Violet, *An Humble Declaration . . . touching the Transportation of Gold and Silver Bullion . . .* (1643), p. 22.   [2] *Ibid.*, p. 21.

currency. The first notes issued by the goldsmiths were, as we have seen, bailee notes, or non-assignable warehouse receipts. The next type of money receipt issued by the goldsmith was a promissory note representing a holding of cash withdrawable on demand, and this note developed the quality of assignability. Demand deposits, however, were soon followed by time deposits, a practice which, as the ledgers of Backwell clearly show, was a feature of the private banking of the goldsmiths in the years immediately following the Restoration.

The bailee receipts were really "accountable notes," the type which we find the earliest cashiers of the Bank of England issuing to customers as counter receipts for cash deposited. Like the earliest promissory notes, they represented deposits which were withdrawable on demand. The note in both cases was fully backed by a deposit. But with the introduction of time deposits there emerged the custom of issuing another type of note, a note which was not connected with a specific deposit, and which was therefore not necessarily a personal note made out in a customer's name.

The third class of notes was accepted by the public simply on the banker's integrity. They were notes which possessed no specific metallic backing, and were issued in accordance with the banker's calculations as to the possible demand by his customers for gold and silver coins. The banker now became a recognised purveyor of assignable instruments, and his "running cash note" payable on demand, or credited as cash in his ledgers, filled a breach in the nation's currency. Bank credit was accepted as currency, and the development of banking became closely connected with the evolution of paper money.

Thus by the time that Sir Robert Vyner and Backwell were the leading banker capitalists of the Lombard Street of Charles II, the private banking of the goldsmiths was indispensable in the "business of remittances," and in the purveying of currency. Two great difficulties had been surmounted—distance and credit; the goldsmith banker was a reliable person for transmitting money overseas, and his notes were accepted as transferable instruments by the traders of

Q

the day. When this stage was reached the private banking of the goldsmiths had become an integral part of the commercial life of Stuart England. "The goldsmiths' notes," wrote Sir Henry Pollexfen in 1697,[1] "were taken upon an implicit faith, or else not probable that one goldsmith would have been indebted to the people when the Fire of London happened above £1,200,000."

How the system of paper credit initiated by the goldsmith banker worked is described in some detail by a contemporary of Pollexfen. "If a Merchant in receiving his Debts," states this writer, "Collects a Number of Goldsmiths Notes, suppose Nineteen Hundred Pound Notes, and he hath one for the like Sum of as Eminent a Merchant as any in the City, all on Demand, he carries these to his Goldsmith, who will give a Note for Two Thousand Pounds on Demand, and in the Margent write thus :

> 1900 Cash
> 100 Merchant's Name
> ――――
> 2000

implying the Merchant's Note must be made good, if not received; and as any Body would think, thus Expressing Goldsmiths Notes as Cash, entering them so in their Cash book, and the Merchant's Note into a Bill book, take them as Money (and are liable, and frequently do, to pay that Money the next Hour, or Moment after they so take them) and yet upon the insolvency of a Goldsmith, any of them were due from, they demand such Money of the Merchant notwithstanding."[2]

There is ample evidence to show that during the reign of Charles II the private banking of the goldsmiths had become regularised into the operations of deposit, of discount and of note issue. The shop of the goldsmith banker functioned as an agency for the distribution of loanable funds, and as a source of paper money which was accepted by the general

[1] *A Discourse of Trade, Coyn and Paper Credit*, pp. 66–67.
[2] *A Proposal to the Bank of England and the Banks now Setting up with some Considerations about Goldsmiths Notes* (1695), p. 1.

public as a means of payment.   The banker was now a recognised keeper of "running cash," and a mobiliser of idle surpluses, and was, therefore, a vital factor in the economic activities of the day.

How did the three operations of deposit, of discount and of note issue come together, and whence did the deposits of money originate?   The evidence, as we have seen, shows that the money scrivener was a custodian of deposits before the goldsmith, and that the goldsmith was a dealer in bills of exchange before he became a recognised deposit keeper. The stages in the evolution of the goldsmith into a banker in the modern sense therefore appear to be : (1) the loaning of money out of personal profits obtained as craftsman and bullion merchant, i.e. personal money-lending; (2) money-lending, accepting money and valuables in trust, money-changing, and discounting of bills of exchange, i.e. money-lender, bailee, exchanger and bill broker; (3) money-changing, discounting, the accepting of interest-bearing deposits returnable on demand, which the depositor placed at the goldsmith's disposition, and the issuing of fully backed promissory notes which were recognised under the Law Merchant as assignable instruments; (4) money-changing, discounting, accepting deposits which were not returnable on demand, and issuing promissory notes, which were not necessarily backed by coin and bullion, and which, whether " payable to an individual or their order or unto bearer," were finally recognised by Act of Parliament,[1] as instruments which are "assignable or indorsable over in the same manner as inland Bills of Exchange are or may be according to the Custom of Merchants."[2]

The acceptance of money deposits for loaning out at interest was a distinct advance from the old type of loan, which a financial intermediary like the scrivener or the broker obtained from a "money-master," and advanced at extortionate rates to the borrower.   When the goldsmith developed the practice of using his deposits as advances to

[1] 3 & 4 Anne, c. 8 (1704).   This Act is entitled "An Act for giving like Remedy upon Promissory Notes as is now used upon Bills of Exchange, and for the better payment of Inland Bills of Exchange."
[2] Ibid., s. 1.

trade or to the State, a system of private banking emerged which was recognised by people with surplus funds as a distinct organisation for the mobilisation and the administration of such funds. The depositor, however, was given no special security; he was simply a type of bondholder receiving a receipt for the amount deposited, which, if made out to bearer, he could transfer by mere delivery, and if to order, by indorsement. "The Bankers," wrote Mun,[1] "are always ready to receive such sums of money as are put into their hands by men of all degrees who have no skill or good means themselves to manage the same upon the exchange to profit. It is likewise true that the Bankers do repay all men with their own, and yet reserve good gain to themselves, which they do as well deserve for their ordinary provision or allowance as those Factors do which buy or sell for Merchants by Commission: And is not this likewise both just and very common?"

Thus there emerged an assignable instrument which did not represent actual coin or bullion held by a goldsmith. In addition, there emerged the note written by a depositor which enabled him to withdraw money or pay another person. This was the "drawn note" or cheque, which, as has been shown, was not a novel instrument but a copy of a similar device used in obtaining money from the Exchequer of Receipt. The goldsmith banker, however, used the cheque not only to enable the customer to withdraw money but also to transfer credit in his ledgers from one account to another.

The deposits held by the goldsmith bankers formed a great monetary pool from which the mercantile enterprises of the later Stuarts were financed. But such enterprises under the earlier Stuarts were also greatly assisted by the goldsmith who dealt in bills of exchange—the "exchanging" goldsmith, "the goldsmith about the cittie exchanges," of whose operations we hear at least two decades before those of the "running cash" goldsmith. The discounting of a bill of exchange was a form of loan, and traders in this way obtained funds from the "exchanging" goldsmiths who had not yet developed into keepers of deposits.

[1] *Englands Treasure by Forraign Trade* (1664), pp. 124–25.

Thus between the crude money-lending and money-changing goldsmith of Elizabethan times—the Hoare or the Martin who as a wealthy craftsman advanced money, and changed foreign coins out of his profits as a jeweller, lapidary and bullion merchant—and the goldsmith banker who was a recognised keeper of demand deposits and a discounter of bills of exchange, a type of goldsmith crafts-man emerged who advanced money on good trade bills, but whose dealings were necessarily restricted because his loanable funds were not obtained from depositors.

The next stage—the accepting of demand deposits—was undoubtedly reached under Sir Thomas Vyner and Back-well in Cromwellian times, but there is no evidence to show that these outstanding bankers or any others accepted time deposits prior to 1660. It was not the custom of the Crom-wellian banker to accept deposits at a week's or a month's "warning." By the time of Defoe the distinction between demand and time deposits had long been operative. " Our Banks" [the Bank of England and the Orphans Bank], wrote this well-known writer in 1697, " are indeed nothing but so many Goldsmiths Shops where the Credit being high (and the Directors as high) People lodge their Money . . . if you lay it at Demand they allow you nothing, if at Time 3 per cent., and so wou'd any Goldsmith in Lombard Street have done before." [1] When the practice of time deposits had been established the goldsmith banker had a freer hand to experiment with the issue of promissory notes in excess of his holding of coin and bullion.

Under the Commonwealth, therefore, the current account was firmly established. But whence came the deposits? The profits of traders, as already stated, accounted for large sums that found their way to the strong-rooms of the " keepers of running cashes " dwelling in Lombard Street, Cheapside and the Strand. So also did the surplus earn-ings of master mariners engaged as ocean carriers, a trade which the Navigation Acts attempted to foster. Many of the customers of the goldsmith bankers were sea captains. Then, again, large sums were obtained from the clergy, while tallies, Treasury-Exchequer money orders, " barrs "

---

[1] *Essay on Projects*, p. 40.

of bullion imported from Holland, France and Portugal, the rents of the nobility, the money of widows and orphans, and the debts collected under letters of attorney at the Exchequer by the bankers for their customers rapidly increased the balances in the shops of the goldsmiths.

By the Restoration the deposits of the goldsmith bankers had reached a big total.   Even before this event the bankers had conducted large transactions in the floating debt of the State represented by tallies.   Both Sir Thomas Vyner and Backwell were, prior to 1660, big discounters of tallies, and after the appearance in 1665 of the repayment order which accompanied the tally the bankers' dealings in this connection greatly increased.[1]   There is, also, documentary evidence which shows that the goldsmith's promissory note which was not actually backed by gold had made its appearance in the early years of the post-Restoration régime. The earliest of Backwell's ledgers, dated 1663, bears testimony to this important development, and there are many entries in this particular account book which show that customers paying in Backwell's notes were credited with their face value.   By 1665 the cheque was functioning, while two years later Charles II made his disastrous experiment with the fiduciary " orders of the Exchequer," the first official issue of State paper money in England, of which the bankers accepted large quantities.

The fiduciary orders led directly to the partial suspension of cash payments at the Exchequer in January 1672, the so-called " Stop " of the Exchequer.   The real nature of this episode seems to have been misunderstood by modern writers.   There was no " seizure of the Exchequer "[2] by Charles II.   The King did not " lay violent hands upon a sum of £1,400,000,"[3] nor did he " shut up the Exchequer " and " pay no one."[4]   What actually happened was that an attempt was made to remedy the shortage of currency by issuing, in anticipation of the Additional Aid of 1667,

[1] See Appendix 8, infra.
[2] W. Graham, The One Pound Note in the History of Banking in Great Britain, p. 337.
[3] O. Airy, Charles II (1904), p. 269.
[4] Bagehot, Lombard Street, p. 91.

Government paper orders, as payments for stores to naval and army contractors, or for the purpose of raising loans on the security of the Aid. If this device had been limited to one particular tax it might have been a successful experiment, and the Exchequer might have functioned as a bank of issue. But the orders were soon issued in anticipation of other sources of revenue, such as the Hearthmoney, the Customs and the Excise. Large numbers of the orders, and also of tallies and repayment orders which when issued represented loans already made to the Exchequer, had been discounted by the bankers. What Charles II did in January 1672 was to refuse repayment of, and interest on, these, and it was not until 1677 that he commenced the regular payment of interest on his loans to the bankers.

In the meantime, however, many of the goldsmiths received payments of interest, and also part payments of loans, at the Exchequer. The records kept by the Exchequer officials show that even in 1672, the very year the " Stop " was declared, several such payments were made to the goldsmith creditors of the State.[1] This proves that the " Stop " was not a complete one even so far as the goldsmiths were concerned. Numerous payments were made to the other creditors of the State who were hardly affected by the " Stop," while many payments were also made to various goldsmiths between 1672 and 1674 when Charles made an interim grant of £140,000 for two years as interest on his debt to the goldsmiths. It is thus clear that certain generally accepted opinions about the reign of Charles II need careful revision.

When the Government next experimented with fiduciary paper money the Bank of England had been in existence for two years. The issue of Exchequer bills in 1696 was a far more cautious experiment than that of Charles II. These bills were issued in order to fill the big breach made in the currency by the calling in of coins for the Recoinage of 1696–99. The Bank assisted the Treasury in their circulation, and they were accepted in payment for all taxes except the Land Tax. They were not forced upon the

[1] See Appendix 13, *infra.*

public, but as they were negotiable and interest-bearing, were issued in smaller denominations than the Bank of England note minimum of £20, and later were made exchangeable for ready money at the Bank, they became very popular with the general public. There was, therefore, no tendency to an accumulation of the bills in the shops of the goldsmiths or in the Bank of England.

These two experiments show that the shortage of metallic currency was a serious problem in the England of the Stuarts. Hence the numerous schemes for supplementing the currency, which are a conspicuous feature of the literature of the day, and which throw much light on the development of banking theory, the development of the ideas of theorists with reference to the effects of banking service on the economic system.

Many, for example, were the schemes that were published with reference to the issue of " bills of credit " with merchandise as a basis. This was the idea of a store bank, the forerunner of the land bank idea. " Credit that shall never fail," wrote Dr. Mark Lewis in 1677,[1] " founded upon our own Commodities will in greater payments every way answer Money; for Money is nothing but a Medium of Commerce." Lewis suggests that the Chamber of London should " set up an office " to receive goods as pawns " upon which they will advance Bills of Credit to two-thirds, three-fourths, or four-fifths of the value or higher according as the nature of the goods are." He gives the following form of such bills : [2]

> Guildhall Jan. the 10th 1676
> There is due unto A.B. 100 l. for Goods deposited in the Office there which we promise to pay at the end of Seven Months
>
>   C. D.
>   E. F.

The issue of " bills of credit " backed by merchandise was the chief function of the London Office of Credit, the

---

[1] *Proposals to increase Trade and to Advance His Majestys Revenue*, p. 2.

[2] *Ibid.*, p. 7.

ill-fated Bank of the City of London, set up in 1683. It was, we are told, "neither Bank nor Lumbard because the foundations of Credit in Bank is Money and here 'tis Goods and Merchandise. . . . For after the same manner and limitations in every respect, as goods are received, stored and preserved in a Lumbard, shall they be in this Office, and Credit shall be delivered out and transferred exactly after the manner it is in forraign Banks. Each party that either raiseth or receiveth Credit, having his Folio in the Bank-Book and is Registered Debitor and Creditor, according to that he receiveth and payeth." [1]

The store bank was also, as we have seen, advocated by Petty, who, while admitting " durable Commodities " as a basis of credit, did not forget to include money deposits; [2] by Cradocke, with his deposits of " rich pictures and hangings " and " wines and tobacco "; [3] and by Murray, with his " magazines at Devonshire-house without Bishopsgate for the reception of any Goods for which Credit shall be given for two-thirds or three-fourths of their value according to the quality thereof." [4]

From merchandise or " durable commodities " as a basis for the extension of credit was but a short step to land. Hartlib, Cradocke and Murray suggested land as one of the securities for issuing " bills of credit," while the promoters of the Bank of the City of London advertised that they were prepared to grant credit to the " mortgagors of Land or Houses to the Bank." [5] But the theory that land was the best basis for paper money was not actually applied to banking until after the foundation of the Bank of England, when the four land banks were launched. "The Governors of the Land Bank," states the prospectus of Asgill and Barbon's Land Bank,[6] " will lend Money on Land or Houses at 3l. 10s. p. cent. per annum to all persons that shall convey

---

[1] A Description of the Office of Credit, p. 1.
[2] A Treatise on Taxes and Contributions (1662), p. 9.
[3] An Expedient for Taking away all Impositions and for Raising a Revenue without Taxes (1660), p. 5.
[4] A Proposal for the Advancement of Trade (1676), pp. 4–5.
[5] The many Advantages the Bank of the City of London will afford to the Public, and to all sorts of Traders (1684).
[6] An Account of the Land Bank, p. 1; B. M., Burney Collection, 113 a.

their Estates according to the settlement which is thus: Their Estates are to be convey'd in Trust for the Payment of the Principal and Interest to the Governors of the Land Bank. And upon further Trust, that the said Governors may have Power to charge the said Lands with Notes or Bills of Credit for the said Moneys so borrow'd and Interest for the same."

Such notes were actually issued by the proprietors of this land bank. But the theory of land banking was a fallacious one. It assumed that the provision of a security for the ultimate redemption of paper money is the same thing as the provision for redemption at any time. "Bills of credit," based on land, were regarded with suspicion by the general public because their issuers gave no guarantee that they were immediately redeemable at the demand of the holder.

Two other principles strongly advocated by the seventeenth-century banking theorists were copied from the continental banks. These were the "assignation of debts" by transfer of book credits, and the "receiving and paying" of all bills of exchange "in bank." Thus in 1641 we find Henry Robinson in his *Englands Safety in Trades Encrease* [1] pointing out that when the bank, which he proposed, "hath once got credit," "payments may be done by assignation, or turning them over from one to another without any reall assuring of monies, which besides saving trouble to tell so much money, becomes exceeding beneficiall to a Commonwealth, increasing the trade and traffic so much more as all the monies this Bank hath gained credit for doth import."

And so, also, Hartlib, a few years later, stressed the same principle, which was "the manner of the Banks beyond the Sea." Money deposited in a bank, he states, "instead of being carried out and delivered" should be "passed (person to person) by assignation only of the Ownership of so much money which (in the language of the place) is called credit in Bank or Bank-credit." [2]

This method of debt settlement between individuals by

---

[1] Pp. 34–35.   [2] *An Essay upon Master W. Potters Designe*, p. 2.

book transfers from one deposit account to another was termed on the Continent payments in " bank money." It was one of the outstanding characteristics of the Bank of Amsterdam, and has been described in detail by Dunbar.[1] The transfers were made on the authority of an order of the depositor making the payment, who either presented it at the bank in person or through a representative, but the actual transfer was not effected until the day after the order was received.[2] With the appearance of the " drawn note " or cheque in the private banking of the goldsmiths such transfers were carried out immediately the cheque was presented to the banker.

The assignation of debts by means of transfers in the books of a bank was a direct descendant of the method of offsetting debts in the great mediæval continental fairs. The author of *Observations upon the Bank of England*, a pamphlet which appeared in 1695, gives a clear description of this practice of cancelling indebtedness, which was termed *virement de parties*, or *scontration*. " At the City of Lyons in France," states this writer,[3] " there is, and hath of a long time been, a very convenient way and method of transferring Debts upon a sort of Register or Protochole which some have called a Bank. They also transfer Bills of Debt as in most other places of Trade in Christendom; so that great payments are made and but little Money used, and Returns of Money from one place to another made safe and easie, this being a sort of generall Ballance of Accounts, than any Transportation of Money."

The practice of compelling traders to present all bills of exchange over a certain amount for payment in a bank was one of the regulations of the Bank of Amsterdam. But this practice never took root in England. The goldsmiths and other financiers were allowed to carry on their dealings in bills of exchange without any restriction, and

---

[1] *Chapters on the Theory and History of Banking* (2nd ed., 1906), pp. 100–1.

[2] For a copy of the order see S. Ricard, *Traité Général du Commerce* (enlarged ed., 1781), I, p. 77.

[3] P. 11.   See also R. Ehrenburg, *Capital and Finance in the Age of the Renaissance*, p. 285; H. Sée, *op. cit.*, pp. 78–79 and 178; and P. Huvelin, *Le Droit des Marchés et des Foires*, pp. 563–64.

even when the Bank of England was established there was no regulation compelling traders to take any of their bills direct to the Bank for payment. Among the advocates of the Dutch method were Lambe, Lewis and Hartlib. Hartlib, however, went so far as to suggest that " all payments above ten or twenty pounds " should be " enjoyed by authority to be made in Bank-credit." [1]

Dealings in bills of exchange, both inland and " outland," greatly increased between the Restoration and the Revolution. The promissory notes of the goldsmith bankers were readily taken by the traders of the post-Restoration period in exchange for commercial bills, and so, later, were the notes of the Bank of England. The popularity of the inland bill is evident from the ledgers of Backwell, and the increasing use of this instrument is one of the reasons why the branch banks, the " petty Chambers " advocated by Beeckman and Cary, did not mature. A second reason was the fact that London was pre-eminently the commercial centre of Stuart England, the industrial north had not yet emerged, Liverpool, Manchester, Sheffield and Leeds were mere villages. A third reason was the increasing number of provincial people who kept deposits with the London bankers upon whom they could draw either an inland bill or a cheque. A fourth reason was the use made of the commercial letter of credit, a seventeenth-century example of which is thus given by Hatton in his much-studied *Merchant's Magazine*,[2] an important Stuart commercial treatise which reached its fourth edition in 1701 :

"I entreat you to furnish the Bearer hereof Mr. Mathew Meanwell the sum of Fifty Six Pounds Sterling at such time as he shall require the same, and place it to my Accompt for which this Letter of Credit, together with his Receipt, shall be your sufficient Voucher and Warrant, giving upon Payment a Line or two of Advice to
　　　　　　　　　　　your real Friend and Servant
To Mr. Nicholas Neverfail,　　　　　Samuel Standfast.
Merchant in Hull.
London May 1. 1697.

[1] *An Essay upon W. Potters Designe*, p. 32.　　　[2] P. 247.

A· fifth reason was the persistence of the practice among provincial traders of carrying sums from place to place for the settlement of debt. ·

The transporting of metallic money for the settlement of debt was criticised by Beeckman, who urged that it should be forbidden and that the inland bill should be abolished. He therefore proposed the establishment of four " Grand Chambers of Accompts " in London, and county or divisional " Chambers," which should be authorised to establish " Petty Chambers " in the " principal towns of trade throughout the kingdom," and that sums to be remitted from town to town should be paid into these " Chambers." Cash could then " be remitted to any place, as desired, with as great expedition as the General Post can reach it; the Party having his money so remitted paying for the same three pence per pound, or something more or less according to the distance of place from whence it shall be so remitted." [1]

But the inland bill of exchange was, in the latter half of the seventeenth century, too popular an instrument· to be superseded by any novel scheme for the remitting of money from one English town to another. The form of this type of bill is thus given by Hatton : [2]

> Norwich, June 1. 1697
> At four Days sight pay unto Mr Miles Moneylove, or his Order One hundred thirty two Pounds, value received of Edmund Easie and place it to Accompt as per Advice of
> Your Humble Servant
> David Draw-well
>
> To Mr Paul Punctual
> at the Ship in Grace-
> church-Street, London.

Such bills made payable to order were recognised by the Law Merchant as early as Cromwellian times as assignable by indorsement. Chief Justice Holt declared that inland bills were subject to the same law as " outland " or foreign bills. It is a noteworthy fact that the general recognition

---

[1] *Proposals . . . to raise Five Hundred Thousand Pounds per Annum to the Government*, p. 2.
[2] *Merchant's Magazine*, p. 238.

of the assignability of bills of exchange payable to order corresponds with the development of goldsmith banking in England. The emergence of banking law based on test cases in the Courts of Common Law contributed towards the banker's security. But it was not until the case of *Williams* v. *Williams* in 1693 that the goldsmith's promissory note payable to order was held by the Courts of Common Law to be an assignable instrument. This decision held good for ten years, when its reversal by Holt resulted in the famous Act of 1704, which declared all kinds of promissory notes negotiable. " If you pay a Debt with a Bill that is payable to you or Order," wrote Hatton in the fourth edition of his *Merchant's Magazine* in 1701,[1] " you must first write your Name on the backside of the Bill, which is Assigning it, as practised among Traders. But if you pay a Debt with a Note payable to such a one or Bearer, then you only deliver the Note. And it is the Wisdom in Bankers that pay part of a Bill or Note to make the Indorsement cross that part which is most wrote on, to avoid Deceipt by taking off the Indorsement."

Thus when the Bank of England was launched in 1694, the status of the credit instruments of the day had been clearly defined both by the Law Merchant and the Common Law. A " custom of Bankers " had emerged, and had been duly regularised. The business of the Bank could, therefore, be firmly based on the principles of deposit, of discount and of issue, of which that of issue was the most important. " No Bank in the World," wrote Sir Theodore Janssen in 1697,[2] " ever was so happily constituted; no Bank hath so great a Revenue settled upon so good a Fund and so little paid for it."

[1] P. 203.   [2] *A Discourse concerning Banks*, p. 4.

APPENDIX 1

THE EARLIEST EXAMPLES OF GOLDSMITHS' RECEIPT NOTES

In possession of Messrs. Hoare, 37, Fleet Street, London, and published by permission of this well-known banking house. The first of these is the earliest known specimen.

Undecimo die Decembris 1633

Receaved ye day and year above written of William Hale Esq. for a post ffyne charged upon Rowland Hale Esq. upon ye accompt of Henrie Coghill Esquire High Sheriffe of ye Countie of Herts ye some of three poundes and five shillings of current English money I say receaved as aforesaid

By me

Lawrence Hoare.

June the 9th 1671

Rec^d of Mr Richard Green p order of Mr Robt Everret the summe of one hundred seaventy and five pounds and is for the use of and uppon the Accompt of Wm Hale Esq.   li   175

I say rec^d————

for my Mr Robt Tempest

p Richard Hoare

THE PRIVATE ACCOUNTS OF SAMUEL PEPYS AND NARCISSUS
LUTTRELL. FROM THE EARLIEST OF MESSRS. HOARE'S
LEDGERS

By permission of Messrs. Hoare.

The ledger from which the accounts of these two famous
diarists are taken belonged to Richard Hoare, goldsmith banker.
It will be observed that Mr. Pepys' account is overdrawn.

SAMUELL PEPYS ESQ is Dr

			£	S.	D.
Jan 1680	18	By £017 : paid Mrs Hollinshead p. note from Dr	17	—	—
Febr	9	,, £010. 15 paid Dr p. his rec^t	10	15	0
Mar	9	,, £005 paid Mr Moses Pitty p. note from Dr	5	—	—
,,	9	,, £010. 15 paid Dr p. his rec^t	10	15	0
,,	17	,, £014. 0 paid Mr Edw Hollinshead for Mr Hollinshead p. note from Dr	14	00	0
Apr	11	,, £010. 16. 8 paid p. his rec^t	10	16	8
,,	13	,, £008 paid Mr Godfrey Richards p. note from Dr	8	—	—
May	2	,, £12. 16. 8 paid Dr p. his own rec^t	12	16	8
June	11	,, £10. 16. 8 ,, ,, ,, ,, ,,	10	16	8
,,	20	,, £12. 18. 0 ,, ,, ,, ,, ,,	12	18	—
Aug	13	,, £07 paid Mr Robert Hasellwood p. note from Dr	7	—	—
,,	20	,, £24. 10. paid Mr Robert Scott p. note from Dr	24	10	(
,,	26	,, £30. 0 paid the Lady Bernard p. note from Dr	30	—	—
Sep	26	,, £16. 05. 0 paid Dr p. his rec^t	16	05	0
Nov	9	,, £15. 16. 8 ,, ,, ,, ,,	15	16	8
		,, £10 paid Dr on the 29 of January	10	—	—

SAMUELL PEPYS ESQ is Cr

			£	S.	D.
Dec 1680	13	ffor £200 rec^d of Cr p note	200	(	

NARCISSUS LUTTRELL ESQ is D^r

			£	S.	D.
Mar 1681	18	By £200 paid Mrs Catherine Love my note for	200	00	0
May 1682	25	,, £150 paid Dr in pt of my note for £500	150	00	0
June	2	,, £50 paid Mrs C. L. p. note from Dr	50	00	0
July	13	,, £200 paid ditto p. note from Dr	200	00	0
,,	19	,, £100 paid Mr Henry Turner p. note from Dr	100	00	0
			700	00	0

NARCISSUS LUTTRELL ESQ is C^r

			£	S.	D.
Mar 1681	10	ffor £500 rec^d of Cr p. note	500	00	0
	15	,, £200 rec^d of Cr p. note	200	00	0
			700	00	0

R

APPENDIX 3

OTHER EXAMPLES OF PRIVATE ACCOUNTS FROM THE LEDGERS OF GOLDSMITH BANKERS

The following account is taken by permission of Messrs. Hoare from the earliest of their ledgers. The customer's inspection certificate is appended.

WILLIAM HALE Esq is D^{btr}

			£	S.	D.
June 5 1676	By £80 paid Mr. Jacob Lucy p. Mr Tho Williams p. note from D^{btr}		80	0	
10	„ £100 paid Mr John fford p. note from D^{btr}		100		
22	„ £100 paid Mr Rich Parker p. note from Mr Nicolas Clerke		100	(	
11	„ £54–10–10 paid Mr Wm Morgan for Sr John Auston		54	10	10
12	„ £73–10–0 paid Mr Harner for Capt Haddock		73	10	0
	„ £160 paid D^{btr} p. his rec^t		160	0	0
	„ £50 paid John Hoskins Esq for the Lady Williamson		50	0	0
12	„ £155–10–0 paid Mr Nicholas Clerke		155	10	0
			773	10	10

July 12 1676

This account seen and allowed by mee
Will Hale

WILLIAM HALE Esq is C^r

			£	S.	D.
May 26 1676	ffor £180 recd of Mr Richard Green p. the hands of Mr George fford p. order of Mr Robt Everet		180	0	0
June 22	„ £300 recd of Mr Nicholas Clerke		300	0	0
July 4	„ £503–6–8 recd of Mr Richard Clapham		503	6	8
			983	6	8

July 12 1676

By this account seen and allowed by mee this day Mr Hoare is debtor to mee two hundred and nine pounds fifteen shillings and ten pence and no more   209 15 10

Will Hale.

242

The following accounts are taken by permission of Messrs. Glyn, Mills & Co. from Alderman Edward Backwell's ledger, dated 1664 (Ledger L).

ROBERT LYE.

Dr.

			£	s.	D.
1664					
March 25	To Ballance in Ledger, K, f. 117		500 : 00 : 00
	Paid for Interest—Simple interest only of the £1775 : 05 : 00 as per Interest folio 114........................		027 : 05 : 00
April 18	To him		600 : 00 : 00
April 20	To the Earl of St Albans		266 : 13 : 07
April 27	To him		373 : 06 : 05
Sept 16	For a Bill on Mr Denew		445 : 00 : 00

	2212 : 05 : 00
To Int. acc°	8 : 00 : 00
	2220 : 05 : 00

ROBERT LYE.

Cr.

		£	s.	D.
Due in Jany.	By a Tally on the farmers of the Customes dated the 16th March 1663 given mee on the 24th March 1663 which is putt to Dbt of the farmers in folio 199	1775 : 05 : 00
Sept 17	By Mr Denew	445 : 00 : 00

2220 : 05 : 00

JAMES BLACKBIRD

Cr.

		£	S.	D.
March 31	By Bill drawn at 2ᵈᵃ sight paya to Majʳ Ashton value of Mʳ Bulstroode	200	00	00
March 31	By Bill drawn at sight paya to Mʳ Allexʳ Horton or order value of him	200	00	00
Apr 11	By Bill drawn on him at sight paya to Nath Garrerd	150	00	00
Apr 13	By Bill drawn on him at 2ᵈᵃ sight paya to Mʳ Loft value received of himself	240	00	00
Apr 21	By Bill drawn on him paya to Nich Pickering Esq	100	00	00
May 3	By Bill drawn on him at sight paya to Capt Jeffrey 200 li another to Majʳ Walters 100 li another to Majʳ Ashton 100 li value of Mʳ Bulstroode	400	00	00
May 27	By Bill drawn at sight paya to Oglethorpe	97	03	09
		2970	03	09

THE OWNERS OF THE SHIPP ROYAL KATHERINE

Dr

1664

	£	s	d
To Bal. from Ledger K, f. 443	80	0	0

Cr

	£	s	d
By Sʳ And Riccards	2	10	0
By Mʳ Rich. Foley (his share)	37	10	0
By the shipp Royal Katherine			
for my owne 32ⁿᵈ part of her stock	37	10	0
for seamen's wages I paid	2	10	0
	80	0	0

ITEMS SELECTED FROM AN EXCHANGE ACCOUNT IN ONE
OF THE LEDGERS OF ALDERMAN EDWARD BACKWELL
GOLDSMITH BANKER

By permission of Messrs. Glyn, Mills & Co.

EXCH^A ACC^T.

Dr

1664			£ s. D.
Apr	20	Allowed Mr Lindsay in folio 204 for pvision of receiving £302. 10. 00 in Edinburgh ½ p. cent and for paying it mee in Berwick 1 p. cent	4 : 10 : 00
June	8	To Mr Decosta	2 : 10 : 00
Sept	20	To a Broker	0 : 14 : 00

Cr

Mar	29	By exch^a & Int of 400 li Bristoll	10 : 00 : 00
Mar	31	By 100 for Yorke	1 : 00 : 00
Apr	5	By 200 for Dublin	10 : 00 : 00
May	7	By 100 from Chester	1 : 00 : 00
May	19	By 250 for Amster	6 : 09 : 00
May	24	By 60 from Bristol	1 : 00 : 00
May	24	By Thomas Seward folio 420 *	3 : 00 : 00
June	11	By 50 from Exon	0 : 15 : 00
July	1	By Dolin's bills	2 : 04 : 06
July	2	By 100 from Exon	0 : 10 : 00
July	5	By 350 from Yorke.......................	3 : 10 : 00
July	7	By 95. 8. 4 from Plim°	0 : 09 : 04

* The following entry appears on the Cr. side of Seward's
Account, folio 420 :

By his bill given for Edinburgh negotiated with Jno⎫ £ s. D.
Lindsay fol. 204
52 : 10 : 00   Out of which dt deducted   ⎬ 49. 10. 0.
 3 : 00 : 00   ⎭

─────
49 : 10 : 00

APPENDIX 5

ENTRIES, DATED 13TH NOVEMBER 1656 TO 2ND JULY 1657, FROM A CROMWELLIAN EXCHEQUER BOOK RECORDING THE RECEIPT OF "MONEYES PAYABLE" BY SIR THOMAS VYNER AND EDWARD BACKWELL, GOLDSMITH BANKERS, "UPON THEIR CONTRACT FOR THE SPANISH PLATE AND MONEY"[1]

Receipt Books (Pells), P.R.O., Recs. Ex. R., E. 401/1931, fols. 17–180.

Each amount recorded is preceded by the following description :

"Of Sr Thomas Vyner, Knt and Edward Backwell Cittizen and Goldsmith of London in part of the Moneyes payable by them upon their contract for the Spanish plate and money lately brought by generall Montague."

The following are the recorded amounts between the dates specified :

Folio in Receipt Book.	Date received at the Exchequer.	Amount of the instalment.		
		£	S.	D.
22	13 November 1656	2,000.	0.	0.
29	22 ,, ,,	1,000.	0.	0.
35	24 ,, ,,	1,200.	0.	0.
40	5 December ,,	10,000.	0	0.
40	5 ,, ,,	2,000.	0.	0.
41	5 ,, ,,	10,000.	0.	0.
41	5 ,, ,,	10,000.	0.	0.
43	9 ,, ,,	1,000.	0.	0.
54	25 ,, ,,	5,700.	4.	7.
55	26 ,, ,,	4,000.	0.	0.
56	30 ,, ,,	4,000.	0.	0.
57	31 ,, ,,	1,500.	0.	0.
73	27 January 1657	10,000.	0.	0.
97	28 February ,,	5,000.	0.	0.
106	16 March ,,	6,000.	0.	0.
116	28 ,,	4,000.	0.	0.
123	18 April	8,000.	0.	0.
133	1 May	6,000.	0.	0.
180	2 July ,,	5,000.	0.	0.

[1] In the contract between Sir Thomas Vyner and Backwell on the one hand and the Council of State on the other it was arranged that the whole of the Spanish prize-money was to be brought to Portsmouth by Montague, and conveyed in waggons to London to be coined at the Mint under the direction of the two goldsmith bankers. For this privilege they agreed to make a preliminary advance of £50,000 to the Government between 31st October and 16th November 1656. S.P. Dom., Interregnum, Council of State, I, 77, fols. 462–65.

APPENDIX 6

A TREASURY WARRANT, DATED 15TH JULY 1664, AUTHORIS-
ING THE DRAWING OF AN ORDER FOR PAYMENT OF
£357 4s. 9d. DUE TO EDWARD BACKWELL FOR RECOINING
THE CROSS AND HARP MONEY

Warrant Books (Auditor's), P.R.O., Recs. Ex. R., E.403/3032,
fol. 3.

Edw. Backwell.   After my hearty Consideracons etc His Matie
by his Lres of Privie Seale bearing Date the xxx^th
day of May in the xvj^th yeare of his Maties Reign
having directed the sume of ccclvij^li iiij^s ix^d to be
paid out of the Excheq^r to Edward Backwell Esq
being soe much due unto him for recoyning of the
Crosse and Harpe money att the rate of cx^li for
every hundred pounds according to an agreement
made betweene his Matie and the said Edward
Backwell These are to will and pray you to drawe
an ord^r for the payment of the said sume of
357li. 4s. 9d. unto the said Edward Backwell or
his Assignes according to the Divisions of his
Maties said Lres of Privie Seale And cause Tallies
to be strucke for the same upon the ffarmers of
his Maties Customes for their halfe yeares rent
ending att Michas next And for soe doing this
shalbe your warrant Given at Southton House
the 15th of July 1664.

l. s. d.
357 4 9

Customes
Mich. 1664.

Southampton.

To my loving ffriend
Sr Robert Long.

247

A TREASURY WARRANT, DATED 25TH OCTOBER 1664, FOR THE
PAYMENT OF £8,000 AND £1,500 TO EDWARD BACKWELL,
THE FORMER SUM AS A FREE GIFT FOR LOANS TO
CHARLES II, AND THE LATTER AS AN ALLOWANCE FOR
RECEIVING THE DUNKIRK MONEY

Warrant Books (Auditor's), P.R.O., Recs. Ex. R., E.403/3032,
fols. 12–12a.

Mr. Backwell for Reward of Loane of Money —80⁰⁰ li. and 1500 li. for receiving the Dunkirke Money

Tallies upon London Excise for the yeare ending in Novemb 1665

After my hearty Commendacons Whereas Edward Backwell Esq hath advanced the sume of Two hundred eighty six thousand forty two pounds for several occasions of His Matie as Navy Guards etc for which he received the ordinary consideracon of six pounds p. cent from the tyme of payment thereof till the precise day it was repaid His Matie being sensible that to furnish these his occasions and that the said Edward Backwell might not be unprovided when he was called upon for them was forced to admit large proporcons of other mens monies in Banck (which he payes interest for) than otherwise he would doe which putts him upon greater uncertainties than others who deale in common loanes where a precise day of payment is ffixt And His Matie further reflecting upon ye necessary attendance and expenses undergone in his service resolving henceforth that upon view of these Accompts stated upon simple Interest to determine himself what to allowe further as a free gift hath by his Lres of Privie Seale dated the fourteenth day of September last (for the services aforemenconed) directed the sume of eight thousand pounds to be paid to the said Mr. Backwell as of His Maties free gift and without Accompt or any other allowance to be paid by him other than what is usually paid for the Navy or Household Affayres And whereas the said Edw. Backwell did by His Maties Comands transport himselfe with his servants into ffraunce to count and receive the sume of ffoure Millions and five hundred thousand Livres agreed to be paid to His Matie by the ffrench king

248

upon the rendring of Dunkirke His Matie for the great paines and charge in that service and likewise in respect of the hazard in securing it against all false counting and false monies hath determined to make him an allowance in grosse of the sume of 1500 li and by his Lres of Privie Seale above menconed hath directed the same to be paid without accompt These are therefore to pray and require you to drawe severall orders for payment of the severall sumes of 8000 li and 1500 li to the said Edward Backwell for the respective services aforementioned as by the Privie Seale is authorised And let Tallies be struck for the same on the ffarmers of His Maties Excise of London Midd and Surrey on the year ending in November 1665 And for soe doing this shalbe your warr^t

Southampton.

Southton House
October 25th 1664
To Sr Robert Long Baronet
  Auditor.

APPENDIX ·8

A LIST OF TALLIES STRUCK· ON THE HEARTH DUTY HELD BY SIR ROBERT VYNER, GOLDSMITH BANKER

Warrant Books (Auditor's), P.R.O., Recs. Ex. R., E.403/3039, fol. 33*b*.

		l.	s.	d.
Sr George Carteret	12 July 1666	3000.	0.	0.
Trer of the Navy	the same	3000.	0.	0.
Earl of Sandwich	5 ffebry 1666	3000.	0.	0.
	the same	3000.	0.	0.
Sr George Carteret	26 Aprill 1667	10000.	0.	0.
	the same	10000.	0.	0.
	the same	10000.	0.	0.
	the same	10000.	0.	0.
		52000.	0.	0.

A PRIVY SEAL, DATED 25TH AUGUST 1669, AUTHORISING PAY-
MENT TO EDWARD BACKWELL OF £4,650 16s. 8d. AS
INTEREST, ALLOWANCE AND GRATUITY ON SEVERAL
LOANS TO CHARLES II AND AN ATTACHED "GENERAL
ACCOMPT OF INTEREST"

Privy Seal Books (Pells), P.R.O., Recs. Ex. R., E.403/2611,
fols. 17b–19b.

Edward Back-
well Esq.

Charles the Second by the grace of God King of
England, Scotland, ffraunce and Ireland Defend^r
of the ffaith to the Com^rs of Our Treary now being
And to the Trear under Trear and Com^rs of our
Treary for the tyme being Greeting Whereas
upon an Interest Account of Edward Backwell Esq
stated by Richard Aldworth Esq one of the Seaven
Auditors of our Revenue for money by him advanced
unto our Excheq^r and unto severall psons upon
severall occasions for our Service made up to the
ffoure and twentieth of June last it appeareth that
the said Edward Backwell hath advanced for our
Service within the tyme of the said Account at
severall tymes in the said Account menconed

Advanced
157,683l. 4s. 10d.

severall sumes of money amounting in the whole
to the sume of one hundred ffifty seaven thousand
six hundred and eighty three pounds four shillings
and tenn pence whereof was repaid unto him at or
before the said ffoure and twentieth of June last
the sume of eighty six thousand six hundred eighty

Repaid
86,688l. 9s. 2d.

eight pounds nine shillings and two pence and then
remayned unpaid of the Principall money the sume
of seaventy thousand nine hundred ninety ffour
pounds fifteene shillings and eight pence ffor which
severall sumes so advanced as aforesaid there is
due to the said Edward Backwell for interest at
six pounds p. cent p. annum from the severall
tymes the same stands charged in the said Account
to the respective days of repayment of the said
eighty six thousand six hundred eighty eight
pounds nine shillings and two pence pt thereof and
of the said sume of seaventy thousand nine hundred

ninety ffoure pounds ffifteen shillings eight pence
being the residue unpaid to the tyme of makeing
up of the said account the sume of two thousand
seaven hundred and sixty pounds ffifteen shillings
tenn pence and for foure pounds p. cent p. annum
being two thirds more of all the said interest which
we are graciously pleased to allow unto him as
gratuity for his good Service in the seasonable
supply of the said money for our Service as aforesaid and for his charge and expense in furnishing
the same the sume of eighteene hundred fforty five
pounds seaventeene shillings and two pence both
sumes due for the interest at six pounds p. cent
upon the said account with the allowance of two
thirds more of the said interest amounts to the
sume of ffoure thousand six hundred and ffourteene
pounds thirteene shillings together with more which
is due to him for interest and allowance at the rate
aforesaid for the sume of nine hundred and sixty
pounds by him advanced for payment of our
ffootemen and charged on the Additional Aide
over and above the sume of one hundred pounds
which was paid unto him by Sir Edward Griffen
Trear of our Chamber in part of the said interest
and allowance for the said nine hundred and sixtie
pounds the whole of all which sumes for interest
and allowance by way of Gratuity amount to the
full sume of ffoure thousand six hundred ffifty
pounds sixteene shillings and eight pence. Our
will and pleasure therefore is and wee doe hereby
Com̃and and authorise you out of our Treasure
now or hereafter being or remayning in our Receipt
of the Exchequer to pay or cause to be paid to the
said Edward Backwell or his Assignes the said
sume of ffour thousand six hundred and ffifty
pounds sixteene shillings and eight pence in full
satisffaccon of all Interest and Charge for the
ffurnishing and advancing of the said severall
principall sumes of one hundred fifty seaven
thousand six hundred eighty three pounds ffoure
shillings and tenn pence and nine hundred and
sixtie pounds advanced as aforesaid without any
Accompt Interest or other Charge to be sett upon
him his Executors or Assignes for the same or any
part thereof. And because the said Principall
sumes of money were advanced furnished and repaid
at severall tymes or still remayning due as aforesaid
which is not pticularly menconed in these our lres

of Privy Seale but are exactly expressed and conteyned in the aforesaid Account of the said Auditor Aldworth Our will and pleasure therefore is that together with these our lres of Privy Seale you send it to the Receipt of our Exchequer the said Interest Account And that you have direcion to have the same kept there and entred upon Record together with these our lres of Privy Seale to the end no further demands be hereafter made of us our heires or successors for the said interest and allowance or any part thereof. And these our lres shall be your sufficient warr^t and discharge in this behalfe. Given under our Privy Seale at our Palace of Westminster the ffive and twentieth day of August in the one and twentieth yeare of our Reigne

25th August
1669

Tho Watkins. Dep. Comit. de Sandwich.

Scr xvij die Novemb 1669

GENERALL ACCOMPT OF INTEREST and Allowances due from his Matie to Edward Backwell Esq for Moneys by him paid into the Exchequer and Advanced to severall persons by way of Loane for use of his Matie as by the Particular Accompts (relation thereunto being had) may appeare viz.

PRINCIPALL		INTEREST due to Edward Backwell Esq to 4th June 1669
29,000	Advanced to the right hono^ble Arthur Earle of Anglesey for the use of the Navy upon Security of the Eleaven Moneths Tax as p. Accompt Ro. A.	l. s. d. 400. 2. 0.
04,500	Paid into the Exchequer for the said Earle to be by him imployed for the use of the Navy upon Security of the Customes as p. Accompt Ro. B	055. 14. 6.
25,000	Paid into the Exchequer by order of the right hono^ble ye Lords Commissio^rs of ye Treary upon Security of the Customes as p. Accompt Ro. C	291. 2. 3.
02,000	Paid into the Exchequer by order of the said Lords Commissio^rs of ye Treasury upon Security of ye Eleaven Moneths Tax as p. Accompt Ro. D	055. 11. 3.
1,918. 15. 0.	Advanced to the right hono^ble Henry Lord Viscount Arlington upon Security of the Customes as appeares p. Accompt Ro. E	057. 1. 6.

		INTEREST due to Edward Backwell Esq to 4th June 1669
PRINCIPALL		

PRINCIPALL		INTEREST
0,600. 00. 0.	Advanced to Sr Robert Southwell K^t upon Security of the Customes as appeares p. Accompt Ro. F	l. s. d. 016. 19. 3.
3,000. 00. 0.	Advanced to the Marquis de Mountbrun upon Security of ye Eleaven Moneths tax as p. Accompt. Ro. G	073. 10. 9.
3,185. 18. 9.	Advanced to Sir William Temple Baronet upon Security of the Customes as p. Accompt Ro. H	062. 16. 1.
0,200. 00. 0.	Advanced for pulling downe Houses about ye Tower Assigned this Accomptant upon Capt Geo. Wharton as p. Accompt Ro. J	004. 17. 4.
0,463. 5. 6.	Remainder of a Privy Seale dated 19 January 1665 Secured this Accomptant upon the Royall Ayd as p. Accompt. Ro. K	013. 15. 6.
1,000. 00. 0.	Advanced to Sir John ffinch Ambassador in Italy upon Security of the Customes as p. Accompt. Ro. L	019. 7. 11.
30,000. 00. 0.	Paid into the Exchequer for Sir Tho. Littleton and Sir Tho. Osborne for the use of the Navy upon Security of the Customes as p. Accompt. Ro. M	652. 8.
10,000. 00. 0.	Paid into the Exchequer upon Security of the Crowne Lands as appeares p. Accompt. Ro. N.	267. 12. 6.
20,000. 00. 0.	Paid into the Exchequer for Sir Edw. Griffen Treasurer of the Chamber upon Security of the Customes as p. Accompt. Ro. O	408. 9. 9.
2,700. 00. 0.	Paid into the Exchequer for Ralph Montague Esq upon Security of the Customes as p. Accompt. Ro. P	066. 11. 6.
0,920. 00. 0.	Paid into the Exchequer for Sir William Godolphin upon Security of the Customes as p. Accompt. Ro. Q	021. 12. 6.
0,400. 00. 0.	Paid into the Exchequer for Sir Peter Wyche upon Security of the Customes as p. Accompt. Ro. R	008. 12. 3.
6,750. 00. 0.	Paid into the Exchequer for the right hono^{ble} Henry Lord Howard upon Security of the Customes as p. Accompt. Ro. S	062. 2. 7.
5,000. 00. 0.	Paid into the Exchequer for which no Particular Security is yet assigned this Accomptant as p. Accompt. Ro. T	022. 3. 10.

PRINCIPALL

3,000. 00. 0. Paid into the Exchequer for the right honoᵇˡᵉ Edward Earle of Sandwiche p. Wardrobe upon Security of the Customes as p. Ro. V.

l.   s.   d.
5. 18.   2.

6,657. 16. 4. Principall due to this Accomptant the 25th December 1668 secured upon the Eleaven Moneths Tax and Customes as p. Accompt. Ro. W

173. 00. 5.

0,322, 10. 0. Paid the Lord Chamberlain of his Maᵗⁱᵉˢ Household and Sir Charles Cotterell for Senior Oniatto on Security promised upon the Customes as p. Accompt. Ro. X

006. 3. 11.

0,500. 00. 0. Advanced to the right honoᵇˡᵉ Charles Earle of Carlisle yᵉ 18ᵗʰ ffebruary 1668 on Security promised upon the Customes as p. Accompt. Ro. Y

009. 12. 4.

0,215. 00. 0. Paid yᵉ Lord Chamberlain of his Maᵗⁱᵉˢ Household for yᵉ Portugall Agent on Security promised this Accomptant upon yᵉ Customes as p. Accompt. Ro. Z

004. 18. 10.

0,350. 00. 0. Paid Peter du Moulin upon Security promised this Accomptant on yᵉ Customes as p. Accompt. Ro. AA

008. 10. 2.

_____

157,683. 04. 10.

To which add ⅔ᵈˢ

2,768. 15. 10.
1,845. 17. 2.

_____

4,614. 13. 0,

0,960. 00. 0. Advanced to Sir Edward Griffen Knᵗ for payment of his Maᵗⁱᵉˢ ffootemen a yeares sallary upon Security of the Additional Ayd as p. Ro. BB.

36. 03. 8.

_____

158,643. 4. 10.

4,650. 16. 8.

Edward Backwell
Tho. Watkins, Dep. Comᵗⁱˢ
de Sandwich
George Usher, Clerke to
Richard Aldworth Esq.
Auditor

Scr. in Offic. Clici. Pellin
xvij die November 1669

APPENDIX 10

THE INTEREST ACCOUNT OF JOHN PORTMAN, GOLDSMITH BANKER, ATTACHED TO A PRIVY SEAL, DATED 31ST MARCH 1671, AUTHORISING PAYMENT OF £497 17s. 6¼d. AS INTEREST AND "CHARGES" ON A LOAN OF £9,608 16s. 1d. ADVANCED BY THIS BANKER

Privy Seal Books (Pells), P.R.O., Recs. Ex. R., E. 403/2611, fols. 12a–13.

THE ACCOMPT OF JOHN PORTMAN OF LONDON, GOLD-SMITH, for the Interest of Severall Sumes of money by him advanced upon the Creditt of severall tallies unto the Right Honble George Carteret late Trear of His Maties navy at severall tymes for His Maties use between the 30th day of March 1666 exclusive and the 23rd of Aprill 1667 inclusive, as also of several sumes of money by him received upon those tallies and interest rebated therefore stated by order of the Right Honble the Lords Commissioners of His Maties Treasury signified by Sr George Downing their Lord^{ps} Secretarie

as followeth

THE KING DEBTOR TO THE ACCOMPTANT
viz for

Money lent	The tyme when	Interest there-fore due to ye 14th of December 1667 when the last money was paid.	For what tyme the interest is become due.
l. s. d.		l. s. d.	
0460. 01. 03.	30th March 1666	047. 01. 02.	20 Monthes 14 Dayes
0668. 04. 00.	Ditto	068. 07. 01.	20 Monthes 14 Dayes
1000. 00. 00.	7th Aprill 1666	101. 03. 00.	20 Monthes 7 Dayes
1000. 00. 00.	10th May	095. 13. 01¾	19 Monthes 4 Dayes
2500. 00. 00.	31th December 1666	143. 05. 00½	11 Monthes 14 Dayes
0500. 00. 00.	29th January 1667	026. 03. 00¼	10 Monthes 14 Dayes
0500. 00. 00.	29th March 1667	021. 04. 07¾	8 Monthes 15 Dayes
0240. 00. 00.	27th Aprill 1667	009. 02. 02½	7 Monthes 18 Dayes
1207. 17. 06.	18th Aprill 1667	047. 08. 09¼	7 Monthes 26 Dayes
1532. 13. 04.	23th Aprill 1667	058. 18. 07½	7 Monthes 26 Dayes
9608. 16. 01.	Totall	618. 06. 08½	Total of Interest
7168. 05. 04.	Money Repaid	319. 12. 02¼	⎰Interest due to the ⎱King p. Contra ⎰Deducted
2440. 10. 09.	The Remayne		
		298. 14. 06¼	Then Remaynes
		199. 03. 00.	⎰The Kings Addiconall ⎱allowance of ⅔rd
		497. 17. 06¼	The Totall of Interest due to the Accomptant

Mr. John ffen late Agent to Sr George Carteret in pursuance of an Order of his Ma^{ty} and the Councell made oath the 13th of febr 1668 before Mr Baron Atkins that ye severall sumes of money in this Account mençoned were advanced by Mr. Portman unto Sr George Carteret at or upon the severall dayes and yeares above mençoned

Mr. John Portman sworne ye 10th of December 1668 before Baron Spelman deposeth ye like as to ye money advanced and the tymes when soe advanced and also depòseth that ye sume of 7168: 05: 04 was repaid him upon the several dayes and Yeares in the Accompt mençoned

THE ACCOMPTANT DEBTOR TO THE KING FOR MONEY REPAID AND INTEREST THEREFOR

Money repaid	The tyme when	By whom	Interest therefor to ye 14th of 10 BER 1667	Ffor what tyme the interest is become due
l. s. d.			l. s. d.	
2500. 00. 00.	17th October 1666	Thos Weedon rec^d of the Royall Ayd in Com. Bucks.	173. 11. 11.	13 Monthes 27 Dayes
0768. 05. 04.	15th ffebruary ditto	The same received	038. 04. 10¼	9 Monthes 29 Dayes
0500. 00. 00.	27th ffebr 1666	Repaid by Mr John ffen	023. 17. 11¼	9 Monthes 17 Dayes
2800. 00. 00.	15th June 1667	Mr. Strickland rec^d of ye Royall Ayd for Yorkshire	083. 06. 11½	5 Monthes 29 Dayes
0200. 00. 00	28th Novemb. 1667	Mr. Hollinghead rec^d of ye Royall Ayd for Stafford		
0400. 00. 00	14th Decemb. 1667	Mr Sands rec^d of ye Royall Ayd of Cumberland	000. 10. 06¼	0 Monthes 16 Dayes
7168. 05. 04.	Totall money repaid		319. 12. 02¼	Interest due to the King

And then Remayned due to the said Accomptant ye 14th Decemb 1667

PRINCIPALL 2440. 10. 09
INTEREST   497. 17. 06¼

l. s. d.
2938. 08. 03¼

viz

Mem^d The Accomptant hath severall Tallies assigned to him for pt of the remayning Principall amounting to 2400 l. of which pt is received and pt not as he informeth.

s

I cannot find by the Privy Seale for Interest allowed to
Sr George Carteret nor by the Papers recd from Auditor
Phellipps any mencon made of loans to Sr George Carteret
by this Accomptant who doth informe me that this is the
first money lent that ever hee hath advanced to the said
Sr George Carteret for the Kings Service

C Bickerstaff

Ex. p. Wm. Chislett: Dep. Auditor
   Scr. viii die Novembr 1669

A PRIVY SEAL, DATED 21ST MAY 1671, TO SIR ROBERT VYNER FOR THE PAYMENT OF £9,063 15s. 7d. AND £22,865 8s. 8d FOR GOLD CHAINS, MEDALS, PLATE AND JEWELS SUPPLIED TO CHARLES II.

Privy Seal Books (Auditor's), P.R.O., Recs. Ex. R., E.403/2573, fols. 102–102b.

Sr ROBERT
VYNER

Sir Gilbert
Talbot received
from Sr Robert
Vyner several
pcells of Plate
Jewells Chaines
and Medalls

m
ix lxiijli xvs vijd

Crowne gold
vje xij ounces
given away in
Chaines and
Medalls to
Ambassadors

Gilt Plate
for Christenings
and Gifts.

Charles the Second by the Grace of God King of England, Scotland ffraunce and Ireland Defender of the ffaith etc   To the Comrs of Our Treary now being and the Trer under Trer and Commisiors of Our Treary for the time being Greeting   Whereas it appears by Certificate of Sr Gilbert Talbot Knt Master of Our Jewell House bearing date the xxvth day of March 1671 that he hath received into Our Jewell House from Sr Robert Vyner Our Goldsmith divers Chaines Medalls and other Gold Works wth some Jewells and also severall parcells of Gilt Plate wth some money by him disbursed amounting in the whole to the sume of twenty two thousand eight hundred sixty five pounds eight shillings and eight pence viz ffor twenty five thousand seaven hundred sixty foure ounces two penny weight of white Plate for Our Stores most of it curiously wrought and enchased which its severall prices doth Amount to the sume of Nyne thousand sixty three pounds fifteene shillings and seaven pence, ffor six hundred and twelve ounces sixteene pennyweight, ffourteene grains of Angell and Crowne gold given away in Chaines and Medalls to Ambassadors and others wth a George and Garter to the Prince of Orange from the fourteenth of ffebruary One thousand six hundred sixty eight to the five and twentyeth of March One thousand six hundred seaventy and wch Amounts unto for Gold Jewells and Workmanshipp three thousand five hundred fifty eight pounds six shillings and three pence Also for eighteen thousand three hundred fifty two ounces one quarter of amount of gilt Plate given at Christenings and for New Yeares gifts wch at severall Prices doth amount unto Eight thousand nyne hundred and ffive pounds ffifteen shillings and two pence ffor new making repairing and golding severall parcells of Our Store Plate the sume of One thousand and ninety pounds seaventeene shillings and sixpence Also for engraving seaven hundred and fifty two peeces of Plate wth Armes, And three hundred and eighty one peeces wth G R and Crowne and one Christall Glasse, the sume of One hundred forty eight pounds eight pence

Moneys disbursed to ye Cutler and Casemaker

Also by money by him disbursed to the Cutler and Casemaker for Knives Blades and Cases fforty three pounds thirteene shillings sixpence And also for money paid to Walter Brydall, Thomas Tindall and John Gilbert Officers of the said Jewell House for Parchment Vellum Ink Paper Wood Coales and other Necessaries from January the tenth One thousand six hundred and sixty seaven to July the tenth One thousand six hundred and sixty eight and from January the tenth One thousand six hundred and sixty eight to January the tenth One thousand six hundred and seaventy fifty five pounds the particulars of all which pcells of Gold Plate and other things as recd certified by Our said Master of Our Jewell House to be delivered in by the said Sr Robert Vyner from the ffourteenth of ffebruary one thousand six hundred and sixty eight aforesaid to the xxv^{th} of March last One thousand six hundred seaventy one And doth now at large appeare in the Books of Our said Jewell Office wch sume of twenty two thousand eight hundred sixty five pounds eight shillings and eight pence soe due to the said Sr Robert Vyner Wee are graciously pleased shall be satisfyed unto him Our Will and pleasure therefore is And Wee doe hereby command and authorize you out of such Our Treasure now or hereafter being and remayning in the Receipt of Our said Excheq^r to pay or cause to be paid unto the said Sr Robert Vyner or his

m. c.
xxii viij lxv^{li}
viij^s viij^d

assignes the said sume of twenty two thousand eight hundred sixty five pounds eight shillings and eight pence of lawfull money of England in full satisfacon and payment for all the said Chaines Medalls Plate Jewells Gold Workes and other things by him delivered into Our said Jewell Office

Without Accompt

aforesaid the same to be by him received without accompt imprest or other charge to be set upon him his executors or administrators for the same or any pt thereof And these our Lres shall be your sufficient Warrant and discharge in this Behalfe Given under Our Privy Seale at Our Palace at Westminster the one and twentyeth day

May the 21 1671

of May in the three and twentyeth yeare of Our Reigne

Tho. Watkins Dep
Com de Sandwich

APPENDIX 12

COPIES, ENTERED IN AN EXCHEQUER ORDER BOOK, OF THE ORIGINAL PAYMENT ORDERS AUTHORISING "REWARD AND COMPENSATION" TO EDWARD BACKWELL FOR LOANS AMOUNTING TO £14,169

Order Books (Pells), P.R.O., Recs. Ex. R., E.403/2772, fols. 148b–149.

The following entries are the last five for December 1671. The "Stop" was declared on 5th January 1672.

XXIX die Decemb 1671

Edward Backwell Esq Reward for Loane

By Order dated the xiij day of July 1671 To Edward Backwell Esq or his Assigns the sume of Two hundred twenty six pounds seaventeene shillings eight pence by way of Reward and Compensation for procuring the

ccxxvj^{li} xvij^{s} viij^{d}

Int. at 6 li. p. cent. pd 5th July 1671

sume of iiij^{m}ciiij xj^{li} by him lent unto His Ma^{ty} the xxvjth day of ffebry 1669 upon the Creditt for repayment thereof out of the Customes for the moneth of June 1671 and is at iiij^{li} p. cent. p. annum from the xxvjth day of ffebry 1669 to the vth day of

Out of the last farme of the Customes

July 1671 : Per lras de Privat Sigill dat xvjth die August 1667
Ashley. J. Duncombe.

Squibb

Edward Backwell Esq for Loane

By Order dated the vj day of September 1671 To Edward Backwell Esq or his Assigns the sume of one hundred and ninety pounds eighteene shillings tenn pence by way of Reward and Compensation for procuring the

xx
ciiijx^{li} xviij^{s} x

Int. at 6 li. p. cent pd 5 September 1671

sume of MMMcxxj^{li} by him lent unto His Ma^{ty} the xxvjth day of ffebry 1669 upon the Creditt of repayment thereof out of the Customes for the moneth of August 1671 and is at iiij^{li} p. cent p annum due from the xxvjth of ffebry 1669 to the iiijth day

Out of the last farme of the Customes

of September 1671 : Per lras de Privat Sigill dat xvjth August 1667
T Clifford J. Duncombe

Squibb

261

Edward Back-well Esq Re-ward for Loane	By Order dated the viij day of December 1671 To Edward Back-well Esq or to his Assignes the sume of two hundred twenty foure pounds nineteene shillings tenn pence by way of Reward and Compensation for the	ccxxiiij^{li} xix^s x^d
Int. at 6 li. p. cent pd. 30 Sept 1671	procuring the sume of MMMvxliij^{li} by him unto His Ma^{ty} the xxvjth day of ffebry 1669 lent on the Creditt of the Customes on the moneth of September 1671 And is at iiij^{li} p. cent p. annum from the said xxvjth day of ffebry 1669 to the xxvijth day	
Out of the last farme of the Customes	of Septemb last 1671 · Per lras de Privat Sigill dat xvjth die August 1667 Ashley. J. Duncombe	Squibb
Edward Back-well Esq Re-ward for Loane	By Order dated the second day of Novemb 1671 To Edward Backwell Esq or to his Assigns the sume of thirty pounds eleaven shillings two pence by way of Reward and Com-	xxx^{li} x^s ij^d
Int. at 6 li. p. cent pd 3 Nov 1671	pensation for procuring the sum of iiijl xvj^{li} by him lent unto his Ma^{ty} the xxvj day of ffebry 1669 on the Creditt of the Customes on the moneth of March 1670/1 And at iiij^{li} p. cent p. annum from the said xxvjth day of ffebry 1669 to the xvith day of	
Out of the last farme of the Customes	October 1671 : Per lras de Privat Sigill dat xvjth die August 1667 Ashley J. Duncombe.	Squibb
Edward Back-well Esq Re-ward for Loane	By Order dated the second day of Novemb 1671 To Edward Backwell Esq or to his Assigns the sume of One hundred ninety nine pounds five shillings by way of Reward and Compensation for procuring the sume	xx ciiijxix^{li} v^s
Int. at 6 li. p. cent pd 3 Novemb 1671	of MMMxxxviiij^{li} by him lent unto his Ma^{ty} the xxvjth day of ffebry 1669 on the Creditt of the Customes on the moneth of Aprill last 1671 And is at iiij p. cent p. annum from the said xxvjth day of ffebry 1669 to the xvj	
Out of the last farme of the Customes	day of October 1671 : Per lras de Privat. Sigill dat xvjth die August 1667	Squibb
	Ashley J Duncombe	

APPENDIX 13

ENTRIES FROM AN EXCHEQUER INTEREST ACCOUNT RECORDING PAYMENTS OF INTEREST TO GOLDSMITH BANKERS IN THE YEAR OF THE "STOP" OF THE EXCHEQUER

Declaration Books (Pells'), P.R.O., Recs. Ex. R., E.405/314, fols. 115–34.

Folio in Account.	Banker.	Interest Paid. £ s. D.	Date to which paid.	Amount of loan. £ s. D.	Teller paid by.	Date paid.
115	Benjamin Hinton	1. 4. 3.	21 Dec. 1671	53. 6. 8.	Doyle	25 Ap. 1672
120	Isaac Meynell	2. 5. 1.	,,	86. 10. 10.	Loving	15 May 1672
120	,,	1. 2. 11.	,,	46. 10. 10.	,,	,,
120	,,	2. 13. 1.	,,	100. 7. 6.	Doyle	,,
121	Edward Backwell	5. 17. 4.		260. 18. 4.	Squibb	4 July 1672
123	Sir R. Vyner	60. 0. 0.	4 June 1672	2,000. 0. 0.	Doyle	17 July 1672
123	John Colville	24. 0. 0.	21 Dec. 1672	1,000. 0. 0.	Squibb	22 July 1672
123	Dorothea Colville	30. 0. 0.	25 June 1672	1,000. 0. 0.	,,	9 Aug. 1672
123	,,	30. 0. 0.	,,	1,000. 0. 0.	,,	,,
123	,,	15. 0. 0.	,,	500. 0. 0.	,,	,,
123	,,	15. 0. 0.	,,	500. 0. 0.	,,	,,
124	,,	15. 0. 0.	,,	500. 0. 0.	,,	,,
124	,,	15. 0. 0.	,,	500. 0. 0.	,,	,,
124	,,	15. 0. 0.	,,	500. 0. 0.	,,	,,
124	,,	6. 6. 6.	,,	210. 17. 8.	,,	,,
133	Henry Lewis	237. 2. 10.	,,	8,571. 9. 4½	Loving	2 Sept. 1672
134	Sir R. Vyner	150. 0. 0.	,,	5,000. 0. 0.	Doyle	19 Sept. 1672
134	,,	150. 0. 0.	,,	5,000. 0. 0.	,,	,,
134	,,	150. 0. 0.	,,	5,000. 0. 0.	,,	,,

THE FIRST TWO ITEMS OF AN EXCHEQUER "ACCOMPT OF
MONIES" DUE TO DOROTHEA COLVILLE, ADMINISTRA-
TRIX OF JOHN COLVILLE, GOLDSMITH BANKER, FOR
INTEREST. ("MRS. COLVILLE'S ACCOMPT OF INTEREST
FOR 47,360 li.")

Exchequer of Receipt, Miscellanea, "A Booke for Entringe of the
Accompts of Goldsmiths and others," P.R.O., Recs. Ex. R.,
E.407/33, fols. 37–39b.

AN ACCOMPT OF MONIES due to MRS. DOROTHEA COLVILLE RELICT
AND ADMINISTRATRIX OF JOHN COLVILLE LATE OF LONDON,
GOLDSMITH, for interest after the rate of 6 li p. cent. p.
annum (making the interest principall every six moneths)
of the principall sume of 47,360 li payable to her upon
orders for which Interest is payable in the Exchequer.

ON THE HEARTH MONEY

l s. d.			s. d.
20,000. 00. 00.	Upon 4 orders Nos 1062: 1063: 1064: 1065 from 1st December 1671 to 25th of the same moneth	24 dayes	78. 18. 0.
	l s. d. 78. 18. 00 from 25th Dec 1671 to 25 June 72 .... 2. 7. 3.	6 mo	2. 07. 03.
	81. 05. 03 from 25 June 72 to 25 Dec 72 .... 2. 08. 08	6 mo	2. 08. 08.
83. 13. 11	83. 13. 11		
20,083. 13. 11 602. 10. 01	from 25 Dec 72 to 25 June 73 ...	6 mo	602. 10. 01.
20,686. 04. 00 620. 11. 08	from 25 June 73 to 25 Dec 73 ...	6 mo	620. 11. 08.
21,306. 15. 08 639. 04. 00	from 25 Dec 73 to 25 June 74 ...	6 mo	639. 04. 00.
21,945. 19. 8	1945–19–08		

l. s. d.		l. s. d.
5,000. 00. 00	Upon an order No 1063 from 1st Dec 71 to 25th of the same mo. 24 dayes	19. 14. 06.
	l. s. d.	
	19. 14. 06 from 25 Dec 71 to 25 June 72 .... 6 mo	00. 11. 08.
	11. 08.	
	20. 06. 02 from 25 June 72 to 25 Dec 72 .... 6 mo	00. 12. 02.
	12. 02	
	20. 18. 04 from 25 Dec 72 to 25 June 73 ...:............ 6 mo	00. 12. 06.
	12. 06	
21. 10. 10	21. 10. 10	
5,021. 10. 10	from 25 June 73 to 25 Dec 72 ... 6 mo	150. 12. 10.
150. 12. 10		
5,172. 03. 08	from 25 Dec 73 to 25 June 74 ... 6 mo	155. 03. 03
155. 03. 03		
5,327. 06. 11	327–6–11	

A PRIVY SEAL, DATED 30TH JUNE 1674, FOR THE PAYMENT OF £300 TO EDWARD BACKWELL, AND £2,000 TO SIR ROBERT VYNER AS ALLOWANCES FOR KEEPING IN READINESS FOR THE SERVICE OF THE STATE THE SUMS OF £33,333 6s. 8d. AND £145,000 RESPECTIVELY

Privy Seal Books (Auditor's), P.R.O., Recs. Ex. R., E.403/2573, fols. 147–147b.

Edward Back-well and Sir Robert Vyner

Charles the Second by the Grace of God King of England, Scotland, ffraunce and Ireland   Defender of ye ffaith etc   To the Com^rs of Our Treary, Treasurer, Chancellor and Under Treasurer of Our Exchequer now and for the time being Greeting Whereas upon the first of Aprill One thousand six hundred sixty eight it was by you the Com^rs of Our Treary represented unto Us in Councill that Edward Backwell Esq did crave interest after the rate of Six pounds p. cent p. ann. for the sum of thirty three thousand three hundred thirty three pounds six shillings eight pence which by order of Our late High Treasurer of England he kept in his hands from August One thousand six hundred sixty six to January following when it was lent by Advance upon the Customes   And whereas it was upon the five and twentyeth day of June One thousand six hundred sixty and nine likewise represented to Us in Councill that Sr Robert Vyner Knt and Bart did receive interest after the rate aforesaid for the sume of one hundred forty five thousand pounds wch by Our Order he kept in his hands above two moneths and afterwards in the moneths of October, November and December one thousand six hundred sixty six paid the sum unto the then Treasurer of Our Navy   Both which services Wee Ourselfe remembring were graciously pleased at the respective time when the same was soe represented unto Us to Order that for in satisfaction of such their keeping in readynesse the said moneys   Allowance should be made the said Edward Backwell of the sume of three hundred pounds and to the said Sr Robert Vyner of the sume of two thousand pounds   Our will and pleasure therefore is   And Wee doe hereby

these presents Authorize and require you · and
every of you to whom it shall or may appertaine
that out of such Our Treasure as now is or shall be
remayning in Our Receipt of Excheq^r arising by.
or out of the Rents issues or proffits of Our said
Customes and Subsidies or out of any other moneys
remayning in Our Excheq^r you pay or cause to be
paid to the said Edward Backwell or his Assignes
the said sume of three hundred pounds and to the
said Sr Robert Vyner or his Assignes the said sume
of two thousand pounds in full payment and satisfaction of all Interest and Consideracon for such
their keeping in readynesse the several sums of
money before menconed to be by them respectively
soe kept as aforesaid and of all demands whatsoever
for touching or concerning the same or any part or
parcell thereof the said severall sumes to be taken
to the said Edward Backwell and Sr Robert Vyner
and their Assignes respectively with out Accompt
Imprest or other charge to be sett upon them or
any or either of them for the same or any part
thereof And these our Letters shall be your
sufficient Warrant and discharge in this. behalfe
Given under our Privy Seale att our Palace of
Westminster the thirtyeth day of June in the
three and twentyeth yeare of Our Reign
                                        J Mathen

APPENDIX 16

AN EXCHEQUER "ACCOMPT OF MONIES" DUE TO JOSEPH HORNBY GOLDSMITH BANKER, FOR INTEREST. ("MR. HORNBY S INTEREST ACCOMPT FOR 13,734 li.")

Exchequer of Receipt, Miscellanea, "A Booke for Entringe of the Accompts of Goldsmiths and others," P.R.O., Recs. Ex. R., E.407/33, fols. 20–20*b*.

An Accompt of Monies due to Joseph Hornby of London, Goldsmith, for interest after the rate of 6 li p. cent. p. annum (making the interest principall at the end of every six moneths) upon orders of loane registered on severall branches of his Maties Revenue according to his Maties Lres Patents in that behalfe

UPON THE CUSTOMES

l s. d.			s. d.
934. 00. 00	Upon an order N° 31 on the qr ended Xmas 1671 from 16 Novemb 70 to 16 May 71	6 mo	28. 00. 04.
28. 00. 04			
962. 00. 04	from the 16th May 1671 to 16 Nov foll	6 mo	28. 17. 02.
28. 17. 02			
990. 17. 06	from the 16th Novemb 71 to 16 May 72...	6 mo	29. 14. 06.
29. 14. 06			
1,020. 12. 00	from the 16th May 72 to 16 Novemb foll	6 mo	30. 12. 04.
30. 12. 04			
1,051. 04. 04	from the 16 Novemb 72 to 16 May 73	6 mo	31. 10. 08.
31. 10. 08.			
1,082. 15. 00	from the 16 May 73 to 16 Nov foll	6 mo	32. 09. 07.
32. 09. 07			
1,115. 04. 07	from 16 Novemb 73 to 16 May 74...	6 mo	33. 09. 01.
			214. 13. 08.
2,000. 00. 00	Upon an order N° 14 on the qr ended Lady day 73 from the 25 Dec 72 to 25 June 73	6 mo	60. 00. 00.
60. 00. 00			

268

l s. d.			l s. d.
2,060. 00. 00.	from 25 June 73 to 25 Dec. foll	6 mo	61. 16. 00.
61. 16. 00			
2,121. 16 00	from 25 Dec 73 to 25 June 74	6 mo	63. 13. 00.
			185. 09. 00.
800. 00. 00	Upon an order N° 20 on the qr Lady day 73 from 5 Oct 71 to 5 Apr 1672	6 mo .	24. 00. 00.
24. 00. 00			
824. 00. 00	from the 5th Apr 72 to 5 Octr. foll	6 mo·	24. 14. 04.
24. 14. 04			
848. 14. 04	from 5 Octr. 72 to 5 Apr 73	6 mo	25. 09. 02
25. 09. 02			
874. 03. 06	from the 5th Apr 73 to 5 Oct foll ...	6 mo	26. 04. 05.
26. 04. 05			
900. 07. 11	from the 5th Oct 73 to 5 Apr 74 ·...	6 mo	27. 00. 02.
			127. 08. 01.

UPON THE ADDITIONAL EXCISE

10,000. 00. 00	Upon 2 orders N°ˢ 46 & 47 from 25 Decemb 72 to 25 June 1673	6 mo	300. 00. 00.
300. 00. 00			
10,300. 00. 00	from 25 June 73 to 25 Dec 73	6 mo	309. 00. 00.
309. 00. 00			
10,609. 00. 00	from the 25 Dec 73 to 25 June 74...	6 mo	318. 05. 04.
			927. 05. 04.

PRINCIPALL	INTEREST
934	214. 13. 8.
2,000	185. 9. 0.
800	127. 8. 1.
10,000	927. 5. 4.
13,734	1,454. 16. 1.

The Totall of the Interest due to Joseph Hornby by this Accompt without making the interest principall at the end of every six moneths is 1396 li. 2s. 7d. And the total of the Interest arising by making the interest principall every six moneths is 58 li. 13s. 6d. making in the whole the sume of 1454 li. 16s. 01d. which is 19 li. 5s. 5d. lesse than two yeares interest of his principall sume of 13734 li. for which Interest is payable in the Exchequer

7th October 1674   R. Howard

A TREASURY WARRANT, DATED 21st JULY 1674, FOR THE PAYMENT OF INTEREST ON THE STATE DEBT TO THE GOLDSMITH BANKERS

Treasury Warrants (1671–5), Brit. Mus., Additional MS., 28075, fols. 74–75.

July 1674.

Goldsmiths
Interest

A warrant for the paym^t of Interest after the rate of 6 l. p. cent. per. ann. for 2 years past for all such moneyes as are now due to Sr Robert Vyner, Edward Backwell, Dorothea Colville, Isaac Meynell, Jeremiah Snow, John Portman, Robert Welstead, George Snell, Bernard Turner, Thomas Rowe, Joseph Hornby, Gilbert Whitehall, John Grymes, Henry Lewis, Richard Stratford, Robert Ryves, Thomas Price, Thomas Temple, Thomas Pardoe, and Isaac Collier upon orders payable at the receipt of the Excheq or Tallyes levyed therupon any branch of his Maj^{ties} Revenue either in their owne names or assigned to them or any of them makeing the Interest Principal at the end of every 6 months Provided the Interest money be paid by virtue of this grant doe not exceed 140,000 l. the same to be paid out of his Maj^{ties} Revenue of excise by eight quarterly paym^{ts} the first to be made ye 15th day of March next & if upon acc^{ts} stated the said interest shall not amount to 140,000 l.—the overplus to be paid towards the interest wch shall grow due to them above the said 2 yeares subscribed by Mr Att Genl by warr^t und^r his Maj^s signe mannuall

My very good Lord
I have been acquainted wth this Docq^{tt}

Danby

21 July 1674

A GOLDSMITH BANKER'S CONDITIONS OF OFFICE UPON
BEING APPOINTED CASHIER AND RECEIVER OF EXCISE

Miscellaneous Treasury Papers, Brit. Mus., Additional MS.,
28078, fol. 436.

Mr RICHARD KENT enters upon being Cashier and Receiver
of the Whole Duty of Excise upon these CONDITIONS following
viz.

First   He undertakes to pay weekly to Sir Stephen Fox for y^e
Forces at least £3,000 a weeke and to furnish at the end of
Musters as much Money as shall pay them their full pay
And may amount to about the sum of 210,000 l. all
which shall be lent or advanced by him upon Talleys at the
rate of 6 per cent interest and no more, Which interest is to
commence two lunary months after the end of each Muster
according to the method of former Interest accompts.   And
in case ye Muster be changed to Calendar Months then interest
is to begin at ye end of two calendar months after the end of
each Muster so that ye forces will be paying four months
before the Interest begins for the first two and then Interest
of the whole establishment for the first Muster for two
months is to be received till such time as the tallys shall be
paid   Always to bee understood in this and all other loans
that when any part of the said Tallys shall be paid the
Interest of that part ceases.

Secondly   He undertakes to lend Mr. Cofferer for his Majesty's
House within three days after he shall be invested in this
Office the sume of 15,000 l. the pay of his Majesty's Household Establishment to the 1st April 1674, And to lend
3,000l. a month beginning October 1674 for the carrying on
the constant steady expense of his Majesty's House,   And
also to send the rest of what shall be assigned for his Majesty's
House at the end of three months after the half year is
expired viz in January for the half year ending at Michale-
mas past and in July for the half year ending at Lady Day
past, Interest of which sume so lent to Mr Cofferer is to begin
from the time of lending and to be secured by Talleys on
the Excise and the Interest to determine as aforesaid.

Thirdly   And for all payments assigned by Tallys on the said
Excise provided they do not anticipate the said revenue
about twelve or at furthest fifteen months   He undertakes
to lend at such times as shall be directed by my Lord
Treasurer's Lett^s   Interest of which loanes are to begin
from the time of lending and to determine as aforesaid.

Fourthly In regard the said Cashier will now become the only Interest Accomptant, it will be necessary that his accompts of Interest be audited and paid at the end of each half year viz in July and January, and that there may be no occasion of mistrust that all loans of Money be made known to the Comptroller of ye Excise who may be on all Transactions a good voucher for the Auditor to proceed in the making up the Accompts of Interest.

Fifthly For security of his Majesty's Treasure at ye Excise Office it will be needful for the Cashier to have Convenient accommodation of Houseroom at ye said office which is humbly prayed may be referred to Mr Chiffinch. . . .

It is to be understood that though there is no mention made of above 6 per cent. Interest to be allowed for all moneys to be lent as aforesaid by ye said Cashier yett that by way of gratuity or reward he is to have 2 per cent more for all that he lends except to ye Forces which is not to vary from what is proposed.

APPENDIX 19

A GOLDSMITH BANKER'S ASSIGNMENT, DATED 11TH SEPTEMBER 1677

Assignment Books (Pells'), P.R.O., Recs. Ex. R., E.406/27.

Sir Robert Vyner
Assignment of
the Sum of
12l. 16s. to

Whereas Peter Aylworth Cittizen and Cloth-worker of London hath delivered up unto me Sir Robert Vyner of London. Knight and Baronet all his security for, and hath discharged me of, two hundred and thirteen pounds nine shillings and nine pence, which I owed unto him, and is content to accept of an assignment of a proporconable part of the Rent or yearly sum of twenty five thousand and three pounds nine shillings and ffour pence granted unto me my heires and assigns by his Matie, and payable out of the hereditary Revenue of Excise by virtue of his Maties Lres Patent dated the thirtieth of Aprill last past. Know all men therefore by these presents that I the same Sir Robert Vyner in consideracion thereof, and in pursuance of the trust reposed in me by the said Lres Patent, have granted and assigned and doe hereby grant and assigne unto the said Peter

Peter Aylworth

Aylworth and his heires the sum of twelve pounds and sixteen shillings yearly, being his proporconable part of the said yearly summe of twenty-ffive thousand and three pounds nine shillings and ffour pence in satisfacion for his said debt, to receive and enjoy the said yearely sum of twelve pounds and sixteen shillings, the said Peter Aylworth his heires and Assignes, for ever, to commence from the ffirst day of the Nativity of St. John Baptist last past before the date hereof to the proper use and benefit of him the said Peter Aylworth and his heires and assignes for ever in satisffacon of his said Debt under the Condicons in the said Lres Patent menconed. And I doe hereby for my selfe, my heires, Executors, and Administrators, Consent and grant to and with the said Peter Aylworth, his heires and Assignes, that I the said Sir Robert Vyner, my heires and assignes, shall and will at any time hereafter upon reasonable request and at the

T

273

Cost and Charge in Law of the said Peter Aylworth, his heires and assignes, doe any such further Act or Acts unto the said Peter Aylworth, his heires and Assignes, for the better securing, recovering, obtaineing, receiving, and enjoying of the said twelve pounds and sixteen shillings p. annum to him and them subject to the condicons in the said Lres Patent expressed as by him or them or by his or their councell in the Law shall be reasonably advised and required. And I shall doe noe Act or thing whereof the said Peter Aylworth his heires or assignes may or shall be hindered, barred, or delayed in recovering obtaining receiving or enjoying the promise granted or menconed to be granted as aforesaid In witness whereof I have hereunto sett my hand and seale this eleventh day of September Anno Domini 1677 in the nine and twentieth yeare of the reign of our soveraigne Lord Charles the Second by the Grace of God of England, Scotland, Ffrance, and Ireland, King, Defender of the Ffaith &c.

Signed, Sealed and
Delivered in the presence of

Robert Vyner.

Jo. Marsh　　　　Bern^d Eales.
Nic^o Smith　　　Robt Vyner Junr.

APPENDIX 20

A TREASURY WARRANT, DATED 3RD JANUARY 1686, FOR THE
PAYMENT OF INTEREST TO RICHARD KENT AND
CHARLES DUNCOMBE, GOLDSMITH BANKERS

Warrant Books (Pells'), P.R.O., Recs. Ex. R., E.403/3000, fol. 21.

Lord Treasurer Rochester's Warrant to Sir Robert Howard, Kt., Auditor of His Majesty's Receipt of Exchequer, to draw one or more. orders for payment of interest to Richard Kent and Charles Duncombe.

After my hearty commendacons By vertue of his Majesty's Letters of Privy Seale bearing date the 25th day of March 1685 These are to pray and require you to draw one or more orders for payment to Richard Kent and Charles Duncombe Esq^s or their assignees of the Sum of one thousand three hundred and seaventy pounds ten shillings and nine pence for interest after the rate of ffive pounds per cent per Annum for severall sumes of money by them advanced and lent for the service of his present and late Majesty the sume appearing to be due to them by an accompt thereof made upp to the 25th December last 1686 by Mr Auditor. Aldworth and allowed the 31st of the same Month and lett the same be satisfyd out of any his Majesty's Treasure now or hereafter being and remaineing in the Receipt of the Exchequer not appropriated to particular uses by Act of Parliament ffor which this shall be your Warrant.   Whitehall Treasury Chambers January the 3rd 1686.

To my very loving ffriend Sir   Rochester
    Robert Howard Kt Auditor of his
    Majesty's Receipt of Exchequer.

THE FIRST MINUTES OF THE COURT OF DIRECTORS OF THE BANK OF ENGLAND

By permission of the Governor and Company of the Bank of England.

The Court Minute Books of the Bank of England, Lib. A, fols. 1–3.

THE CHARTER

for Incorporating ye Govern^r and Company of the Bank of England was sealed this 27th July 1694 at Powis House. And so soon as the same had pafsed the Seale

        Sir John Houblon as Govern^r
        Michael Godfrey Esq. as Dep^{ty} Govern^r

And

Sr John Huband Barr^t ⎫
Sr Willm Gore   ⎪
Sr Henry Furnese   ⎪
Robert Raworth   ⎬ as Directors
John Smith   ⎪
Obadiah Sedgwick &   ⎪
Willm Patterson Esq^{es} ⎭

Tooke the severall Oathes respectively appointed by the said Charter before the R^t hono^{ble} Sr John Somers K^{nt} Lord Keeper of ye Great Seale of England.

A Court of Directors
at
Mercers Hall
27 July 94 (Afternoon)
(at ye Opening of ye Charter)

Present

Sr John Houblon Govern^r
Mich^l Godfrey Esq Dep^{ty} Govr

Wm Patterson	Obad: Sedgwick
Abra: Houblon	John Lordell
John Smith	Sr Wm Scawen
Sr Hen: Furnese	Jam^s Denew
Sr Wm Gore	Tho: Goddard
Theo: Jansen	Robt Raworth
Sr James Houblon	John Ward
Gilb^t Heathcott	Jam^s Bateman Esq^{es}

Directors

Of whom these persons following not having taken the Oathes appointed by the Charter, now took the same before the Govern^r and Dep^ty Govern^r who had been sworne (as aforesaid) before the Lord Keeper

Sr Jam^s Houblon	John Ward
Sr Wm Scawen	Tho: Goddard
Jam^s Denew	Brooke Bridges
John Lordell	Theod: Jansen Esq^es

The Method of giving Receipts for running-Cash was Debated, whether one certain Method, or more than one, should be observed and what method in particular

And these were Proposed

1st By keeping Accompts in Books wth the Creditors
2^d By endorsing Notes given
3^d By Charging Notes on the Bank.

And upon putting the Question after a long Debate, It was Resolved that, these three Methods shall be observed & none other

1st To give out Running-Cash-Notes and to endorse on them what is paid off in part.
2^d To keep an Accompt with ye Creditor in a Book or Paper of his owne.
3^d To accept Notes drawn on ye Bank.

And It is Ordered that no Creditor shall use any two of the said methods, but if having used one of them, he shall think fitt to change it for another, giving notice thereof to ye Court he is at liberty to use any one of the said Methods.

Upon Debate concerning the payment of the Second ffourth part of the Subscripcons; and what Discompt to allow for the same payment thereof

It was Ordered

That such who pay in the same before the 1st of October next, shall be allowed two pence p diem p cent Discompt, from the time of the payment till the said 1st October—But this is to be allowed only for the Second-ffourth part.

THE BANK OF ENGLAND'S EARLIEST REGULATIONS FOR
THE KEEPING OF A "DRAWING ACCOUNT," DATED
12TH JANUARY 1698

By permission of the Governor and Company of the Bank of
England.

The Court Minute Books of the Bank of England, Lib. C,
fols. 61–63.

THE COURT doth resolve and order That the following
method should be putt in practise and observed for the accommodation of those who by approbacon in writing of the 3 Directors
in Waiting or any 3 other Directors should keep their cash with
the Bank by a Drawing Acco^t.

A Distinct
Cash-Book

1. That a Cashier with a distinct Cash-book be appointed for the Receipts and Payments of all persons that shall keep a Drawing Acco^t, and that nothing else be entered in the said Cash-Book to prevent mistakes by intermixing of busine∫s.

A Particular
Leidger.

2. That a particular leidger be appointed for the Acco^{ts} of the said persons.

A Wast Leidger.

3. That to prevent any mans overdrawing that there be (over and above the said leidger) another wast leidger, to be kept by a Sub-Accomptant that shall attend at the Cash-book, and post every article in figures only (for brevity sake) as they shall be entred. So that the Cashier shall at all times be able to knowe the ballance of every man's acco^t, The said two leidgers to be often compared to prevent mistakes, And as a further expedient to prevent overpaym^{ts} That no Teller be permitted to take in notes drawne on the Bank Except only from the Drawer himselfe.

None p^d more
than their
Ballance.

4. That the Cashier do not accept or pay upon any man's accompt beyond the Ballance.

Drawn Notes p^d
at sight.

5. That the Cashier shall pay or discharge every drawne note at the sight thereof (so far as the Drawer has creditt) And not suffer any person to carry away such note with a promise of paym^t.

No credit for
bills till paid.

6. That no person shall have creditt for any Bills or Notes till they are actually received except in the case of fforreign and second bills as hereafter directed.

Bill Journal and Alphabet &c.

7. That such Bills or Notes shall be entred distinguishably in the Bill Journall from whence they may be carried to the Creditt of each man's acco^t as soon as they shall be received, And that every person when he begins to draw on the Bank be required to enter his name and sett his seale in an Alphabet for that purpose with his additions and habitacon, which may help the person who keeps the Bill-Journall to know what Bills belong to those persons acco^{ts}, And serve for the comparing of hands when doubted, And that all Notes drawn shall be numbred signed and sealed by ye Drawer.

Conveniences to persons keeping Cash with ye Bank.

Ordered also that the following conveniences be allowed to persons that shall keep their Cash with the Bank.

For Bills under £5,000 Discount^d.

1. That fforreign bills be discounted by direction of the Gentl in Waiting at 4½ per cent not exceeding £5,000 with any one person.

Bill not above 3 days to run discounted gratis.

2. That fforreign bills not having above 3 days of Grace to run shall be discounted gratis, by order of the Directors in Waiting.

2^d Bills allowed as Cash.

3. That Second Bills be allowed as Cash (at the discretion of the Directors in Waiting) not exceeding £1,000 with any person at one time, and so as the bearer of such bill be a person well known.

On January 19th 1698 it was ordered " that there be added to the said method the following article, viz.

8th. That all persons do make up their Acco^t with the Bank once in every Month."

APPENDIX 23

THE BANK OF ENGLAND'S EARLIEST PUBLIC STATEMENT OF ACCOUNTS, DATED 10TH NOVEMBER 1696

Presented to Parliament on 4th December 1696. *Journals of the House of Commons*, XI, p. 614.

STOCK FOR THE HONOURABLE THE GOVERNOR AND COMPANY OF THE BANK OF ENGLAND

Dr	£	s.	d.	Cr	£	s.	d.
To sundry Persons, for sealed Bank-Bills standing out	893,800.	0.	0.	By Tallies on several Parliamentary Funds as *per* List thereof annexed with interest	1,784,576.	16.	5.
To Ditto due on Notes, for running Cash	764,196.	10.	6.	By Half a Year's Deficiency of the Fund of 100000 l. per Ann. in the 2d year	50,000.	0.	0.
To Monies borrowed in Holland	300,000.	0.	0.	By Mortgages, Pawns, other securities, and Cash	266,610.	17.	0.
To Interest due upon Bank Bills standing out	17,876.	0.	0.				
Balance ...	125,315.	2.	11				
	2,101,187.	13.	5		2,101,187.	13.	5.

London, November 10. 1696.
Examined by Order of the Court of Directors,
Per Tho Mercer, Accountant.

THE SAID LIST OF TALLIES ON PARLIAMENTARY FUNDS

	£	s.	d.
On the 4th Year's Land-Tax	431,924.	0.	4.
On Continued Impositions on East India Goods	94,960.	12.	3.
On the 4th Year's Customs	200.	15.	9.
On the 3d Year's Land-Tax	122,029.	4.	7.
On the Post-Office Security	60,629.	1.	8.
On the 2d Year's Customs	109,014.	13.	8.
On Wines, Vinegars &c	184,823.	18.	3.
On the Coal Act	174,775.	19.	6.
On the 3d Year's Customs	130,713.	13.	1.
On Marriages, &c	431.	12.	0.
On Joint-Stocks	2,884.	1.	1.
On 2/3 Excise	34,667.	19.	2.
On the Reversionary Annuities	141,865.	16.	2.
On the Salt-Act	250,000.	0.	0.
On Paper and Parchment	11,310.	4.	6.
Interest grown due thereon	44,345.	4.	5.
	1,784,576.	16.	5.

London, November 10. 1696.
Examined by Order of the Court of Directors,
Per Tho Mercer, Accountant.

BIBLIOGRAPHY

THE following list brings together the various sources, manuscript and printed, referred to in the text, notes and appendices.

I. MANUSCRIPT SOURCES

1. BANK RECORDS.

   (a) The Bank of England.

   The Court Minute Books: the four earliest known as Lib. A, Lib. B, Lib. C, and Lib. D (dated 1694–1705); "The Book conteyning the Subscriptions"; The First Stock Book; and the Bank's valuable collection of early paper money.

   (b) Messrs. Hoare, 37, Fleet Street, London, E.C.

   The earliest documents, and the ledgers of Richard Hoare preserved in Hoare's Bank.

   (c) Messrs. Glyn, Mills & Co.

   The earliest documents and ledgers preserved in Child's Branch of Messrs. Glyn, Mills & Co., 1, Fleet Street, London, E.C., including the Records of Messrs. Child, Vol. I, 1670–1700; Vol. II, 1704–1753; Vol. III, A–G; Vol. IV, H–Z; the earliest ledgers of Alderman Backwell, dated 1663–71, and the "Dunkirk Ledger," dated 1657–78; the earliest ledgers of Sir Francis Child.

2. THE GUILDHALL OF LONDON.

   The records of the Orphans' Fund preserved in the Guildhall, London: the Orphans' Ledgers; the Common Serjeant's Books; and the Orphanage Book, dated 1639–44.

3. THE ADVOCATES' LIBRARY, EDINBURGH.

   The Halifax Papers.

4. GOLDSMITHS' HALL, LONDON.

   The Wardens' Accounts and Court Minute Books of the Goldsmiths' Company.

5. THE HOUSE OF LORDS.

   Report of the Accounts Commission of 1669 (MSS. No. 213).

6. THE CHURCH OF ST. MARY WOOLNOTH, LOMBARD STREET, LONDON.

> The Parish Registers.

7. THE PUBLIC RECORD OFFICE.

> (a) Exchequer Accounts, Various.
>> Mint, E. 401, Bdles. 296/4 and 304/12, relating to the transactions of Sir Richard Martin; E. 101, Bdles. 302/24 and 303/5, 7, and 8, relating to the transactions of Sir Martin Bowes.

> (b) Records of the Exchequer of Receipt.
>> 1. E. 401/1930, 1994, 1995, Receipt Books (Pells'), dated 1654–56, 1656–58, 1694 and 1694–95 respectively.
>> 2. E. 401/2583. 2584, Registers of Receipts for Loans on Privy Seal, dated 1597 and 1604–5 respectively.
>> 3. E. 401/2590, Register of Repayments of Loans on Privy Seal, dated 1597.
>> 4. E. 403/1330, 1331, Special Series of Exchequer Issue Rolls, dated 1696–97.
>> 5. E. 403/2430–2435, Registers of Orders for Repayment, dated 1666–70.
>> 6. E. 403/2510, Auditor's Patent Book for Tallies, dated 1673–78.
>> 7. E. 403/2573, Privy Seal Books (Auditor's), dated 1671.
>> 8. E. 403/2611, Privy Seal Books (Pells'), dated 1669.
>> 9. E. 403/2721, 2728, 2729, 2730, 2772, Order Books (Pells'), dated 1597–99, 1608–9, 1609–10, 1611–12 and 1671 respectively.
>> 10. E. 403/3000 and 3019, Warrant Books (Pells'), dated 1684–85 and 1674–88 respectively, the latter entitled "The Bankers' Booke of Interest."
>> 11. E. 403/3032 and 3039, Warrant Books (Auditor's) dated 1664 and 1667 respectively.
>> 12. E. 404/619, Original Orders for Payments (1660–70).
>> 13. E. 405/314, Declaration Books (Pells'), dated 1672.
>> 14. E. 406/1–26, Assignment Books (Goldsmiths'), dated 1676–1705.
>> 15. E. 406/27–44, Assignment Books (Pells'), dated 1677–1704.
>> 16. E. 406/89, Certificates of Exchequer Bills, dated 1696–99.

17. E. 406/206, 207, Warrants and Contracts for Exchequer Bills, dated 1696–98.
18. E. 407/33, 34, Miscellanea, " A Booke for entringe of the Accompts of Goldsmiths and others," (two parts), dated 1674–77.
19. E. 407/79, Original Debentures (1636–1800).
20. E. 407/119, 120, 123, 125, Thorpe's Exchequer Papers.
21. E. 407/134(2), Papers relating to Exchequer Bills, dated 1697–1835.

(c) Records of the Treasury.

1. T. 29/8–11, Treasury Minute Books, dated 1695–96 to 1698–1700.
2. T. 29/627, Special Minute Book compiled during Anne's reign.
3. T. 48/6, The Lowndes Papers.
4. T. 51/15, Warrants, Early.
5. T. 52/4, Warrants, King's.

(d) Records of Chancery Proceedings.

1. Early.
    (a) Bdle. 407/44, *Fulwoode* v. *The Mayor and Sheriffs of London.*
    (b) Bdle. 608/24, *Brown* v. *Doughty.*
    (c) Bdle. 713/12, *Ardyson* v. *Mayor, Aldermen and Sheriffs of London.*
    (d) Bdle. 725/7, *Barnes* v. *Mayor and Sheriffs of London.*
2. James I.
    (a) Bdle. D. 7/63, *Harman* v. *Wild.*
    (b) Bdle. G. 16/75, *Gyttens* v. *Davenant.*
    (c) Bdle. H. 2/29, *Hodges* v. *Chubb.*
    (d) Bdle. H. 13/4, *Hedges* v. *Gregory and Atwood.*
3. Series II (1621–60).
    (a) Bdle. 337/70, *Beecher* v. *Quarles.*
4. Before 1714 (Hamilton).
    (a) Bdle. 224/83, *Vyner* v. *Rowe, Green and Stone.*
    (b) Bdle. 354/12, Sir Robert Vyner's bill of complaint.
5. Before 1714 (Mitford).
    (a) Bdle. 64/81, *Vyner* v. *Bulkley, Stroode and Moore.*
    (b) Bdle. 127/48, The Answer of S. Moore.
6. Before 1714 (Reynardson).
    (a) Bdle. 35/66, *Vyner* v. *Clipsham and Castle.*
    (b) Bdle. 97/19, *Vyner* v. *Joyner.*

(e) Exchequer Bills and Answers.

London and Middlesex, E. 112, Nos. 863, 931, 977, 982, 987, 1006, 1133, 1276, 1277, 1278, 1324, 1360, 1395, 1408, 1529, 1533, 1561, 1568, Charles II; and 28, James II.

(f) State Papers, Domestic.

Elizabeth: 19, No. 2; 36, No. 95; 71, Nos. 4, 9, 24 and 77; 73, Nos. 43 and 70; 77, No. 55; 110, No. 51; 150, No. 73; 241, No. 38; 244, No. 33; 249, No. 54; 251, No. 80; 261, No. 36; 262, Nos. 96, 97, 109, 114 and 135; 263, Nos. 8, 9 and 10; 264, No. 145; 265, No. 121.
James I: 130, Nos. 29–32; 163, No. 10.
Charles I: 39, No. 17; 107, No. 17; 478, No. 96.
Interregnum: 9, No. 64; 24, No. 21; 25, No. 101; 102, No. 27; 124, No. 20; 129, No. 75; A. 59, last folio; I. 77, fols. 462–65.
Charles II: 40, Nos. 131–32; 68, No. 138.

(g) State Papers, Foreign.

Elizabeth: 14, letters dated 12th May and 30th August 1560; 15, letter dated 24th June 1560; 30, letters dated 2nd and 8th September 1561; 40, letters dated 11th and 16th August 1562.

8. THE BRITISH MUSEUM.

(a) Additional MSS.

5755: Original Documents relating to the Exchequer Offices and Board of Works, fols. 24–57.
17677: State Correspondence between England and the Netherlands, QQ.
20721: MSS. relating to the Revenue of England 1685–99, fols. 11, 34, 37–38.
27877: Register of Accompts of Collectors of a Public Loan.
28074–5: Treasury Warrants, 1671–75.
28078: Miscellaneous Treasury Papers, 17th century, fols. 284, 286.
28621: Original Letters and Miscellaneous Papers, 1517–1727, fols. 17–26.
31025: Exchequer Bills, 1697–1720.
32471: Public Revenue, etc., 17th century, fol. 16.
33038: Newcastle Papers, CCCLIII, fol. 100.
34355: Letters from Charles Montague, Chancellor of the Exchequer to William Blathwayt, Secretary at War.

(*b*) Cottonian MSS.

> Otho, E. X : Papers relating to Mines, Coinage, Weights and Measures, fol. 94.

(*c*) Harleian MSS.

> 660 : Various Tracts on Coins, Weights, Measures, etc., fol. 107.
> 1282 : Public Accounts, 1689–97, fols. 1–15.
> 1492 : Minutes of the Commissioners of Accounts.
> 7421 : A Copy of ye Earl of Ranelagh's Report.

(*d*) Lansdowne MSS.

> 12 : Burghley Papers, 1569–70, fol. 29.
> 30 : *Ibid.*, 1580, No. 37.
> 32 : *Ibid.*, 1581, fols. 14–22.
> 60 : *Ibid.*, 1589, fol. 45.
> 108 : *Ibid.*, undated, fol. 90.
> 113 : *Ibid.*, undated, fol. 29.
> 351 : Scheme for the erection of Pawn-houses or Mounts of Piety, fols. 18–40.
> 801 : Brief Memoirs relating to the Silver and Gold Coins of England, by Hopton Haynes, fol. 49.

(*e*) Royal MSS.

> 18B, XVIII. A Project for raysing of a Stocke out of . . . the unlawful dealinges · of · thievinge brokers, by T. Huniman.

II. CASES FROM THE PRINTED LAW REPORTS

Martin v. *Boure* (1602).
Oaste v. *Taylor* (1613).
Herbert v. *Lowns* (1621).
Edgar v. *Chut* (1663).
Cooksay v. *Bouverie* (1682).
Vernon v. *Bouverie* (1682).
Sarsfield v. *Witherby* (1686).
Carter v. *Downich* (1686).
Hodges v. *Steward* (1691).
Coggs v. *Horton* (1691).
Williams v. *Williams* (1693).
Bromwich v. *Lloyd* (1696).
Taswell and Lee v. *Lewis* (1696).
Nicholson v. *Sedgwick* (1698).
Anonymous, (1698).
Anonymous (1699).
Bank of England v. *Newman* (1699).
Carter v. *Palmer* (1701).
Jordan v. *Barloe* (1701).
Ford v. *Hopkins* (1701).

Anonymous (1702).
Ward v. *Evans* (1702).
Clerke v. *Martin* (1703).
Buller v. *Crips* (1704).
Walmsley v. *Child* (1749).
Glyn v. *Bank of England* (1750).
Miller v. *Race* (1758).
Grant v. *Vaughan* (1764).

III. ACTS OF PARLIAMENT

3 Rich. II, c. 3 (1379).
3 Hy. VII, c. 5 (1486).
3 Hy. VII, c. 6 (1486).
4 Hy. VII, c. 11 (1487).
11 Hy. VII, c. 8 (1494).
37 Hy. VIII, c. 9 (1545).
1 Ed. VI, c. 6 (1547).
5 and 6 Ed. VI, c. 20 (1552).
13 Eliz. c. 8. (1571).
43 Eliz. c. 12 (1601).
1 Jas. I, c. 21 (1604).
19 Jas. I, c. 19 (1621).
21 Jas. I, c. 17 (1623).
12 Chas. II, c. 9 (1660).
12 Chas. II, c. 13 (1660).
12 Chas. II, c. 18 (1660).
13 Chas. II, stat. 1, c. 14 (1661).
15 Chas. II, c. 1 (1663).
17 Chas II, c. 1 (1665).
4 Wm. & M., c. 3 (1693).
5 Wm. & M., c. 5 (1694).
5 and 6 Wm. & M., c. 7 (1694).
5 and 6 Wm. & M., c. 10 (1694).
5 and 6 Wm. & M., c. 20 (1694).
6 and 7 Wm. & M., c. 5 (1695).
6 and 7 Wm. & M., c. 17 (1695).
7 Wm. III, c. 1 (1696).
7 and 8 Wm. III, c. 10 (1696).
7 and 8 Wm. III, c. 19 (1696).
7 and 8 Wm. III, c. 31 (1696).
8 Wm. III, c. 1 (1696).
8 Wm. III, c. 3 (1696).
8 Wm. III, c. 6 (1696).
8 and 9 Wm. III, c. 20 (1697).
8 and 9 Wm III., c. 22 (1697).
8 and 9 Wm. III, c. 28 (1697).
8 and 9 Wm. III, c. 32 (1697).
9 Wm. III, c. 3 (1697).

9 and 10 Wm. III, c. 17 (1698).
9 and 10 Wm. III, c. 44 (1698).
10 Wm. III, c. 1 (1698).
10 and 11 Wm. III, c. 22, (1699)
12 and 13 Wm. III, c. 11 (1700).
12 and 13 Wm. III, c. 12 (1700).
3 and 4 Anne, c. 8 (1704).
5 Anne, c. 13, (1707).
6 Anne, c. 6 (1707).
6 Anne, c. 16 (1707).
6 Anne, c. 22 (1707).
7 Anne, c. 7 (1708).
7 Anne, c. 8 (1708).
9 Anne, c. 7 (1710).
10 Anne, c. 19 (1711).
12 Anne, c. 11 (1713).
12 Anne, stat. 2, c. 16 (1713).
1 Geo. I, c. 19 (1715).
1 Geo. I, c. 20 (1715).
3 Geo I, c. 7 (1717).
6 Geo. I, c. 4 (1720).
13 Geo. I, c. 3 (1726).
7 Geo. II, c. 8 (1734).
16 Geo II, c. 13 (1742).
15 Geo. III, c. 51 (1775).
17 Geo. III, c. 30 (1777).
21 Geo. III, c. 60 (1781).
23 Geo. III, c. 82 (1782).
37 Geo. III, c. 34 (1797).
39 and 40 Geo. III, c. 60 (1781).
53 Geo. III, c. 68 (1816).
59 Geo. III, c. 49 (1819).
7 Geo IV, c. 6 (1826).
7 Geo IV, c. 46 (1826).
3 and 4 Wm IV, c. 98 (1833).
4 and 5 Wm. IV, c. 15 (1834).
5 and 6 Wm. IV, c. 35 (1836).
17 and 18 Vict., c. 90 (1854).

IV. DICTIONARIES, ENCYCLOPÆDIAS, AND YEAR BOOKS

The Dictionary of National Biography.
The Oxford New English Dictionary.
Macleod, H. D., *Dictionary of Political Economy* (1863).
Palgrave, Sir Robert H. Inglis, *Dictionary of Political Economy* (revised ed., 1923–26).
Postlethwayt, M., *Universal Dictionary of Trade and Commerce* (1751–55).
Thomson, W., *Dictionary of Banking* (6th ed., 1926).
Walford, C., *The Insurance Cyclopedia* (1871–80).
The Encyclopædia Britannica (12th and 13th editions).
The Jewish Encyclopædia (1925 edition).
The Bankers' Almanack and Year Book, known as the *Banking Almanac, Directory, Year Book and Diary* from 1845–1919.

V. SEVENTEENTH-CENTURY PERIODICALS

London Gazette, Post Boy, Flying Post, Old Postmaster, John Houghton's *Collection for Improvement of Husbandry and Trade.* All these are in the Burney Collection, British Museum.

VI. MODERN PERIODICALS

American Historical Review, Archæologia, Banker, Cambridge Historical Journal, Connoisseur, Economic Journal, Economica, Harper's Magazine, Journal of Economic and Business History, Journal of the Institute of Bankers, Journal of Political Economy, Law Quarterly Review, The Old Lady of Threadneedle Street, The Pamphleteer, The Times, Transactions of the London and Middlesex Archæological Society, Quarterly Journal of Economics.

VII. OFFICIAL PUBLICATIONS AND LAW REPORTS

Acts of the Parliament of Scotland, IX, X, XI.
Burrow, Sir J., *Reports of Cases argued and determined in the Court of King's Bench, 1756–72* (4th ed., 1790).
Calendar of State Papers, Colonial, America, and West Indies, 1661–68.
Calendar of State Papers, Domestic, 1649–50; ibid., *1650*; ibid., *1653–54*; ibid., *1673–75*; ibid., *1676–77.*
Calendar State Papers, Foreign, Elizabeth, 1569–71.
Calendar of Treasury Books, I–VIII (1904–23).
Calendar of Treasury Papers, 1557–1696 (1868).
Carthew, T., *Reports of Cases adjudged in the Court of King's Bench, 1686–1701* (1741).

Croke, Sir George, *Reports of Select Cases adjudged in the Courts of King's Bench and Common Pleas in the reigns of Queen Elizabeth, King James and King Charles I* (1790–92).

English Reports, XXI, Chancery I (1902).

Gairdner, J., and Brodie, R. H., *Letters and Papers, Foreign and Domestic of the Reign of Henry VIII*, XIX, Pts. I and II (1903, 1905); XXI, Pt. I (1910).

Giuseppi, M. S., *A Guide to the Manuscripts preserved in the Public Record Office*, I (1923).

Historical Manuscripts Commission, *Reports* and *Calendars :*
  MSS. of Marquis of Salisbury, Pts. I and II (1883).
  Thirteenth Report, App., Pt. I (1891).
  MSS. House of Lords, 1693–95, I, New Series (1900).
  MSS. of Marquis of Downshire, I, Pt. I (1924).
  MSS. of the Duke of Portland, Pt. II (1890).

Holt, Sir J., *Report of all the Cases determined by Sir John Holt, 1688–1700* (1738).

Journals of the House of Commons, XI.

Journals of the House of Lords, XV.

Keble, J., *Reports of Cases in the Court of King's Bench at Westminster from the XII to the XXX year of the Reign of King Charles II* (1685).

Levinz, Sir C., *Reports of Sir C. Levinz . . . in French and English* (1722).

Lord Raymond, *Reports of Cases . . . in the Courts of King's Bench and Common Pleas* (4th ed., by J. Bayley, 1790).

Lutwyche, Sir Edward, *Reports of the Resolutions of the Court on divers Exceptions taken to Pleadings and other Matters in Law* (1718).

Parliamentary Papers (arranged chronologically).
  1792–93, XI, *Reports from Committees of the House of Commons.*
  1792–93, XXXVIII, 780(3), *Million Bank, Statement of Transactions.*
  1797, XII, *Twenty-first Report from the Select Committee on Finance.*
  1810, III, 349, *Report from the Select Committee on the High Price of Bullion.*
  1812, VI, 268, *Report from the Select Committee on the Orphans' Fund.*
  1822, IV, 481, *Report from the Select Committee on the Orphans' Fund.*
  1829, III, 309, *Report from the Select Committee on the Orphans' Fund.*
  1831, X, 313, *First Report of the Commissioners of Public Accounts.*
  1831–32, VI, 722, *Report from the Committee of Secrecy on the Bank of England Charter.*

1842, XVIII, 1, *Report on Exchequer Bills.*
1852–53, XXII, 916, *Report from the Select Committee on Coal Duties (Metropolis).*
1857–58, XXXIII, 33, *Return of the National Debt.*
1868–69, XXXV, 366, *Accounts of the Net Public Income and Expenditure.*
1898, LII, C–9010, *History of the Earlier Years of the Funded Debt.*
Reports of the Deputy Keeper of Public Records, III, App. II; IV, App. II; V, App. II; VI, App. II; VII, App. II.
Salkeld, W., *Reports of Cases adjudged in the Court of King's Bench* (1795).
Shower, Sir B., *Reports of Sir B. Shower of Cases adjudged in the Court of the King's Bench in the reign of King William III* (1708–20).
Statutes at Large.
Statutes of the Realm.
Vesey, F., senior, *Cases in Chancery, 1747–58* (1771).

VIII. CONTEMPORARY PRINTED BOOKS AND PAMPHLETS, TO 1700

(With the British Museum references.)

Ames, W., *Conscience with the Power and Cases thereof* (1639). 4372. bb. 6.
Anon. (arranged alphabetically).
A Bank Dialogue between H. C. and a Country Gentleman (1696). 8223. e. 7 (8).
A Description of the Office of Credit (1665). 1139. d. 13.
A Hue and Cry after a Man Mid-wife (1699). C. 20. f. 2 (211).
A List of the Several Annuities to which the Million Bank are intituled (1695). 816. m. 10 (10); 8223. e. 7 (11).
A Proposal to the Bank of England and the Banks now setting up, with some Considerations about Goldsmiths Notes (1695). 816. m. 10 (6).
A safe and easy Method for supplying the want of Coin and raising as many millions as the occasions of the Publick may require (1695). 108. g. 48 (5).
An Abstract of the Proposals for the Bank on the Tickets of the Million Adventure (1695?), 816. m. 10 (10).
An Account of the Constitution and Security of the General Bank of Credit (1683). 1029. e. 8 (13).
An Account of the Land-Bank (1695). 712. m. 1 (53).
Angliæ Tutamen (1695). 1029. e. 41.
Bank Credit, or, the Usefulness and Security of the Bank of Credit examined in a Dialogue . . . (1683). 104. d. 58.

U   BANKING

Corporation Credit: or a Bank of Credit made current by common consent in London (1682). 1139. d. 12.

England's Interest, or, the great Benefit to Trade by Banks or Offices of Credit (1682). 1138. e. 12.

London's Liberties (1651). E. 620 (7).

Mr. J. Asgill his Plagiarism detected and his Assertions of which he pretends to be the Author proved to be taken out of Mr. Briscoe's Discourse on the Late Funds (1696). 104. k. 33.

Proposals for National Banks (1695?). 1139. f. 21.

Reasons for Encouraging the Bank of England (1695). 8223. b. 11.

Several Objections sometimes made against the Office of Credit fully answered (1682?). 1029. e. 8 (13).

Some Considerations ordered against the Continuance of the Bank of England (1700?). 1139. f. 68.

The Arguments and Reasons for and against Engrafting upon the Bank of England with Tallies (1697). 8227. g .5.

The Case of Richard Thompson and Company (1678). 1417. h. 42.

The Many Advantages the Bank of the City of London will afford to the Public and all sorts of Traders (1684?). 1029. e. 8 (12).

The Monthly Account of the Land Bank (1695), Nos. 4 and 6. 712. m. 1 (46).

The Mystery of the New-Fashioned Goldsmiths or Bankers (1676).

The Schedule containing the Draught of the Charter [of the Bank of England] (1698). 8223. e. 7 (15).

The Scheme for the Proposals for Making a Fund for granting Annuities for Lives . . . .With the terms of joyning the same to the Million Bank (1695?). 712. m. 1 (54).

The Tryal and Condemnation of the Trustees of the Land Bank at Exeter Exchange for murdering the Bank of England at Grocers Hall (1696?). 712. m. 1 (51).

Asgill, J. *Remarks on the Proceedings of the Commissioners for putting in Execution the Act passed last Sessions for establishing of a Land-Bank* (1696). 245. k. 16 (2).

— *Several Assertions proved in order to create another Species of Money than Gold or Silver* (1696). 245. k. 16 (1).

B., I. *The Merchants Avizo* (1607), 712. b. 1.

B., T. *The Several Forms of Instruments relating to the Affairs of Merchants and Traders* (1674). 6305. a. 3.

Barbon, N. *A Discourse of Trade* (1690). 1138. b. 2.

Beeckman, D. *Proposals . . . to raise Five Hundred Thousand Pounds per Annum to the Government and Increase Dealings of all Kinds* (1696). 8245. a. 57 (122).

Benbrigge, J. *Usura Accommodata, or, a Ready Way to rectify Usury* (1646). E. 353. (22).

Billinghurst, G. *Arcana Clericala* (1674). 6305. a. 3.

Brewster, Sir Francis. *Essays on Trade and Navigation* (1695). 436. a. 2.

Briscoe, J. *An Account of the National Land Bank* (1695?). 816. m. 10 (6).

　An Account of the Value of the Estates in the Several Counties subscribed towards the Fund of a National Land Bank (1695). 712. m. 1 (43); 712. m. 1 (51); 8223. e. 7 (5).

　An Answer to a late Pamphlet intituled Reasons offered against the intended project commonly called the National Land Bank (1696). 8223. e. 7 (9).

　A Discourse on the Late Funds of the Million Act, Lottery Act and Bank of England (1694). 518. f. 62 (3).

　An Explanatory Dialogue of a late Treatise, intituled, A Discourse on the late Funds of the Million Act, Lottery Act and Bank of England (1694). T. 2029 (18).

　The following Proposals for, and Accounts of, a National Land Bank have been printed in London . . . (1695). 8223. e. 7 (5).

　Proposals for raising Money for the National Land Bank (1695). 816. m. 10 (11).

　To the Lords Spiritual and Temporal and Commons in Parliament assembled (an Address respecting a National Land Bank), (*Advice to the Free-Holder* 1696). 712. m. 1 (45).

Bullinger, H. *Decades* (1577). English trans. by T. Harding (1850).

Carr, W. *The Traveller's Guide and Historian's Faithful Companion* (1690). 1051. b. 9.

Cary, J. *An Essay on the Coyn and Credit of England* (1696). T. 1814 (1).

　Essay on the State of England in relation to its Trade, its Poor, and its Taxes, for carrying on the Present War against France (1695). 1029. a. 5 (1).

　An Essay towards the Settlement of a National Credit in the Kingdom of England (1696). 1029. a. 5 (2).

Challoner, J. *Proposals . . . for Passing an Act to prevent Clipping and Counterfeiting Money* (1694). 816. m. 10 (40).

Chamberlen, H. *A Bank Dialogue, or Doctor Chamberlen's Land-Bank explained by way of Question and Answer* (1695). 8223. e. 7 (6).

　A brief Narrative of the Nature and Advantages of the Land Bank (1695). 816. m. 10 (5).

　A few Proposals recommending . . . the Establishing a Land Bank (1700). 1139. c. 15.

　A Proposal of Dr. Hugh Chamberlen . . . for a Bank of Secure Current Credit to be founded upon Land (1695). 8223. e. 7 (3).

　Dr. Chamberlen's Petition and Proposals for a Land Bank to increase Trade (1693). 8225. f. 6.

Dr. Chamberlen's Proposals to make England Rich and Happy (1690).

Manuale Medicum (1685).   1039. f. 28 (1).

Papers relating to a Bank of Credit upon Land Security proposed to the Parliament of Scotland (1693).   1139. h. 18.

The Constitution of the Office of Land Credit declared in a Deed (1696).   8223. e. 7 (12).

Chamberlen, P.   *The Poore Mans Advocate* (1649), 1027. i. 16 (4).

Child, Sir Josiah.   *A New Discourse of Trade* (2nd ed., 1694). 712. c. 5.

Cleriac, E.   *Usance du Negoce* (1656).   1140. f. 20.

Cooke, J.   *Unum Necessarium* (1648).   1102. h. 1 (5).

Cradocke, F.   *An Expedient for taking away all Impositions and for raising a Revenue without Taxes* (1660).   518. h. 1 (3).

   Wealth Discovered (1661).   518. h. 1 (4).

Dafforne, R.   *The Merchants Mirrour* (2nd ed., 1636).

Dekker, T.   *English Villanies* (1631).   C. 27. b. 13.

Defoe, D.   *An Essay upon Projects* (1697).   1029. b. 24.

De Laune, T.   *Angliæ Metropolis* (1690).   578. a. 3.

Fanshaw, T.   *The Practice of the Exchequer Court* (1658). E. 1928. (1).

Fleetwood, W.   *A Sermon against Clipping* (1694).   1103. a. 1 (1).

Ford, Sir Edward.   "Experimented Proposals how the King may have Money" (1666), *Harleian Miscellany*, Vol. IV, pp. 195–96.

Godfrey, M.   *A Short Account of the Bank of England* (1694), 712. m. 1 (25).

Gerbier, Sir Balthazar.   *Some Considerations on the two great Staple Commodities of England* (1651).   1029. e. 8 (1).

Guicciardini, L.   *Descrittione di tutti Paesi Bassi, altrimento detti Germania Inferiore* (1567).   570. h. 9.

H. E.   *Decus and Tutamen* (1696).   1139. c. 25.

Harrys, W.   *The Market or Fayre of Usurers* (1550).   C. 38. c. 59.

Hartlib, S.   *An Essay upon Master W. Potters Designe : Concerning a Bank of Lands to be erected throughout this Commonwealth* (1653).   234. e. 32 (1).

Holmwood, T.   *Trade Revived* (1660).   1027. c. 26.

Howes, E.   *The Annales or General Chronicle of England* (1615). 2072. g.

Janssen, Sir Theodore.   *A Discourse concerning Banks* (1697). 104. d. 53.

Jordan, T.   *The Goldsmiths Jubile* (1674).   9930. g. 62.

Lambe, S.   *Seasonable Observations* (1657).   712. m. 1 (26), and in Somer's *Tracts*, II.

Leigh, E.   *England Described* (1659), 577. a. 4.

Leti, G.   *Historia, e Memorie recondite sopra alla vita di Oliviero Cromvele* (1692).   G. 1884 (5).

Lewis, M. *A Short Model of a Bank* (1678). . 8223. a. 36.
   A large Model of a Bank (1678). 1139. f. 19.
   Proposals to the King and Parliament (1679). 518. h. 1 (7).
   *Proposals to Increase Trade and to Advance His Majestys
   Revenue* (1677). 1029. e. 61.
Malynes, G. de. *A Treatise of the Canker of England's Common-
   wealth* (1601). 1391. a. 15.
   Consuetudo, Vel Lex Mercatoria (1622), 5805. b. 27.
Marius, J. *Advice concerning Bills of Exchange* (1651). E.
   1397. c. 24.
Mellis, J. *A Briefe Instruction and Maner how to keepe bookes of
   Accompts after the order of Debitour and Creditour* (1588),
   712. a. 39.
Molloy, C. *De Jure Maritimo* (1676). 502. e. 9.
Mosse, M. *The Arraignment and Conviction of Usurie* (1595),
   695. a. 36.
Mun, T. *England's Treasure by Forraign Trade* (1664). 1029. a. 1.
Murray, R. *Proposals for the Advancement of Trade* (1676).
   712. m. 1 (90).
   A Proposal for a National Land Bank (1695). 104. d. 57.
North, Sir Dudley. *Discourses upon Trade* (1691). 8223. b. 5.
Pacioli, L. *Sūma de Arithmetica, Geometria Proportioni et
   Proportionalita* (1494). I B, 23272.
Peele, J. *The Maner and fourme how to keep a Perfect Reconyng
   after the order of the most worthie and notable accompts of
   Debitour and Creditour* (1553). 8223. c. 16.
   *The Pathe Way to Perfectnes in th' accomptes of Debitour
   and Creditour* (1569). C. 54. k. 3.
Petty, Sir William. *Quantulumcumque concerning Money* (1682).
   8223. a. 69.
   Treatise of Taxes and Contributions (1662). 518. h. 32 (1).
   Political Arithmetic (1690). 523. a. 30.
Pollexfen, Sir Henry. *A Discourse of Trade, Coyn and Paper
   Credit* (1697). 1139. c. 8.
Potter, W. *Humble Proposals to the Honourable the Council for
   Trade* (1651). 1029. e. 7.
   The Key to Wealth (1650). E. 1067 (2).
   The Tradesman's Jewel (1650). E. 614 (9).
Powell, T. *The Art of Thriving . . . Together with the Mysterie
   and Miserie of Lending and Borrowing* (1635–36). G. 16365.
Proclamation by the Mayor, MDCLXXI, dated Guildhall
   November 7th. 21. h. 5 (48).
Roberts, L. *Merchants Mappe of Commerce* (1638). 30. f. 19.
Robinson, H. *Englands Safety in Trades Encrease* (1641).
   Certain Proposals (1652). 1102. h. 1 (8).
Scarlett, J. *The Stile of Exchanges* (1682). 510. a. 27.
Scobell, H. *Collection of Acts and Ordinances . . . 1640–1651*
   (1658). Circ. 61. b.

Stow, J. *A Survay of London* (1598). 578. b. 1.
Stubbes, P. *The Anatomie of Abuses* (1583). 697. a. 35 (2).
Temple, Sir William. *Observations upon the United Provinces of the Netherlands* (5th ed., 1690). 1196. b. 8.
Turnor, T. *The Case of the Bankers and their Creditors fully stated and examined* (1675). 104. d. 52.
Vernon, J. *The Compleat Compting House* (1678). 523. a. 29 (1).
Violet, T. *An Appeal to Cæsar* (1660). 104. f. 26.
    Petition against the Jews (1661). 714. h. 12 (6).
Whately, T. *Now is the Time, or, The Proposal of the Loan Bank Seasonable* (1694). 816. m. 10 (1).
West, W. *Symbolæographia* (1590). 514. a. 26.
Wilson. T. *A Discourse uppon Usurye* (1572). G. 19352.

IX. LATER PRINTED BOOKS, AFTER 1700

(Including Pamphlets, and Articles in Periodicals, Dictionaries and Encyclopædias).

Airy, O. *Charles* II (1904).
Anderson, A. *An Historical and Chronological Deduction of the Origin of Commerce* (1787–89).
Andréadès, A. *History of the Bank of England* (1909).
Angell, J. W. *The Theory of International Prices*, Harvard Economic Studies, Vol. 28 (1926).
Anon. (arranged alphabetically).

   A Short View of the apparent Dangers and Mischiefs from the Bank of England (1707).
   Arguments against prolonging the Bank (1708).
   Remarks upon the Bank of England with regard more especially to our Trade and Government (1705).
   The Anatomy of Exchange Alley (1719). Reprinted in J. Francis, *Chronicles and Characters of the Stock Exchange*, pp. 359–83.
   The History of the Bank of England from the Establishment of that Institution (1798).
   Vyner, A Family History (1885).

Ashley, Sir William. *An Introduction to English Economic History and Theory* (1892–93).
    "The Tory Origin of Free Trade," *Quarterly Journal of Economics*, XI (1897), pp. 335–71.
Aveling, J. H. *The Chamberlens and the Midwifery Forceps* (1882).
Bagehot, W. *Lombard Street* (1873).
Baker, A. F. *Banks and Banking* (1892).
Bannister, S. *The Writings of William Paterson* (1859).
Baring, Sir F. *Observations on the Establishment of the Bank of England and on the Paper Circulation of the Country* (1797).

Bauer, S. "Barbon, Nicholas, M.D.," Palgrave's *Dictionary of Political Economy*, (1923–25).
"Balance of Trade (History of the Theory)," *ibid.*
"Nicholas Barbon," *Jahrbücher für Nationalökonomie und Statistik*, XXI (1890), pp. 561–90.
Bell, W. G. *Fleet Street in Seven Centuries* (1912).
Beer, G. L. *The Origins of the British Colonial System* (1908).
The Old Colonial System (1912).
Bidwell, W. *Annals of an East Anglian Bank* (1900).
Bisschop, W. R. *The Rise of the London Money Market* (1912).
Bland, A. E., Brown, P. A., and Tawney, R. H. *English Economic History, Select Documents* (1914).
Bond, Sir Edward A. "Extracts from the Liberate Rolls relative to Loans supplied by Italian Merchants to the Kings of England in the Thirteenth and Fourteenth Centuries," *Archæologia*, XXVIII (1839), pp. 207–326.
Bourne, H. R. F. *Famous London Merchants* (1890).
Broom, H. *Constitutional Law viewed in relation to Common Law* (1866).
Buckley, H. "Sir Thomas Gresham and the Foreign Exchanges," *Economic Journal*, XXXIV (1924), pp. 589–601.
Burgon, J. W. *Life and Times of Sir Thomas Gresham* (1839).
Burnet, G. *History of My Own Times* (1724–34).
Byles, Sir J. B. *A Treatise on the Law of Bills of Exchange, Promissory Notes, Bank Notes and Cheques* (18th ed., 1923).
Cannan, E. "Early History of the term Capital," *Quarterly Journal of Economics*, Vol. 35 (1920–21), pp. 469–81.
The Paper Pound of 1797–1821 (1919).
Cary, J. *Discourse on Trade* (2nd ed., 1745).
Cave, C. H. *A History of Banking in Bristol* (1899).
Chaffers, W. *Gilda Aurifabrorum* (1883).
Chalmers. *A Digest of the Law of Bills of Exchange, Promissory Notes and Cheques* (2nd ed., 1881).
Chitty, J. *A Practical Treatise on Bills of Exchange, Promissory Notes and Bankers Checks* (1834).
Clapham, J. H. *Economic History of Modern Britain* (1926).
Collins, C. M. *The History, Law and Practice of Banking* (1882).
Coleridge, E. H. *The Life of Thomas Coutts, Banker* (1920).
Comyns, Sir J. *A Digest of the Laws of England* (5th ed., 1882).
Conant, C. A. *A History of Modern Banks of Issue* (5th ed., 1915).
Cranch, W. "Promissory Notes before and after Lord Holt," *Select Essays in Anglo-American Legal History*, III (1909).
Cuneo, C. *Memorie sopra l'antico Debito Publico Mutui, Compere e Banca di S. Giorgio in Genova* (1844).
Cunningham, W. *The Growth of English History and Commerce* (5th ed., 1921–22).
"Economic Change," *Cambridge Modern History*, Vol. I (1902), Chap. XV.

Davis, A. M. " Currency and Banking in the Province of Massa-chusetts-Bay," *American Economic Association Publications*, Series 3, Vol. II, No. 2.

Day, C. *A History of Commerce* (3rd ed., 1922).

De Fraine, H. G. " Tallies," *The Old Lady of Threadneedle Street*, Vol. II, No. 13 (March 1924).

Des Essars, P. " A History of Banking in Latin Nations," Vol. III, pp. 1–379, of *A History of Banking in all Nations* (1896).

Dietz, C. F. *English Government Finance, 1485–1558* (1920). University of Illinois Studies in the Social Sciences.

Dowell, S. *A History of Taxation and Taxes in England* (1888).

Dowling, S. W. *The Exchanges of London* (1929).

Dunbar, C. F. " The Bank of Venice," *Quarterly Journal of Economics*, Vol. VI (1892), pp. 308–35, and *Economic Essays* (1904).
  " Early Banking Schemes," *Quarterly Journal of Economics*, Vol. II (1888), and *Economic Essays*.
  Chapters on the Theory and History of Banking (2nd ed., 1906).

Easton, H. T. *History of a Banking House (Smith, Payne and Smith)* (1903).
  History and Principles of Banking (1924).

Ehrenberg, R. *Capital and Finance in the Age of the Renaissance* (1928), English translation by H. Lucas of *Das Zeitalter der Fugger* (1896).

Fairman, W. *The Stocks examined and compared* (1795 ?).

Fay, C. R. *Great Britain from Adam Smith to the Present Day* (1928).

Ferrara, F. " Gli antichi banchi di Venezia," *Nuova Antologia*, Vol. XVI (1871).

Fisk, H. E. *English Public Finance from the Revolution of 1688* (1921).

Forbes, W. *A methodical Treatise concerning Bills of Exchange* (1703).

Foxwell, H. S. Introduction to Phillippovich, *History of the Bank of England* (1911).
  Introduction to Andréadès, *History of the Bank of England* (1909).

Francis, J. *The History of the Bank of England* (1848).
  Chronicles and Characters of the Stock Exchange (1849).

Gardiner, S. R. *History of the Commonwealth and Protectorate* (1894).

Gay, J. "Epistle to Mr. Thomas Snow, Goldsmith, near Temple-Bar." *Poets of Great Britain* (ed. R. Anderson) (1795), Vol. 8, p. 306.

Gilbart, J. W. *The History, Principles and Practice of Banking* (1834).
  A Practical Treatise on Banking (6th ed., 1858).

Godwin, W. *History of the Commonwealth of England* (1824–28).
Gooch. *Political Thought in England from Bacon to Halifax* (1914).
Goris, J. A. *Étude sur les Colonies Marchandes Méridionales à Anvers de 1488 à 1567* (1925).
Graham, W. *The One Pound Note in the History of Banking in Great Britain* (1886).
Granger, J. *A Biographical History of England* (1824).
Gras, N. S. B. *The Evolution of the English Corn Market* (1915). Harvard Economic Studies, Vol. 12.
Gross, C. *Select Cases concerning the Law Merchant 1270–1638* (1908). Selden Society Publications.
Grindon, L. H. *Manchester Banks and Banking* (1877).
Guizot, F. P. G. *Histoire de la République d'Angleterre* (1850–56).
Gutteridge, H. C. "The Origin and Historical Development of the Profession of Notaries Public," *Cambridge Legal Essays* (1926).
Hall, H. *Antiquities and Curiosities of the Exchequer* (1898).
Hallam, H. *The Constitutional History of England* (1854).
Hankey, T. *Banking: Its Utility and Economy* (1860).
Hatton, E. *A New View of London* (1708).
The Merchant's Magazine (1701).
Hawkins, E. *The Silver Coins of England* (2nd ed., 1876).
Hawtrey, R. G. *Currency and Credit* (2nd ed., 1923).
Henne, A. *Histoire du Regne de Charles-Quint en Belgique* (1858–65).
Hewins, W. A. S. *English Trade and Finance, chiefly in the Seventeenth Century* (1890).
Hoare, Sir Richard C. *Pedigrees and Memories* (1819).
Holdsworth, W. S. *A History of the English Law*, VIII (1925).
Holzapfel, P. H. *Die Anfänge der Montes Pietatis, 1462–1515* (1903).
Horton, C. D. *The Silver Pound* (1887).
Houblon, Lady Alice Archer. *The Houblon Family, Its Story and Times* (1907).
Howarth, W. *Barclay and Company Limited* (1901).
Some Olde Curiosities (1890).
Howell, T. B. *A Complete Collection of State Trials* (1812).
Huguenot Society of London. Publications, XVIII (1891), *Denizations and Naturalisations of Aliens in England and Ireland.*
Huvelin, P. *Le Droit des Marchés et des Foires* (1897).
Hughes, J. *Liverpool Banks and Bankers, 1760–1837* (1906).
Hyamson, A. M. *A History of the Jews in England* (2nd ed., 1928).
Ingram, J. K. "Early European Banks," Palgrave's *Dictionary of Political Economy.*
Institute of Bankers. *Catalogue of the "Maberly Phillips" Collection of Old Bank Notes, Drafts, etc.* (1906).
Jackson, Sir Charles J. *English Goldsmiths and their Marks* (2nd ed., 1921).

Jacob, W. *An Historical Inquiry into the Production and Consumption of the Precious Metals* (1821).
Jacobs, J. " Banking," *The Jewish Encyclopædia* (1925).
Jencken, H. D. *A Compendium of the Laws on Bills of Exchange, Promissory Notes, Cheques, and other Commercial Negotiable Instruments* (1880).
Jenkinson, H. " Exchequer Tallies," *Archæologia*, Vol. LXII (1911), pp. 367–80.
    A Manual of Archive Administration (1922).
Jenks, E. " On the Early History of Negotiable Instruments," *The Law Quarterly Review*, IX (1893).
Joplin, T. " On the General Principles and Present Practice of Banking in England and Scotland," *The Pamphleteer*, XXIV (1824).
    An Analysis and History of the Currency Question (1832).
Judges, A. V. " Philip Burlamachi, a Financier of the Thirty Years' War," *Economica* (November 1926).
Justice, A. *A General Treatise of Monies and Exchanges* (1707).
Kayserling, M. " Suasso," *The Jewish Encyclopædia*.
Kennedy, W. *English Taxation, 1640–1799* (1896).
Kennet, W. *A History of England* (1706).
Kingsford, C. L. *The Stonor Letters and Papers, 1290–1483* (ed. for R. Hist. Soc., 1919).
Klarwill, V. von. *The Fugger Newsletters* (1924).
    Ibid., second series (1926).
Knight, C. *London* (1875–78).
Knight, F. " Historical and Theoretical Issues in the Problem of Modern Capitalism," *Journal of Economic and Business History*, Vol. I. (1928–29).
Knight, M. M. " Recent Literature on the Origins of Modern Capitalism," *Quarterly Journal of Economics*, Vol. XII (1927).
Lattes, E. *Le liberta delle banche a Venezia dal secolo XIII al XVII secondo i documenti inediti del R. Archivio dei Frari* (1869).
Lawson, W. J. *History of Banking* (1855).
Lecky, W. E. H. *A History of England in the Eighteenth Century* (1892).
Lewis, G. R. *The Stannaries* (1908). Harvard Economic Studies, No. 3.
Lipkind, G. ." Medina, Sir Solomon de," *The Jewish Encyclopædia*.
Lloyd, S. *The Lloyds of Birmingham* (1907).
Luttrell, N. *A Brief Historical Relation of State Affairs from September 1678 to April 1714* (1857).
Macaulay, Lord. *The History of England from the Accession of James II* (1858–61).
Macleod, H. D. *The Theory and Practice of Banking* (5th ed., 1892).

Macpherson, D. *Annals of Commerce* (1805).
Madox, T. *The History and Antiquities of the Exchequer* (1769).
Maitland, W. *The History and Survey of London* (1739).
Malden, H. E. *The Cely Papers.* Camden Society Publications,
    (1900).
Marsden, R. G. *Select Pleas in the Court of Admiralty* (1894–97).
    Selden Society Publications.
Martin, F. *Stories of Banks and Bankers* (1865).
    The History of Lloyds (1876).
Martin, J. B. *The "Grasshopper" in Lombard Street (History
    of the Banking House of Martin & Co.),* (1892).
Matthews, W. P. *The Bankers' Clearing House* (1921).
Matthews, W. P., and Tuke, A. W. *History of Barclays Limited*
    (1926).
Mees, W. C. *Proeve eener Geschiedenis van het Bankwesen in
    Nederland, gedurende den tijd der Republiek* (1838).
Mitchell, W. *An Essay on the Early History of the Law Merchant*
    (1904).
Monroe, A. E. *Monetary Theory before Adam Smith* (1923).
    Harvard Economic Studies, No. 25.
Motley, J. L. *The Rise of the Dutch Republic* (1903).
Nasse, E. "Das venetianische Bankwesen im 14. 15. und 16.
    Jahrhundert." *Jahrbücher für Nationalökonomie und
    Statistick,* Vol. 34 (1879).
Noble, T. C. *Memorials of Temple Bar* (1869).
Nougier, L. *Des Lettres de Change* (1839).
Overall, W. H., and H. C. *Analytical Index to the Series of
    Records known as the Remembrancia preserved among the
    Archives of the City of London* (1878).
Palgrave, Sir Robert H. Inglis, " Banks and Banking," *Encyclo-
    pædia Britannica* (1910–11).
Papillon, A. F. W. *Memoirs of Thomas Papillon of London,
    Merchant, 1623–1702* (1887).
Pennant, T. *Some Account of London* (1790).
Pepys, S. *Diary,* H. B. Wheatley's edition (1893–99).
Philippovich, E. von. *History of the Bank of England and its
    Financial Services to the State* (1911).
Phillips, M. " Bank Note Collecting," *Connoisseur,* Vols. 5 and
    6 (1903).
    *A History of Banks, Bankers and Banking in Northumber-
    land, Durham and North Yorkshire* (1894).
Picciotto, J. *Sketches of Anglo-Jewish History* (1875).
Pirenne, H. " The Stages in the Social History of Capitalism,"
    American Historical Review, Vol. 19 (1914), pp. 494–515.
    Histoire de Belgique (1900–20).
Postan, M. " Credit in Medieval Trade," *Economic History
    Review,* Vol. I (1927–28).
Postlethwayt, J. *The History of the English Revenue from the
    Revolution in 1688 to Christmas 1753* (1759).

Powell, E. T. *The Evolution of the Money Market* (1915).

Power, E. " The English Wool Trade in the Reign of Edward IV," *The Cambridge Historical Journal*, II, 1 (1926).

Price, F. G. H. " Some Notes on the Early Goldsmiths and Bankers to the close of the Seventeenth Century." *Transactions of the London and Middlesex Archæological Society*, Vol. V (1881), pp. 255–80.

  A Handbook of London Bankers 1667–1876 (1876).

  The Signs of Old Lombard Street (1887).

  Temple Bar, or Some Account of " Ye Marygold," No. 1 *Fleet Street* (1875).

Prideaux, Sir Walter S. *Memorials of the Goldsmiths' Company* (1896).

Ranke, L. von. *The History of England mainly in the Seventeenth Century* (Oxford translation, 1875).

Reddie, J. *An Historical View of the Law of Maritime Commerce* (1841).

Rees, J. F. *Fiscal and Financial History of England* (1921).

Relton, F. B. *An Account of the Fire Insurance Companies* (1893).

Rhodes, W. E. " The Italian Bankers in England and their loans to Edward I and Edward II," *Historical Essays*, edited by T. F. Tout and J. Tait (1907).

Ricard, S. *Traité Général du Commerce* (1705, and enlarged ed., 1781).

Richards, R. D. " The Early History of the term Capital," *Quarterly Journal of Economics*, Vol. XL (1925–26).

  " The Origin of the Cheque," *Banker*, Vol IX (1929).

Richardson, R. *Coutts & Co., Bankers* (1892).

Ridley, Hon. Jasper. " Thomas Coutts, Banker," *Banker*. Vol II (1926).

Rogers, J. A. T. *The First Nine Years of the Bank of England* (1887).

Rose, J. H., Newton, A. P., and Benians, E. A. *The Cambridge History of the British Empire*, Vol. I (1929), edited by.

Roth, H. L. *The Genesis of Banking in Halifax* (1914).

Ruding, E. *Annals of the Coinage of Britain and its Dependencies* (3rd ed., 1840).

Salter, F. R. *Sir Thomas Gresham* (1925).

Scott, W. R. *The Constitution and Finance of English, Scottish and Irish Joint Stock Companies* (1910–12).

Scroggs, W. O. " English Finances under the Long Parliament," *Quarterly Journal of Economics*, Vol. 21 (1907).

Scrutton, T. E. " General Survey of the History of the Law Merchant," *Select Essays in Anglo-American Legal History*, III.

Sée, H. *Modern Capitalism* (English trans. by H. B. Vanderblue and G. F. Doriot, 1928).

Seligman, E. R. A. *Curiosities of Early Economic Literature* (1920).

Sharpe, R. R. *London and the Kingdom* (1894).

Shaw, W. A. *Select Tracts illustrative of English Monetary History* (1896).
"The Treasury Order Book," *Economic Journal*, Vol. XVI (1906), pp. 33–40.
The History of the Currency, 1252–1894 (1895).
"The Beginnings of the National Debt," *Historical Essays*, edited by T. F. Tout and J. Tait (1907).

Silberling, N. J. "Financial and Monetary Policy of Great Britain during the Napoleonic Wars," *Quarterly Journal of Economics*, XXXVIII (1923–24).

Sinclair, Sir John. *The History of the Public Revenue of the British Empire* (1803–4).

Smith, A. *The Wealth of Nations*, E. Cannan's edition (1920).

Smith, A. L. "Taxation and Finance (1689–1714)," *Social England*, edited by H. D. Traill and J. S. Mann, Vol. IV (1901).

Sombart, W. *The Jews and Modern Capitalism* (1913).

Somers, Lord Keeper. *Argument on his giving Judgment in the Bankers' Case, 1696* (1733).

Stauber, A. *Das Haus Fugger* (1900).

Stephens, T. A. *A Contribution to the Bibliography of the Bank of England* (1897).

Story, J. *Commentaries on the Law of Bills of Exchange* (4th ed., 1860).

Strype, J. *J. Stow's Survey of the Cities of London and Westminster* (1720 edition).

Suter, A. B. *The Worthies of St. Dunstan's* (1856).

Sykes, E. *Currency and Banking* (6th ed., 1925).

Sykes, J. *The Amalgamation Movement in English Banking, 1825–1924* (1926).

Symes, J. E. "The Economic Revival (1558–1584)," *Social England*, edited by H. D. Traill and J. S. Mann, Vol. III (1901).

Taswell-Langmead, T. P. *English Constitutional History* (8th ed., 1919).

Taylor, O. H. "Tawney's Religion and Capitalism and Eighteenth-Century Liberalism," *Quarterly Journal of Economics*, Vol. XLI (1927).

Tawney, R. H. *The Agrarian Problem of the Sixteenth Century* (1912).
"Religious Thought on Social and Economic Questions in the Sixteenth and Seventeenth Centuries," *The Journal of Political Economy*, Vol. XXXI, Nos. 4, 5 and 6 (1923).
Wilson's Discourse upon Usury (1925), Introduction.
Religion and the Rise of Capitalism (1926).

Tawney, R. H., and Power, E. *Tudor Economic Documents* (1924).

Thomas, A. H. *Calendar of Early Mayor's Court Rolls preserved among the Archives of the City of London at the Guildhall* (1924).

Thomas, F. S. *The Ancient Exchequer of England* (1848).

Thornton, E. *An Enquiry into the Nature and Effects of the Paper Credit of Great Britain* (1802).

Thurloe, J. *A Collection of the State Papers of John Thurloe* (1742).

Tooke, T. *A History of Prices and of the State of the Circulation from 1793 to 1837* (1838).

Turberville, A. S. *The House of Lords in the Reign of William III* (1913).

Turner, B. B. *Chronicles of the Bank of England* (1897).

Unwin, G. *Industrial Organisation in the Sixteenth and Seventeenth Centuries* (1904).

" Commerce and Coinage, " *Shakespeare's England* (1916).

Usher, A. P. " The Origin of the Bill of Exchange," *Journal of Political Economy*, Vol. XXII (1914), pp. 566–76.

Valentine, A. H. " Brokers, Jew," *The Jewish Encyclopædia*.

Van der Borght, R. " A History of Banking in the Netherlands," *A History of Banking in all Nations*, Vol. IV, pp. 191–95.

Van Dyke, P. " A Captain of Industry of the Sixteenth Century," *Harper's Magazine*, European edition, Vol. 59, pp. 276–84 (1909–10).

Wagenaar, J. *Amsterdam* (1760–67).

Warren, H. *The Story of the Bank of England* (1903).

Weber, M. ' Die protestantische Ethik und der Geist des Kapitalismus,' *Archiv für Sozialwissenschaft und Sozialpolitik Statistik*, Bd. 20 (1905).

Westerfield, R. B. *Middlemen in English Business, 1660–1760.* Transactions of the Connecticut Academy of Arts and Sciences, Vol. 19 (May 1915), pp. 111–445.

Wheatley, J. *An Essay on the Theory of Money and Principles of Commerce* (1807).

Whitwell, R. J. " Italian Bankers and the English Crown," *Transactions of Royal Historical Society*, New Series, Vol. XVII (1903).

Williams, B. *The British Empire* (1928).

Wiszniewski, Prince Adam. *Histoire de la Banque de Saint-Georges de Gênes* (1865).

Wolf, L. *The Re-settlement of the Jews in England* (1881).
Cromwell's Jewish Intelligencers (1891).
Crypto-Jews under the Commonwealth (1894).
The First English Jew (undated).

INDEX

BOOKS TO READ

THE RESTORATION OF EUROPEAN CURRENCIES.

By D. T. JACK, M.A., Dept. of Political Economy, University of Glasgow. Demy 8vo. 230 pp. 10s. 6d.

An attempt is made in this book to discuss certain of the methods which have been employed within recent years to reform the disorganized currency systems of Europe. The author, in his Introduction, makes a general survey of the whole problem, and then proceeds to examine the position of each country separately for the sake of simplicity.

RESTORING CURRENCY STANDARDS.

By E. L. HARGREAVES, Ph.D. Demy 8vo. 110 pp. 6s.

This book deals with the monetary history of America, France, and Austria during the period 1780–1813. The author has unearthed much forgotten history which is so like that of recent years as to suggest the adage " there is nothing new under the sun."

MODERN MONETARY SYSTEMS.

By BERTRAND NOGARO, Professeur à la Faculté de Droit de l'Université de Paris. Translated into English. Demy 8vo. 250 pp. 15s.

Extract from the Introduction.—This book is " intended to give an explanation of monetary phenomena to-day which shall be consistent with the truths of economic science. The first part comprises an historical account of monetary systems and of their operation. In the second and third parts an attempt will be made to deduce the theoretical conclusions and to work out some of their implications in practice."

Financial News.—" The historical account of modern monetary systems is interesting and valuable in that it is up to date and contains a good deal of information which is not readily accessible elsewhere."

THE AUSTRIAN CROWN: Its Depreciation and Stabilization.

By J. VAN WALRÉ DE BORDES, LL.D., with an Introduction by Sir HENRY STRAKOSCH, K.B.E. Demy 8vo. 252 pp. 15s.

The notable and successful work which the League of Nations accomplished in improving the monetary position of Austria is here described by a member of the League Secretariat.

The Economic Journal.—" This book is a very able attempt to test and re-state current theories in the light of actual facts, carefully observed. It is neither a mere catalogue of events nor a series of deductive generalizations based on general tendencies, but a close inquiry into the phenomena accompanying the depreciation and stabilization of the Austrian crown, with an application of the results to general theories about the value of money . . . it is indeed one of the best books on currency questions which has appeared for some time."

P. S. KING & SON, LTD.

14 GREAT SMITH STREET, WESTMINSTER

BOOKS TO READ

WEALTH : A Brief Examination of the Causes of Economic Welfare.

By EDWIN CANNAN, Emeritus Professor of Political Economy in the University of London. *Third and Revised Edition.* Crown 8vo. 330 pp. 5s.

First published in 1914, nearly 20,000 copies have been sold to date, and the book has been translated into Spanish, Japanese, Chinese, Polish, and Braille. In this, the third edition, the book has been entirely re-set, much new matter added, and the price reduced to 5s. There are also many alterations in casual allusions and examples which have been made necessary by the effects of the War, especially the great decline in the purchasing power of money.

THE FOREIGN EXCHANGES, being the Newmarch Lectures for 1922–23.

Delivered by A. W. FLUX, C.B., M.A. Demy 8vo. 220 pp.   10s. 6d.

Illustrated by several diagrams and charts showing the course of the exchanges.

The Times Literary Supplement.—" This book forms a useful introduction to the study of post-war exchanges, and concentrates on the actual nature of international exchange, set free from the central idea of currency exchange. This imparts a sense of reality to the discussion which will be welcomed by the ' plain man,' for whom the book is intended."

A HISTORY OF PRICES AND OF THE STATE OF THE CIRCULATION FROM 1792 TO 1856.

By THOMAS TOOKE, F.R.S., and WILLIAM NEWMARCH, F.R.S. Originally published (1838–57) in 6 vols. Now re-issued in 4 vols. With an Introduction by Professor T. E. GREGORY, D.Sc. (Econ.).

£4 4s.

A facsimile reproduction of the original work, the value of which is considerably augmented by the comprehensive Introduction written by Professor Gregory. This Introduction is also issued as a separate volume, price 2s. 6d. per copy.

THE EVOLUTION OF PROVINCIAL FINANCE IN BRITISH INDIA. A Study in the Provincial Decentralization of Imperial Finance.

By B. R. AMBEDKAR, D.Sc. (Econ.), sometime Professor of Political Economy at the Sydenham College of Commerce and Economics, Bombay. With a Foreword by EDWIN R. A. SELIGMAN, Professor of Economics, Columbia University, New York. Demy 8vo. 290 pp. 15s.

Extract from Foreword.—" The value of Mr. Ambedkar's contribution to this discussion lies in the objective recitation of the facts and the impartial analysis of the interesting development that has taken place in his native country. The lessons are applicable to other countries as well; nowhere, to my knowledge, has such a detailed study of the underlying principles been made."

P. S. KING & SON, LTD.

14 GREAT SMITH STREET, WESTMINSTER

*

BOOKS TO READ

AMERICAN BANKING METHODS.

By LEONARD LE MARCHANT MINTY, Ph.D., B.Sc. (Econ.), B.Comm., Certified Associate of the Institute of Bankers, with an Introduction by Sir DRUMMOND DRUMMOND FRASER, K.B.E., M.Comm. Demy 8vo. 460 pp. 15s.

The Financial News.—" The book is interesting not only on account of the full and detailed information it affords, and of the similarities and contrasts in practice it presents, but because, incidentally, and apart from definite intention, it throws an instructive light on the financial conditions and influences which have shaped, and are still shaping, business conditions on the other side."

A STUDY OF INTEREST RATES.

By KARIN KOCK. Demy 8vo. 264 pp. 12s. 6d.

This book is an examination of the factors governing the rates of interest on different kinds of loan in a modern loan market. In studying the changes in the margin between the different rates, the author has analysed the development during the after-war boom and depression of the American, English and Swedish loan markets.

The Times Literary Supplement.—" The first of a series of economic studies by writers connected with Stockholm University, this volume contains a careful examination of the different types of loans and interest rates, the factors determining and influencing them, and their inter-relations. The book gives evidence of practical knowledge of market conditions as well as of the literature of the subject."

BANKING POLICY AND THE PRICE LEVEL : An Essay in the Theory of the Trade Cycle.

By D. H. ROBERTSON, M.A., Fellow of Trinity College, Cambridge, Lecturer in Economics in the University of Cambridge. *Second Impression.* Crown 8vo. 106 pp. 5s.

The purpose of this book is to examine critically the doctrine that the Trade Cycle is due to purely monetary causes and could be abolished by a monetary policy designed to keep the general price level stable. The merits and limitations of such a policy are discussed together with some other matters bearing on the problem of industrial stabilization. In the course of the argument some new light, it is believed, is thrown on certain aspects of the Theory of Money and Banking, and on the nature of the burden indicated by Inflation.

RUSSIAN CURRENCY AND BANKING, 1914–24.

By S. S. KATZENELLENBAUM, Professor of Economics in the First State University of Moscow, Member of the Board of Directors of the State Bank of the Union of Soviet Socialist Republics. Demy 8vo. 198 pp. 9s.

In publishing this treatise in English a double aim is kept in view. On the one hand, it is desired to make the British public acquainted with the changes that have taken place in the last few years in the currency and credit system in Russia; on the other, to make known to those interested in theoretical problems the views of the author regarding the laws governing the depreciation of paper currency.

Financial News.—" He has treated his subject with a scientific mind, and deserves, therefore, the attention of all interested in the greatest economic experiment of history of which Russia has been and is the scene."

P. S. KING & SON, LTD.
14 GREAT SMITH STREET, WESTMINSTER

BOOKS TO READ

THE AMALGAMATION MOVEMENT IN ENGLISH BANKING.

By J. SYKES, B.A., M.Com., Assistant Lecturer in Economics, University College, Exeter.   Demy 8vo.   243 pp.   10s. 6d.

Manchester Guardian Commercial.—" The variety of sources from which he has drawn his information proves that he has not only great patience in the study of documentary and statistical evidence, but also a refreshing boldness (very rare among academic students) in getting information directly from great bankers and financiers.   His work overflows with facts and figures which will be useful to any future student of the subject."

A HISTORY OF THE BANK OF ENGLAND.

By A ANDRÉADÈS, C.B.E., Professor of Public Finance in the University of Athens.   With a Preface by Professor H. S. FOXWELL, M.A.   *Second Edition.*   Demy 8vo.   455 pp.   15s.

Manchester Guardian.—" The book discloses not only wide research on the part of the writer, but also a deep sympathy with the subject which carries the reader along with it.   It is certainly *the* History of the Bank, and derives special interest from being the work of a foreigner, who naturally does not view his subject from exactly the same standpoint as ourselves.   As a history it appears to be marvellously comprehensive, and the review of the surrounding conditions affecting general finance at various periods is both accurate and intelligent."

ENGLAND AND THE NEW GOLD STANDARD, 1919 TO 1926.

By WILLIAM ADAMS BROWN, Junr.   320 pp.   11 Charts.   15s.

An account of the Transition from the Old Gold Standard to the New: 1919 to June, 1920, Gold Regains a World Market.   The Sterling-Dollar Exchange finds its Own Level—June, 1920, to February, 1922.   Gold—as an Instrument of Deflation.   The Sterling-Dollar Exchange reflects Unsolved Problems of Reconstruction—March, 1922, to February, 1924. · Gold Inflation begins and is checked.   The Sterling-Dollar Exchange Marking Time—February, 1924, to April, 1925.   The Disappearance of the Gold " Premium." England Returns to the Gold Standard.   The Conflict of Opinion and Economic Interest in England.   The New Gold Standard.   The New Gold Standard begins.

Bankers' Magazine.—" The author has been at great pains to obtain an analysis of the relationship of South Africa and India to the world's gold demands, and some of the statistics given in this connection are very enlightening.   The book contains references to a very wide range of authorities, and the author's view on the stabilization of world prices on a gold standard basis are not the least interesting feature."

P. S. KING & SON, LTD.

14 GREAT SMITH STREET, WESTMINSTER

BOOKS TO READ

THE EVOLUTION OF THE INDIAN INCOME TAX.

By J. P. NIYOGI. Demy 8vo. 340 pp. 12s. 6d.

The object of the present volume is to trace the history of income tax in India from 1860 onwards, to study the existing system, and to offer some criticisms derived from a comparative study of British and Indian income tax laws.

THE INCOME TAX IN GREAT BRITAIN AND THE UNITED STATES.

By HARRISON B. SPAULDING, Ph.D. Demy 8vo. 320 pp. 12s.

In both Great Britain and the United States the income tax is the principal source of public revenue, and a comparative study of the income tax laws of these two great English-speaking nations has long been needed. This book is an attempt to meet this demand.

Financial News.—" The study is careful, and, in detail, full, and for the inquirer in search of comparative facts the book is a valuable compendium."

PEOPLES' BANKS: A Record of Social and Economic Success.

By HENRY W. WOLFF. *Fourth Edition.* Newly revised and completed. Demy 8vo. 452 pp. 10s. 6d.

Giving a History of the Origin and Extension of Co-operative Banking, and a description of the various forms in use in different countries.

ELEMENTS OF STATISTICS.

Fifth Edition (1926). Demy 8vo. 459 pp. Numerous Diagrams. 18s.

This book is intended to form a general introduction to the theory and practice of statistics for all persons whose business is to handle them, or to whom a general understanding both of the utility of statistical results and the limitations of statistical investigation is important.

Banker's Magazine.—" The standard text-book for students of statistical methods . . . .the new edition is particularly suitable for actuarial students."

Insurance Magazine.—" This excellent work, in the words of the preface, ' is intended to form a general introduction to the theory and practice of statistics for all persons whose business is to handle them.' The present problem of the cost of living cannot be investigated scientifically without the use of Index-numbers, and the chapter on this method of investigation is particularly illuminating and appropriate, especially as examples and instances have been brought up to date."

P. S. KING & SON, LTD.

14 GREAT SMITH STREET, WESTMINSTER

SD - #0019 - 280922 - C0 - 229/152/19 - PB - 9780428177928 - Gloss Lamination